HUMAN RESOURCE MANAGEMENT
FOR PUBLIC ORGANIZATIONS

An Essential Guide

HUMAN RESOURCE MANAGEMENT
FOR PUBLIC ORGANIZATIONS
An Essential Guide

Publisher | Chung Kyu Sang
Printed by | Sungkyunkwan University Press
First Published 2015. 6

Authors | Sung Min Park, Reginald Ugaddan
Production Editor | Shin Chul-ho
Designer | Chorokbanana

Sungkyunkwan University Press
25-2 Sungkyunkwan-ro, Jongno-gu
Seoul 110-745, Korea
Tel | 82-2-760-1253~4, Fax: 82-2-762-7452
http://press.skku.edu

ISBN 979-11-5550-111-5 93350

This work was supported by the National Research Foundation of
Korea Grant funded by the Korean Government(NRF-2013S1A3A2055042).

HUMAN RESOURCE
MANAGEMENT
FOR PUBLIC ORGANIZATIONS

An Essential Guide

Sung Min Park & Reginald Ugaddan

Sungkyunkwan University Press

Preface

Public personnel management is the administration of and policymaking for people and positions in the public sector and is critical to the successful implementation of government programs. The HRM for Public organizations: An Essential Guide outlines the important role of human resource management (HRM) policies and practices in increasing quality of service, government efficiency, and effectiveness of public organizations. Collectively, the book will address pressing issues in managing public human resource—emerging workplace conditions such as diversity, aging workforce, labor relations, decreasing government budget, work and life issues, and among others. The text is designed to explore in detail many of the complex issues that public managers are facing in the workplace today and ones that they will face in the future. It introduces the underlying organizational and management principles of public administration and emphasizes the importance of developing the knowledge, skills, abilities, and fostering the drives of public employees. Also, the readers—researchers, students of HRM, OB, public management—may benefit in understanding that effectiveness of government services rests heavily on the knowledge, skills, abilities, and motivations of the people in the public organizations. The recruitment, selection, training and development, performance appraisal, compensation, and other HRM functions are influential factors of individual and organizational performance. Thus, this book will help address knowledge and skills gap on analyzing public human resource management system and explore various approaches that may contribute in enhancing public management and delivery of public services.

Essentially, this book is an in-depth analysis of the literature, problems, and directions of public personnel issues. The book is divided into 3 main parts: 1) The Core Human Resource Environment: structure and functions of the public HR departments, core principles of HRM, politics of public human resource management, human resource management perspectives (e.g., macro and micro, international and national, top-down and bottom-up, political and managerial, traditional and NPM, quantitative and qualitative, and efficiency and equity perspectives), public human resource management reforms, declining trust in government; budget issues; downsizing and upsizing; demands for effective, productive, and creative government; alternative work schedules (AWS); centralization and decentralization of HR activities; e-Government—reforming and reengineering of government processes, and/or the holistic internal and external environment of HRM; 2) The Core Functions of Human Resource Management: Acquiring and training human resource—recruiting, selection and job placement, training employees, HRD, succession planning, SHRM, comparative perspective of SHRM and HRM; Motivating and Utilizing Human Resources—theories of motivation, leadership and OB (e.g., public service motivation (PSM), self-determination theory (SDT), goal-setting theory, expectancy theory, equity theory, Herzberg's two-factor theory and McGregor's theory X and Y, and among others); Position management: classification, evaluation, and compensation—fundamental personnel strategies, rank-in-job and rank-in-person, job design and analysis, performance appraisal, performance management, performance management and pay-for-performance, pay systems, pay or salary structure; and 3) The Core Issues and Special Topics in Human Resource Management: diversity management, equal employee opportunity (EEO), affirmative Action (AA), employee friendly policies (e.g., health and wellness programs, flexible work policies, family and work programs, traditional employee friendly policies), e-HRM and the role of information technology in the public human resource management, and the public sector unionism, trends on public sector unionism, and laws on labor relations and standards.

HRM for Public organizations: An Essential Guide integrates theories, concepts, cases, and some practical issues in the aegis of public sector human resource management. Each chapter of the book is designed in this manner: First part is the Preview which provides an introductory discussion of each of the main topics. Second part is the Theory Synopsis which outlines and provides a thorough discussion of the relevant topics within the core sections of the book. It presents the relevant theories and conceptual explanation for each of the topics as well as the sub-topics. Specific cases are included to provide a practical view of the HRM theories, concepts, and issues and learners are encouraged to address the gaps on those cases through a Problem-Based Learning (PBL) approach. In each chapter, the PBL table is provided for the students to provide a thorough analysis of their country or agency's distinct issues as presented in each of the topics. Third part is the Reviews. This section pitch in important discussion or on hand practical questions, and/or theoretical questions that may embolden and widen the learners' understanding of the topics presented in the chapter. Lastly, the Ending Credit will point out and present studies of issues and different factors related to each topic in the book sections. These studies were adopted from prominent academic journals in the field of public management, public administration, organizational behavior, human resource management, and among others. The suggestions for further readings are specifically linked to the contents of the chapters within the core sections of the book.

An Essential HRM Framework

Our approach in this book follows the Essential HRM Framework (in Figure 1). Typically, HRM in different context—private or public sector—may be exposed to the same and/or varying elements of environment, leadership, culture, organizational structure, processes, and also people's attitudes and behaviors. These core factors surrounding HRM have vital impact on the efficacy of the organization. In the public sector, HRM have been exposed to various bureaucratic practices as well as public ideologies that may foster or hinder the effective delivery of public service and organizational effectiveness in the public sector.

HRM strategies or functions are not in isolation that are free from external influences—environmental stimuli. As the framework implies, HR planning, recruiting or staffing, human resource development (e.g., individual development (ID), career development (CD), and organizational development [OD]), motivating and utilizing human resource, appraisal, compensation, and labor relations are affected and are dependent with the external and internal environment of the organization. The external environment includes factors such as political, environmental, socio-cultural, technological, economic, private competition, and legal. These factors are indispensable and inevitable in an organizational setting either public or private. The internal environment may have something to do with the different elements that may portray organizational culture, climate, or values. The most observable organizational values would include democratic values, diversity, organizational fairness, equity, justice, and among others. It may also include organizational policies and practices such as merit systems, rank-in-

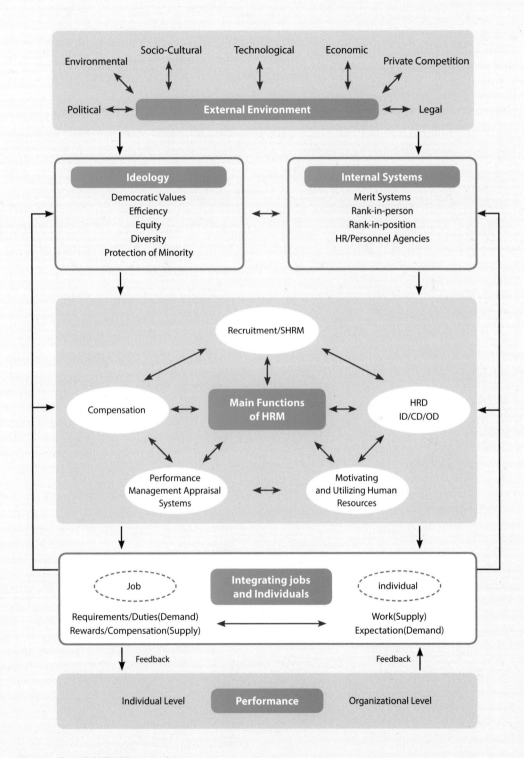

Figure 1. Essential HRM Framework

person and rank-in-position system. In this book, the external environment, ideology, and internal systems composed Part 1, "The Core Human Resource Environment".

The central component of the book dwells on the discussion of the main functions of HRM: recruitment and SHRM, HRD—ID, CD, and OD, motivation and utilization of HR, performance management and appraisal systems, and compensation. In this core element, and as the model shows, that HRM functions influences job and individual integration. The job requirement and duties demands works (individual level), and individual expectation demands job rewards and compensation. These elements comprised the Part 2, "The Core Functions of Human resource Management," of the book. Part 3 of the book presents The Core Issues and Special Topics in HRM.

Sung Min Park
Reginald Ugaddan
Sungkyunkwan University

| C o n t e n t s |

| PART 2| THE CORE FUNCTIONS OF HUMAN RESOURCE MANAGEMENT

| PART 3| THE CORE ISSUES AND SPECIAL TOPICS IN HUMAN RESOURCE MANAGEMENT

THE CORE HUMAN RESOURCE ENVIRONMENT

Public Personnel Administration and Management

Framework

Human Resource Management for Public Organizations: An Essential Guide

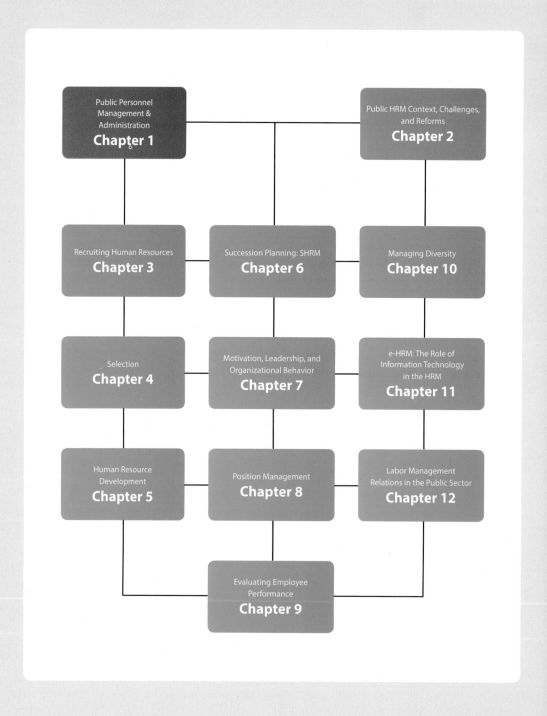

Learning Outcomes

After going through this chapter, you should be able to:

- Define public personnel administration (PPA) and management.
- Understand the conceptual foundations of PPA and management.
- Describe the typical differences of PPA and approaches in the private and nonprofit sectors.
- Identify the prevailing issues in the modern PPA.
- Describe the different HRM perspectives and explain how it relates to PPA.
- Discuss the operating characteristics of public human resource management.

Preview

Public personnel management is widely regarded as an important element of effective public administration and a component of democratic society (Donald & Nalbandian, 2003). The personnel management—human resource management (HRM)—policies, strategies or practices may determine the service quality, efficiency and effectiveness of public sector organizations. The human resources in the public sector organizations must have the necessary competencies—knowledge, skills, and abilities (KSAs)—to provide efficient and professional public service and accomplish government goals. While the government strives to elevate the level of its performance and address the pressing issues of public governance, there are continuing challenges that limit the maximization of its services such as tighter funding which requires the government to do more with less, issues on human resource capacity, and employee's motivations (Burke, Allisey, Noblet, 2013). Internationally, these are crucial issues that personnel management must address in order to ensure that organizational goals are attained. Figure 1.1 shows the relationship of public personnel management, individual competency (e.g., knowledge, skills, and abilities), human resource behavior (e.g., motivation) and organizational performance.

Figure 1.1
Impact of Public Personnel Management

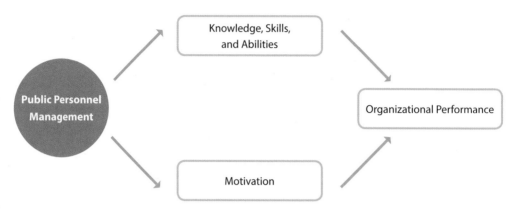

Understanding *public personnel management*—as a critical element for the satisfaction of the government's mandate reflected in established laws, policies or the constitution, will provide the necessary and effective approaches to public human resource planning, acquisition, development, and sanction (PADS). Clearly, it deals with the relationship between the organization and the maximization of individual competencies to achieve desired or mandated goal, mission and objectives. The relationship, however, is reciprocal, interactive and at times contradictory because the performed task is perceived to be meaningful to both the individual and the organization (Berman, Bowman, West, & Van Wart, 2012). The individual may consider tasks as a fulfillment of a motivation (e.g., intrinsic, extrinsic motivation), while the organization may contemplate on it as a utilization and maximization of human capital.

Public personnel management, then, is a colossal aspect of public organizational management. Public managers must be able to maximize the use of government resources—including human resource or capital—effectively and productively to address the needs of the society. Personnel management policies and practices such as workforce planning, recruitment, selection, job analysis, training and development, compensation, performance evaluation, labor management relations, and other functions on human resource administration can significantly affect individual behavior—also career development, and the total performance of the organization— service quality and citizen's satisfaction.

Why Focus on Public Personnel Management?

Definitely, focusing on public personnel management (PPM) is due to its important role for the effective and efficient operations of public organizations. The rationale behind the need to aim serious attention at PPM may include the following (Burke, Allisey, Noblet, 2013, p. 2): *a.* lack of attention in the HRM literature, *b.* role of public sector services and the role of human resources in achieving these services, *c.* civil service investment and its maximization, and *d.* workforce-related challenges in the public sector. *First,* discussions on contemporary human resource management failed to recognize the uniqueness of public sector personnel management—government or public funding, strict compliance with existing laws and regulations, public sector values, and indispensable external and internal influences on personnel practices and policies—in relation with the private sector. *Second,* the nature of services produced by the government—public goods and services—requires competent and reliable workforce. The work performed by the government through its employees must not be tainted with any incompetence or failures. The manner in which personnel administration or management is undertaken can influence the capacity of the public organization to execute the roles and responsibilities to an acceptable or exceptional level. *Third,* considering the enormous government budget allocated and spent for general government services which include civil servant's wages and salaries there is a need for the government workforce to show that these monies were spent to achieve better services for the citizens. In *Figure 1.2*, OECD countries allotted almost half of their GDP for general government expenditures. In 2012, the World Bank reports that the average percentage of GDP for operating activities of the public sector in providing good and services all over the world have reached 28.5%. *Lastly,* the foreseeable challenges of the future and extensive civil service reform require an objective grasp of the circumstances where public organizations will operate; for instance, the changing trend in the workforce demographics, unpredictable economic and political shifts, and the growing threat of terrorism or military extremism. Also, the U.S. Merit Systems Protection Board recognized the importance of having motivated, engaged, and skilled employees in the light of severe cuts to public spending, looming retirement, and public debates over the value of federal employees.

For the public sector leaders, public personnel management is unimpeachable factor of public management that is critical for organizational performance. Understanding the essentials of managing people and prioritizing personnel management can bring important developments on how the public sector can effectively and efficiently deliver public goods and services for the members of the community.

The remainder of this chapter sets the stage of *public personnel management* which includes the detailed discussion of its scope and context. Recognizing some ambiguities on the definition, functions, and role of PPM (relative to personnel administration and human resource management) in the public sector, we begin explaining its conceptual foundations and the typical differences with the private and non-profit sectors. The various traditional and contemporary HRM perspectives are tackled in relation and within the ambit of public personnel management. Finally, it will present reform trends in the public sector organizations and the challenges they bring in public management.

Figure 1.2
General government expenditures as a percentage of GDP (2001, 2009 and 2011)

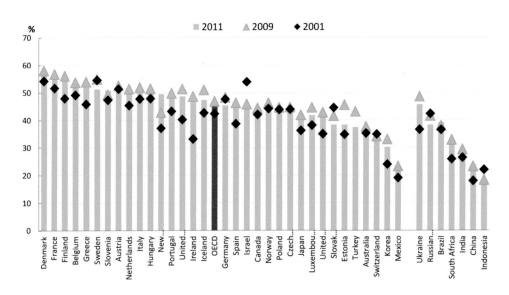

Source: OECD National Accounts Statistics (database). Data for the Other major economies
(excluding the Russian Federation) are from the IMF Economic Outlook (April 2013).

Making Sense of the RealWorld

One of the distinguishing characteristics of the pivotal development in the public personnel management is the rapid changes in the environmental context surrounding public sector organizations. The following video clips are supplemental materials that may help the learners widen the understanding on the topics discussed in this chapter.

Title	Gist	Source
The Workforce is Changing Rapidly: How Will You Manage?	The video clip provides a general scenario of the changing workforce demographics all over the world. This phenomenon warrants a careful consideration for effective workforce planning in all sectors, especially in the public organizations.	http://www.youtube.com/watch?v=2XIQkDldpml

a. What makes public personnel management "public," that is, what differentiates PPM from approaches in the private or non-profit sectors?

b. Based on your experience or knowledge, what are the most important or critical issues in PPA today? Do you have any comments or experience you can tell us about?

c. From a HRM perspective, what demographic and other trends should be monitored closely by public employees?

© Randy Glasbergen
glasbergen.com

"We have 22 different kinds of coffee, 8 types
of creamer and 5 different sweeteners.
That counts as diversity, doesn't it?"

Theory Synopsis

Public Personnel Administration, Management, and Public HRM

The terms *public personnel administration* (PPA), *public personnel management* (PPM), and public *human resource management* (HRM) must not be confused and used nonchalantly. These three denotes the same thing—the administration and management of public sector employees. Various scholars and practitioners used these terms in different ways but their meaning is more of the same. Generally, public HRM concern about the "*people part*" of public employees' administration and management, including hiring and promotion, training and development, compensation and benefits, retirement, and other related issues of public organization's workforce. As a tributary of human resource or public personnel management, PPA looks for ways to help civil servants thrive and be a productive force of the organization, and continuously find ways to improve organizational policies and practices associated with personnel planning, acquisition, development, discipline, and grievances or labor management relations. PPA functions as the connector between the public organization and its people working within it. PPM, as in the traditional lens of human resource management, is viewed as a means of moving people along to achieve organizational goals through staffing, performance, change management and achievement of administrative objectives. In essence, these three are *"workforce centered"* that focuses on "the challenges of attracting, retaining, motivating, and developing the large and diverse pool of highly qualified people" working with public entities like government offices.

Public personnel administration can also be understood in terms of the general context in which it operates. In most part, PPA operates within the sphere of public sector organizations and focuses on civil service, collective bargaining, affirmative action (AA) (wiseGeek, 2015). These three fields in the personnel management are associated on how human resources are oriented, trained, and protected by the public organizations. For example, civil service concerns on the protection of worker's rights and efficient public management; collective bargaining denotes on the labor management relations with regards negotiated work benefits and conditions; and affirmative action that ensures employment opportunities for the individuals who belong to protected classes (wiseGeek, 2014).

In the context of this textbook, PPA, PPM, or Public HRM is to be understood in the same sense—they are defined and to be comprehend as similar concept.

Public Personnel Management/HRM Functions

Generally, *public personnel management* has four main functions or purposes (wiseGeek, 2014; Llorens & Bataglio, 2009; Donald & Nalbandian, 2003) which can easily remembered through the acronym "**PADS**". These include, *first*, **planning** that is usually undertaken in the top level of the organization. The budget preparation and human resource planning (e.g., human resource allocation based on knowledge, skills, and abilities; job analysis; job classification; evaluation), and setting for pay and benefits. The purpose of this specific function provides the opportunity for the employees to be informed of what are to expect in the organization, thus will result for a smooth relationship between the organization and the employees, or better management and labor relations (wiseGeek, 2014; Llorens & Bataglio, 2009).

Second is **acquisition.** This is associated with the selection and recruitment of employees. This function requires the personnel manager or administrator to device ways in creating job postings, assessment, evaluation, maintaining HRM information system, and employ advance recruitment strategies and evaluation schemes (Llorens & Bataglio, 2009). Indispensable in the acquisition of human resource, this function includes interviewing job applicants, then recruit and retain the finest among them (wiseGeek, 2014), the equal employment opportunity (EEO), and affirmative action (AA). *Third* is **development**. The main focus of this function is motivation, training and development (TD), and performance evaluation. Motivating employees may go in parallel with the TD and performance evaluation. Employees must undergo the process of regular activities that will enhance their knowledge, skills, and ability to address pressing issues in their work and the organization. Personnel manager or administrator may develop enhanced performance appraisal techniques that may properly fir the needs of the organization, for example under merit pay system or at-will systems in the federal agencies of the United States.

Fourth is **sanction.** This function typically deals with the employer-employee relations (wiseGeek, 2014) such as handling and implementing existing labor relations and standards laws, grievance machineries and systems, workplace safety, and employment rights. The purpose of this function is to maintain the smooth working relationship between the employer (e.g., government agency) and the employees (e.g., unionized and un-unionized employees) through compliance and satisfaction of mutual obligations of the two parties (Donald & Nalbandian, 2003).

In most cases, public personnel management and administration executes functions of planning, acquisition, development, and sanctions within the limits provided and defined in existing civil service laws, regulations, and policies. Unlike in the private sector, personnel management are done within the prescribed policies and strategies of the management, however, in the public sector organizations cannot jump over the limits specifically provided in the language and intention of laws and regulations. For example, in cases of labor and management dispute in the public sector, the substantial satisfaction of "procedural due process" provided in settling disputes and actions afforded to employees (Goldman, 2007; cited in Riccucci, 2007). Due process is an elusive concept (Goldman, 2007), however, whatever infringement or curtailment of employee's right must satisfy the due process rule. If not, any action or decisions made are deemed *void ab initio* and with no force at all. This would be different in the private sector—they may have a different way on handling grievances and retaining employees. Basically, they must provide an opportunity for a party to be heard—in cases of firing an employee—and may follow a distinct labor and management dispute settlement that are usually provided by the statute. Employee retention programs focus on the importance of keeping good employees, and it includes programs such as training, development, and tuition assistance to help build loyalty and reduce turnover. Many public organizations are able to be as efficient as they are because of the talent, skill, and passion of their workforce, and people in the personnel administration field typically work to be sure these remains true over time.

Table 1.1 summarizes the main functions of PPM and the corresponding purpose attached to each functions.

Table 1.1 Public Personnel Management Functions

Function	Purpose
PLANNING	Budget preparation and human resource planning; dividing tasks among employees (job analysis, classification, and evaluation); deciding how much jobs are worth (pay and benefits)
ACQUISITION	Recruitment and selection of employees
DEVELOPMENT	Orienting, training, motivating, an evaluating employees to increase their competencies
SANCTION	Establishing and maintaining expectations and obligations that employees and the employer have toward one another; discipline, grievances, health and safety, and employer rights

Source: Klinger Donald, E., & Nalbandian, J. (2003).
Public Personnel Management: Contexts and Strategies. New Jersey.

Organizational Environment and Relevant Issues

Another way to think about *public personnel management and administration* is in terms of the organizational environment in which it exists. Almost all agencies (e.g., public, nonprofit, private) have personnel management system — *what* are the different elements that may affect their operations often a little bit different. The external and internal environment continues to influence the operations of the public organizations. For instance, political factors, economic factors, legal changes, socio-cultural changes, technological changes, private competition, and among others (Pynes, 2008) challenge the functions of public personnel management and administration. These environmental factors are discussed in detail in Chapter 2. A visual depiction of the various internal and external environmental factors of public personnel management is shown in Figure 1.3.

The public personnel managers need to take cognizance of various issues and trends in the public sector environment such as, the changing workforce demographics, decreasing trust in the government, budget cuts, contract or alternative work arrangements, downsizing and upsizing, demands for productivity, emerging workplace and virtual government, reforming and reengineering initiatives, centralization and decentralization of human resource activities, and increased managerial flexibility (Berman et al., 2012). These trends and issues are critical factors that affect the operations and have important implications on public personnel management and administration. Each trend will be discussed and considered in whole in Chapter 2, under the subsection *Environmental Context and Challenges for Public HRM.*

Figure 1.3
The Environmental Context of PPM

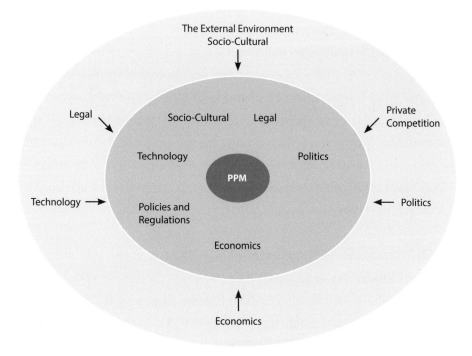

HRM Perspectives

The field of Human Resource Management (HRM) has evolved significantly over the past 90-100 years (Wright & Boswell, 2002). Studies have been initiated on HRM dwelling on various perspectives—macro, micro, international and national, top-down and bottom up, political and managerial, traditional and NPM, quantitative and qualitative, and efficiency and equity perspectives. Each of these areas appeared to be separate and distinct; however, a line can be drawn across these areas to show connections and interrelationship.

Macro and Micro Perspective

Consistently, studies have shown that HRM can be characterized into macro perspective (strategic) and micro perspective (functional) (see Mahoney & Deckop, 1986; Fisher, 1989). The dichotomization was brought by different issues and trends surrounding the field—such as the transition from traditional personnel administration to contemporary HRM approach, and from human resource planning to strategic human resource design (Wright & Boswell, 2002). Also, the splitting of HRM into macro and micro perspectives provided the clear distinction between tying human resource to strategy and other strategic issues (e.g., mergers, international HRM, downsizing, etc.) and the fundamentals of the functional HRM such as selection and training, compensation, and performance appraisal (Fisher, 1989; Wright & Boswell, 2002).

Traditionally, the *macro perspective* of public HRM is associated with strategic components of human resource based on reforms, equal employment opportunity (EEO), diversity, labor relations and standards. On the otherhand, the *micro perspective* of public HRM focused on the functional aspect of HRM which includes recruitment and selection, human resource development (e.g., OD, CD, ID) job evaluation and compensation, motivation and leadership, strategic human resource management, and among others. In the research arena, *micro* HRM perspective was explored looking at the impact of numerous HR practices on individual performance (e.g., work productivity, turnover, absenteeism, etc.) satisfaction, quality of work produced, or on some individual characteristics (e.g., knowledge, skills, abilities, attitudes, intention or disposition, behavior, etc.) (Wright & Boswell, 2002).

International and National/Domestic Perspectives

HRM was also viewed based on international and national context. Undoubtedly, there has been a dramatic growth of interest in international human resource management (IHRM) which can be applied to various emerging multinational or international organizations. For many years, researchers argued that international organizations must follow the HRM concepts and principles developed and applied in the United States to be successful (Fisher, 1989). However, this was outmoded by the "divergence approach" that recognized the critical role of culture in managing people in an international context and the necessity to develop a unique perspective that integrates various cultural variables (Fisher, 1989; Ricks, Toyne, & Martinez, 1990).

As compared to domestic or national HRM perspective, IHRM must take serious cognizance of the different cultural norms as well as social values of all employees. The unique composition of the international organization requires the coherence and applicability of management strategies to one's cultural orientation. In the IHRM research arena, Ferris and colleagues (1990) suggested that "researchers must be wary of the interaction of different cultural-based norms and social values, the adaptability of management issues from one culture to another, the legal and economic differences that exist, and the different learning styles and response styles due to socio-cultural differences" (p. 395). The diverse cultural origins of employees necessitate the application of various management approaches that may encompass the socio-cultural values of the people in the organization. By this alone, the difference between national or domestic HRM and IHRM may be drawn. Any organization operating in a global context, must be wary of the welfare of their people, thus, must find ways to become intimately connected in their people's personal lives and give them necessary support through various means (Ferris et al., 1990). Figure 1.4 provides a visual mapping of HRM&D approaches across nations—Global HRM&D comparative HRM&D, and national HRM&D.

Figure 1.4
Mapping the Boundaries of HRM&D

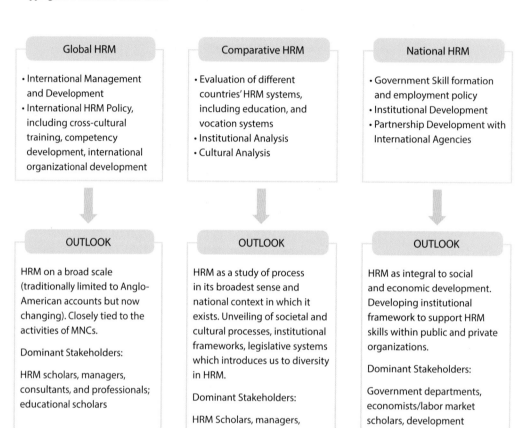

Global HRM	Comparative HRM	National HRM
• International Management and Development • International HRM Policy, including cross-cultural training, competency development, international organizational development	• Evaluation of different countries' HRM systems, including education, and vocation systems • Institutional Analysis • Cultural Analysis	• Government Skill formation and employment policy • Institutional Development • Partnership Development with International Agencies
OUTLOOK	OUTLOOK	OUTLOOK
HRM on a broad scale (traditionally limited to Anglo-American accounts but now changing). Closely tied to the activities of MNCs. Dominant Stakeholders: HRM scholars, managers, consultants, and professionals; educational scholars	HRM as a study of process in its broadest sense and national context in which it exists. Unveiling of societal and cultural processes, institutional frameworks, legislative systems which introduces us to diversity in HRM. Dominant Stakeholders: HRM Scholars, managers, consultants, and professionals	HRM as integral to social and economic development. Developing institutional framework to support HRM skills within public and private organizations. Dominant Stakeholders: Government departments, economists/labor market scholars, development sociologists, UNDP, WB, OECD, ILO, INGOs, and NGOS

Source: Metcalfe, B. D., & Rees, C. J. (2005). Theorizing advances in international human resource development. Human Resource Development International, 8(4), 449-465.

Political and Managerial Perspectives

The political perspective on HRM puts emphasis on the influence of politics on human resource management functions, for instance in the selection and recruitment process, human resource development (HRD) (e.g., organizational development, individual development, and career development), performance evaluation, and other main areas that politics may intervene. For Ferris et al (1990), they identified three categories that have been the subject of research in the field—staffing and/or employment interview decisions, performance evaluation process, and career success. These categories are critical components of HRM that may give a serious blow in achieving positive organizational results. For instance, *first,* the selection process may decide the kind of employee or [the employee-management relationship in that matter] that will be integrated in the organization if they are recruited and selected based on political backing or influence. However, a study shows that the results of interview for those who employed "self-promotion tactics" in the application process have higher ratings than those who employed "ingratiation tactics" or the political-backing strategy (Kacmar, Delery, & Ferris, 1992; cited in Ferris et al., 1990).

Second, the role and influence of politics in the performance evaluation is unimpeachable fact. Theory and results of studies recognized that supervisors rating employees' performance may be driven by political goals and agenda, thus undermining the objectivity of the evaluation (see, for example, Cleveland & Murphy, 1992). As pointed by Ferris and colleagues (1990), "rating errors may not simply be errors of omission, but errors of commission as well" (p. 398).

Lastly, the career success category are deemed to be influenced by politics either through extrinsic (e.g., salary, job level, number of promotions, etc.) and intrinsic (job and life satisfaction) career success (Judge & Bretz, 1994). These arguments can also be associated with the findings derived from the study reported by Ferris, Judge et al. (1994), in which "ingratiation tactics" or political-backing strategy resulted in higher outcomes while "self-promotion tactics" had a negative impact on career success. Table 1.2 depicts the shared responsibility for personnel functions of the elected and appointed officials, managers and supervisors, and personnel directors and specialists.

Table 1.2
Shared Responsibilities for Personnel Functions

Function	Level		
	Elected and Appointed Officials	Managers and Supervisors	Personnel Directors and Specialists
PLANNING	Estimate revenues; set program priorities	Manage to mission within a budget	Develop job descriptions, implement pay and benefit plans
ACQUISITION	Influence values that guide the selection process	Hire and fire employees	Develop hiring rules and procedures
DEVELOPMENT	Define agency and program goals and priorities	Make sure employees have clear goals, skills, feedback, and rewards	Develop training and evaluation systems
SANCTION	Determine appropriate personnel systems	Counsel and discipline employees and policies	Develop policies and programs for drug testing, discipline

Source: Klinger Donald, E., & Nalbandian, J. (2003).
Public Personnel Management: Contexts and Strategies. New Jersey.

The managerial perspective on the otherhand, must be understood in a manner that HRM functions are dealt with objectivity where decisions and actions are based on strategic direction of the organization and the specific goals and objectives that they are mandated to achieve.

Traditional and NPM Perspectives

In the public sector, the traditional HRM perspective has been greatly associated with the "ideals of justice, fairness, equality, transparency and stability"… "job security, regular and predictable salary increments, generous pensions, promotion based on seniority, a focus on equal opportunities, and paternalistic and collectivist approaches to managing the employment relationship" (OECD, 2005; Truss, 2013; cited in Burke, Noblet, & Cooper, 2013, p. 21). Traditionally, HRM is perceived within the bounds of the bureaucratic principles characterized by centralization, hierarchical structures, and rule-based decision-making (Brown, 2004; Burke et al., 2013). Table 1.3 shows that traditional core functions of HRM.

However, various scholars argued that the traditional and old public sector approaches are no longer plausible in addressing the emerging and diversifying needs of the society. The New Public Management (NPM) emerged as an alternative—but some denotes it as an innovative approach to public sector government—to the traditional approach on managing people in the organization. One of the manifestations of this transition is that, if in the traditional HRM, the seniority matters as an indicative requirement for promotion, in the NPM, looks at the performance appraisals outcome as the basis for an upward movement in the organization.

Table 1.3
Traditional Core Functions of Public Human Resources Management (HRM)

Function	Task Involved
PLANNING	Job Analysis Classification Compensation Workforce Planning
ACQUISITION	Recruitment Assessment Selection Equal Employment Opportunity (EEO) Affirmative Action (AA)
DEVELOPMENT	Training Performance Management Safety and Health
SANCTION	Employee Relations Labor Relations/Collective Bargaining

Source: Llorens, J. J., & Bataglio, R. P. (2009). Human resources management in a changing world: Reassessing public hum human resources management education. Review of Public Personnel Administration, 30(1), 112-132.

Other HRM Perspectives

- Top-down vs. Bottom-up Perspectives
- Quantitative vs. Qualitative Perspective
- Efficiency vs. Equity Perspectives

HR Core Traditional Values

Public personnel management or administration typically exists within the context of continuously interacting—or conflicting—values such as the protection of individual rights, organizational effectiveness, selection by merit (e.g., neutral competence), administrative efficiency, demographical representativeness, political responsiveness, centralization and formalization, security of tenure, and a rational-legal bureaucracy (see also Klinger & Nalbandian, 2003). Looking with these core values, one may also provide a conclusive idea on the differences between the public and private sector organization's personnel management for instance on the political context (wiseGeek, 2014).

Individual Rights

It gives emphasis on the respect and ensures the protection of individual rights against arbitrary and capricious actions or decisions by the government with regards, job security, and other issues that may affect the individual employment. By the language and spirit of law, civil servants must remain apolitical, thus must be insulated from any political pressures such as participating in any campaign sortie, making contributions, or directly engaging in the electoral practices. Also, it afforded protection for those unionized members of the organization—that compliance of the provisions of the collective bargaining agreements are fully observed, respected and implemented. The observance of the individual rights includes and not limited to what was provided in the Bill of Rights such as the equal protection of the laws and due process.

Merit Selection

Proponents of merit selection (e.g., neutral competence) emphasized on the need to professionalize the ranks of the government. For example, for the recruitment of government positions that requires important knowledge, skills, and abilities (KSA), and formal or required education to such position. The merit selection may observe the principles of the *"square peg on a round hole"*. Meaning, misfits must be eliminated and discouraged.

Demographical Representativeness

This reflects the equal opportunity of every individual to be employed in the government given the required competence, or satisfaction of the requirements for employment. Given that equal employment opportunity (EEO), this is "designed to eliminate discrimination passively by protecting fairness in employment process and decisions" (Klinger & Nalbandian, 2003, p. 161)   and affirmative action (AA) that is, "designed to deal with the failure of passive non-discrimination to eliminate discrimination by enforcing diversity" (Klinger & Nalbandian, 2003, p. 161).

Social Equity

It emphasizes fairness to every groups of the society (e.g., women, racial minorities, disabled, and veterans) or those that may have been sidelined or disadvantaged due to some occurrences—such as economic changes. Generally, social equity is concerned of justice or fairness based on employment preferences with regards membership in a protected class or group.

Organizational Effectiveness

It is the belief that reflects the aspiration towards an effective and efficient public sector organization; that is the recruitment and selection process are based on the applicants and employee's competencies and not on political considerations.

Political Responsiveness

It denotes on the responsiveness of the government on the people's will. Meaning, the individual's political loyalty are best ensured based on the objective qualifications provided on the job requirements (KSAs), merits, and/or training and educational attainment. In cases of political, appointees, in a given context, a political leader may appoint a certain employee as a "political appointee" by virtue of his appointing authority. However, the nature of the appointment and functions are determined and decided by the appointing authority or by the personnel management as the case may be.

Other Important HR Core Values

- A Career Service of Security of Tenure and Lifelong Employment
- A Rational-Legal Bureaucracy
- Administrative Efficiency
- Centralization and Formalization

Public Personnel Management in Developed and Developing Countries

Public personnel management in the U.S. and in developing countries has evolved as a dynamic equilibrium among competing values and systems for allocating scarce public jobs in a complex and changing environment. These stages are shown in Table 1.4 (United States) and Table 1.5 (Developing Countries).

Table 1.4
Evolution of Public Personnel Systems and Values in the United States

Stage of Evolution	Dominant Value(s)	Dominant System(s)	Pressure for Change
One (1789-1828)	Responsiveness	"Government by elites"	Political parties + Patronage
Two (1828-1883)	Responsiveness	Patronage	Modernization + Democratization
Three (1883-1933)	Efficiency + Individual Rights	Civil Service	Responsiveness + Effective Government
Four (1933-1964)	Responsiveness + Efficiency + Individual Rights	Patronage + Civil Service	Individual Rights + Social Equity
Five (1964-1980)	Responsiveness + Efficiency + Individual Rights + Social Equity	Patronage + Civil Service + Collective Bargaining + Affirmative Action	Dynamic equilibrium among four competing values and systems
Six (1980-now)	Responsiveness + Efficiency + Individual Accountability + Limited government + Community Responsibility	Patronage + Civil Service + Collective Bargaining + Affirmative Action + Alternative mechanisms + Flexible employment relationships	Dynamic equilibrium among four competing values and systems, and three anti-governmental values and systems

Source: Klinger Donald, E., & Nalbandian, J. (2003). Public Personnel Management: Contexts and Strategies. New Jersey.

Table 1.5
Evolution of Public Personnel Systems and Values in the Developing Countries

Stage of Evolution	Dominant Value(s)	Dominant System(s)	Pressure for Change
One	Responsiveness	"Government by elites"	Political parties + Patronage
Two	Responsiveness	Patronage	Modernization + Democratization
Three	Efficiency + Individual Rights	Civil Service + Patronage	Responsiveness + Effective Government
Four	Responsiveness + Efficiency + Limited Government	Patronage + Civil Service + Collective Bargaining + Privatization	Dynamic equilibrium among four competing values and systems, and anti-governmental values

Source: Klinger Donald, E., & Nalbandian, J. (2003). Public Personnel Management: Contexts and Strategies. New Jersey.

Traditional HR Systems

Patronage System

Patronage System is the system that allows a political leader—legislator or executives—to appoint employee in a particular position in a temporary nature. Such job is a co-terminus job which will be dissolved at the whims of the appointing authority, or at the expiration of the appointing authority's term of office.

Civil Service System

Civil Service System amplifies on the importance of professionalizing the civil service (see also Klinger & Nalbandian, 2003). In doing this, it requires an objective and strict compliance of existing selection and recruitment process for public servants; and is based on the public workforce strategic planning, and fair treatment of employees. It also demands the provision of various traditional or contemporary benefits afforded for public employees (e.g., family friendly policies, pension, health benefits, etc.), respect and protection of constitutional and moral rights as a worker, and a civil service that is totally insulated against "partisan politics"

Collective Bargaining Systems

In substantive compliance of showing real faith on the rights of individuals, the collective bargaining system echoes the importance of individual right to association—such as joining a labor union or federation—and must ensure the faithful compliance of whatever has been agreed [after proper approval of higher office(s), for example the legislature in case of U.S. government] in the CBA. Basically, this system wants to ensure that a smooth relationship exists between the management and labor side.

Affirmative Action Systems

This system encourages the government to give due credence for those misrepresented sector in the government labor force, for example female, minority groups, disabled applicants, and other disadvantaged group. However, for this system to work, the public sector must recognize that there is an imbalance in the workforce (Klinger & Nalbandian, 2003); and that they are qualified based on the established standards. The court may as well intervene in cases where the government failed to recognize that there is such an inequality or disproportion in the public sector workforce.

New Managerial Values

The emergence of contemporary and "innovative" management approach—New Public Management (NPM) has opened a new arena of debate and ideas on public management. Relative to the traditional system of HRM, new managerial values surfaced: rule-bound culture and a performance-based culture; a new model of public management: NPM Model (e.g. managing results, performance measurements); efficiency and cost effectiveness of the personnel system itself; strategic HR management in support of the agency's mission; alternative organization: NGO, non-profit organizations; and flexile employee relationships: at-will systems...without civil service "bumping rights". Figure 1.5 depicts NPM and Post-NPM Reform Values.

Figure 1.5
NPM and Post-NPM Reform Values

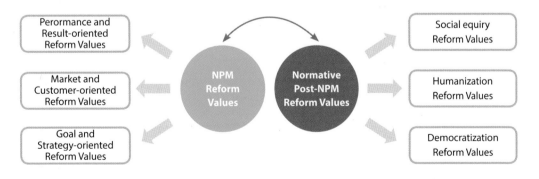

Source: Park, S. M., & Joaquin, M. E. (2012). Of alternating waves and shifting shores: the configuration of reform values in the US federal bureaucracy. International Review of Administrative Sciences, 78(3), 514-536.

Case Brief

Hiring the Unqualified

Congress of the United States, House of Representatives
Washington, DC 20515-0502
Congressman Wally Herger's Comments
Regarding USDA Civil Rights Programs
Woodland, California

I appreciate Secretary Glickman's leadership in providing this forum for both federal employees and the interested public to discuss United Stated Department of Agriculture (USDA) civil rights programs. I am a strong supporter of the Civil Rights Act of 1964.

The laudable goal of that landmark piece of legislation was the abolition of discrimination. Regrettably, the USDA civil rights programs fall far short of that lofty goal. Indeed, current USDA civil rights programs show an obsession with matters of race and gender, and an unfair and counterproductive commitment to quotas in both hiring and promotion opportunities.

I will submit for the record today United States Forest Service job announcements which specify that—and I am now quoting from these job postings—"Only unqualified applicants may apply," "Only applicants who do not meet X-118 standard will be considered," and "Only applicants who do not meet the Office of Personnel Management (OPM) qualifications requirements will be considered under this announcement."

Mr. Secretary, I submit to you that it is not a civil right to land a job for which one is unqualified. If we, as a nation, are to ever move beyond conflicts over race and gender, we must become color blind. We must let excellence be our standard, because excellence can come and does come in a variety of colors. We must return to the original vision of Dr. Martin Luther King, Jr., who hoped for a day in which all of us are judged by the content of our character, and not the color of our skin.

The affirmative action programs of the USDA are nothing more than quota programs. As such, they are divisive and morally indefensible. They guarantee workplace hostility, and set race relations backward, not forward. They stigmatize the very people who are supposed to benefit from the program. What message is sent to the employee who applies for a position which requires that he or she demonstrate that he or she has yet met minimal standards associated with the position? This is ludicrous, and it must end. We cannot remedy past discrimination by engaging in more discrimination. The best solution for past discrimination is no more discrimination at all.

I have heard from hundreds of Forest Service employees who have deluged my office with job announcements that contain bizarre preconditions, which effectively preclude them from the advertised position.

I will provide to you today a job announcement, which contains the requirement that the successful applicant must show a (quote) "demonstrated commitment to civil rights or contribution to a diverse workforce." Forest Service employees have complained that his appears to be "code language" designed to exclude many otherwise qualified non-minority males. By USDA definition, non-minority males do not contribute to a diverse workforce. And how is the job applicant expected to "demonstrate" his commitment to the Forest Service civil rights program? This appears to require the passing of an ideological litmus test as a requirement for employment or promotion. This has an Orwellian overtone, and is flatly wrong.

Many of my constituents who are Forest Service employees do not support the USDA civil rights programs, and are involved in a lawsuit to protest this kind of quota hiring. These employees surely do not demonstrate commitment to the program over which they are suing and thus they are, by definition, unable to meet the evaluation criteria for this advertised position. Not only is quota hiring unfair and divisive, it can also be dangerous. I am today submitting a "white paper" produced by the Plumas National Forest, in which the following statements appeared:

> In a growing number of instances, we are not filling positions when there are no women applicants. In the past three months we have re-advertised, left vacant, or filled with unqualified temporaries eleven permanent fire positions because we could not find female applicants. If the position is in fire prevention or forest fuels management, the job simply doesn't get done and we face the consequences of additional person-caused fires and untreated hazardous forest fuels. The Plumas attempted to fill five Positions from the roster, but could only reach two women. Both women declined our offers. No offers were made to men. All fire positions are presently vacant or filled with unqualified temporary employees.

I find the preceding statements both shocking and appalling. Regrettably, it was not an isolated incident. Both public safety and our natural resources can clearly be compromised by this wrong-headed policy. Quota hiring is also expensive. The quota hiring system has led to an explosion of Equal Employment Opportunity complaints within the Forest Service. Forest Service employees have informed me that the costs of these Equal Employment Opportunity Commission (EEOC) complaints, including sizable financial awards, are often "charged" to the timber of fire budget of the affected forest. Thus, we see less money committed to the resources on the ground as available funding is consumed by contentious legal squabbles. This situation is a disservice to both the taxpayers and our federal employees.

On several occasions, my inquiries to the Forest Service regarding this matter have been met with the response that, while these problems may have existed in many years ago, they have now been corrected. Regrettably, there are recent job postings, which clearly indicate that quotas are, in fact, the status quo within USDA. Documents are attached for your review. Mr. Secretary, I urge you to scrap the current fatally flawed quota system and install in its place a merit and skill-based approach to both hiring and promotions.

Because the Forest Service civil rights program has been particularly harmful, I have introduced legislation—the Forest Service Employment Opportunity Act of 1997— to assist the Forest Service in moving beyond the failed status quo. I encourage the Administration to support this legislative remedy. Working together, we can put past problems behind us by fashioning hiring and promotion policies that are fair to everyone. The current programs have clearly failed to achieve the desired outcomes of nondiscrimination and fairness. USDA must do better. Thank you.

1. Discuss your reasons for either continuing or discontinuing the Forest Service's practice of reserving certain designated positions to be filled by unqualified applicants.

2. What is the implied correlation between an increase in EEOC complaints and the filling of positions with unqualified applicants?

3. What options are available for achieving the Forest Service's goal of increased diversity without compromising the merit system?

This case was adopted from: Reeves, T. Z. (2006).*Cases in public human resource management*. Thomson Wadsworth.

Student Activity:

Mapping-out for the public sector human resource management (public personnel management or administration); identify the extent wherein traditional HR systems and new managerial values are evident in your organization or country. Write about these values and their contributions as well as their negative impacts to the organization. Use the case analysis table below to provide a clear organization of your thoughts.

HRM in the Public Organizations: An Essential Guide

Case Analysis

	Step	Contents		
1	Environments/ Conditions/ Backgrounds	Please explain the situation briefly. (1-2 pages)		
2	Problem Definitions	In your own perspective, please be as specific as possible when pointing out the problem. (2-3 pages)		
3	Actual Case Studies	Please explain by providing specific examples. (Newspaper articles, news clips, or interviews) (2-3 pages)		
4	Alternatives	Possible Alternative(s)	Pros in your Country Context	Cons in a your Country Context
		①		
		②		
		③		
		Please propose more than three policy alternatives. (2-3 pages)		
5	The Best Solutions	Why did you choose this alternative as the best solution? What are the expected effects and potential contribution? (2 pages)		

1. How does traditional personnel administration differ from HRM?

2. If you were in charge of reforming civil service in your country, what do you think the best way to reduce anti-reform sentiments during the reform period?

3. What if you fail to continue the process? If you made a successful case, how would you transfer, export, and generalize the reform values/initiatives to other organizational/institutional/national settings?

Ending Credits

Research Digest

Building bridges over troubled waters: Merit as a guide

Facts

In 1883, nearly two years after President James A. Garfield had been shot by a federal office seeker, who believed he had been treated unfairly in his job search, Congress passed the Pendleton Act. The act was intended to restore professional competence to the federal service and significantly limit the intrusion of politics into its composition and conduct. The Pendleton Act had three main provisions: (1) It provided that admission to the federal service be based on open, competitive testing; (2) it prohibited fi ring federal employees for any reason other than cause; and (3) it provided that no political pressure or coercion be exerted on federal employees for contributions or specific actions.

The act also directed that federal work be arranged in hierarchical classes and that appointment and promotion occur in accordance with that structure. The Pendleton Act, in classic incremental American fashion, initially covered only 10 percent of new employees. Other members of the service could be "blanketed in" by special order of the president (Ingraham 1995; Van Riper 1958). Over time, and with ebbs and flows, they were. Seventy years later, during the Eisenhower administration, the system established by the Pendleton Act had expanded to cover 86 percent of the U.S. federal service (Pfeiffer 2000, 30).

In this less than spectacular fashion, the administrative system that is now most frequently referred to as the *merit system* was born and grew. It never abolished patronage, nor was it intended to. Its own top administrative unit — the Civil Service Commission — was oddly disjointed, having responsibility for both advising the president on political appointments and ensuring that those appointees did not intrude into the operations of the civil service. The hierarchical classification system stipulated by the law ensured that bureaucratic processes and operations would be key characteristics of the system as it grew. Each of these contained the seeds of dysfunction. But more fundamentally, except for a brief time immediately preceding and following the passage of the Pendleton Act, the system did not earn the respect of the citizens whom it was designed to serve. Hugh Heclo observes, "Repeatedly, the energy behind civil service reform has come from exploiting public dissatisfactions and distrust of government. ... What the public is not prepared to accept, indeed what it has been persistently educated to reject in a political culture of bureaucrat bashing, is the idea that the civil service itself could be a high professional calling " (2000, 230 – 31). Did the system, despite these problems, instill merit, the objective it sought? Should we now be referring to the contemporary civil service system as a *merit* system?

Current interchangeability of the terms would suggest so. In fact, some debates about federal government reforms that are now on the table suggest that changing the procedures of the civil service system would fundamentally attack the concept of merit (Partnership for Public Service 2005). We know, however, that civil service systems are not meritorious in many ways. We also know that characteristics of systems that are designed to foster merit and those of systems notable only for bureaucratic features have become intricately commingled. Rendering civil service synonymous with merit has become commonplace but has caused untold confusion, obfuscation, and dissatisfaction.

Indeed, former President Jimmy Carter advocated for the Civil Service Reform Act of 1978 by arguing that there was "no merit in the merit system!" (Ingraham, 1995, 76). The president was talking about the worst characteristics of a rigid civil service system and bureaucracy: excessive rules, slowness, and apparent lack of accountability and sensitivity to the world beyond bureaucratic boundaries. That does not characterize merit. Indeed, it is these dysfunctional bureaucratic characteristics of the civil service system that have been the targets of past and contemporary reforms, including those aimed at better presidential direction and control. Merit and meritorious service have not been maligned. That is also true in relation to the current emphasis on performance. These reforms do not undermine merit and are, in fact, compatible with merit *if public action is meritorious in pursuit of better performance.*

Issues
1. Civil service and Merit System.

2. Civil Service is associated with dysfunctional, bureaucratic government personnel practices.

3. The civil service system must be reformed if merit principles (ideals) are to be preserved.

Arguments/Findings
Throughout the article, it was argued that effective consideration of reform of the federal service necessarily separates and preserves the ideal of merit from the bureaucratic structures that are often described as the merit system. Reform of the structures that characterize the civil service must be considered, but from a different

perspective. Many elements of those structures have been widely conceded to be dysfunctional and costly, and in fact, some of them have already been reformed in single agencies. Others are current targets of change. None of the past or current changes proposes to abandon merit.

The global environment in which the U.S. federal service operates demands a new emphasis on the dimensions of merit that comport with its original intent: to guarantee the presence of a well-qualified, talented, responsive workforce that functions well in rapidly changing conditions. Recent analyses of the current global environment describe it as "permanent whitewater" or a "constant spin cycle" (McAllister, forthcoming; Sanders 2005). The e old structures will attempt to withstand such turbulence in classic bureaucratic fashion: They will become more insular, less responsive, and less effective. Reforming them is fundamental to successfully meeting new challenges.

Current reform proposals envision a federal public service of the future that is different from today' s service, but none advocates eliminating a well- qualified and competent federal workforce. None suggests that the entire workforce be employed "at will." And none suggests that merit has run its course. Rather, contemporary views of merit envision it as the energizing force of the goals and ideas that guide reform. Merit as a value and an ideal can or cannot reside in mechanisms created to attain it, but those mechanisms can generate their own value by pursuing merit and effectively structuring the business of government. Sadly, in the federal government, the present civil service is not meeting these positive objectives. Simply put, the existing civil service structures and processes are not providing merit a happy home. Some structure or set of structures is obviously necessary to carry the value forward. That is why both the ideal of merit and the best means of attaining it are critical elements of effective reform. Structural changes to the bureaucratic systems surrounding civil service should not proceed without the pursuit of merit as their most fundamental objective. But they must proceed.

Source: Ingraham, P. W. (2006). Building bridges over troubled waters: Merit as a guide. Public Administration Review, 66(4), 486-495.

Further Readings

- Berman, E. M., Bowman, J. S., West, J. P., & Van Wart, M. R. (Ed.) (2012). *Human Resource Management in Public Service: Paradoxes, Processes, and Problems.* Fourth Edition. Sage Publications.

- Kim, P. S. (Ed.) (2010). *Civil Service System and Civil Service Reform in ASEAN Member Countries and Korea.*

- Brown, K. (2004). Human resource management in the public sector. *Public Management Review, 6*(3), 303-309. .

- Llorens, J. J., & Bataglio, R. P. (2009). Human resources management in a changing world: Reassessing public human resources management education. *Review of Public Personnel Administration, 30*(1), 112-132.

- Ingraham, P. W. (2006). Building bridges over troubled waters: Merit as a guide. *Public Administration Review, 66*(4), 486-495. & Thompson, J. R. (2006). The federal civil service: The demise of an institution. *Public Administration Review, 66*(4), 496-503.

- Denhardt, R. B., & Denhardt, J. V. (2000). The new public service: Serving rather than steering. *Public Administration Review, 60*(6), 549-559.

- Park, S. M., & Joaquin, E. M. (2012). Of alternating waves and shifting shores: The configuration of reform values in the U.S. federal bureaucracy. *International Review of Administrative Sciences, 78(3),* 467-489.

References

Alfes, K., Shantz, A. D., Truss, C., & Soane, E. C. (2013). The link between perceived human resource management practices, engagement and employee behaviour: a moderated mediation model. *The international journal of human resource management*, 24(2), 330-351.

Berman, E. M., Bowman, J. S., West, J. P., & Van Wart, M. R. (2012). *Human resource management in public service: Paradoxes, processes, and problems.* Sage.

Burke, R. J., Allisey, A. F., & Noblet, A. J. (2013). The importance of human resource management in the public sector, future challenges and the relevance of the current collection. *Human resource management in the public sector*, 1-16.

Cleveland, J. N., & Murphy, K. R. (1992). Analyzing performance appraisal as goal-directed behavior. *Research in personnel and human resources management*, 10(2), 121-185.

Ferris, G. R., Hochwarter, W. A., Buckley, M. R., Harrell-Cook, G., & Frink, D. D. (1999). Human resources management: Some new directions. *Journal of management*, 25(3), 385-415.

Ferris, G. R., Judge, T. A., Rowland, K. M., & Fitzgibbons, D. E. (1994). Subordinate influence and the performance evaluation process: Test of a model. *Organizational behavior and human decision processes*, 58(1), 101-135.

Fisher, C. D. (1989). Current and recurrent challenges in HRM. *Journal of Management*, 15(2), 157-180.

Goldman, D. D. (2007). Due Process and Public Personnel Management. *Public Personnel Administration and Labor Relations*, 217.

Judge, T. A., & Bretz, R. D. (1994). Political influence behavior and career success. *Journal of Management*, 20, 43–65.

Kacmar, K. M., Delery, J. E., & Ferris, G. R. (1992). Differential Effectiveness of Applicant Impression Management Tactics on Employment Interview Decisions1. *Journal of Applied Social Psychology*, 22(16), 1250-1272.

Klinger Donald, E., & Nalbandian, J. (2003). Public Personnel Management: Contexts and Strategies. *New Jersey*.

Llorens, J. J., & Battaglio, R. P. (2009). Human resources management in a changing world: Reassessing public hum human resources management education. *Review of Public Personnel Administration, 30*(1), 112-132.

Mahoney, T. A., & Deckop, J. R. (1986). Evolution of concept and practice in personnel administration/human resource management (PA/HRM). *Journal of Management*, 12(2), 223-241.

Murphy, K. R., Cleveland, J. N., Skattebo, A. L., & Kinney, T. B. (2004). Raters who pursue different goals give different ratings. *Journal of Applied Psychology*, 89(1), 158.

Metcalfe, B. D., & Rees, C. J. (2005). Theorizing advances in international human resource development. *Human Resource Development International*, *8*(4), 449-465.

Pynes, J. E. (2008). *Human resources management for public and nonprofit organizations: A strategic approach* (Vol. 30). John Wiley & Sons.

Riccucci, N. M. (Ed.). (2007). *Public personnel administration and labor relations*. ME Sharpe.

Ricks, D. A., Toyne, B., & Martinez, Z. (1990). Recent developments in international management research. *Journal of Management*, *16*(2), 219-253.

WiseGeek (2015). What is Public Personnel Administration? Retrieved from http://www.wisegeek.org/what-is-public-personnel-administration.htm

Wright, P. M., & Boswell, W. R. (2002). Desegregating HRM: A review and synthesis of micro and macro human resource management research. *Journal of management*, *28*(3), 247-276.

Public HRM Context, Challenges, and Reforms

Framework

Human Resource Management for Public Organizations: An Essential Guide

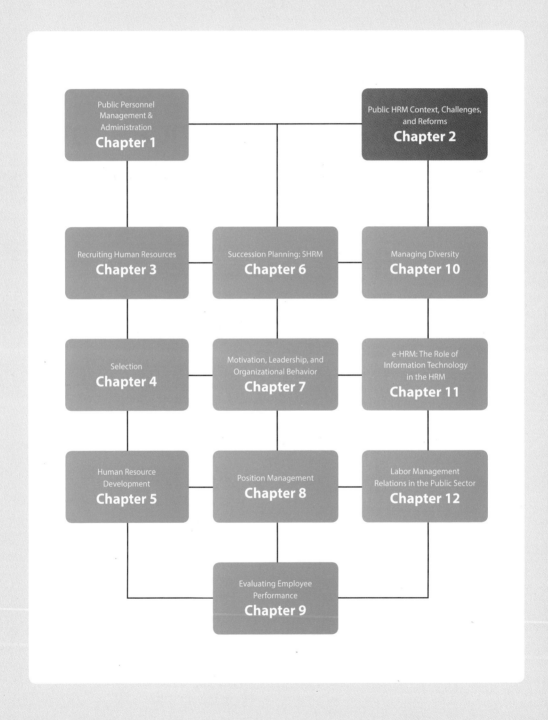

Learning Outcomes

After going through this chapter, you should be able to:

- Understand and determine the environmental context of Public HRM.
- Assess the contribution and impact of various environmental contexts on effective public sector organizational management.
- Describe the different trends and/or reforms in the public sector and determine how they contribute in the effective management.
- Identify how the Public HRM challenges are evident in the current or past public sector organizations.
- Identify the various reform trends within the ambit of public management and determine the contributions in the effective operations of public organizations.

Preview

Managers in the public sector organization need to be watchful of various developments, trends, or changes in the environmental context of *Public HRM* (Berman et al., 2013). These trends and developments are important because they may cause significant changes in the personnel management strategies, policies, practices, as well as systems that may impact employee's behavior and attitudes (e.g., quality of services and goods delivered), productivity, and the overall organizational performance. As people is one of the important resources in the organization, human resource strategies and practices (e.g., recruitment & selection, training & development, compensation, motivation, etc.) are required to be the most appropriate and effective levers that may thwart any organizational backlash brought by the unpredictable environmental context of public sector organizations. Even in the most advanced nations, public HR strategies and practices are developed to stand the shocks of unstable external and internal environmental climate. Thus, it entails malleable strategies and practices to provide rooms for immediate and fitting changes in the current HR systems.

Figure 2.1 emphasizes the possible link of environmental context, reforms, challenges, and organizational performance: external factors such as environmental context, reforms (e.g., civil service reforms), and challenges (e.g., dynamic environmental changes such as ageing workforce, declining trust in government, etc.) are important dimensions that may strongly affect public HR strategies and HR practices. Eventually, these human resource practices can produce outcomes that are correlated with the quality of works produced as well as the employee's productivity that may contribute on the total organizational performance.

Figure 2.1
The Possible Link of Environmental Context, Reforms, Challenges, and Organizational Performance

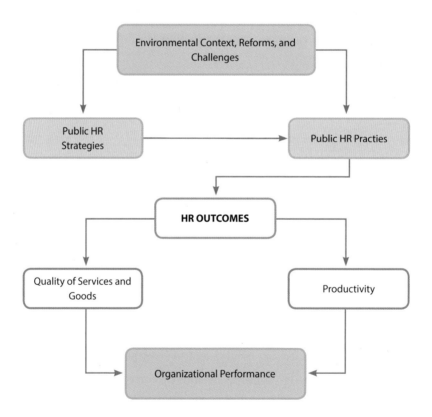

One of the key factor in enhancing and developing an effective and efficient public sector organization, is to recognize the significant influences of various challenges—external and internal challenges—on the functions of public organization. External challenges may include those that are the results of uncertain political, economic, legal, socio-cultural, and technological factors. Internal challenges may include "leadership development, employee motivation, labor turnover, managing HR during economic downturn and the role of unions in organizational change" (Burke, Noblet, & Cooper, 2013, p. 9). In this section, along with the various civil service reforms in the selected ASEAN member-countries, some of the important reforms in the U.S. civil service will be discussed.

Making Sense of the RealWorld

The development, changes, or reforms across the government require public managers to be mindful on the adaption of HRM approaches. The following video clips provide information on the reform initiatives in the UK civil service and how they addressed the key issues on public HRM. As an offshoot of various environmental factors, reforms are made as a measure for survival. The main objective of reform is to build a dynamic and adaptable workforce in order to ensure that public sector organization is efficient and effective as possible. Among the specific HR initiatives that have been introduced in UK is the modernization of civil service.

Title	Gist	Source/Link
Modern Civil Service	The changes in the environmental circumstances of the UK public sector have encouraged the adaption of modern and innovative ideas in the civil service.	http://www.youtube.com/watch?v=rlfihe8xCVM&index=5&list=PLIBDZ8I17toqlgZBn2dQmVUyKC76fJf-G
Reform Across Government	As a result of various inevitable changes, the government must undergo reform preserve its importance and relevance in the society.	http://www.youtube.com/watch?v=mdqs-R4FEWU&index=4&list=PLIBDZ8I17toqlgZBn2dQmVUyKC76fJf-G

a. What are the impacts of various environmental factors on effective public sector management? Can you cite an example in your country or agency?

b. What are the major civil service reforms that you can recall in your country or agency? Can you state some of the contributions of these reforms in the effective public sector organization management?

c. Compare and contrast the Civil Service reforms in your country and other country, for example US or Korea.

"The computer says I need to upgrade my brain to be compatible with the new software."

Theory Synopsis

Environmental Context and Challenges for Public HRM

Across the world, public HRM confront serious challenges brought by many environmental factors that influence the operations of the organization. In the public HRM parlance, environment is understood to be anything that is outside the organization and is capable of influencing the present and future activities of the organization (Kew & Stredwick, 2010). There is a need to know the different external influences, including political, economic, socio-cultural, technological, legal, and among others, affecting the directions, shape, and performance of the organization. Public sector organizations can either be reactive or proactive towards the environmental changes. It's a matter of choice; however, public organizations may not afford to sit comfortably without addressing the changes forthrightly. A reactive posture behaves on changes as they occur or "act when being attacked" behavior—which is one-step backward or organizations deals with unexpected changes without any plan of taking it down. The proactive posture displays a gung-ho attitude on addressing any environmental changes—behaves one-step ahead on any changes or organizations have foreseen possible changes then prepare and identify applicable HR levers that can be applied for such change.

The public organization, like all other organizations is not insulated to any environmental alterations. At time when environmental changes occur, it produces specific challenges to the public organization. These are either external or internal in nature that challenges the resoluteness of existing organizational strategies and practices. Thus, the succeeding discussions will try to review some of the important environment context and the potential challenges that public organizations face; and then briefly address how practical and proactive HRM practices can make a difference in helping public organizations achieve their missions despite these challenges. The basic and evident key drivers of external contexts of public organizations are provided in Table 2.1.

Table 2.1

The External Contexts of Public HRM

Context	Key Drivers
Economic	Macro-economic policy, markets and prices, price levels, global trends, market structures, profits, public spending, taxation, consumption and investment spending, wages and salaries, public services, imports and exports, exchange rates, balance of payments, employment and unemployment, labour and capital markets, social enterprise, social entrepreneurship
Socio-Cultural	Demography by size, age, other social characteristics and geographical distribution, working population, gender, ethnicity, education and training, religion, social values and beliefs, immigration, multiculturalism
Technological	Information and communication technologies, biotechnology, medical advances, nanotechnology, robotics, technological change, research and development, e-Government, e-HRM, e-HRIS,
Legal	Contract law, employment law, health and safety, consumer protection law, company law, codes of practice, regulatory bodies, the legal system and the courts, the Court of Justice, civil service law,
Political	Party politics, government, opposition, public administration, public policy, legislature, local government, pressure groups, public opinion, international and local institutions, international organizations

Source: Farnham, David. 2010. "Human Resource Management and its External Context." Published by CIPD.

As a public sector organization with the citizens as the clients, there are vast numbers of actors that are critical in the efficient and effective management of public resources. The attitudes and behaviors of various actors in the environment determine the possible degree of impact of the environment contexts. For example, the role of political executives, legislature, organized interest groups, courts, private sector, employees, and the public may cause significant changes in the above-mentioned external contexts— economy, politics, technology, legal, and socio-cultural. The policy strategies and approaches of new political leaders may require an overhaul of the existing HR strategies and practices; the demands of the general public for effective and efficient government services may encourage public sector organizations to reform; new laws passed in the legislature and jurisprudences may also summon significant changes in the administration of public human resource; the influence of employees groups (e.g., labor unions) may demand for some amendments on labor-management relations (e.g., labor relations and standards) policy; the strong voice of the organized interest groups and the inevitable role of the private sector on governance may bring influential challenges for the public sector to find ways and means to innovate and be creative in the affairs of the government. In sum, these actors are, in one way or the other, the catalysts of change in the public HR environment context. Figure 2.2 shows the different environmental actors.

Figure 2.2
The Actors in the Environment

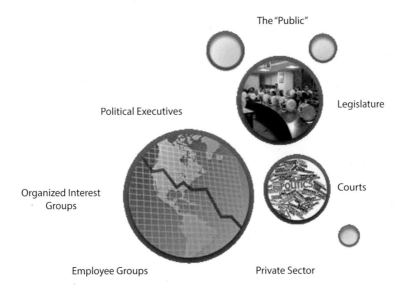

Political Executives

The "Public"

Legislature

Organized Interest
Groups

Courts

Employee Groups

Private Sector

Economic Context

In the economic context, numerous indicative trends are discernible that can bring significant influence on public HRM. One of this is the fiscal crisis that is both evident in developed and developing economies. For instance, a deficit on the fiscal balance—difference between government revenues and expenditures—is seriously harmful for the sustainability of public funds (OECD, 2013) which may result to the adaption of government austerity measures (e.g., slice wage bills, budget cuts, refuse to hire replacement for retirees, etc.) and streamlining of government functions and resources. In 2002, most of the U.S. states projected a budget gap of $25.7 billion which forced them to lay off government employees, imposed an across-the-board budget cuts, reorganized programs, and enacted early retirement scheme (Pynes, 2004). The firing rate of government workers in U.S. has not changed since 2001 (The Economist, 2012) and continuously enacted policy strategies that may mitigate the inevitable impact of economic downturn.

The factors that may affect the economic change is brought by macro-level economic condition, the global economic trends, downturns in major industries, market structures, investments, and among others. There are instances wherein the private sector whines on how public sector deals with the economic changes, such as faithfully implementing austerity measures. They complain that the burden of the stern measures was laid more on the private than in the government sector. For instance, though Greek government employees were able to avoid lay-offs and the "state sector remains bloated", "... the retrenchment in spending is still for real: contract employees have not had their agreements renewed and some workers who were worried about future pension cuts took early retirement instead" (The Economist, 2012). Figure 2.3 displays the schematic impact of economic condition on government input (e.g., budget, human resource, etc.), then to government activities and programs, and eventually the total impact on government performance through various outcomes.

Figure 2.3
The Impact of Economic Condition on the Government

Among the immediate challenges that economic change can bring is the reduction of government budget and downsizing or rightsizing.

- *Budget Cuts.* There are various factors which may lead to declining government budgets such as political pressures, tax holidays or limitation policies, and outright budget cuts. However, the glaring impact of economic downturn may push the government to take drastic steps to consolidate public finance, effectively respond to fiscal pressures, and reduce budget deficits. The trimming of budget requires the government agencies, bureaus, and/or departments to initiate mandated reforms and curbing present and future spending. This may include stoppage or a moratorium on recruitment of new employees while some existing employees might be forced to retire due to possible cuts on pension benefits.

- *Downsizing.* The common solution to economic difficulties is downsizing— retrenchment and reduction of number of employees in either private or public sector. It is also known as "rightsizing" because it intends to trim down the size of the government [or the workforce] into right size in accordance with the available financial resources. Some argue that downsizing or rightsizing is necessary in increasing the effectiveness and efficiency in reducing cost. In the U.S., the federal civilian workers declined from 2.7 million in 2006 to 2.15 million in 2010. The retrenchment is obviously not without any backlash on public HRM. The streamlining may enforce lay-offs, buy-outs, or offering of early retirement packages (Berman, et. al. 2013). *Downsizing* may leave the public managers to look into how the remaining employees will be maximized or to be 'stretched' in order to achieve positive organizational outcomes. However, in some instances *downsizing* or *rightsizing* in the one hand, and *up-sizing* on the other were embraced as an effective tool to address the issue of needed government size (see the case of Korea).

Socio-Cultural Context

In the social context, one of the key drivers is the changing demographic composition (Pynes, 2004) or the population trends in the society (Farnham, 2010). The extent of change has resulted from various phenomenons such as immigration, ageing workforce—such as the eventual exodus of baby boomers, birth rate—falling birthrates such as in South Korea and Japan; and higher birthrates in other parts of the globe, especially in developing countries like Philippines and Indonesia. There is, however, an augmentation of labor force (e.g., growing number of migrant workers) provided by the higher immigration and higher birthrates (Farnham, 2010). In South Korea, and as they bridged on the multicultural and multiracial society, an increasing number of migrant workers from south-east Asia was able to help provide potential labor force for small- and medium-sized enterprises and even major industries in the country. Even in other developed nations, the demographic characteristics and composition of the labor force are continuously changing. In the U.S., the 2012 survey provides the people of color made up 36% of the total labor force, which is non-Hispanic white is approximately 99,945,000 (64%); 24,679,000 (16%) are Hispanic; 18,758,000 (12%) are African American; and 8,202,000 (5%) are Asian; and about 3% do not identify themselves to any ethnic categories (Burns, Barton, & Kerby, 2012). Not only will there be an increase change in the ethnicity of employees but also the increase numbers of women in the labor force (see Figure 2.4 on the total population of women in general government compared to women in labor force in the OECD member countries), thus an increasing diversity in workplace. This will open up the issue of diversity management and the shift in the employees' attitudes and values, such as seeking for a work-life balance (WLB) or alternative work policies that will give them the opportunity to have time for the family (Pynes, 2004).

Figure 2.4

The women in general government compared to women in labor force

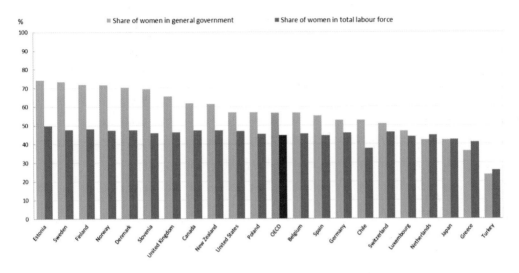

Sources: International Labour Organization (ILO), LABORSTA (database)
and OECD Labour Force Statistics (database).

A major challenge that needs careful consideration is the resulting impact of ageing society. In the government, there is a growing concern that the exit of baby boomers may result to considerable loss of knowledge, skills, abilities, and competence, or literally a "brain drain" in the human resource. In the U.S., approximately 10,000 employees' reach retirement age every day though all of them are not immediately retiring. Along with the other challenges, this social development requires proactive public HR strategies considering the demand and supply of human resource. The U.S. Bureau of Labor Statistics' employment projections for over the decade of 2012-22 (see Table 2.2), roughly 50.6 million job openings are expected wherein 67.2% are predicted to come from the replacement need (BLS, 2013). The public and also the private sector organizations must head off the problem and prepare a comprehensive public HR plan that will include selection and recruitment, human resource development (HRD) that will focus on educating and training workers to fill the job skills gaps of the retiring employees and newbies, fair compensation and rewards structure, and motivation and retention of competent workforce.

Table 2.2

Civilian labor force by age, sex, race, and ethnicity, 1992, 2002, 2012, and projected 2022

[Numbers in thousands]

Group	Level				Change			Percent change			Percent distribution				Annual growth rate (percent)		
	1992	2002	2012	2022	1992-2002	2002-2012	2012-2022	1992-2002	2002-2012	2012-2022	1992	2002	2012	2022	1992-2002	2002-2012	2012-2022
Total, 16 years and older	128,105	144,863	154,975	163,450	16,758	10,112	8,475	13.1	7.0	5.5	100.0	100.0	100.0	100.0	1.2	0.7	0.5
Age, years:																	
16 to 24	21,617	22,366	21,285	18,462	749	-1,081	-2,823	3.5	-4.8	-13.3	16.9	15.4	13.7	11.3	0.3	-0.5	-1.4
25 to 54	91,429	101,720	101,253	103,195	10,292	-467	1,942	11.3	-0.5	1.9	71.4	70.2	65.3	63.1	1.1	-0.0	0.2
55 and older	15,060	20,777	32,437	41,793	5,717	11,660	9,358	38.0	56.1	28.8	11.8	14.3	20.9	25.6	3.3	4.6	2.6
Sex:																	
Men	69,964	77,500	82,327	86,913	7,536	4,827	4,586	10.8	6.2	5.6	54.6	53.5	53.1	53.2	1.0	0.6	0.5
Women	58,141	67,364	72,648	76,537	9,223	5,284	3,889	15.9	7.8	5.4	45.4	46.5	46.9	46.8	1.5	0.8	0.5
Race:																	
White	108,837	120,150	123,684	126,923	11,313	3,534	3,239	10.4	2.9	2.6	85.0	82.9	79.8	77.7	1.0	0.3	0.3
Black	14,162	16,565	18,400	20,247	2,403	1,835	1,847	17.0	11.1	10.0	11.1	11.4	11.9	12.4	1.6	1.1	1.0
Asian	5,106	6,604	8,188	10,135	1,498	1,584	1,947	29.3	24.0	23.8	4.0	4.6	5.3	6.2	2.6	2.2	2.2
All other groups[1]	-	1,544	4,703	6,145	-	3,159	1,442	-	204.6	30.7	-	1.1	3.0	3.8	-	11.8	2.7
Ethnicity:																	
Hispanic origin	11,338	17,943	24,391	31,179	6,605	6,448	6,788	58.3	35.9	27.8	8.9	12.4	15.7	19.1	4.7	3.1	2.5
Other than Hispanic origin	116,767	126,920	130,584	132,271	10,153	3,664	1,687	8.7	2.9	1.3	91.1	87.6	84.3	80.9	0.8	0.3	0.1
White non-Hispanic	98,724	103,349	101,892	99,431	4,625	-1,457	-2,461	4.7	-1.4	-2.4	77.1	71.3	65.7	60.8	0.5	-0.1	-0.2
Age of baby boomers	28 to 46	38 to 56	48 to 66	58 to 76													

1The "all other groups" category includes (1) those classified as being of multiple racial origin and (2) the race categories of (2a) American Indian and Alaska Native and (2b) Native Hawaiian and Other Pacific Islanders.
Note: Dash indicates no data collected for category. Details may not sum to totals because of rounding.

Source: News Release on "Employment Projections 2012-22". December 19, 2013.
Bureau of Labor Statistics, US Department of Labor. www.bls.gov/emp

Thus, among the resulting challenges for the public HRM brought by the socio-cultural change are the changing workforce environment and the possible emergence and adoption of "blended workforce" or alternative work arrangement.

- *Changing Workforce Environment.* The changing workforce demographics is due to continuous immigration or *diaspora* to various countries, the raising concern for the right to equal employment, and the retirement of Baby Boomers. The labor force is increasingly diverse—such as that of the U.S. and UK—wherein women, person of color, LGBT, and people with disabilities are widely dispersed in the work environment. In the U.S. public sector, workers are becoming older or the baby boomers (Bond, Galinsky, & Swanberg, 1998; Pitts, 2005), thus requires a serious effort on establishing sustainable selection and recruitment approach.

- *Contract or Alternative Work Arrangements or Blended Workforce*. The imminent impact of *Baby Boomers'* hegira posed a serious concern for public managers on sustaining an increased efficiency and effectiveness on delivering public goods and services. In the U.S. federal government, public managers have a keen interest in the enactment of "alternative work arrangements", "nonstandard work arrangements", "contingent work", "flexible staffing arrangements," and "just-in-time employment practices" (Thompson & Mastracci, 2008) to boost the federal government human resource capacity. These strategies are related but distinct on a given context. Nonetheless, they refer to the participation of external labor forces or workers that are non-permanent, contracted, temporary, and part-time employees in the conduct of government functions. As pointed by Mastracci and Thompson (2005), the scheme of contracting with external labor market involves the use of core-ring staffing model—the core are the internal labor forces (e.g., full-time or permanent workers in the organization) while the ring are those external labor forces (e.g., contractors, part-time) (Berman, et. al., 2013). This is denoted as the *"blended workforce"*. Blended workforce is defined by the Society for Human Resource Management (SHRM) as, "a workforce that is comprised of permanent full-time, part-time, temporary employees and independent contractors" (Thompson & Mastracci, 2008, p. 4).

Technological Context

In the technological sphere, there have been tremendous technological innovations that influence how things in the public or private sector organizations are being done (Pynes, 2004). These ground-breaking technological advancements have serious organizational and managerial implications. For example, the internet's impressive growth in 1993 was followed by numerous electronic applications and software (e.g., email, intranets, facebook, YouTube, Skype, video conferencing, google search engine, Wikipedia, etc.) allows communication and transmission of information easy and accessible anytime and anywhere. Along with the initial stage of government reform effort, advanced countries like U.S. turned into developing a digital government through virtual agencies—following the web portal model used in the economy, is organized by client—for example, students, seniors, small-business owners, or veterans; each side site is designed to provide all of the government's services and information from any agency as well links to relevant organizations outside government. Internet access such as the web portals of the government that were made available 24/7 would provide a new structure that can define the relationship between state and citizen to be simpler, more interactive, and more efficient. Jane Fountain (2001) described this as virtual state—it's "a government that is organized increasingly in terms of virtual agencies, cross-agency and public-private networks whose structure and capacity depend on the internet and web".

The continuous development of technology affects all aspects of the organization, including communication between individuals, within organizations, amongst organizations, and increasingly between individuals and machines (Farnham, 2010). The introduction of e-Government has made tremendous changes in the public sector organizations. Figure 2.5 depicts the technology enactment framework that is useful in the analysis of virtual state or agency. Technologies render physical space and distance irrelevant in many business, working and human transactions. This effectively makes ICTs the first global, technological transformation process. They radically affect how people work, what they do at work, and how people are managed within organizations. Thus, public organizations need to recruit and hire people with a new set of skills and orientations to fit the new culture. Key challenges facing organizations will be the ability to attract and hire qualified applicants and to provide training for incumbent employees so that the benefits of technology can be realized.

Figure 2.5
Technology Enactment: An Analysis Framework

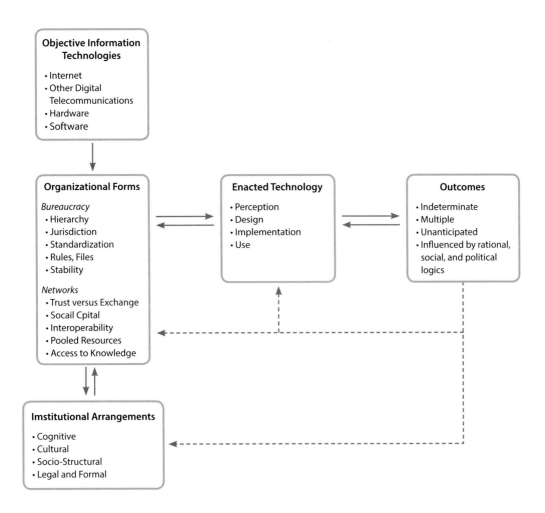

Source: Fountain, J. E. (2004).Building the virtual state: Information technology and institutional change. Brookings Institution Press.

As a result of technological change, the public sector organizations may face the challenges brought by emerging virtual workplace and virtual government and reforming and reengineering initiatives.

Emerging virtual workplace and virtual government. Due to the technological development, innovative organizations adapted a more flexible working time and place such as telecommuting and flexi-time (Berman et. al., 2013). Technology makes it possible to telecommute, work from virtual offices and communicate with businesses and individuals across the globe. Flexible work schedules are popular because so many duties and responsibilities can be accomplished from an employee's home or while the employee is traveling. The private sector initially became the test case for telecommuting arrangements, and the federal government followed suit in its attempt to be competitive with industry in attracting qualified candidates. Remote reporting relationships are also a factor of improved technology. Managers or team members who live and work in different cities, and even different countries is becoming more common. Thus, these initiatives provide an enormous change in the employee-employer relationship as well as the citizen and the government (Berman et. al., 2013).

Reforming and Reengineering Initiatives. Technology has made difficult things easy and possible. The Government Process Reengineering (GPR) or Business Process Reengineering (BPR) such as the e-Services, e-Commerce, e-Petition, etc. was widely enacted in the public sector organizations. For example, online filings of taxes, application for driver's license, among others are made available for the citizens to transact electronically with the government.

Political Context

In the political sphere, the influence of politics remains to be very strong. The main political institutions that have been impacting the public HR are the executive department, legislative department, as well as local political bodies. The organizations in the public sectors have to plan responses to the political pressures emanating from these bodies, using appropriate strategies, policies and practices if they are to prosper or at least survive. They do this by drawing upon the support of organized pressure groups, political lobbying or campaigning publicly (Farnham, 2010).

Another ongoing and political development is privatization that can also be caused by the tight government funds and demand from the public for efficiency and productivity.

These are normally offset by increased state regulation of private and public businesses on the grounds of accountability and the public good. Both the corporate and public sectors have to address the legal requirements arising out of regulation, such as employment legislation or health and safety law. On the one hand, they have to reward, train and develop existing staff to retain them. On the other, they have to compete with one another for scarce skills and competencies in the open labor market. These are challenges that follows suit upon taking into a transition from public to private enterprise. The role of the public organization is crucial in ensuring that the public goods and services transferred for a market value must ensure that the general public will take what it deserves.

Political change is as daunting as how we think of it. They may give a slight change or an amendment to existing public HR strategies and policies, or may totally overhaul the system. In one way or the other, these political alterations are challenged by the *decreasing trust towards the government* or can bring great challenges such as *citizen's demands for more efficiency and productivity.*

 - *Decreasing Trust in the Government*. Confidence in the government is crucially important in whatever policies and programs the government would want to undertake. A decline in trust would result to low rates of policy compliance and may derail the gains of policy strategies. In OECD countries, by 2012 an average of four out of ten people claimed that they trust their government (OECD, 2013). In Figure 2.6, it shows that the average confidence in national government for OECD countries is 40 percentage points. Switzerland and Luxembourg have the highest citizen's confidence while U.S., Japan, and Korea score below the OECD average.

Figure 2.6

Confidence in national government in 2012 and its change since 2007

Arranged in descending order according to percentage point change between 2007 and 2012

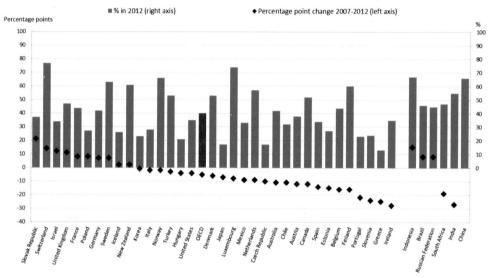

Note: Data refer to percentage of "yes" answers to the question: "In this country, do you have confidence in each of the following, or not? How about national government?" Data for Chile, Germany and the United Kingdom are for 2011 rather than 2012. Data for Iceland and Luxembourg are for 2008 rather than 2007. Data for Austria, Finland, Ireland, Norway, Portugal, the Slovak Republic, Slovenia, and Switzerland are for 2006 rather than 2007.

Source: Gallup World Poll

- *Demands for Productivity.* As the citizens' confidence in the government is declining, the demand for productivity is at its high. The public sector organization, at all levels, are pressured to increase productivity given the limited resources and along with the various challenges that are just around them. The call for efficiency and productivity entails efforts to continuously motivate people within the organization. Public managers must determine effective rewards and incentives structure, HRD, and compensation mechanisms that can help boost employees' motivation.

Legal Context

As a government entity, public sector organizations must observe enacted laws, policies, rules and regulations, executive orders (EOs), memoranda, administrative orders (AOs) promulgated or directed by those of authorities, as well as court rulings, orders, or jurisprudence. The legal landscape where public organizations are operating requires strict and substantive compliance of these laws and orders. For instance, reform initiatives, employee protection, equal employment opportunity act, and enforcement of employment contract demands a faithful compliance of the requirements of the law. For public HR, they must comply with all the legal constraints and obligations, monitor them, as well as evaluate and provide feedback on it.

As the law requires compliance, public HR maybe challenged by some of the important reform initiatives in the public sector, such as the *centralization and decentralization of human resource activities* and *increased managerial flexibilities*.

Figure 2.7
Delegation of key HRM responsibilities to line Ministries in central government (2010)

	General management of pay systems (salary levels, progressions)	Flexibility of working conditions (number of hours, etc.)	Allocation of budget envelope between payroll & other expenses	Performance appraisal systems	Management of the variable portion of pay benefits; performance related pay	Number & types of posts within organisations	Recruitment into the civil service
Australia	◉	◉	◉	◉	◉ ○	◉	◉ ○
Austria	●	●	◉	●	◉	●	◉
Belgium	●	●	◉	○	○ ◉	◉	◉
Canada	●	○	◉	◉	● ○	◉	◉
Chile	●	●	●	○	●	○	◉
Czech Republic	●	◉	●	◉	◉	◉	◉
Denmark	○	● ◉	●	◉ ○	◉ ○	◉	◉ ○
Estonia	◉	◉ ○	◉	◉ ○	◉	◉	◉
Finland	◉	○ ◉	○	◉	◉ ○	◉	◉
France	●	○ ◉	● ◉	◉	○ ◉	● ◉	◉
Germany	●	● ◉	● ◉	◉	○	◉	◉
Greece	●	●	◉	●	●	○	◉
Hungary	●	◉	● ○ ◉	◉	● ○ ◉	● ○ ◉	◉ ○
Iceland	●	◉ ○	◉	n.a.	○ ◉	◉	◉ ○

Ireland	●	●	●	◉	● ◉	●	●
Israel	● ○	○	◉	●	● ○	●	○
Italy	●	○	◉	●	◉ ○	◉	◉
Japan	○	○	○	○	○	○	○
Korea	●	○	○	○	○	○	○
Mexico	○	● ○ ◉	○	●	○	○	● ○
Netherlands	●	● ◉	●	● ◉	◉	◉	◉ ○
New Zealand	◉	◉	◉	◉	◉	◉	◉
Norway	●	● ◉	◉	◉	◉	◉	◉ ○
Poland	◉ ○	○ ◉	○	◉ ○	◉ ○	◉	○ ◉
Portugal	◉	◉	◉	n.a.	◉	◉	◉
Slovak Republic	● ○	○	◉	○	n.a.	◉	○
Slovenia	◉	◉	◉	○	◉	◉	◉
Spain	●	●	●	○	◉	○	○ ◉
Sweden	◉	◉ ○	◉	◉ ○	◉ ○	◉	◉ ○
Switzerland	○	● ◉	○	●	◉ ○	◉	◉ ○
Turkey	●	○	●	●	●	●	○
United Kingdom	◉	◉	●	◉	◉	◉	◉
United States	●	n.a.	◉	◉	◉	◉	◉
Brazil	●	●	●	●	●	●	●
Russian Federation	n.a.	◉	n.a.	◉	◉	n.a.	◉
Ukraine	●	◉	◉	◉	●	◉	● ◉
Total OECD33							
●	20	12	11	8	7	6	2
○	6	11	7	7	11	7	8
◉	9	19	19	16	21	23	26
○	1	3	0	5	8	0	8

● Central HRM body (which sets the rules and is closely involved in applying them) and/or Ministries of Finance.
○ Central HRM body but with some latitude for Ministries/Departments/Agencies in applying the general principles.
◉ Ministries/Departments/Agencies within established legal and budgetary limits.
○ Unit/team level
n.a.: Not available.

Source: 2010 OECD Survey on Strategic Human Resources Management in Central/Federal Governments.

- *Centralization and Decentralization of Human Resource Activities.* There is an ongoing decentralization of HRM activities not only in the U.S. but also in most of the OECD member members (see Figure 2.7). This effort provides the line agencies to have direct and greater responsibility on some of the HRM functions, thus gave them more flexibility and discretion in the human resource administration and management (Berman et. al., 2013).

- *Increased Managerial Flexibility.* Along with the decentralization of some HRM activities, one of the civil service reforms, especially in the U.S. federal agencies, is the greater discretion given to the public managers to decide on recruitment, compensation, discipline, and termination of employees (Berman et. al., 2013).

Civil Service Reform

Public Sector Reform in Korea and ASEAN Countries
The Case of Philippines, Indonesia, and Korea

Most of governments of the world, like the United States, have been undergoing continuous reforms. These reforms are the results of incessant changes in the environmental context of the public sector organizations, without which may impede the effective delivery of public goods and services, or worst may cause the demise of a government institution (see Ingraham, 1993). In this section, the trajectories of the public sector reform in Korea and some ASEAN member countries (i.e., Philippines and Indonesia) will be discussed and briefly explore the reform impacts on human resource management.

Box 2.1

Civil Service Reform in Indonesia

Civil Service Reform in Indonesia

Civil service reform is one of the most important elements of the reform initiatives in Indonesia. As a general backdrop of public sector reform, Indonesian government aims to reduce corruption, collusion, and nepotism in order to establish meritocracy and depoliticized public administration. As pointed by Prasojo (2011), civil servants in the country have been known for being "unresponsive, oversized, with low incentive, and low morale, and driven by corruption" (p. 101). Since 2006, the government of Indonesia focused on the following civil service reform initiatives.

A. Establishment of Performance Measurement

- The introduction of performance-based budgeting—government agency's budget allocation will be based on its target performance—wherein every institution must provide a well-defined performance measurement during the process of budget allocation. Every employee is also required to have a "performance contract". Then, every year, the government institution/agency must submit a Government Institution Performance Accountability Report (LAKIP) to provide an overview of their accomplishments.

- Legal Basis: Law No. 17/2003 on State Finance

B. Development of New Incentive System

- It emphasizes on the adoption of competency-based personnel placement, opening of new offices for public service, streamlining internal organizational structures, introduction of performance measurement, and introduction of performance incentives. This reform has provided a more transparent and accountable incentive system.

C. Development of an Assessment Center and Integrated Information System

- The main objective of this initiative is to provide a comprehensive civil servant's profile which includes career, rotation, and improvement. This has four major components: (a) competence dictionary; (b) standard competencies required of a public official; (c) methods and instruments of competence measurement; and (d) competence profile of each civil servants and officials.

D. Open Bidding for Promotion

- The filling-up of available government position is done through an open bidding. This gives an open and equal opportunity for the employees to apply for any vacant positions, and recruitment is based on merit and fitness—"competence, career achievement, work performance, work period, work location, career rank, record of discipline, and special requirements needed" (p.105).

The government is still on the process of reflecting major civil service reform into law. The Indonesian government has proposed three bills on administrative reforms which cover state apparatus, civil service, and government code of ethics (Sijabat, 2012). The "State Civil Apparatus Bill" plan to make the Indonesian government streamlined, ethical, and professional. Some of the important reform ideas included in the bill are the following:

- New Strategic Resource Management
- Civil Service as a Profession

- Position-Based System
- Merit System
- National Selection System
- Differentiation Status
- Distribution of Civil Service Authorities and Management

This is an excerpt of the article written by Eko Prasojo entitled "Exploring Public Sector reform in Indonesia", a manuscript included in the book, **Public Sector Reform in ASEAN Member Countries and Korea** edited by Pan Suk Kim. Published on December 30, 2011.

Other source: Ridwan M. Sijabat, *Government Makes Last Ditch Effort at Reform*, THE JAKARTA POST (June 8, 2012)

Box 2.2

Civil Service Reform in the Philippines

Decentralization and the Civil Service Reform in the Philippines

In 1991, the Philippine government started decentralization initiatives which include "substantial transfer of power, authority, responsibility, and accountability to the sub-national institution or local government units" (Brillantes & Flores, 2011, p. 229). Decentralization is one of the various public sector reform initiatives in the Philippines that have brought significant impact on the personnel management aspect of the government. Figure 2.8 depicts the overall public sector reform and governance framework in the Philippines.

Figure 2.8 Public Sector Reform and Governance Framework

In the Philippines, the civil service reform is a supporting strategy that can give help on the effective decentralization. The civil service reform must be seen as one of the major components in order for the government to achieve its goal—efficient delivery of government goods and services. In the context of decentralization, reform of the civil service requires the process of modifying existing rules and regulations, adapting a workable incentive system, and HRM strategies in order to obtain efficient and dedicated government employees in a decentralized environment.

Challenges on Civil Service Reform due to Decentralization

Among the challenges of decentralization on civil service reform initiatives are the issues such as:

- Under what conditions are to be considered in the devolution or deconcentration of human resource management to a lower tier of government?

- What are the important or crucial capacity requirements in order to make the system work?

The decentralization or total transfer of power and resources to the local or lower tier of government requires building the local capacity to provide a welcoming environment for the moving employees. Thus, this warrant comprehensive readiness or capacity—human resource, physical resource, as well financial resource. Issues of budget constraints and shortage, practically, my impede the development. As many have argued, decentralization of human resource management is more likely to succeed in local governments that have the resources available.

Box 2.3

Civil Service Reform in South Korea

Civil Service Reform in South Korea

Korea initiated public sector reforms under the emerging philosophy of New Public Management (NPM). During the Kim Dae Jung administration, reform initiatives have been introduced to cope with the worsening financial crisis in 1997 (Kim & Moon, 2002) and sought to have a "small and efficient but better government" (Jang, 2011). Since then, Korea has carried out drastic reforms in the public sector management, for instance in the public personnel management.

On the article written by Jang (2011) in the book entitled, "Discover Korea in Public Administration" published by Korea Institute of Public Administration (KIPA), he pointed important reform initiatives which will be discussed in the succeeding section.

A. The Civil Service Commission

▪ The Civil Service Commission has undergone series of changes from 1948 to present. Table 2.3 shows these changes.

Table 2.3
Changes to the Central Personnel Agency

The Republic	The Central Personnel Agency	Year
1st and 2nd Republics	Civil Service Exam Committee and Ministry of Government Administration	Civil Service Exam Committee and Ministry of Government Administration (1948), Secretariat of State Council (1955)
3rd and 4th Republics	Ministry of Government Administration	1963-1979
5th and 6th Republics Kim Young-sam Administration	Ministry of Government Administration	1980-1998
Kim Dae-jug and Roh Moo-hyun Administration	Ministry of Government Administration and Home Affairs (MOGAHA)	1998-1999
	Dual System of MOGAHA and Civil Service Commission (CSC)	1999-2004
	Civil Service Commission (CSC)	2004-2007
Lee Myung-bak Administration	Ministry of Public Administration and Security	2008-2012
Park Geun-hye Administration	Ministry of Security and Public Administration (MOSPA)	2012-2014
	Ministry of Personnel Management	2014-present

Sources: Choi, 2008; Jang, 2011; Wikipedia

B. Open Position System/Open Employment System

- The open position system allows a more open, flexible and competitive personnel system in order to recruit well-deserving personnel through a fair and open system from both public and private sector. The Open Employment System (OES) allowed private employees to apply in grades 1-3 in the Korean civil service (Kim, 2000).

C. Senior Civil Service

- Senior civil service was first introduced in the Roh Moo-hyun administration as an initiative to enhance the "government-wide personnel system by selecting, assigning, developing, advancing, rewarding, and managing senior civil servants" (Jang, 2011, p. 297). See Table 2.4 for the composition of SCS in Korea.

Table 2.4
Senior Civil Service Employment Method

	Outside of the Ministry		
	Open Positions	Open Recruitment	Autonomous Personnel Positions
Characteristics	Competition with non-civil servants and among ministries	Competition among ministries	Internal decision by minister
Ratio	20%	30%	50%

Source: Park & Joo, 2010; cited in Jang, 2011

D. Performance Management System

- Before Korea follows the system of rank-based pay but later on changed it to performance-based pay system. It was first introduced in 1994 by the Kim Young-sam administration linking performance and pay; then later on changed by Kim Dae-Jung administration into Performance-related Pay System (PRP).

Table 2.5
The Payment Scope and Performance Pay Rate by Appraisal Grade

	Appraisal Grade			
	Excellent (S)	Outstanding (A)	Normal (B)	Unsatisfactory (C)
Scope	Upper 20%	30%	40%	Bottom 10%
Performance Pat rate (of basic salary)	15%	10%	6%	0%

Source: MOPAS, 2009; cited in Jang, 2011

E. Personnel Exchange System

- This system was introduced in 2002 in which middle manager level civil servants (Grade 4 and 5) are given the opportunity to work in the private sector within a three-year leave.

F. 360 Degree Feedback Appraisal System

- It was introduced in the Korean government in 2003. This is a multi-layer performance evaluation approach that allows supervisors, coworkers, subordinates, and the citizens or clients to evaluate civil servant's performance.

This is an excerpt of the article written by Hoseok Jang entitled "Public Personnel Management", a manuscript included in the book, Discover Korea in Public Administration edited by Eung-kyuk Park, Chang-seok Park, and Bernard Rowan. Published on April 2012 by The Korea Institute of Public Administration.

A Focus on U.S.

There has been a recurring administrative reform in most of the countries to improve public management and public service. Generally, most governments seek reforms to achieve a government that is efficient, economical, and with enhanced performance. For instance, in Condrey's comparison of four models of public HRM (2005) (see Table 2.6), the emphasis of the traditional government model is on efficiency (Lim, 2006) while the succeeding government models (e.g., reform model, strategic model, and privatization or outsourcing model [Condrey, 2005]) introduced reforms that were directed towards better work and less cost. In the past two decades in the U.S., there has been an increased interest on civil service structural reforms and frequent introduction and inclusion of administrative changes in the public agenda (Berman et. al., 2013; Battaglio & Condrey, 2006). These reform initiatives were instigated by the concepts of "reinventing government" and "new public management (NPM)" (Battaglio & Condrey, 2006). The introduction of the aforementioned reform concepts have resulted with significant changes in the public personnel management, such as the "diminution or outright demolition of job security in the public sector, replaced with at-will employment arrangements" (Battaglio & Condrey, 2006, p. 119).

As presented in Table 2.6, the transition and adoption of various strategies in each model reflects an important approach that encourages the government to improve efficiency and enact policy and/or strategy to promote economy. The privatization or outsourcing model, for example, has introduced schemes that directly tap private sector to engage in the delivery of public goods and services (e.g., contracting-out, sales of government assets, load shedding, etc.).

Discussing the major civil service reforms, the *"The Tides of Reform"* of Paul Light (1997) is a rich and reliable reference to look at and in understanding the overall government performance. Using the Light's four reform philosophies—scientific management, war on waste, watchful eye, and liberation management, Berman and colleagues (2013) examined some of the possible implications of these philosophies on the current human resource management. Thus, the succeeding discussion of the four reform philosophies will present the brief analysis made by Berman et al. (2013) and also identify some the significant effects they brought on the public HRM.

Table 2.6
A Comparison of Four Models of Public Human Resource Management

Function	Traditional Model	Reform Model	Strategic Model	Privatization or Outsourcing Model
Service Delivery	Centralized	Decentralized	Collaborative	Contract
Goal Orientation	Uniform enforcement of rules, policies, and procedures	Manager-centered	Respectful of human resource management and organizational goals	Effective contract negotiator and administrator
Communication Pattern	Top-down	Two-way	Multidirectional	Reports and contract monitoring
Feedback Characteristics	Formal and informal complaints	Muted	Continuous	Muted

Function	Traditional Model	Reform Model	Strategic Model	Privatization or Outsourcing Model
Value orientation	"Merit"	Immediate responsiveness to organizational mission and goals	Effective organizational functioning coupled with a respect for effective human resource management practices	Efficiency; private sector preference
Role of human resource manager	Enforcer of "merit"	Diminished authority and control	Organizational consultant	Contract negotiator and administrator
Perception of human resource management profession	Hindrance to effective organizational functioning	Adjunct collection of skills	Full managerial Partner	Diminished
Role of Education	Public personnel administration	Adjunct to managerial skills	Human resource management, general management, practical focus	Contract negotiation and administration skills

Source: Condrey, 2005; Battaglio & Condrey 2006.

A. SCIENTIFIC MANAGEMENT

Scientific management is the first tide of reform. It focuses on enhancing government efficiency and effectiveness drawing on hierarchy, specialization, division of labor, and a clear-cut and well-defined chain of command. The basic philosophy of scientific management as argued by Frederick Taylor, the father of scientific management, is that, we could find "one best way" in which an employee can perform task as interchangeable as a part of a machine. The emphasis was on the structure and rules in which experts apply the "scientific principles of administration" such as the POSDCORB—planning, organizing, staffing, directing, coordinating, reporting, and budgeting (Berman, et al., 2013).

The major statutes that reflect this tide of reform are the 1939 Reorganization Act and the 1990 Chief Financial Official Act (Berman et al., 2013; 2006).

On the implication of scientific management on human resource management, Berman and colleagues (2013, p. 25) concluded that:

> 66
>
> *Scientific management has implications for human resources. It emphasizes conformity and predictability of employee' contributions to the organization (machine model), and it sees human relationships as subject to management control. Hallmarks of scientific management such as job design (characterized by standard procedures, narrow span of control, and specific job description instituted to improve efficiency) may actually impede achievement of quality of performance in today's organizations where customization, innovation, autonomous work teams, and empowerment are required.*
>
> 99

This scientific management has influenced numerous human resource management practices such as on establishing standard procedures, span of control, and job description. Even in the existing or present-day human resource management, scientific management has brought important initiatives that emphasizes on performance management, financial incentives, and performance evaluation (Berman et al., 2013; 2006). As argued by many HR luminaries and practitioners, performance management is undoubtedly an important tool to enhance government productivity and efficiency. For instance, the performance appraisal and evaluation can give important impact on how to improve existing motivation approaches for the employees to maximize knowledge, skills, abilities, or efforts towards governmental goals. It also provides reliable and objective information on vital human resource management approaches such as dismissal, compensation, and rewards and promotion. The scientific management philosophy can help identify the major lapses on HRM practices in order to improve performance and/or to continuously motivate good performers to maintain and reach the maximum level of performance.

B. WAR ON WASTE

War on waste is the third reform tide that focuses on economy. The main actors that pursue this goal are the state auditors, investigators, inspectors general, and also the mass media. The war on waste reform was inspired by various welfare fraud hearings and includes regulatory policies for preventing wasting government money (Mikesell, 2003). Among the significant statutes under this reform is the enactment of 1978 Inspector General Act and the 1992 Federal Housing Enterprises Financial Safety and Soundness Act which signaled the seriousness of government in curbing internal corruption (Berman et al., 2013). However, the passage of the 1993 Hatch Act reform Amendments provided contradictory principles to this reform—instead of tightening the political participation of the federal employees, it relaxed the provision that limits it (Berman et al., 2013).

There are various implications for human resource management that can be derived from the tide of war on waste. Typically, it resulted to more internal controls, oversight, regulations, directives, tight supervision, and accountability. Public sector organizations set-up well-defined and detailed processes, rules and regulations, standard operating procedures or guidelines which include internal administrative procedures, whistle-blowing systems, and multi-layered audit reviews that are prominent in a fat bureaucracy (see also Bertok, 1999). However, these approaches provide wariness both on the employees and public managers because of the tendency to strictly following rules and regulations, or literally following rigorously "by the book". As provided in Berman et al (2013), "Managers concerned with controlling waste try to minimize idle time, avoid bottlenecks, install time clocks, audit travel vouchers and long distance phone records, inventory office supplies, and monitor attendance and punctuality" (p. 26). Thus, may the government may take advantage of temporary employees—contracting out—and service privatization to contain government spending (Berman et al., 2013).

C. WATCHFUL EYE

The third tide of reform is the watchful eye stresses on fairness and openness. In here, the Congress and the Courts are the main institutional actors that play a crucial role in ensuring justice and fairness; while whistleblowers, the media, interest groups, and the public are the main citizens' actors that may give a serious blow to whatever injustices, unfairness, or unethical conduct in the government. The statutory manifestation of this reform is the enactment of the 1946 Administrative Procedure Act which provides important provisions on how the government organizations must operate as defined by the statute; and was clearly expressed on the *1989 Ethics Reform Act* (Berman et al., 2013; 2006). The latter provides mechanisms on curbing lobbying influences and for promoting ethics in government (Berman et al., 2013; 2006).

As to the implication of the watchful eye on human resource management, Berman and colleagues (2013) concluded:

> *Concern about ethical conduct of employees' leads to greater scrutiny in the hiring process to ensure integrity, as well as job-related competence of new recruits. Attentiveness to ethics also minimizes the illegitimate use of hiring criteria such as sex, race, age, and the handicap status. Such scrutiny should minimize arbitrary decisions to fire employees….Managers should seek congruence between the standards espoused by the organization and the behavior of public workers.*

Clearly, the watchful eye intends to lead employees in the public agencies towards ethical values and an ethical human resource management practices. For instance, in the recruitment and dismissal criteria of employees such as gender, age, and race must employ ethical conduct of fairness and openness. For this reason, many public human resource managers make efforts to create an organizational culture of openness, careful record keeping, and transparency (Berman et al., 2013; 2006).

D. LIBERATION MANAGEMENT

The final tide of reform is the *liberation management* emphasizes on the transition of the regulated and controlled public sector management into a high-performing market-based management. The government reinvention was popularized and led by former Vice President Al Gore and the National performance Review (NPR) initiatives wherein it seeks to promote economy and efficiency of government operations through rationalizing administrative procedures, empowerment of public managers, and emphasizing on getting things done rather than the process (Kellough, 1999). The major actors here are the frontline employee, teams, and evaluators while the defining statute is the 1993 Government Performance and Results Act. Kettl (2000) observed that the continuing reinvention in the public sector is now almost inevitable in the federal agencies of the United States. Reinvention efforts have been directly correlated with increase productivity.

Case Brief

Continuities and Changes in Korean Government Innovations

The Kim Dae-Jung administration actively pursued (or at least proclaimed) a small and entrepreneurial government through downsizing, restructuring, and privatizing initiatives, whereas the Roh Moo-Hyun administration promoted an "enabling" government rather than a small government, and pursued balance, fairness, and a concern for the underprivileged—elements that are often undervalued in efficiency-driven New Public Management reforms. Pursuing more process-focused innovation than previous administrations, the current administration puts more emphasis on the establishment of sustainable government innovations and an autonomous innovation system by changing administrative processes, administrative software systems, and administrative culture and practices. The administration continues to monitor and assess its government innovation programs through innovation assessment programs and autonomous integrated administrative systems (such as the On-nara System) in order to institutionalize and ensure sustainable government innovations. Promoting an enabling government and dealing with the continuing economic downturn, the Roh Moo-Hyun administration gave up on downsizing and upsized the public sector by increasing the number of public servants by about 50,000. This shift from small government to big government has been criticized for promoting inefficiency. Reversing the Roh Moo-Hyun administration's policy, the Lee Myung-Bak administration adopted a strong policy of downsizing and streamlining government. Promoting a practical and utilitarian government, the Lee administration pursues a small but strong government by reducing the number of cabinet level departments from 18 to 15 as well as downsizing the body of civil service. The administration also promotes large scale department and bureau in order to support downsizing effort.

1. Give your own ideas and comments on the PBL table including your opinion on this downsizing and upsizing of the Korean government? Make use of the sets of the discussions provided in the book. Also, discuss your own suggestion(s) and recommendations in reforming or addressing the public personnel management systems of the country.

2. From a comparative point of view (if applicable), please discuss the relevance and importance of these initiatives (i.e., evaluations, recommendations, lessons, and best practices) to current management issues in your country. Also, include your own ideas on what possible reforms that can best fit your country.

This case was adopted from: "Continuities and Changes in Government Innovations: Prospects and Lessons" by Moon M. Jae in the publication, Transforming Korean Public Governance: Cases and Lessons. ISSUE BRIEF PUBLIC GOVERNANCE OECD/KOREA POLICY CENTRE. November 2008. www.oecdkorea.org

Student Activity:

Getting to know the various environmental factors, challenges and reforms that is typical in every nations, write down the different environmental context surrounding the public human resource management in your country or agency and discuss how they affect the current HRM policies and practices. Use the case analysis table below to provide a clear organization of your thoughts.

HRM in the Public Organizations: An Essential Guide

Case Analysis

	Step	Contents		
1	Environments/ Conditions/ Backgrounds	Please explain the situation briefly. (1-2 pages)		
2	Problem Definitions	In your own perspective, please be as specific as possible when pointing out the problem. (2-3 pages)		
3	Actual Case Studies	Please explain by providing specific examples. (Newspaper articles, news clips, or interviews) (2-3 pages)		
4	Alternatives	Possible Alternative(s)	Pros in your Country Context	Cons in a your Country Context
		①		
		②		
		③		
		Please propose more than three policy alternatives. (2-3 pages)		
5	The Best Solutions	Why did you choose this alternative as the best solution? What are the expected effects and potential contribution? (2 pages)		

Reviews

1. If you were in charge of reforming civil service in your country, what do you think the best way to reduce anti-reform sentiments during the reform period? What if you fail to continue the process?

2. If you made a successful case, how would you transfer, export, and generalize the reform values/initiatives to other organizational/institutional/national settings?

3. What is the war on waste? What are its implications for HRM? What is the watchful eye? What are its implications for HRM? What is liberation management? What are its implications for HRM?

4. How do you define the term, "(neo) managerialism"? What are the core assumptions/ hypotheses of the principal-agent theory which could explain the manager-employee dyads?

Ending Credits

Research Digest

The Effects of Personnel Reform Systems on Georgia State Employees' Attitudes: An Empirical Analysis from a Principal-Agent Theoretical Perspective

Facts
In the United States, reform efforts aimed at improving the economy and efficiency of government operations have been made with relative frequency and regularity.

Then initial event that sparked public human resource management reform was the Pendleton Act of 1883, which depoliticized civil service reform. This Act created a merit system, tenure, examinations, and a neutral administrative structure (Ingraham et al. 2001). The administrative reform proposals generally assume that government administrative structure, culture, and procedures are hierarchical and inflexible, as well as unresponsive to stakeholders and to administrative and political leadership. Public personnel systems and practices are sometimes maligned as inferior to the private ones and are regarded as ineffective for increasing the organizational productivity and performance. While the logic of public personnel reforms has been driven by different philosophical sub-components such as managerial, political, or technical reasons, the main purposes of personnel reform in the government are to enhance the level of public managers' job flexibility, managerial empowerment, and work motivation, as well as to make public agencies more business-like and hence more productive organizations using market-friendly strategies (Kellough and Nigro 2006).

Most of the public management reform cases in the developed and market economy countries (the USA, Western Europe, and New Zealand, for example) were mainly adopted and implemented by a 'top–down' rather than by a 'bottom–up' approach from a 'strategic decision-making' perspective (Pollitt and Bouckaert 2004: 26, 184). This top–down reform strategy allows 'elite decision-makers' to have more discretion and authority in their choices of means and methods for public management reform (Pollitt and Bouckaert 2004: 26). The Georgia civil service reform, for example, was initiated by former Governor Zell Miller and the Georgia General Assembly, who had the strong political will to radically reform the entire Georgia civil service system. Before implementing dramatic civil service reform, the state of Georgia had a traditional and rigid centralized personnel system, originally designed to secure the values of merit, political responsiveness, and social equity within legal-bureaucratic public administration arrangements (West 2002). In 1996, for the purpose of transforming the entire state human resources management systems and policies, the state of Georgia launched two major reform initiatives of its personnel system: (1) the GeorgiaGain program; and (2) the Civil Service Reform Law (Act 816). The GeorgiaGain program was implemented in 1995–6 and involved such changes as reforming the employee performance evaluation processes, implementing a new wage and salary structure,

95

developing new training and development practices, and designing the current pay-for-performance system (Kellough and Nigro 2002, 2006). Act 816 in 1996 stipulated that all state employees hired or promoted after 1 July 1996, be at-will or unclassified in their positions, which means that those at-will employees have neither property interest in their employment nor a right to due process protections regarding dismissal, grievance, or appeals procedures.

Georgia's 1996 civil service reform, with a focus on reform results (e.g. increasing performance) rather than implementation processes, tried to remove long-standing civil service job protection and procedural due process rights for new job hires; furthermore, to restructure public managerial functions and ultimately to ensure efficient organizational systems, reformers pursued deregulation, decentralization, and market-oriented initiatives through the process of privatization (West 2002). The new goals and objectives in the reform agenda were to create performance- and mission-oriented cultures and privatized organizational systems that emphasize increased managerial flexibility through streamlining HRM processes and reducing red tape, focusing on efficiency and cost effectiveness in the use of human and financial resources in state agencies.

Reformers in Georgia also sought to achieve these goals by enhancing line agency managers' flexibility, streamlining adverse action procedures, decentralizing and simplifying merit system operations, and realigning the role of the central personnel department. For that reason, many substantial functions and roles were required to be decentralized, forcing the role of the Georgia merit system to change from one of regulator to that of agency partner or consultant, instituting 'at-will' or 'unclassified' employment status for new hires to minimize the procedural barriers in terminating unsatisfactory employees. The purported advantages, such as better customer service, less bureaucracy, employee empowerment, and enhanced motivation and performance, have been expected from the reforms in Georgia.

Overall, there are a few key characteristics common among personnel management reform initiatives, especially at the state level in the United States. First, we can observe an abrupt shift among three values – 'representativeness, neutral competence, executive leadership – that traditionally have characterized public service practices' (Bowman et al. 2003: 286). The concept of the merit system, which protects employees from political attack, was replaced in several state agencies (e.g. Georgia and Florida civil service positions) with employment at-will, a doctrine that 'allows termination of workers for no reason or any reason not contrary to law' (Muhl 2001; Bowman et al. 2003: 287).

Second, a more unbiased and accurate performance monitoring system, which is tied to job-related performance standards, was required to increase employees' job motivation or organizational effectiveness. Third, reformers contended that the states' human resource systems needed to absorb the idea that government should be operated entrepreneurially and that state employees' pay increases should be associated with their performance and productivity. Finally, in order to meet a more competitive and market-oriented working environment, state employees have requested adequate resources and training opportunities for their career development and knowledge advancement.

Based upon these philosophical and practical reform rationales with the administrative, political, and legislative supports from Georgia state government, four distinct personnel reform systems were developed in the state of Georgia: (1) a monetary incentive system (i.e. a merit pay system); (2) a performance monitoring system (i.e. a job performance appraisal system); (3) a knowledge incentive system (i.e. a knowledge management and training system); and (4) a discretionary controlling system (i.e. an at-will employment system). These reform rationales, which borrowed from a principal–agent theoretical approach, mainly intend to deregulate and decentralize the traditional civil service structures and procedures.

Issue(s)
Whether or not the four reform systems (exogenous variables) would directly or indirectly (and also positively or negatively) influence organizational outcomes (endogenous variables).

Findings

The results of three statistical models confirmed that the four latent constructs of managerial reform systems are conceptually separate and distinct and that all four personnel reform systems directly and indirectly affect organizational outcome variables. Among these four effects, this study supports the evidence that discretionary controlling and performance monitoring systems can be the most powerful and effective managerial tools to enhance the level of work motivation and job satisfaction as well as to decrease state employees' turnover intentions.

The empirical findings in this study suggest several managerial strategies which managers or supervisors (i.e. principals) in the public sector should consider. First, the use of a well-established merit pay system, which links individual performance ratings to annual salary increases and differently rewards higher and lower levels of employee (i.e. agent) performance, could encourage poor performers to improve their work productivity in public organizations (Kellough and Nigro 2002, 2006). It is essential for the organization to establish funding resources for the performance-based pay and a long-term commitment to continued funding to support the extrinsic rewards for public employees that are high performers (Freyss 2004: 79–80). Second, objective and reliable performance monitoring systems should be used to 'build on job-specific criteria and to meet the standard of job-relatedness'; adopting several technical and procedural tools; and focusing a manager's attention solely on the objective, job-related criteria for assessing performance (Daley 2005: 499). The public organization will need to develop clear goals for the organization and clear standards of performance by which it may evaluate employees. As the agent comes to accept the organization's goals and the direction of the organization, the agent's path for success will become clear, ultimately encouraging both cooperation with the organization and innovation for the organization. Finally, the decentralization of personnel management systems giving the greater discretion to agencies and supervisors could be used to create an organizational environment which promotes managerial flexibility and competitiveness in public organizations. In addition, the reduction of merit system protections (e.g. the adoption of an at-will employment system) could be adopted to facilitate the important personnel processes and functions, to successfully remove poor-performers from the workplace, to abolish the inefficient rules and regulations, and to enhance managerial authority over personnel policy in public organizations. In sum, one system alone is not enough to attract and retain the best employees for service to the public, but a system design that takes into account employees' generic work environments and effective compensation, evaluation, and discipline systems with the custom-fit job design component will be necessary.

In the current research, despite several significant findings, some theoretical weaknesses as well as methodological and data limitations suggest that the empirical results of this study should be carefully interpreted. First, as a theoretical downside, the relationship between employees and supervisors is not exactly the same as that suggested by the principal–agent theory, especially in public organizations. That is, there should be multiple agents and principals in the contractual process, who actually have or are willing to develop a multidimensional or pooled interdependence relationship rather than a bilateral and reciprocal interaction. In the pooled relationship, we expect that there is little or no formal interaction or coordination among organizational participants, and thus no principal–agent relationship (O'Toole and Montjoy 1984). Moreover, in the public sector, not only the agent but the principal would also encounter informational asymmetry problems, leading to a violation of the major assumption of the agency theory. In this regard, agency theory may not fully account for the social dynamics of principal–agent dyads in specific circumstances, for example, in the public sector (Parks and Conlon 1995).

Source: Park, S. M. (2010). The Effects of Personnel Reform Systems on Georgia State Employees Attitudes: An empirical analysis from a principal–agent theoretical perspective. Public Management Review, 12(3), 403-437.

Further Readings

- Berman, E. M., Bowman, J. S., West, J. P., & Van Wart, M. R. (Ed.) (2012). *Human Resource Management in Public Service: Paradoxes, Processes, and Problems.* Fourth Edition. Sage Publications.
- Kim, P. S. (Ed.) (2010). *Civil Service System and Civil Service Reform in ASEAN Member Countries and Korea.*
- Condrey, S. E. (Ed.). (2005). Handbook of Human Resources Management in Government. *John Wiley & Sons.*
- Park, S. M. (2010). The Effects of Personnel Reform Systems on Georgia State Employees Attitudes: An empirical analysis from a principal–agent theoretical perspective. Public Management Review, 12(3), 403-437.
- Battaglio, R. P., & Condrey, S. E. (2006). Civil Service Reform Examining State and Local Government Cases. Review of Public Personnel Administration, 26(2), 118-138.
- Lah, T. J., & Perry, J. L. (2008). The diffusion of the Civil Service Reform Act of 1978 in OECD countries: A tale of two paths to reform. Review of Public Personnel Administration.

References

Battaglio, R. P., & Condrey, S. E. (2006). Civil Service Reform Examining State and Local Government Cases. Review of Public Personnel Administration, 26(2), 118-138.

Berman, E. M., Bowman, J. S., West, J. P., & Van Wart, M. R. (2012). *Human resource management in public service: Paradoxes, processes, and problems*. Sage.

Bertok, J. (1999). OECD Supports the Creation of Sound Ethics Infrastructure: OECD1 Targets Both the "Supply Side" and the "Demand Side" of Corruption. *Public Personnel Management*, 28(4), 673-687.

Burke, R. J., Allisey, A. F., & Noblet, A. J. (2013). The importance of human resource management in the public sector, future challenges and the relevance of the current collection. *Human resource management in the public sector*, 1-16.

Burns, C., Barton, K., & Kerby, S. (2012). The state of diversity in today's workforce: as our nation becomes more diverse so too does our workforce.

Condrey, S. E. (Ed.). (2005). Handbook of Human Resources Management in Government. *John Wiley & Sons*.

Eko Prasojo entitled "Exploring Public Sector reform in Indonesia", a manuscript included in the book, Public Sector Reform in ASEAN Member Countries and Korea edited by Pan Suk Kim. Published on December 30, 2011.

Farnham, D. (2010). Human Resource Management and its External Context. *Published by CIPD*

Fountain, J. E. (2004). Building the virtual state: Information technology and institutional change. *Brookings Institution Press*.

Hoseok Jang, Public Personnel Management", a manuscript included in the book, Discover Korea in Public Administration edited by Eung-kyuk Park, Chang-seok Park, and Bernard Rowan. Published on April 2012 by *The Korea Institute of Public Administration*.

Ingraham, Patricia W. 1993. Of Pigs in Pokes and Policy Diffusion: Another Look at Pay-for-Performance. *Public Administration Review* 53 (4): 348 – 56.

Kellough, J. E. (1999). Reinventing public personnel management: Ethical implications for managers and public personnel systems. *Public Personnel Management*, 28(4), 655-671.

Kettl, D. F. (2000). The transformation of governance: Globalization, devolution, and the role of government. *Public Administration Review*, 60(6), 488-497.

Kew, J. and Stredwick, J. (2010), Human Resource Management in Context, CIPD, London.

Lah, T. J., & Perry, J. L. (2008). The diffusion of the Civil Service Reform Act of 1978 in OECD countries: A tale of two paths to reform. Review of Public Personnel Administration.

Light, P. C. (2006). The tides of reform revisited: Patterns in making government work, 1945–2002. *Public*

Administration Review, 66(1), 6-19.

Lim, E. G. (2006). The Euro's challenge to the dollar: different views from economists and evidence from COFER (Currency Composition of Foreign Exchange Reserves) and other data.

Mastracci, S. H., & Thompson, J. R. (2005). Nonstandard Work Arrangements in the Public Sector Trends and Issues. *Review of Public Personnel Administration*, 25(4), 299-324.

Mikesell, J. L. (2003). International experiences with administration of local taxes: A review of practices and issues. *Tax Policy and Administration Thematic Group*, The World Bank.

OECD. (2013). Government at a Glance 2013. Retrieved from: http://www.oecd-ilibrary.org/governance/government-at-a-glance-2013_gov_glance-2013-en

Pitt-Catsouphes, M., Swanberg, J. E., Bond, J. T., & Galinsky, E. (2004). Work-life policies and programs: Comparing the responsiveness of nonprofit and for-profit organizations. *Nonprofit Management and Leadership,* 14(3), 291-312.

Pitts, David W. (2005). Diversity, Representation, and Performance: Evidence about Race and Ethnicity in Public Organizations. *Journal of Public Administration Research and Theory,* 15 (4): 615 – 31.

Pynes, J. E. (2008). *Human resources management for public and nonprofit organizations: A strategic approach* (Vol. 30). John Wiley & Sons.

Pynes, J. E. (2004). The implementation of workforce and succession planning in the public sector. *Public Personnel Management*, 33(4), 389-404.

Ridwan M. Sijabat, Government Makes Last Ditch Effort at Reform, *THE JAKARTA POST* (June 8, 2012)

The Economist (2012). Parsing public payrolls. Retrieved from: http://www.economist.com/news/finance-and-economics/21565216-public-sector-employment-shrinking-many-countries-greece-included-parsing

Thompson, J. R., & Mastracci, S. H. (2008). The Blended Workforce: Alternative Federal Models. *Public Personnel Management*, 37(3), 363-380.

United States Bureau of Labor Statistics (2013). Employment Projections: 2012-2022 Summary. Retrieved from: http://www.bls.gov/news.release/ecopro.nr0.htm

PART 2

THE CORE FUNCTIONS OF HUMAN RESOURCE MANAGEMENT

Recruiting Human Resources

Framework

Human Resource Management for Public Organizations: An Essential Guide

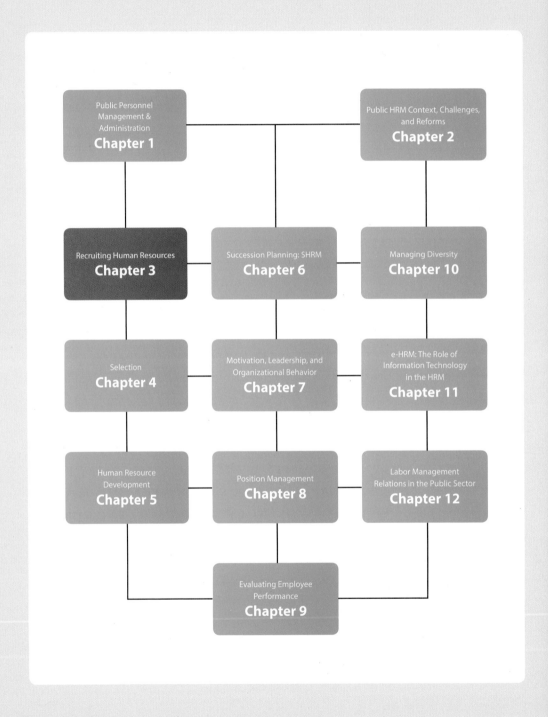

Public Personnel Management & Administration
Chapter 1

Public HRM Context, Challenges, and Reforms
Chapter 2

Recruiting Human Resources
Chapter 3

Succession Planning: SHRM
Chapter 6

Managing Diversity
Chapter 10

Selection
Chapter 4

Motivation, Leadership, and Organizational Behavior
Chapter 7

e-HRM: The Role of Information Technology in the HRM
Chapter 11

Human Resource Development
Chapter 5

Position Management
Chapter 8

Labor Management Relations in the Public Sector
Chapter 12

Evaluating Employee Performance
Chapter 9

Learning Outcomes

After going through this chapter, you should be able to:

- Define the recruitment function.
- Understand the recruitment techniques and strategies used in the contemporary public sector organizations.
- Describe the steps in the public sector recruitment process.
- Understand the relationship of recruitment and selection process.

Preview

To effectively adapt on rapid environmental changes, an agency must be able to recruit and select qualified individuals that possesses and able to develop new and the needed knowledge, skills, and abilities, and responsive to available incentive structure (Pynes, 2008; 2004). The public personnel managers are challenged to meet the demands of the rapidly changing situations in the public sector organizations. They must possess an unparalleled understanding of the trends and changes in the environment and of the ins-and-outs of the government talent acquisition process. For the public sector organizations, "the capacity to acquire capable employees is essential if government is to successfully provide the numerous services associated with modern public service" (Nigro, Nigro, & Kellough, 2013, p. 69). This calls for the necessity that public personnel office must develop and implement well-designed recruitment and selection process that are capable of meeting the needs and in achieving the goals of the organization. To be successful in the government and public sector, recruitment and selection must involve an effective planning process that include the necessary KSAs needed in the government and the present and future employment priorities that clearly supports organizational strategies.

Pynes (2008) defined *recruitment* as the "process of attracting qualified candidates to apply for vacant oppositions within an organization"; while "*selection* is the final stage of the recruitment process, when decisions are made as to who will be selected for the vacant positions" (p. 180). The recruitment and selection processes in the government and public sector tend to be more complex than in the private sector. Since the public sector is faced with various responsibilities (e.g., public safety and security, environmental protection, justice, etc.) (Klinger & Nalbandian, 2003), it demands acquisition of well-qualified people that will occupy important positions in the government. However, the complexity of the recruitment and selection processes may render difficult for the public sector to compete [for the limited pool of qualified applicants] with the private sector which is also in need of highly qualified employees for their organization. As Sullivan (2013) noted, there will be continuous competition for top talents in the competitive labor market due to slack hiring. In this competition, the public sector recruitment and selection approaches must produce new and applicable strategies that can provide them a competitive advantage in the acquisition of talents.

This chapter discusses the recruitment (Chapter 3) issues, processes, and important challenges that are influential in the overall acquisition function of public HRM. While on Chapter 4, it focuses on the philosophical bases, stages of selection process, and other issues surrounding the effective and successful integration of new employees in the environment of public organization. Figure 3.1 presents the typical process of the civil service staffing emphasizing on recruitment.

Figure 3.1
Civil Service Staffing Process: Recruitment

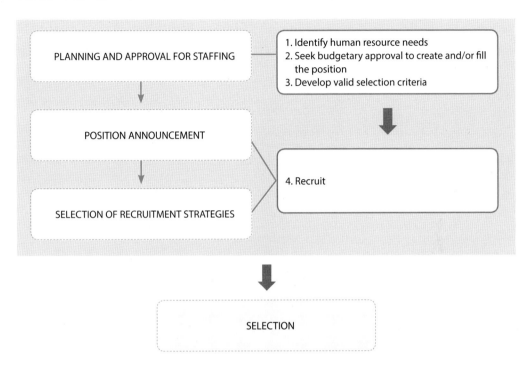

Sources: Berman, Bowman, West, & Van Wart. (2012); Klinger & Nalbandian (2003)

Making Sense of the RealWorld

The development of internet allows various public, non-profit, and private agencies to post online information about job vacancies. Various online recruitment platforms were made available and currently impactful in the recruiting approaches. In the corporate recruiting trends, Sullivan (2013) noted online recruitment trends that will continue to remain relevant in the growing information age. For instance, he posited that *mobile platform, online candidate assessment, live video interviewing, data-driven approach, remote work positions,* and *accelerated internal movement* may continue to be impactful in the organizational recruitment agenda and strategies. These approaches are available and accessible for the public organizations as well, however, has yet to be widely explored. In the United States, the Office of the personnel Management (OPM) in August 2003 enhanced the USAJobs website (www.usajobs.opm.gov) into "Recruitment One-Stop" (Nigro et al., 2013). The kiosk provides federal job information for all job seekers nationwide as well as for the federal agencies finds potential candidates to be recruited (see Figure 3.2 and check for the USAJobs website). The website provides an opportunity for the job seekers to update their resumes in the USAJobs and allows recruiters to review the qualifications of each applicant (Nigro et al., 2013).

Figure 3.2

The USAJobs

Source: www.usajobs.gov

Though the online recruitment system has yet to achieve a mainstream status, practitioners has noted the important contributions it brings in the field of human resource management. To have additional information on online recruitment, check on the following video clips.

Title	Gist	Source
USA Jobs	Presents the process on how to apply on US Jobs using the website.	hhttps://www.youtube.com/watch?v=s8MGO8DC3Jw
Digital e-Recruitment Process Problems on e-Recruitment	The process of e-recruitment and the problems or challenges on e-Recruitment	https://www.youtube.com/watch?v=v780wqrbNGM https://www.youtube.com/watch?v=bvsqqxYwhaw

1. What impact will the current economic conditions of your country and the state (if applicable) have on recruitment, hiring, and retention? Could these conditions change the tide of the labor market and has it already had an effect? If, not, what do you see as the main issues facing your organization/department in the areas of recruitment, hiring and retention?

2. Which is often the first factor that potential applicants review and consider? How do the private, public, and nonprofit sectors compare in this respect?

3. What do you think are the three important steps in recruitment or staffing? What are some differences in recruitment among countries?

4. How can public agencies do a better job of preparing their employees to fill more responsible positions and to be promoted?

5. With extensive delegations and deregulations of the recruitment, testing, and hiring processes, will it be possible to protect the merit principle, ADA, and EEO regulations?

"I'm an expert at multitasking. I can digest food, grow hair, circulate blood, repair cells, make saliva, breathe, blink, walk and talk, all at the same time!"

Recruitment

The rapid changes in the environmental context (discussed in Chapter 1) of public HRM (e.g., labor market change, aging labor force, workforce demographic change—minorities and women), declining public trust in government, changing organizational structure, SHRM, and legal changes) significantly affect the functions of HRM. These changes thwarted existing public personnel administration and management systems and have greatly influenced the efficiency of service delivery. Vacancies in the civil service are a recurring event due to some demographic changes as well as the ageing phenomenon. It may be caused by some internal movements (e.g., employee promotion, retirement, or taking of a leave) or an expansion of program scope and area which requires new employees. According to Pynes (2008), "recruitment is an ongoing process in most organizations; however, often it is not planned and therefore is less successful than it could be" (p. 181). That is, for recruitment to be successful it must follow a well-defined plan that considers the mission of the agency, the job requirements, where to find applicants, and on how to screen them in order to hire the most qualified (Pynes, 2008).

In a comprehensive personnel system, the recruitment and hiring of individuals who possesses the necessary knowledge, skills, and abilities (KSAs) is crucial to continuously fulfill the goals and mission of an organization. Klinger and Nalbandian (2003) describes *knowledge* as those information that allows an individual to perform functions that are based on theories, facts, and principles; *skills* "address the demonstrated *abilities* or proficiencies, which are developed and learned from past work and life experience" (p. 185). It is in this backdrop that all recruitment information, test, and selection decisions must be based on the specific requirements of the job (e.g., competencies) to be done and the organizational goals to achieve. Ideal as it may be, the recruitment and hiring of well-qualified candidates for government posts warrants utmost consideration and serious attention. Thus, the public personnel office must design and implement a recruitment strategy that integrates the values of merit systems in the hiring process—meaning that recruitment and hiring is not based on *who you know* or political patronage but on *what you know*—competency.

It is also true, that there are various contentions surrounding civil service recruitment. Generally, many jobs in the public sector organizations are filled based on political patronage (Nigro et al., 2013). This is among the absurdity in the civil service that must follow a routine procedure of achieving competence. Patronage appointments are believed to mostly have a negative impact on public policy, but attempts are made to prove certain positive effects. The neutral competence of bureaucrats, seen as the key to performance in the public sector (Heclo, 1975) has been targeted by criticism seeking to accommodate the need for increased political responsiveness among bureaucrats. William West (2005) claims that "politics and administration are intertwined" and in order to increase outcomes produced by the public sector there is a need for combining nonpartisan objectivity (characteristic for merit based systems) with responsiveness toward political executives (typical for patronized systems). This view is supported by Bok, Maranto and Moe, which argue that political appointees bring to administration more energy, human capital and higher levels of education than careerists do (Lewis, 2007). They also claim that appointees contribute to a better implementation of their political principals' agenda. Thus responsiveness is the outstanding advantage of patronage, as opposed to careerist bureaucrats, who, according to Dunleavy (1985) tends to make choices based on their own preferences and orientations, thus diverging from the current political agenda. Having political appointees in executive positions may also help mitigate the lack of trust issue that many have in non-elected officials exercising political discretion (West, 2005).

Berman and colleagues (2012) pointed a paradox on organizational perspective stating that "recruitment is the most compelling human resource function, but it is generally acknowledged to be the weakest in most organizations (US Government Accountability Office [GAO], 2003; cited in Berman et al., 2012, p. 99). As argued, it is the weakest because if done properly, the process may be circumvented because it is costly and time consuming, and if not done properly it may sacrifice the subsequent HR functions. Table 3.1 summarizes the paradoxes presented by Berman et al (2012).

Table 3.1
Paradoxes of Recruitment

Paradox	Description
Procurement strategies and techniques	Procurement strategies may be relatively insignificant compared to the sociopolitical environment within which recruitment takes place (i.e., historical recruitment philosophy, declining social status of public employment since the high-water mark in the '30s and '40s, and political leadership.
Fast-track positions	Seemingly abundant employment opportunity but scarcity of desirable positions.
Specialists or generalists?	Generalist training is critical for managers having diverse functions.
Staffing practices	It is the most persuasive HR function but is generally weak.
Pay and benefits	Perception of lower pay and lower job quality.
Balancing competing values	The need for timely recruitment.
Recruitment process emphasis	Which one is to emphasize among KSA, motivation, diversity, and loyalty?
Organizational responsibility to the applicant	Sham recruitment processes.

Approaches on Recruitment

Internal Recruitment

In many public sector agencies, in cases of vacancies caused by retirement, leave, other causes, the current agency staffs are considered first in filling the [vacated] position. This is what they usually call as internal recruitment. This approach is well favored because it saves cost and time as well as an effective mechanism for employee performance management. However, there are limitations for this approach if the position sought to be filled requires a high KSA or a position that needs specialized skills that are not available within the organization. Also, this approach calls for the implementation of a strategic human resource planning (will be discussed in Chapter 6).

External Recruitment

As the name implies, this approach seeks potential applicants from outside the organization. The external labor market is deemed to be relevant if they manifest the job characteristics or criteria defined by the agency and the KSAs are necessary in the organization. The job market can be classified into either *limited* or *general* job market. The limited job market may include those KSAs that are considered highly and limited such as scientists, engineers, managers, and other individuals who possess critical skills. Thus, the geographical area for recruitment should be in a nationwide scale. While in a general job market, the skills sought for the position are common such as clerk, laborer, and technical and direct service providers.

Other Recruitment Approaches

- Centralized Recruitment
- Decentralized Recruitment
- Electronic Recruitment
- Outsourcing

Recruitment Steps

Before proceeding to the discussion of various strategies or methods of recruitment, it will be helpful to determine the various steps and responsibilities involved in the civil service staffing process (see also **Figure 3.1**) which include planning and approval for staffing, position announcement, and selection of recruitment strategies (see also Berman et al., 2012). It must be understood that the recruitment process is a priori stage before the selection (Chapter 4) process.

Figure 3.3
Recruitment Process

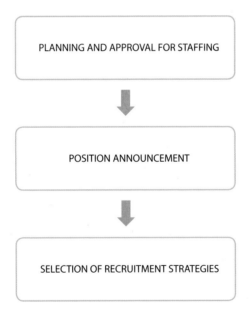

Source: Berman, E. M., Bowman, J. S., West, J. P., & Van Wart, M. R. (Ed.) (2012). Human Resource Management in Public Service: Paradoxes, Processes, and Problems. Fourth Edition. Sage Publications.

In the recruitment process, planning and acquisition of competencies or human resource in various agencies may carry out these steps in different ways. First, in the planning and approval for staffing, it may involve functions (Klinger & Nalbandian, 2003) such as (1) identification of human resource needs, (2) seek budgetary approval for the creation of/or filling of a vacancy, and then (3) develop valid selection criteria. A plan for staffing starts on the needs assessment—identification of human resource needs—that involves labor market analysis and the organizational HR need in the present and future. In essence, it calls for a strategic human resource planning so that issues on HR are proactively dealt with. Upon identification of the HR needs, strategic HR planning must ensure that proper funding is allotted for whatever employee intake. Then, through job analysis the personnel manager must develop minimum and valid criteria as well as the appropriate measures to be used in the selection of employees. It is important to note that, the participation of line managers or those who will be working with the potential hire will be working must be deeply involved in the process (Klinger & Nalbandian, 2003).

Second, the position announcement may not be as complex like the planning and approval for staffing. Since there are no legal restrictions or limitations provided, announcement may take into different forms. Variations may be attributed on issues such as the level of positions sought to occupy. For example, if the position is classified as lower-level position—position that require basic skill and education qualification, the public employer may not need to do a grandiose announcement. It is suffice to do local advertisement or posting information in an appropriate website (e.g., job search website). However, if the position requires high KSA or education requirement, the posting may entail more efforts in order to attract applicants to apply for such position. Posting of job vacancy, of such nature, demands appropriate advertisement styles that treats the government as an entity convincing applicants to file application. In the United States, the federal agencies were criticized due to poor job vacancy and agency advertising efforts (see U.S. MSPB, 2003).

Third, the recruitment strategies may be in different forms. There various methods that can be adapted in communicating and informing the job market on job vacancies in the government. Recruitment strategies may vary depending on circumstances and may entail the combination of two or more. In the United States, federal agencies have been aggressive on recruitment practices (U.S. MSPB, 2006; Berman et al., 2012). In here, we just selected important and relevant strategies for us to consider (see also Berman et al., 2012):

1. *Job Posting.* It is the most common among recruitment strategies. It is typically the posting of job announcements in places that are visible for the public, e.g. post offices, bulletin board in the municipal or city halls. Other countries require, as mandated by rules and regulations, those job vacancies must be posted in public places within a certain period of time. Though practices like this are still happening, contemporary public organizations are posting job information on local dailies and newspapers of general circulation.

2. *Electronic Posting.* In the advent of development of technology and internet, job seekers can now access job information on numerous websites—agency website or other exclusive websites for job finders. Among the available job banks is the U.S. federal government's central website (www.usajobs.opm.gov) and America's Job Bank (www.ajb.dni.us). Even in developing countries the online posting of available or job opening are now widespread.

3. *Personal Contact Recruitment.* This approach has been lauded as one of the most important recruitment source (U.S. MSPB, 2008; Crsipin & Mehler, 2011; Berman, et al., 2012). Generally, it depends on referrals made by employees for those potential recruits in the field; job fairs, and campus visits and presentations.

4. *Mail (and email) Recruitment.* This approach is undertaken for exceptional candidates. It is widely used in the private sector; however, it can also be adopted by public sector organizations in competition for hiring those with high KSAs.

5. *Institutional Capacity Recruitment.* Public agencies may avail of some institutional advertising that may help them promote or advertise job openings or vacancies using the "government access TV, billboards, radio advertisements," and other agency promotional activities.

6. *Headhunting.* Generally, this approach is an external recruitment strategy. This happened wherein the staffing process is entrusted to a third party—*headhunt-*

er—that will find potential recruits. In the public sector, this is usually utilized in recruiting low-level positions but not the middle level positions. While in the private sector, they utilize this approach in seeking to find executives and senior managers for the organization.

It is also worth to consider that in the formulation of an effective recruitment program, Nigro, Nigro, and Kellough (2003, p. 71) suggested to look at the case of the State of Georgia's central personnel agency. The guidelines provide that:

- *The program should permit employees to identify recruitment sources, such as universities and trade schools, that are the most likely to provide enough applicants with the needed skills and abilities.*
- *It should be funded and staffed at the levels required to carry out an active recruitment effort.*
- *In addition to meeting short-term or immediate needs, the program should be designed to meet long-term needs by acquiring entry –level personnel who will later be able to advance and fill more responsible positions.*
- *Recruitment must be seen as the initial step in the selection process and, therefore, it must "ensure compliance with existing federal and state laws and guidelines concerning fairness, equal opportunity, and...minimize potential adverse impact on legally protected groups."*
- *The program should meet the public's expectation that all phases of the hiring process will be "fair" in the sense that merit and EEO are the core values guiding that process.*

Georgia Merit System, 1997, p 1-2

Case Brief

Public Service Recruitment:
The Case of Indonesia, Kenya, and Korea

Human resource management (HRM) is responsible for the attraction, selection, training, assessment, and rewarding of employees while also overseeing organizational leadership and culture, and ensuring compliance with employment and labor laws. Typically, the recruitment and selection process follows the process of (1) defining requirements, (2) attracting candidates, and (3) selecting candidates. Along this backdrop, this section examines the recruitment processes in Indonesia, Kenya, and Korea and discusses the differences that may be derived from them.

INDONESIA

Indonesia is a country located in the Southeast Asia and Oceania. Its archipelago comprises approximately 17,508 islands, 1.9 km2 of land area, and 230 million of estimated population. The Indonesian economy is the world's 16th largest by nominal GDP. In terms of civil service reforms, Indonesia introduced various innovative approaches—open recruitment system that was first initiated in the Ministry of Finance—and are yet to enact other important measures to totally transform and produce efficient and effective government professionals. Along with the reform initiatives, the Indonesian Civil Service provides a systematic management human resource management system that includes functions under the *State Civil Service Agency* (e.g., database record, appointment, registration, and provision of general civil service guidelines), *Ministry of State Apparatus and Bureaucracy Reform* (e.g., supervision, coordination, monitoring, evaluation, and reformation), and the National Institute of Public Administration (e.g., education and training). Figure 3.4 depicts the Civil Service Management of Indonesia.

121

Figure 3.4
Indonesian Civil Service Management

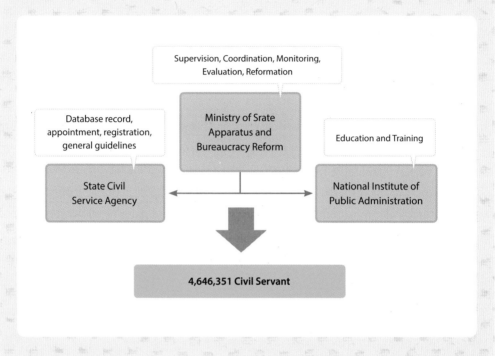

In the recruitment of civil servants, public sector agencies (e.g., local and central government agencies) often look at either internal or external labor market. Current staffs or employees and also qualified applicants from outside the organization are considered in the recruitment process (see Figure 3.6). The announcement of vacancy and recruitment are provided in the government's official website which contains the following information: (a) total and types of vacant position, (b) the requirements which shall be met by applicants, (c) the address and place to which applications are sent, and (d) the deadline of submitting the applications.

In the creation of a new post in the public service, the Indonesian government follow a process (see Figure 3.5) in which each proposal emanates from the local government and/or the central government. Those proposal(s) are submitted in the State Civil Service Agency, and then the latter will move to the Ministry of

State Apparatus and Bureaucracy Reform (MSABR) for technical consideration, preliminary approval, and submission of adjusted formation proposal. Upon satisfaction of all the process, the MSABR give the final approval for the formation.

Figure 3.5
Formation Approval Process

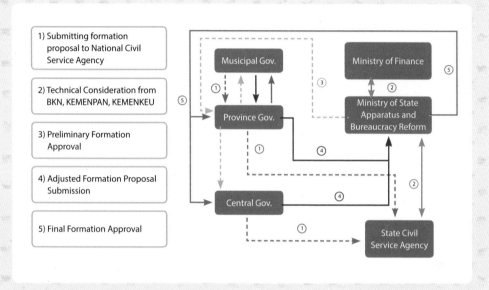

The screening of qualified applicants in Phase I involves the scrutiny of all submitted [required] documents by the applicants. These include the resume or curriculum vitae and other pertinent documents. The Phase II examination will be conducted in writing which will be given to only those who passed the Phase I. The written examination consists of General Knowledge Test (TPU) and Test of Academic Potential (TPA). Then those who succeeded in Phase II will move to psychological test, then health and fitness examination, then interview. It is important to note that, the applicant should be able to satisfy all the requirements and qualify in each examination given.

Figure 3.6
Recruitment Method

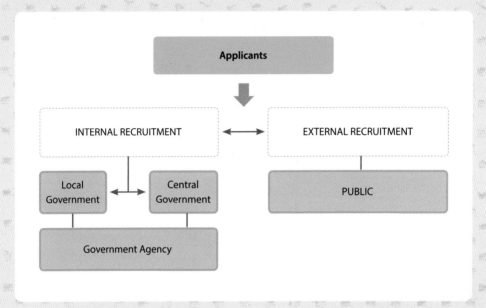

Before the appointment of a civil servant must, it must at least have completed a 1-year and maximum of 2-year probationary period. The appointment will be done by the officials authorized to promote personnel upon satisfactorily met the following guidelines: (1) Each element of work achievement has a good score; (2) Physically and mentally healthy to be appointed as civil servant; and (3) Passed the pre-post education and training.

KENYA

Kenya—*officially the Republic of Kenya*—is a country in Africa that covers 581,309 km2 (224,445 sq. mi), and had a population of approximately 44 million in 2012 (Wikipedia). Kenya is presidential representative democratic republic and has three co-equal branches of government—executive, legislative and judicial department.

The civil service system in the country, like other countries, is still undergoing reform efforts that the fruits are yet to be seen. The public service recruitment, for example, has been greatly challenged by the declining trust in the government and the 'misconception' on the about the public service commission due to interferences from political leadership who happened to be the appointing authority. Also, the influx of candidates from the private sector is increasing, but beneath the surface, this opportunity potentially raises as many problems as it does solutions. While the quantity of candidates may be growing, their quality and relevance for the public sector may not always be. Also, the current Kenyan Constitution posed important limitation and a guideline that in its words are clear and unambiguous. Article 27 (8 and 81b) of the Constitution mandates that, "no more than two-thirds of members of any institution should be of one gender". In the recruitment process (e.g., open competitive examination or non-competitive selection), four major agencies are involved: (1) the ministry involved that needs the civil servant(s); (2) Ministry of State for Public Service (MSPS); (3) Public Service Commission (PSC); and (4) Ministry of Finance (MoF). Figure 3.7 depicts the interaction of the major agencies in the Kenyan civil service recruitment process and Figure 3.9 presents the specific interaction on the recruitment process.

Figure 3.7
Major Agencies Involved in the Recruitment

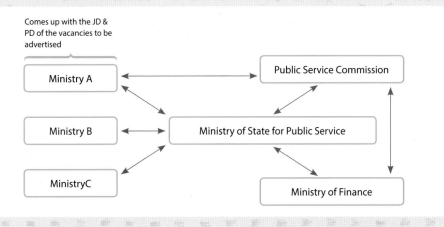

The civil service job grade is categorized into 1-9 grades, horizontal classification (i.e., occupational groups, series, and sub-series), and into two types (i.e., career service and non-career service) (see Figure 3.8).

Figure 3.8
Classification of National Civil Service

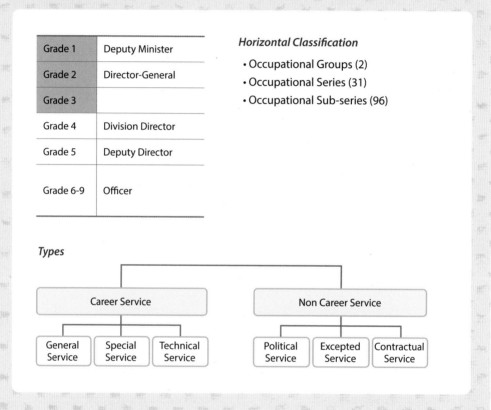

Figure 3.9
Kenyan Civil Servant Recruitment Process

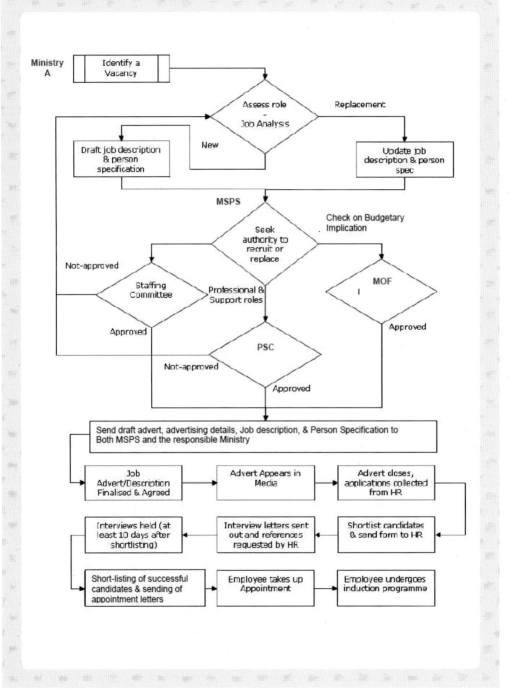

KOREA

In Korea, recruitment for career service in the government is made from 9th, 7th, and 5th grade levels. Generally, the recruitment for 9th grade vacancies were made through new recruitments through competitive written examination—civil service examination—which intend to invite young and new bloods in the government service; while vacancies in the 7th and 5th grade were filled through promotions. To be a candidate for promotion, one should first meet the minimum grade-specific length-of-service requirements, and then climb up through the list of candidates until he/she reaches the top range. In climbing up the list, the results of performance evaluation and training matter to some extent, but seniority is the key. It is in this sense that promotions are mainly seniority-based

In the OECD 2012 report on Human Resources Management Country Profiles, it provides that the Korea's recruitment system is somewhat more career-based compared to the OECD average (see Figure 3.10). As a practice, the recruitment process commonly follows an open and centralized recruitment scheme initiated by the central HRM. The open recruitment is conducted through a tedious civil service examination that is administered by the central HRM while the career-based recruitment system is administered by the central HRM agency and other related agencies. The competitive recruitment ratio in the Korean government civil service was 44.7% in 2010 (OECD, 2012). Also, recruitment focus was laid on gender, person with disabilities, and low income groups in the society. OECD (2012) noted that if the passing rate for certain recruitment examination is less than 30% of the gender proportion; more applicants will be recruited in the gender that is yet to be filled in order to balance the proportion. Also, OECD (2012) pointed that there is a specific quota—wherein 1% of the recruits must be from the low income earning groups and 3% for the persons-with-disabilities.

Figure 3.10
Type of recruitment system used in central government (2005)

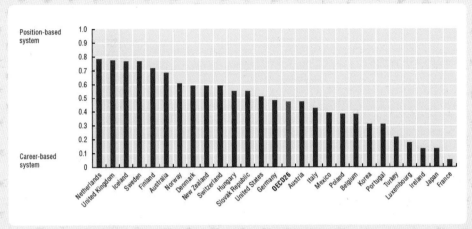

Note: This index describes a spectrum of recruitment systems in place in OECD member countries. It does not evaluate the performance of different systems.

Source: GOVERNMENT AT A GLANCE 2009 © OECD 2009

Apart from the seemingly restricted or limited scope for recruitment system, Korea adopted and introduced "expert recruitment system" (in which a limited number of positions are designated for contract-based appointments from both inside and outside the civil service sector).

Table 3.2
Comparison of the Civil Service Recruitment Factors in Indonesia, Kenya, and Korea

	Indonesia	Kenya	Korea
Recruitment Process	2 processes (Open & Temporary employee)	Same process to all grades	3 Different types in competition exam (Grade 5, 7, & 9)
Entry Exam	Includes writing exams (3)	No writing exams	Includes writing exam (3)
Recruitment done centrally	No. It's done at the Ministerial level	Yes by the PSCK except for non-professions	Yes for the Entry Exam then done by respective Ministries
Any preferences	Not at all	Preference is given to women and people with disabilities	Different process for people with disability
Legal provisions on Gender	Not at all	A provision of not more than two-thirds from the same gender	Has quota system in respect to women (Balanced – Personnel)

In conclusion, public service jobs have become an attraction to many because of the surety of job security and therefore there is need for water tight recruitment process to ensure quality of recruits. The advertisements for public service jobs should at least indicate advancement potential so as to attract best qualities that fear stagnation. There can never be a well cut out solution to recruitment and selection process for all countries. Other than the best practices, the other factors are deemed to vary from one country to the other.

1. What is your opinion on the affirmative action taken by Kenyan government on gender balance?

2. What is your opinion about candidates being subjected to exams during interview? Are they necessary considering that they are already trained professionals?

3. Considering centralized (Central Agency) and decentralized recruitment, which one do you think is the best way of recruitment and why?

4. Do you think that there is need to offer preference to marginalized groups during recruitment and why?

Student Activity:

Public sector organizations have to engage into active recruitment of talents to work in the civil service. Unlike the private sector, public sector seems to be complacent with the recruitment strategies and poorly exploring innovative ways. Using the case analysis table, list down all probable problems in the recruitment process; and then determine what the possible mechanisms that can address problems on recruitment.

HRM in the Public Organizations: An Essential Guide

Case Analysis

	Step	Contents		
1	Environments/ Conditions/ Backgrounds	Please explain the situation briefly. (1-2 pages)		
2	Problem Definitions	In your own perspective, please be as specific as possible when pointing out the problem. (2-3 pages)		
3	Actual Case Studies	Please explain by providing specific examples. (Newspaper articles, news clips, or interviews) (2-3 pages)		
4	Alternatives	Possible Alternative(s)	Pros in your Country Context	Cons in a your Country Context
		①		
		②		
		③		
		Please propose more than three policy alternatives. (2-3 pages)		
5	The Best Solutions	Why did you choose this alternative as the best solution? What are the expected effects and potential contribution? (2 pages)		

Reviews

1. Pynes said, "Interesting places to work can become less interesting," and focus groups, when asked what motivated people to stay with the organization once they were hired, did not usually first mention commitment to the mission, but once brought up, every participant agreed that it was one of the most important factors. Do you think the organizational mission is a superficial motivation? Why else would you choose to work in the public sector?

2. There are arguments stating that smaller organizations have less to offer in terms of salaries, upward movement, benefits, recruitment tools and HR in house functions. Does it make sense for smaller organizations with few employees, but high turnover, and a need to compensate employees creatively through non-financial outlets to invest in their own HR staff member?

Ending Credits

Research Digest

How to attract and retain the best in government

Facts:

How governments can attract and retain the best person for the job is a very complicated but urgent issue for government and business in the war for talent (Hacker, 2001; Michaels at al., 2001; Tulgan, 2002; Berger and Berger, 2003; Losey et al., 2005; Boudreau and Ramstad, 2007; Cheese et al., 2007; Cappelli, 2008; Lawler, 2008). Job markets for talent have become more competitive than ever before so that it is not easy attracting the right person, for the right job, at the right time. It is important to gain and sustain a competitive advantage by finding, hiring, and retaining the right talent with the right structures, systems, processes, and practices in place.

In looking at how to attract and retain the best, first of all, it is necessary to think about the question, 'Why do governments, generally, confront serious recruitment challenges?' Generally speaking, governments' recruiting systems are somewhat passive and very time-consuming with a lot of red tape (Nelson, 2004). The red tape, and too much bureaucracy, needs to be cut out. Also there is generally a lack of attraction for the younger generation. Therefore better, more attractive packages; better compensation, better benefits, better career development programs must be provided for public officials and prospective candidates (Ban and Riccucci, 2002; Kim, 2003; Klingner and Nalbandian, 2003; Berman et al., 2006). Talented and ambitious people will stay with their current employer only if they are offered positive development, motivation, and nurturing (Davis et al., 2007). Without these, there will be a loss of prestige making it difficult to attract young people and competent professionals. Government is often at risk for brain drain, particularly in developing and transitional economies. Poorly planned government staff cutbacks, an aging work force, and competition from the private sector contribute to the brain drain in government. Frequently, it can be seen in the newspapers that bureaucrats are lost to private enterprise where these kinds of packages are offered. Furthermore, when bureaucrats are criticized by the media, or the public, for various reasons, potential candidates for the public service turn away from the public sector to the private sector. Other reasons are lack of financial incentives together with a perception of low morale, and a lack of confidence and trust in the system. These issues must be dealt with, otherwise it will be difficult to attract and retain the best.

Issues
Whether or not different stages of HRM reform can be applicable to all other countries.

Findings
There are several approaches and different stages of HRM reform. It is not feasible to

apply the same strategy to all countries. Effective strategies in advanced countries may not always be the best option for developing countries or transitional economies. For developing countries or transitional economies, for example, the first thing they must do is establish a solid (preferably non-corrupt) civil service system. Then gradually they can adopt a more flexible system in stages. The approaches to government staffing reforms will differ from country to country. In career management, first of all, job security and protection from political interference is essential. In the second stage, an open employment system based on common terms and conditions and/or perhaps a somewhat flexible system can be gradually applied. In doing so, maybe decentralization can take place. While it is fine to have some sort of centralized system in the beginning, at some stage some decentralization or devolution is often chosen.

In the process of HRM reform as well as a paradigm shift in overall public management, the role of the HR director is critical for further developments of a civil service. HR directors should be multi-players (National Academy of Public Administration, 1996: 9). In this case multi-players are first of all HR experts; they should have technical expertise. Second, they have to be advocates; they have to advocate public values, publicness, and the spirit of public administration. They have to resolve conflicts and communicate well. They have to respect basic public values; fairness, diversity, representation. Third, they have to be change agents. In the world of globalization and informatization everyone is competing, one way or another. New ideas are coming up spontaneously. So it is necessary to be agents of change, flexible and responsive to new situations. Fourth, they need to be leaders. Definitions of a leader differ and literature on leadership is abundant. However, in this case, consider a leader as an ethical, creative, and decisive giver; a giver of new ideas and vision, giver of public spirit and trust, giver of motivation and direction. If there is lack of giving of these elements, how can a leader gain respect from his or her employees or subordinates?

Finally, they should be business partners. They should be involved with strategic HR planning, organization design, and strategic change as a part of the management team. If a government agency becomes a world-leading organization then there are other aspects to consider, such as the role of the mission-oriented strategic planner and system innovator. Taken together, multi-players must think about how best to develop

HRM strategies to make government organizations more competitive; they need the skills of an expert, to be the agents of change, advocates, leaders, and business partners. All these are important roles of HR directors.

In sum, the war for talent forces us to respond seriously (Hacker, 2001; Michaels at al., 2001; Tulgan, 2002; Berger and Berger, 2003; Losey et al., 2005; Boudreau and Ramstad, 2007; Cheese et al., 2007; Cappelli, 2008; Lawler, 2008). Talent is essential to competitiveness in the new economy so that it is necessary to build up a talent powered organization (Cheese et al., 2007). The talent management process is one of buying vs developing talent. The making vs buying cycle is driven by the larger product, economic and available labor cycles. By using innovation and execution, talent management should be a source of competitive advantage. In that regard, Peter Cappelli (2008) emphasizes four principles for ensuring that each organization has the skills it needs: (1) balance developing talent in-house with buying it on the open market; (2) improve the accuracy of our talent-need forecasts; (3) maximize returns on our talent investments; and (4) replicate external job market dynamics by creating an in-house market that links available talent to jobs.

Thus, HR managers should: aim to fit talent to task; seek greater lateral movement for employees both within the government and between government and the private sector; and reward the best performers and demand change among the worst (Bruel and Gardner, 2004: 9). In order to successfully compete in the talent war, we need to make a new Copernican transformation for sustainable development in government. Nicholas Copernicus (1473–1543) was a true Renaissance man. He could reasonably be described as a multi-player of his time. At the beginning of the 16th century he formulated the hypothesis that the sun, not the earth, was the center of the universe. This definitely had the 'Wow' factor. It encouraged scientists and scholars to question the world as they thought they knew it and initiated change far beyond the revelation of planets circling the sun. Talent is essential to competitiveness in the new economy. Thus HR managers need to initiate far-reaching, much needed change in the world of government in finding a better way of talent management to make government into the model employer of choice.

Kim, P. S. (2008). How to attract and retain the best in government. *International Review of Administrative Sciences, 74(4)*, 637-652.

Further Readings

- Berman, E. M., Bowman, J. S., West, J. P., & Van Wart, M. R. (Ed.) (2012). *Human Resource Management in Public Service: Paradoxes, Processes, and Problems.* Fourth Edition. Sage Publications.
- Kim, P. S. (Ed.) (2010). *Civil Service System and Civil Service Reform in ASEAN Member Countries and Korea.*
- Nigro, L., Nigro, F., & Kellough, J. (2013). The new public personnel administration. *Cengage Learning.*
- Pynes, J. E. (2008). Human resources management for public and nonprofit organizations: A strategic approach (Vol. 30). *John Wiley & Sons.*
- Kim, P. S. (2008). How to attract and retain the best in government. *International Review of Administrative Sciences*, 74(4), 637-652.
- Ban, C., Drahnak-Faller, A., & Towers, M. (2003). Human Resource Challenges in Human Service and Community Development Organizations Recruitment and Retention of Professional Staff. *Review of Public Personnel Administration*, 23(2), 133-153.
- Lavigna, R. J., & Hays, S. W. (2004). Recruitment and selection of public workers: An international compendium of modern trends and practices. *Public Personnel Management*, 33(3), 237-253.

References

Berman, E. M., Bowman, J. S., West, J. P., & Van Wart, M. R. (2012). *Human resource management in public service: Paradoxes, processes, and problems*. Sage.

Crispin, G., & Mehler, M. (2011). Sources of hire: Channels that Influence.

Dunleavy, P. (1985). Bureaucrats, budgets and the growth of the state: reconstructing an instrumental model. *British Journal of Political Science*, 15(03), 299-328.

Heclo, H. (1975). OMB AND PRESIDENCY-PROBLEM OF NEUTRAL COMPETENCE. *Public Interest*, (38), 80-98.

Klinger Donald, E., & Nalbandian, J. (2003). Public Personnel Management: Contexts and Strategies. *New Jersey*.

Lewis, D. E. (2007). Testing Pendleton's Premise: Do Political Appointees Make Worse Bureaucrats? *Journal of Politics*, 69(4), 1073-1088.

Nigro, L., Nigro, F., & Kellough, J. (2013). The new public personnel administration. *Cengage Learning*.

OECD. (2012). OECD Employment Outlook 2012. Retrieved from http://www.oecd.org/korea/Korea_final_EN.pdf

OECD. (2009). Government at a Glance 2009. Retrieved from: http://www.oecd.org/gov/43926778.pdf

Pynes, J. E. (2008). Human resources management for public and nonprofit organizations: A strategic approach (Vol. 30). John Wiley & Sons.

Pynes, J. E. (2004). Human resources management for public and nonprofit organizations: A strategic approach (Vol. 3). John Wiley & Sons.

Sullivan, J. (2013). The Top 25 Recruiting Trends, Problems and Opportunities for 2014. Retrieved from: http://www.ere.net/2013/12/16/the-top-25-recruiting-trends-problems-and-opportunities-for-2014-part-2-of-2/

U.S. Merit Systems Protection Board (MSPB). (2003). *Help wanted: A review of federal vacancy announcements*. Washington, DC

West, W. (2005). Administrative rulemaking: An old and emerging literature. *Public Administration Review*, 65(6), 655-668.

Selection

Framework

Human Resource Management for Public Organizations: An Essential Guide

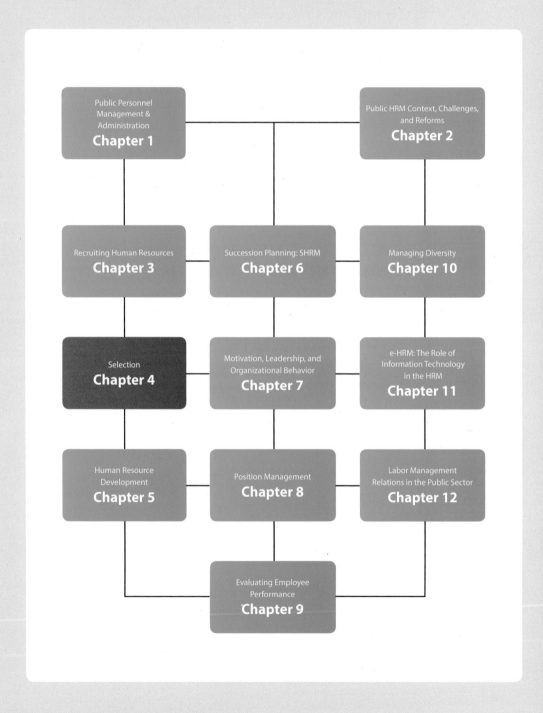

Public Personnel Management & Administration
Chapter 1

Public HRM Context, Challenges, and Reforms
Chapter 2

Recruiting Human Resources
Chapter 3

Succession Planning: SHRM
Chapter 6

Managing Diversity
Chapter 10

Selection
Chapter 4

Motivation, Leadership, and Organizational Behavior
Chapter 7

e-HRM: The Role of Information Technology in the HRM
Chapter 11

Human Resource Development
Chapter 5

Position Management
Chapter 8

Labor Management Relations in the Public Sector
Chapter 12

Evaluating Employee Performance
Chapter 9

Learning Outcomes

After going through this chapter, you should be able to:

- Discuss the stages of selection process.
- Determine appropriate examination methods.
- Identify what are the methods, issues and problems in the selection process.

Preview

The process of selection starts right after all the applications have been received from different identified recruitment strategies (Berman et al., 2012). This is the crucial moment in the staffing process because it involves the interaction with the applicants and making decisions whether to hire them or not. Thus, it is correct to describe it as the most significant "politically sensitive aspect of human resource management" (Ployhart, 2006; cited in Berman et al., 2012). In real sense, selection process has been greatly challenged by political spoils systems that, in a way tarnish the objectivity of the whole civil servant's selection process. Even in the recruitment process, we already learned that political influences was put into debate whether it is contributory on the ineffectiveness of the government services because it trashed-out the merits systems principles. On the other side, it was also argued and perceived to be helpful ineffectively achieving the organizational goals and missions—since the appointing authority have full control of what he perceived to be necessary in the organization. It is a contentious issue that demands objective evidence to show proof that political interventions do not in a way affects the merit systems.

In a more idealistic sense, the principles of the traditional merit systems emphasizes that the selection process is insulated with political intrusions and ensures the objectivity neutrality of the staffing process. Nigro, Nigro, and Kellough (2013) argued that to achieve this, creation of a well-designed and "controlled personnel specialists housed in central personnel agencies or independent commissions" is required (p. 77-78). This emphasized the importance of having an independent body that is not influenced by any outside or external factors—political elements—in the conduct of selection process. It is really important to underscore this issue because the fairness and justice in the selection may come to play. As presented in Chapter 3, there is a paradox on whether or not the recruiting public sector agency should be responsible with the applicants, for example, affording them equal and justifiable consideration in the recruitment and selection process.

Steps or stages in the selection process may differ from one agency to another. This again may depend on whether there is a statute or an existing rules and regulations to follow. In this chapter, however, the steps on the selection process (see Figure 4.1) will be highlighted which includes (1) selection of tests, (2) screening, (3) negotiate and hire, and (4) post-selection considerations (see also Berman et al., 2012). Along with these steps, Klinger and Nalbandian (2003) also provided staffing steps that seems to be adaptable with the process presented by Berman and his colleagues.

Figure 4.1
Civil Service Staffing Process: Selection

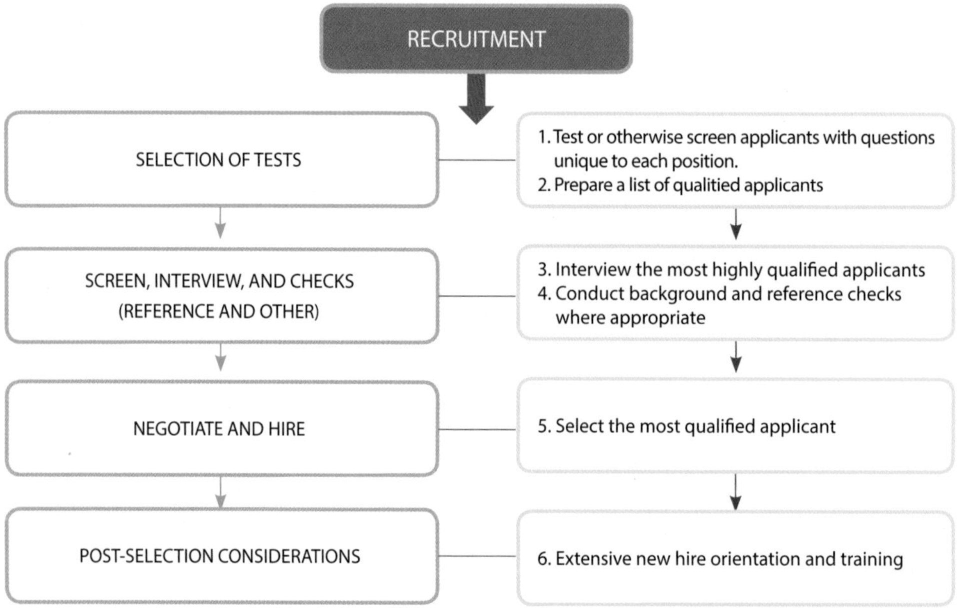

Sources: Berman, Bowman, West, & Van Wart. (2012); Klinger & Nalbandian (2003)

Making Sense of the RealWorld

Seamlessly, recruitment and selection are processes that are connected with each other. After the completion of recruitment stage, the selection process may start to commence following a well-designed process for staffing purposes. There are various approaches that public personnel managers may take into account depending on the circumstances of the public sector agency. In the following video clip, it provides a brief explanation on the recruitment and selection process which may best explain the interrelationship of the two distinct but connected processes.

Title	Gist	Source
Recruitment and Selection	This video clip shows the basics of recruitment and selection process	https://www.youtube.com/watch?v=SYwUfCCMHvk

1. What is your opinion on implementing an all-out merit based selection process for the civil servants? What about merit-based vs. seniority in the promotional hiring? Should the political appointment or patronage-based selection remain in the civil service recruitment and selection process?

2. Is using GPA or class standing to hire new employees a good way of ensuring that agencies will be employing highly qualified applicants?

3. As government employee or a student of public management, what approaches would you like to see in order to improve the selection process in the government? Say, in the local/municipal, provincial, and/or central government?

4. What do you think are the issues that can be confronted in imposing a mandatory drug test for all civil service applicants?

© Randy Glasbergen
www.glasbergen.com

"My short-term goal is to bluff my way through this job interview. My long-term goal is to invent a time machine so I can come back and change everything I've said so far."

Selection

n the last chapter, we tried to determine the recruitment process in which we get into whom to recruit. After doing all the recruitment processes and once the organization has received all the application forms of the applicants, the public sector agency may commence the screening of the applications to determine whether or not the applicants may be a potential candidate for hiring. We will discuss here how potential and eligible candidates are selected. In Figure 4.1 and Figure 4.2, the process provides that, first, in the selection of tests, it includes the screening of applicants with questions that is unique in the position applied and preparing of lists of qualified candidates; *second,* in involves the screening of the most qualified applicants and screen them based on the submitted references and other pertinent documents; *third,* must select the qualified employees and do the negotiation and hiring of possible or potential candidates that can be posted in the vacant position; and *fourth,* conduct an extensive new hire orientation and training activities.

Figure 4.2
Selection Process

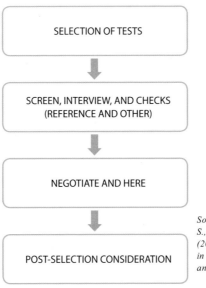

SELECTION OF TESTS

SCREEN, INTERVIEW, AND CHECKS (REFERENCE AND OTHER)

NEGOTIATE AND HERE

POST-SELECTION CONSIDERATION

Source: Berman, E. M., Bowman, J. S., West, J. P., & Van Wart, M. R. (Ed.) (2012). Human Resource Management in Public Service: Paradoxes, Processes, and Problems. Fourth Edition. Sage Publications.

145

STAGE 1:

Selection of Tests

In the process of selecting eligible candidates, it involves various tests which may allow the managers and supervisors (i.e., recruitment and selection committee) to determine the capacity or qualifications of the applicants. Tests do not only include paper-and-pencil or written examination, computer-assisted, but also those that may examine the physical ability, health check-up, skills and ability test, and among others. In the selection of civil servants, the primary consideration is to look into whether an applicant has the necessary knowledge, skills, and abilities required of a given position. The following are some of the tests employed in the public sector selection process (Nigro et al., 2013, p. 78).

- Assessments of minimum qualifications requirements
- Evaluation of training, education, and experience
- Written tests of knowledge and analytic skills
- Job performance tests and simulations
- Oral examinations by individual examiners or boards
- Background checks or investigations
- Medical and physical examination.

The selection process can through four phases in order to arrive at a clean set of potential applicants for hiring. Berman and colleagues (2012) provides useful information on how to deal with the screening of applicants through the four-phased selection process provided below:

Phase 1. Discriminating qualified and unqualified applicants using the basic criteria in the recruitment and selection (e.g., job description, and other special needs on the jobs).

Phase 2. The most highly qualified people are identified and screened based on the documents and other tests initiated. The idea behind this phase is that, to have streamlined candidates that are possible for inclusion in the interview and in-depth study.

Phase 3. Produce one candidate that will be offered the job.

Phase 4. Confirmation of the qualification of the candidate.

Technically, the purpose of selection test is to provide the employer with a reasonably accurate prediction of how applicants are likely to perform in specific jobs (Nigro et al., 2013, p. 79). Test that provides consistent results, even taking the test for the *nth* time will and must yield to the same outcome; such test is considered to be *reliable* (Riccucci, 1991; Nigro et al., 2013; Berman et al., 2012). Tests are considered to be *valid* if they make good distinctions among potential candidates (Berman et al., 2012). Among the examples of test are oral examinations, written tests, physical ability test, an evaluation of training and experience. Regardless of the type of test, there are three major validation strategies that are acceptable to both practitioners and specialists: (1) criterion validity, (2) construct validity, and (3) content validity.

- *Criterion Validity.* This simply requires correlating test scores with a criterion set as an acceptable indicator of job performance. Generally, it criterion validity examines the aptitude or cognitive skills for learning and performing well in the job environment.

- *Construct Validity.* It is a test validity approach that is designed to measure personal traits and characteristics (e.g., intelligence, creativity, integrity, aggressiveness, industriousness, and anxiety). When the test accurately measures the construct, then the test is positively associated with job performance.

- *Content Validity.* If the content of the test closely matches the job content. Meaning the actual duties and responsibilities are closely related with the test.

Table 4. 1 presents the summary of comparative advantages of various selection methods adopted in the public sector. In making a decision on whether or a not a certain method is valid using the test score and job performance as the criterion, it is important to have a well-founded basis that such candidate can be able reflect the result of his test with the job functions. Klinger and Nalbandian (2003) provide a model testing the real relationships between test scores and job performance (see Figure 4.3). They (Klinger & Nalbandian) argued that a true and valid test produces *true positives* and *true negatives.* Meaning, the candidate that scored well in the test will in fact do well in the job; while those who do poor will produce poor job performance. On the other hand, a less valid test tends to produce *false positives* and *false negatives.* Meaning, the candidate did well on the test, but does not turn out to be good on job performance.

Table 4.1
Comparison of Selection Methods

Method	Validity	Reliability	Cost
Bio data	moderate	high	low
References (letters of recommendation)	low	low	low
Aptitude test	moderate	moderate	low
Characteristics of trait test	moderate	moderate	low
Ability test	moderate	moderate	moderate
Performance tests	high	moderate	moderate
Interviews	low	low	high
Assessment centers	moderate	high	high
Probationary appointment	very high	very high	very high

Source: Klinger Donald, E., & Nalbandian, J. (2003). Public Personnel Management: Contexts and Strategies. New Jersey.

Figure 4.3
Relationships between Test Scores and Job performance

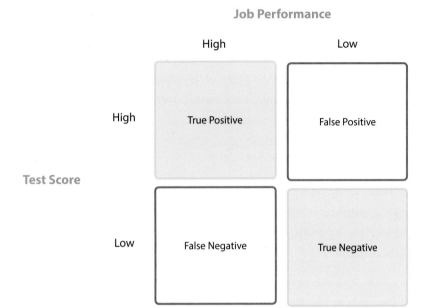

Source: Klinger Donald, E., & Nalbandian, J. (2003). Public Personnel Management:
Contexts and Strategies. New Jersey.

STAGE 2:
Screen, Interview, and Checks (Reference and Others)

In the initial phase of stage 2, it requires the (1) screening of the minimum job requirements (e.g., education and experience), (2) documentary evaluations such as the bio data—curriculum vitae, recommendation letters or references, and (3) written and job performance test.

Minimum Job Qualifications

Establishing a minimum job requirement is a prerequisite for the determination of qualified and eligible candidate. It is important because at its face, the applicant can give diverse and various information about himself which can lead to the decision whether to include him/her in the first list of eligible applicants. Among the minimum job qualifications that can be taken into consideration are the following:

- *Educational Attainment*. There are jobs that require a certain degree or educational qualification in order to perform the job effectively. For example, if the work requires profound knowledge of law, the candidate must at least be a graduate of a law school or   have taken legal management, or any other related courses.

- *Trainings Attended and Work Experience.* The evaluation of previous trainings and work experiences may help the employer the current knowledge, skills, and abilities that the candidates possess.

- *Physical Ability.* There are job that require physical strength to perform duties and responsibilities. At the outset, the applicant may not qualify if he failed to satisfy the physical fitness test.

Documentary Evaluation

An evaluation of the submitted documents can provide the evaluators useful information about the applicant for example, work abilities, effectiveness, and work habits that can be provided by the recommendations and/or references that are mostly from the former employers. Among the important and relevant documents to be evaluated are the following:

- Bio Data or Resume
- Certificates
- Recommendation Letters

Written and Job Performance Test

The written tests are widely used in the public sector recruitment efforts. This is different to that of the general civil service examination that is administered for regular and career employees in the government. In the Philippines, for example, the civil service examination (i.e., civil service profession and/or civil service sub-professional) is taken as a basic requirement in appointing a civil servant. The written examination can be a basis in determining the capacity of the applicant.

The job performance test, as the name implies, wants to test specific skills of the applicants. Generally, this kind of test can provide a confirmation of the knowledge, skills, and abilities of a certain applicant. Thus, can provide a direct measures and information on how an applicant can perform various job elements (Nigro et al., 2013).

After completing the screening all the applicants and have separated all those who are not qualified—narrowing the pool of candidates, the next process would be to conduct an interview.

STAGE 3:
Negotiating and Hiring

From among the eligible candidates who passed through the stages of evaluation and tests, the job negotiation and hiring may come next. However, there are still issues that must be considered in the "must do list" before actually engaging the services of the applicant. For example, there must be efforts to be done to finally ask the applicant if he/she still interested of the job, questions on salary and other benefits, and among others.

- Drug test
- Stipulations on contingencies

STAGE 4:
Post-Selection Considerations

There are other factors that may be considered before the final intake of a new employee. These issues are related with security and other relevant things like drug addiction. That is why; the employment may be put in a conditional status. A drug test is usually administered after all the recruitment and selection processes which may affect the possibility of a civil service employment. After which, the applicant must be informed about the result of the recruitment and selection and will prepare him/her in the integration on the work place. Thus, plans for orientation and training will be prepared.

Case Brief

Deer Valley Hires a New Coach

Every basketball game is won by the team that scores the most points. How important is shooting? Let me put it this way: If you don't shoot well, you're going to spend a lot of time sitting at the end of the bench during games. I don't care who your old man is or how influential he may be; if you don't shoot well, you won't play basketball at Deer Valley High!

It was bad enough for Dave Hollinger to learn that he had been fired as head boys' basketball coach at Deer Valley High School in suburban Phoenix, despite of a winning seasons. But Dave Hollinger also had suffered the humiliation of being informed that he would not be allowed to reapply for his old position, which was now vacant again owing to an abrupt resignation by his successor. In the past, coaches of boys' and girls' sports had assumed that the Deer Valley Unified School District (DVUSD) would automatically renew their coaching contracts unless there was just cause to remove them for poor performance. Removal of coaches usually had been preceded by notice of deficiencies and an opportunity to improve. If not, their contract was not renewed.

Former coach Dave Hollinger believed that DVUSD breached its obligations under his employment agreement when it removed him from his position without adequate notice or opportunity to correct any deficiencies. Further, Dave Hollinger and the union grievance committee asserted that the district failure to provide both pre-disciplinary notice and an opportunity to respond before removal resorted in violation of Dave Hollinger's constitutional due process rights and that the district did not have just cause to terminate his contract as head basketball coach. More fundamentally, Dave Hollinger was angry; he had taken a losing basketball program at Deer Valley and made it into a winner, only to be fired as his thanks!

Finally, Dave Hollinger was upset when DVUSD added insult to injury by engaging in obvious reprisal when it failed to even consider for a head coaching vacancy for the 2003-04 coaching season. Dave Hollinger was prepared to sue the district, if necessary, to gain full reinstatement to his position as head basketball coach with all monies (addenda and summer camp) lost because of the wrongful removal. In addition, Dave Hollinger intended to ask that all adverse material related to his wrongful removal be expunged from his personnel file, supervisory file, and all evaluations maintained by DVUSD central personnel.

There was some glimmer of hope: Dave Hollinger had requested and been granted one final hearing regarding his non-renewable of contract. The district superintendent promised to explain his reasons for not allowing Dave Hollinger to reapply for the coaching position that had once again become vacant.

AN UNHAPPY TENURE IN DEER VALLEY

Dave Hollinger was hired as the head boys' basketball coach at Deer Valley High School for the 1999-2000, 2000-01, 2001-02, and 2002-03 school years. Dave Hollinger's coaching record during these years was 15-5, 14-6, 13-12, and 12-11, respectively. Unfortunately for Dave Hollinger, his teams had failed to defeat their district arch rival, Barry Goldwater High School, during these four years. Despite winning seasons, there were indications that not everyone approved of Dave Hollinger's coaching style. As a social studies teacher in the classroom, Dave Hollinger was quite popular, but some parents and administrators thought Dave Hollinger emphasized winning too much. Another parent, who also happened to be on the school board, believed that Dave did not appreciate her son's abilities as the "sixth man off the bench" for the basketball team. These groups conspired to have Dave Hollinger removed as head basketball coach. There followed a series of events that ultimately would lead to Dave's demise:

1. On March 12, 2000, Wayne Kimbell, Dave Hollinger's predecessor as head basketball coach and current athletic director, evaluated Dave Hollinger's performance as coach during the 1999-2000 seasons. Kimbell subsequently recommended, without meeting with Dave Hollinger, that his contract not be renewed for the 2000-01 season. Kimbell's recommendation was not accepted by the superintendent, and Dave Hollinger continued as head basketball coach for three additional years.

2. In early October 2002, Dave Hollinger and Deer Valley Education Association (DVEA) representative Betty Kim met with Dr. Joseph Schmit, principal of Deer Valley High School, to discuss mutual expectations. Dave Hollinger wanted to avoid potential problems and was concerned that his coach positions might not be renewed the following year. Kim and Hollinger also met with DVUSD Superintendent Dr. Pat Sims and Associate Principal Jerry Simmons during October 2002. All parties agreed that these meetings were positive, with Simmons providing advice to Dave Hollinger regarding ways to improve the basketball program.

3. However, the relationship between coach Hollinger and the district's administrators deteriorated rapidly during the 2002-03 basketball season. DVUSD administrators would later provide a number of instances during the basketball season in support of their contention that they had just cause to not renew Dave Hollinger's contract as head basketball coach for the 2003-04 season. In May 2003, Dave Hollinger was informed by letter that his contract as basketball coach would not be renewed and that district was soliciting applications.

In an attempt to force the issue, Dave Hollinger applied for Dave Hollinger the vacant position. However, Dave was informed that his application could not be accepted for "personnel reasons." When pressed, the district provided the following incidents as the basis of its decisions not to allow Dave Hollinger to apply for the position of head boys' basketball coach:

- Hollinger held an open gym for football players during football season in hopes that some would try out for the basketball team.
- Hollinger encouraged track athletes to play club basketball instead of going for track.
- Hollinger confronted Athletic Director Kimball regarding Junior Varsity Coach Cappelli's intended use of a defensive play during a junior varsity game that Hollinger wished to use in the varsity game.
- Hollinger argued with certain players or had bad player relationships in past years.
- Hollinger allowed basketball players to drive their own vehicles to the Paradise Valley game rather than ride with their parents.
- Hollinger conducted an inappropriate "ass chewing" of players during half-time at an away game in Yuma.
- Hollinger's relationships with coaches in the region suffered because he did not attend the coaches' meeting where conference awards for players were decided.
- Basketballs had been lost after practice.
- Hollinger was inconsistent in disciplining players.
- Team execution was inconsistent throughout the season.
- Hollinger encouraged players to concentrate on only basketball.
- Hollinger prepared an unfavorable evaluation of Assistant Coach Capelli's performance.
- Differences in philosophy between Hollinger and administration were escalated to the community.

Coach Hollinger was shocked to read each of the aforementioned charges and, in each instance, believed he could rebut their substance and validity. Hollinger viewed that charges as myths and half-truths fabricated by some players' parents who believed that their kids should be given more playing time, as well as jealous coaches who secretly wanted his job.

THE FACT-FINDING HEARING

Pursuant to Coach Hollinger's request, Superintendent Pat Sims agreed to convene a "fact-finding" hearing on the matter. Superintendent Sims asked Marcia Lubara, a dispute resolution specialist from Tempe, to conduct the hearing and render an advisory opinion to her regarding whether Dave Hollinger had been unfairly treated.

At the outset of the hearing, Marcia Lubara set forth three issues for her determination and recommendation:

1. Was Dave Hollinger entitled to automatically continue from year to year as head basketball coach?
2. Was DVUSD obligated to establish that there was just cause not automatically continue Dave Hollinger as head basketball coach and, if so, what would be the appropriate remedy?
3. Did DVUSD violate the collective bargaining agreement (CBA) when it denied Dave Hollinger the right to apply and be considered for a vacant head basketball coaching position?

At the beginning of the hearing, the district's legal counsel, Peter Lassen, set forth the district's official view of the matter. Peter Lassen contended that extra duty positions, including coaching assignments, are one-year appointment made at the discretion of DVUSD administrators. Lassen explained that there is no tenure associated with these positions nor is there any justified expectation to continued employment beyond the one-year contractual term. Accordingly, the nonrenewal of Dave Hollinger for the head basketball coaching position for the 2003-04 school years was proper. Furthermore, the position of coach is not afforded the same due process right as that of a certified teacher. Therefore, Dave Hollinger was not entitled to remain as coach, and the district did not have to justify its reasons for prohibiting Hollinger from reapplying for the coaching jobs in the future.

However, fact-finder Lubara reminded everyone at the hearing that the issue of whether DVUSD had just cause to terminate Hollinger's coaching position is only relevant if Hollinger had tenure or a property right as a coach. In other words, Lubara clarified her position: Hollinger is entitled to due process rights as a coach only if the DVUSD accorded these rights through its personnel policies or negotiated said due process rights through collective negotiations with DVEA. Wayne Kimball, athletic director at DVHS, testified that he had understood that coaches were given a one-year contract upon the recommendation of the athletic director to the principal. Mack stated that his practice as athletic director was to evaluate all coaches at the DVUHS and that he used a standard form for this purpose. Kimball testified that he distributed a copy of the Athletic Handbook to all coaches on October 6, 2000; the aforementioned handbook indicates that the coaching contract is for a one-year period.

Wayne Kimball testified that as athletic director, he had provided all coaches with a copy of the Athletic Handbook, which stated that "all coaching assignments are one-year appointments" with a renewal option at the discretion of the principal. Kimball said that the athletic director was subsequently given on advisory role in the decision-making process. Kimball added that the principal's authority to decide upon renewal of coaching contracts was consistently followed in practice as well; Kimball stated that he used a form when evaluating coaches and this evaluation was placed in the coach's personnel file and reviewed by the principal when making the renewal decision. Kimball disagreed with those coaches who signed an affidavit stating that they considered their coaching positions to be automatically renewed unless the resigned or received a poor performance evaluation.

Dave Hollinger testified that his coaching or addenda contract was for $2,400 each basketball season and that he also directed a basketball program in the summer, which netted approximately $1,500. Hollinger stated that past practice was to circulate a memo to coaches at the end of the year to determine if the coach wished to have his or her contract renewed. Hollinger admitted that he received the Athletic Handbook during 2000-01, but not in subsequent seasons. Specifically, Hollinger stated that he did not receive the Athletic Handbook in 2001-02, nor did he see Kimball's accompanying memo of October 6, 2000.

Donald Kline, a DVUHS faculty member and assistant coach during 1999-2000, testified that he was unaware that the Athletic Handbook existed during his service as coach. Kline also indicated that past practice was to allow coaches to either resign or be "due processed" out of a coaching position. Kline stated that a coaching vacancy occurs either through resignation or when one is evaluated out.

Molly France, girls' basketball coach for nine years at DVUHS, stated that coaches were allowed to continue in their coaching positions unless they were evaluated out of them. Robert Ioccoca, an elementary school teacher and assistant baseball coach, testified that coaches were hired by the principal but were removed only by resignation or by being evaluated out. Betty Kim, DVEA representative, stated that she understood that coaches would be terminated only by resignation or by evaluation criteria to be determined ahead of time. Kim stated that all coaching positions the previous year were made "at will," which was a radical departure from past practice, when coaches were given reasons for removal before a nonrenewal decision by the principal. Kim testified that the 2000-04 Collective Bargaining Agreement indicates that coaching positions are "at will" in nature. Sandra Stevens, a member of DVEA's negotiating team, testified that coaches could be terminated only by voluntary resignation of following an evaluation process.

Dave Hollinger stated that the head basketball coach for 2003-04 resigned in November after being hired in October, and that Hollinger had intended to immediately apply for the vacant position. However, Hollinger was not permitted to apply for the job. Betty Kim testified that she sent a letter of protest to Dr. Sims on November 16, 2003, because the district was recruiting for a new basketball coach even though Hollinger was obviously well qualified for the position. Sandra Stevens stated that Wayne Kimball refused to meet with her on November 10 and 11 regarding his refusal to consider Hollinger's application for head basketball coach. Stevens stated that Dr. Bob James, associate superintendent for curriculum and development and acting superintendent, also refused to allow Hollinger to reapply for the position of head basketball coach. James stated that Hollinger could not be rehired for a position from which he had just been terminated, but he could apply for a similar position at Barry Goldwater High School that had become available. Stevens testified that the DVUSD's refusal to consider Hollinger's application constituted a *reprisal* as prohibited by a provision of the 2000-04 Collective Bargaining Agreement. Hearing Officer Lubara ended the hearing and made a recommendation.

1. Did the Deer Valley School District act properly in its decision to terminate Coach Hollinger's employment as head boys' basketball coach?

2. Did the district's action of not considering Coach Hollinger's application for the vacant position violate its own personnel policies and practices?

3. If you were Hearing Officer/Fact-Finder Lubara, what would you recommend to Superintendent Sims?

This case was adopted from: Reeves, T. Z. (2006).Cases in public human resource management. Thomson Wadsworth.

Student Activity:

After learning the processes involved in the recruitment and selection process, try to think of a best practice that can be implemented in your agency. There might be inevitable challenges in its adoption. Thus, following the stages provided in the case analysis table, try to sort out all possible factors that may hasten or slow the process.

HRM in the Public Organizations: An Essential Guide

Case Analysis

	Step	Contents		
1	Environments/ Conditions/ Backgrounds	Please explain the situation briefly. (1-2 pages)		
2	Problem Definitions	In your own perspective, please be as specific as possible when pointing out the problem. (2-3 pages)		
3	Actual Case Studies	Please explain by providing specific examples. (Newspaper articles, news clips, or interviews) (2-3 pages)		
4	Alternatives	Possible Alternative(s)	Pros in your Country Context	Cons in a your Country Context
		①		
		②		
		③		
		Please propose more than three policy alternatives. (2-3 pages)		
5	The Best Solutions	Why did you choose this alternative as the best solution? What are the expected effects and potential contribution? (2 pages)		

Reviews

1. What do you think is the emerging recruitment and selection "best strategies and practices" emerging across the world? What can be the primary challenges for HR managers for adopting these new strategies and techniques?

2. Do you agree with the argument that we need to change pay and staffing systems as two keystones of success in improving public-sector performance?

Ending Credits

Research Digest

Recruitment and Selection of Public Workers: An International Compendium of Modem Trends and Practices

Facts

Not surprisingly, most of the international community is faced with a common set of human resource management (HRM) dilemmas. In the developed world, common problems are:

- The aging of the indigenous civil service, posing the immediate threat of high turnover and a lack of qualified replacements;

- A growing vacuum among "the leadership bench" — the next generation of policymakers and top civil servants who will assume critical roles in directing their governments' efforts to negotiate the troubled waters of the 21st Century;

- The changing definition of *career,* which means that employee loyalty to the organization, is tenuous at best, and which discourages workers from joining government service for the long bail (Green 2002);

- Rapid change (e.g., in technology and economic conditions) that requires a highly fluid *skill mix* in the workforce;

- Strong competition from the private sector for the best and the brightest;

- Budget limitations that reduce compensation and financial incentives, thereby placing government at a disadvantage vis-a-vis business and industry; and

- A negative public image ("government bashing"), which translates into the widespread perception that government is no longer the employer of choice (if it ever was) (Reichenberg 2002).

Compounding these problems are such recent developments as privatization and the outsourcing of many government jobs (a trend that reduces job security and blurs the line between public service and private enterprise), and an erosion of the benefit packages and job security that once were the most effective recruitment tools for government. Adding to this dynamic mix are the widespread demands for "accountability," which often are translated into managerialism — a management focus that harkens back to an earlier era (Classical Management, Scientific Management, or Taylorism) where control functions are heavily emphasized, thereby diminishing some of the intrinsic satisfaction that public service is supposed to provide (Kearney and Hays 1988). Simply stated, today's pressures for greater efficiency in government often make government service less appealing to the very workers whose contributions are needed most.

Of course, less-developed countries face these same challenges, plus even more demanding social, economic and technological barriers. In sum, it is not hyperbole to suggest that many nations are facing a recruitment crisis. At the time when governments need to be most adept at luring talent to public service, their ability to do so has rarely been so constrained and complicated by economic, social and organizational pressures.

Issue(s)

To provide an overview of the types of recruitment and selection initiatives already in place in many nations—both developed and less developed countries (LDCs).

Findings

Despite the real and potential advantages of new strategies and technologies, a few words of caution are necessary. First, the watchword of the new HR era is flexibility, but this can be costly, literally and figuratively (Farnham, 1997). Notably, public personnel systems that are decentralized and deregulated can fall victim to manipulation and exploitation. The headlong rush toward HRM systems that mimic the private sector model is also risky if we ignore the potential downside of this trend. Government and the private sector are not the same, and rushing to adopt private sector approaches without recognizing fundamental differences is a high-risk strategy.

As governments strive for increased responsiveness and flexibility, safeguarding the public service from inappropriate influences may become more difficult. At a minimum, professional public administrators need to be alert to the risks associated with reform. Although there is a critical need to ensure that governments can attract and retain talent, maintaining the neutrality of the public service should be a non-negotiable value.

Another potential threat is posed by the enormous impact of IT on HRM. Although technology offers a wonderful opportunity to improve and expedite HR operations, it also reduces the "human factor" (West and Berman 2001). Technology adds efficiency, but also depersonalizes functions that were built on human interaction and individual judgment. Whether or not this is good or bad is debatable. We pose this question merely as another consideration to factor into the international discussion of HR's transition from a traditional to a virtual tool of line managers.

Ultimately, public organizations must adopt at least some of the recruitment and selection strategies described simply because to do otherwise would be self-defeating. The crises that plague public services in almost all nations are too daunting to permit complacency. The primary challenge for HR professionals is to select the reforms most suitable to their own settings, and to adapt them to local needs. There is no shortage of good ideas, and we hope there will be no shortage of will and creativity in the further implementation of HRM reform. The stakes are far too high for government not to change.

Source: Lavigna, R. J., & Hays, S. W. (2004). Recruitment and selection of public workers: An international compendium of modern trends and practices. Public Personnel Management, 33(3), 237-253.

Further Readings

- Berman, E. M., Bowman, J. S., West, J. P., & Van Wart, M. R. (Ed.) (2012). *Human Resource Management in Public Service: Paradoxes, Processes, and Problems.* Fourth Edition. Sage Publications.
- Kim, P. S. (Ed.) (2010). *Civil Service System and Civil Service Reform in ASEAN Member Countries and Korea.*
- Nigro, L., Nigro, F., & Kellough, J. (2013). The new public personnel administration. *Cengage Learning.*
- Pynes, J. E. (2008). Human resources management for public and nonprofit organizations: A strategic approach (Vol. 30). *John Wiley & Sons.*
- Lavigna, R. J., & Hays, S. W. (2004). Recruitment and selection of public workers: An international compendium of modern trends and practices. Public Personnel Management, 33(3), 237-253.

References

Berman, E. M., Bowman, J. S., West, J. P., & Van Wart, M. R. (2012). *Human resource management in public service: Paradoxes, processes, and problems*. Sage.

Klinger Donald, E., & Nalbandian, J. (2003). Public Personnel Management: Contexts and Strategies. New Jersey.

Nigro, L., Nigro, F., & Kellough, J. (2013). The new public personnel administration. *Cengage Learning*.

Ployhart, R. E. (2006). Staffing in the 21st century: New challenges and strategic opportunities. Journal of Management, 32(6), 868-897.

Riccucci, N. M. (1991). Merit, Equity, and Test Validity A New Look at an Old Problem. Administration & society, 23(1), 74-93.

Reeves, T. Z. (2006).Cases in public human resource management. *Thomson Wadsworth*.

Chapter 5

Human Resource Development

Framework

Human Resource Management for Public Organizations: An Essential Guide

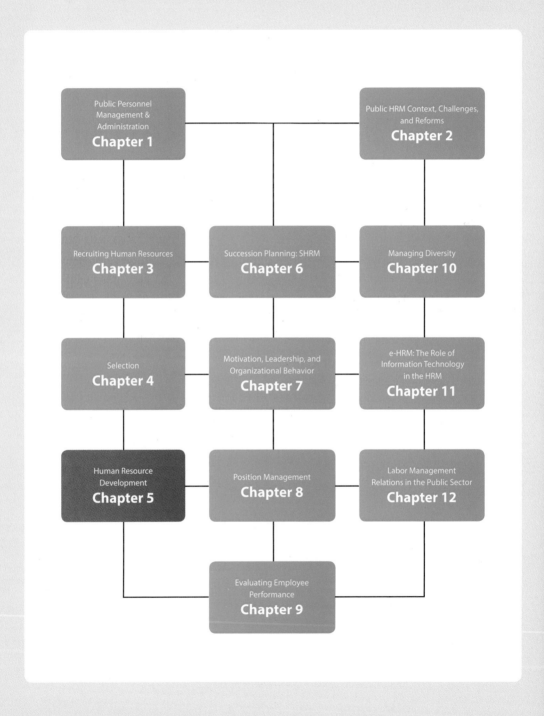

Learning Outcomes

After going through this chapter, you should be able to:

- Understand and define human resource development (HRD)
- Identify and describe the major functions of HRD—Organizational Development (OD), Training and Development (TD), and Career Development (CD)
- Describe the HRD process—such as training needs assessment, design, implementation, and evaluation.
- Develop a strong conceptual understanding of the principles on how to effectively impact learners (i.e., adult learners) and be able to apply these principles to work settings.
- Understand the impact and use of emerging technology on the field of training today; and be able to use appropriate technology to research and develop an effective needs analysis.
- Understand the trend toward performance management, and how this impact today's training professional.
- Develop an appropriate training strategy for today's organization - using both classroom and distance learning technologies.
- Effectively evaluate a training program using appropriate statistical methods and be able to present this effectively to management.
- Understand the appropriate distance learning technology and be able to apply this technology to achieve effective learning.
- Be able to select and use the appropriate technology for effective training follow-up.
- Understand, select, evaluate and apply appropriate technology in business and public settings.
- Develop a strong conceptual understanding of the factors that affect the successful management of innovation and technological change.
- Gain knowledge of human factors that will help students manage technology, training, and development in the public settings.

Preview

In the last few decades, there has been a sort of seismic focus on human resource development (HRD) within work organizations, which are often competitive, turbulent environments confronted with globalization and the continuous evolution of innovation. In order to enhance organizational performance and productivity, HRD is considered an important process that helps employees to acquire new knowledge, skills, and abilities in response to changing work demands (Gardiner, Leat, & Sadler-Smith, 2001). The globalization process has affected to a large extent the way of life of the individual citizens and the communities. This, in turn, has generated new institutional challenges for government institutions and has given rise to a set of complex needs and problems from the society. In such an inevitable phenomenon, the government—as the primary organ of state—has to respond to such needs and challenges to be able to serve well the interests and concerns of the public. Along with the great challenges of the worldwide socio-economic developments brought by free-market, fast approach towards a service economy, changes in workforce demographics, the increasing war on talent, and emphasis on financial performance challenges the human resource (HR) function in its role for creating added value to the organizations (Brockbank et al., 2002; Bucknall & Ohtaki, 2006). Such trend in the global society pushes both the developed and developing countries to cope and impose necessary developmental and progressive changes especially in the government sector.

However, with the challenges brought by globalization and other unpredicted phenomenon that calls for a responsive and flexible civil servant, approaches to HRM initiatives, specifically of the HRD functions likewise faces a demanding revolution. Many private businesses and government entities are moving towards a dimension in order to answer emerging issues and meet organizational needs. HRD can facilitate the provision competencies and implementation of competency-based systems personnel administration and management. It was widely recognized that HRD is moving from a mere rule-based approach to a more results-oriented and deliverables-centered HRM function. To help facilitate the paradigm shift, both public and private organizations recognize the importance of identifying new competencies (NAPA, 1996) and the employment of the most appropriate techniques in accordance with different learning factors (e.g., organizational environment, learners capacity, etc.)

For example, HRD do not only care about the specific learning and development approaches, it also has to intelligently determine the relevant competencies and the surrounding circumstances that affects effective HRD program. In order the public sector organizations to stay relevant and to be able to compete in a rapidly changing environment, they cannot solely rely on particular strategies as a guarantee for organizational success. The government needs to seriously assess its capability in order to survive and win in a highly competitive and fast-changing society. Capability assessment, generally would want to look into the three most important dimensions - individual, organizational and state capability. Simply put, investment in the capacity building efforts of human resources must be the concentration to bring the government organization in the helm success. Accordingly, enhancement of human resources' competencies through human resource development (HRD)—such as training and development, career development, and organizational development—and other capacity building activities will certainly contribute to the establishment of a competent and efficient civil servant.

The certain types of HRD systems designed to utilize and acquire new skills for the workplace can influence individual performance (e.g., job satisfaction, turnover intentions, public service motivation [PSM]) as well as organizational performance (e.g., person-organization fit, organizational commitment, and trust) (Egan, Yang, & Bartlett, 2004; Sturman, Trevor, Boudreau, & Gerhart, 2003). Thus, understanding the role that HRD play in building knowledge and skill in the workplace is essential for the HRD research field.

Understanding the Essentials of HRD

Human capital is the aggregate of people's potentials for lifetime self-development with emphasis on knowledge accumulation and skill and ability advancement. It is the broad concept which embraces a non-commercial, qualitative and quantitative, social and external effect. (Kim, 2006) Training and education is an endeavor to develop human capital, especially artificial process to help individuals acquire knowledge, skill, and ability within organization. Training is an instruction in a myriad of forms and settings, in which both technical and conceptual knowledge and skills are imparted to employees, both non managers and managers (Shafritz, 2001). Good training should meet the needs of organization and must bring performance improvement in the ordinary work place such as management, decision making, and problem solving.

Civil servant can be trained through HRD interventions for diverse purposes, including beefing up technical skills, improving management skills, giving a sense of what is expected from leadership, and creating a common culture and a group spirit among staff and especially among senior management. Training, however, is an integral part of public personnel management. Studies suggest job satisfaction and opportunities for personal development are important factors in enhancing the quality of civil service (Yu & Im, 2002).

Even in a developed country like United States, it was admitted that the role of HRD is not a mere personnel management function that has to be satisfied—or just a compliance of functional routines in the public organization. We can take note of 1989 report of the National Commission on the Public Service (also known as the Volcker Commission's Report) that described the state of public service as "quite crisis" or the slow weakening of the public service in the 1970s and 1980s (Soni, 2004). This phenomenon continued through the 1990s and up until this time but was severed by federal governments' experiences of various human resource challenges such as, retirement wave over the next decade (Lewis & Cho, 2011; Tobias, 2001; cited in Lewis & Cho, 2012) that will eventually result to mounting vacancies throughout the government agencies; turnover rate as evidenced by the fact that one quarter of the federal employees hired from 2006 and 2008 left within 2 years, and two thirds of those who resigned from federal service had less than 5 years of federal experience (Partnership for Public Service and Booz Allen Hamilton, 2010; cited in Lewis & Cho, 2012). As a consequence, federal agencies are confronted with no enough younger people in the pipeline for government jobs (Soni, 2004) and increased competition for employees from the private and nonprofit sectors (French & Goodman, 2011).

However, as Soni (2004) described it as "quiet crisis," referring to the Volcker Commission's report, human resource in the public sector faces challenges constantly. Light (2002) argued that a strong civil service has such five common characteristics indicate a person who is motivated, recruited from the top of the labor market, well-supported, rewarded, and respected. Soni pointed out several problems such as workforce facing massive retirement, but younger workforce tends not to work within government, due to lack of appropriate reward and opportunities to advance. The federal workforce suffer capacity problem and skills gap. Agencies' missions are changing in response to new expectation for government service. Technological advancement is rapid. Younger workforce has different values with current workforce's value. All these problems are caused by lack of recognition of the importance of human capital.

In those situations, the importance of HRD has been emphasized. Uncertainty and complexity has risen in environment, dependency in human resource is also rising, to ensure the performance and survival of organization. Meanwhile, job security is crumbling. In this era, turnover is not strange; but frequently happens. In short, organizations rely on human resource more than previous era, but obtaining human resource who can commit to organization's growth is difficult. It is more significant in public sector, because delivering public service is still depends on human resource. Worse, the budgets that can recruit and train peoples are in crisis, because of financial deficit.

Undeniably, among the HRM functions, HRD is capable of addressing major issues in the ever emerging public sector organizations. Typically, the fundamental purpose of HRD initiatives is to help employees develop skills which, when applied to work, would increase job and organizational performance. The transfer of training or the extent to which employees use their newly gained knowledge, skills and attitudes from learning environment to the workplace is critically important for HRD. Transfer of training is the goal of all HRD's learning and training interventions, without it or the less of it means a failure of HRD program.

Lastly, we can put it that the primordial objective of HRD would want to bring a well-rounded employee that has the necessary KSAs to affect organizational tasks. It is also worthy to note that the employee motivation, commitment, and engagement are enforced and enhanced through HRD programs. For example, employee engagement would like to bring an employee that has an enthusiasm for work, persistent, mentally and emotionally invested in work, committed, and productive (Czarnoswky, 2008; Harter et al., 2002). Along with these lines of argumentation, one can assume that HRD practices can catch light in engaging employees and bring greater results for the organization. As emphasized by Kahn (1990), the psychological meaningfulness that involves sense of return on investment of the self-in-role performances (as cited in Saks, 2006) is achievable from job characteristics. Thus, the numerous HRD interventions (i.e., mentoring, OJT, Off-JT, classroom-based learning, job rotation, etc.) will help in heightening the challenging nature of the job; develop skills and competencies for a more opportunity to contribute in the organization performance. Consistent with Kahn's (1990) meaningfulness theory, Herzberg (1968) pointed out those intrinsic factors (i.e., the importance of contribution and personal growth) motivated employees to be engaged in their work and commitment to attain organizational goals and objectives.

The succeeding discussions in this chapter will focus on the components of HRD, and the HRD process model which will give detailed information on how a distinctive public human resource development is done. This chapter on HRD will frame the concept of training and development within the applicable theory of adult learning and other important factors surrounding the public sector circumstances.

The overarching objective, however, is to learn how to assess, develop, carry out, and evaluates a training program. To get to this objective, we will review the field of training and development, as well as the broader area of human resource development (HRD). This means covering some of the basic concepts of training/HRD, such as motivation and learning theory, needs assessment, and the evaluation of training. Different types of training programs will be examined, including orientation, skills training, team building, management development, organization development, and diversity training.

Making Sense of the RealWorld

Nowadays, emphasis was given on management training and development, and the practical application of various training and development theories in today's organizations. Special emphasis is on the current topics in the field of human resource development, including: training self-directed work teams, managing a diverse workforce, and the practical application of designing programs in today's public sector organization work environment. This includes actual designing of needs analysis and training evaluation programs.

The following video clips provide a glimpse on the role of human resource development in meeting the needs of the organization as well as the approaches that can be employed in the learning process (e.g., adult learners).

Title	Gist	Source
Linking HRD Strategy to Organizational Needs	The purpose of the video is to describe the link between HRD strategy and organizational needs.	https://www.youtube.com/watch?v=eHWDm0hgPPl
Effective Adult training programs: Employee Education for Adult Learners	The video shows how to train employees of different level and/or age—adult learners.	https://www.youtube.com/watch?v=nz6SwliUWoE
Adult Learning In Under Three Minutes	The video presents 3-minute on how to conduct learning activity for the adult learners.	https://www.youtube.com/watch?v=IBSqz-szALl

1. What is the importance of establishing an HRD policy framework in the organization? How to ensure that it does get a funding in the overall investment and development strategy?

2. In your own experience, what efforts initiated by your organization in strengthening human resource capacity and competencies? How are they being implemented?

3. Are there serious issues concerning discrimination in career development and/or training development? What initiatives have been introduced to avoid any discrimination in the organization?

"Yes, I have room in my schedule to attend a Time
Management Seminar...the day after I retire!"

Human Resource Development

From the conceptual inception of human resource development (HRD) in the mid-1960's, it has been conceptualized either from a perspective based development economics or human capital standpoint (Hamlin & Stewart, 2010). Drawing from various definitions of HRD in the academic realm, conceptualizations from HRD practitioners, and/or researchers, there is a big propensity of inconsistency that is prone to differing and confusing interpretation. Garavan et al. (2007) posited that, "HRD remains to be segmented, incomplete, lacking comprehensiveness and coherence, with diverse theories and models offering competing explanations" (Garavan et al., 2007). Notwithstanding the ambiguity, or let us say, an admitted ambiguity of HRD (McLean, 2001). York (2005) defined HRD as, "both an organizational role and a field of professional practice. Its fundamental purpose is to contribute to both long-term strategic performance and more immediate performance improvement through ensuring that organizational members have access to resources for developing their capacity for performance and for making meaning of their experience in the context of the organization's strategic needs and the requirements of their jobs" (York, 2005).

One of the pervasive HRD definitions is that, "HRD is a set of systematic and planned activities designed by an organization to provide its members with the necessary skills to meet current and future job demands" (Werner and De Simone, 2006). In the same manner, Garavan (1991) defined HRD as, "the strategic management of training, development, and of management/professional education interventions, so as to achieve the objectives of the organization while at the same time ensuring the full utilization of the knowledge in detail and skills of individual employees" (Garavan, 1991).

The HRD definition of McLagan and Suhadonik (1989) and Watkins (1989) are worthy of attention for being pervasive and convincing. McLagan and Suhadonik (1989) characterized HRD as, "the integrated use of training and development (TD), career

179

development (CD), and organizational development (OD) to improve individual and organizational effectiveness. In the same manner, Watkins (1989) defined HRD as, "the field of study and practice responsible for the fostering of a long-term, work related learning capacity at the individual, group and organizational level of organizations. As such, it includes, but is not limited to, training, career development, and organizational development (Watkins, 1989). These two conceptualizations emphasized the three fundamental components of HRD – training and development (TD), career development (CD), and organizational development (OD) (see Figure 5.1).

Subsequent to these conceptualizations, for example Matkins (2001) concurred with the earlier theories contemplating that HRD is classified into three fundamental components. In this conceptualization, it can be deduced that training and development (TD) focuses on changing or improving the knowledge, skills and attitudes (KSAs) of individuals (Werner & DeSimone, 2009); career development on the other hand, Greenhaus (1987) posited that CD is "an ongoing process by which individuals progress through a series of stages, each of which is characterized by a relatively unique set of issues, themes, and tasks" (Greanhaus, 1987). Werner & DeSimone (2009) approached organizational development (OD) as "a process of enhancing the effectiveness of an organization and the well-being of its members through planned interventions that apply behavioral science concept" (Werner & DeSimone, 2009).

Notwithstanding, while most definitions on the focused on individual (i.e., training and development and career development) or organizational (organization development) as the targeted activities (McLean and McLean, 2001), there are also conceptualizations that treats HRD as a training and development *per se*. For example, McLean and McLean (2001) pointed out that in terms of scope of activities, HRD considered training as the sole aspect that lies within its boundaries.

Figure 5.1
Fundamental Components of HRD

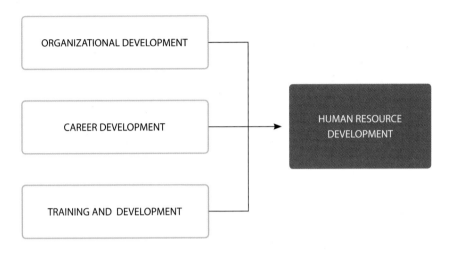

Source: Matkins, 2001, p.66

Though various scholars and practitioners define HRD in different terms, they still present important commonalities. Swanson (2001) defines HRD as "a process of developing and or unleashing human expertise through organization development and personnel training and development for the purpose of improving performance." The former emphasizes learning perspective, while the latter emphasize improving performance. But there is no doubt that HRD is concerned about improving one's capability to accomplishing organization goals. This is advocated by Swanson (2001), in the concept of his "Core HRD beliefs." He suggested that organizations are "human-made entities that rely on human expertise in order to establish and achieve their goals." He also suggested that human expertise is maximized through HRD processes, in the pursuit of mutual benefits of the organizations and the individuals.

Meanwhile, Swanson (2001) argued that the discipline of HRD relies on three core theories to understand and carry out. Three core theories are psychological theory, economic theory and systems theory. Those three core HRD theories and their integration are visually portrayed as a 'three-legged stool.' It represents the full integration of the three theories into the unique theory of HRD. Thomas & Macbey

(1994) argued that HRD consisted of three components; Training and development (T&D), Career development (CD), and Organizational development (OD).

Figure 5.2
Human Resource Development: Definitions, Components, Applications, and Contexts

Cited in: Swanson, R. A. & Holton, E. F. (2009). Foundations of Human Resource Development, 2nd Edition. San Francisco: Berrett-Koehler (p. 5).

As a caveat, HRD should not be treated as a temporary or transient approach for individual and organizational growth. HRD activities must be introduced at the outset when an employee joins the organization—such as employee socialization and orientation—and should continue throughout employment; must be responsive to the work and job changes and should reflect the organizational goals and strategies (DeSimone & Warner, 2012). After defining HRD, we will move on identifying what is its difference with HRM and which position it stands within the context of HRM; identify and describe major HRD functions; recognize competencies of HRD professional; identify contemporary challenges; and will jump into the HRD process.

HRD and HRM

HRM refers to the "effective selection and utilization of employees to best achieve the goals and strategies of the organization and the goals and needs of the individual" (Werner & DeSimone, 2009). Primarily, HRM dwells on the acquisition or obtaining of employees (i.e., recruitment), maintaining employees (e.g., motivation, retention, etc.), and developing of employees (i.e., training and development). HRM also includes functions such as human resource planning, the observance and implementation of equal employment opportunity, staffing (i.e., recruitment and selection), compensation and benefits, employee (labor) relations, health, safety and security, and HRD activities. It covers also functions such as organizational design, performance management and appraisal systems, and research and information systems. By this, we can infer that HRM comprehensively deal with all the aspects of personnel administration and management, in which among them is HRD (extensive definitions of HRD were provided above). Compared to HRM, HRD has three fundamental and major functions: (1) training and development (T&D); (2) organizational development (OD); and (3) career development. The ensuing discussions detail the characteristics of each HRD functions. Figure 5.3 depicts an organizational chart of a large HRM division. On top of all other functions is the Human Resource Management (HRM), while all other functions including HRD are lying below HRM.

Figure 5.3
Organization Chart of Large HRM Divisions

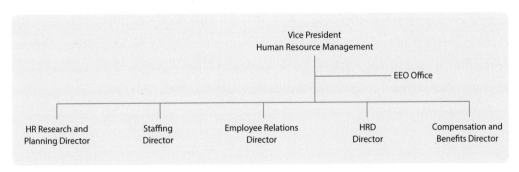

Source: Adapted from DeSimone and Werner, 2012

Fundamental Functions of HRD

Training and Development (T&D)

All workers either in the public or private sector requires in a certain degree to be well-abreast with the demands of the changing environment through training and development. Training and Development is the oldest component of HRD. It focuses on changing or improving the knowledge, skills and attitudes of individuals (Werner & DeSimone, 2009). Training & Development proceed in organization as in Table 5.1. Training is defined as "the efforts to increase the knowledge, skills, and abilities (KSAs) of employee and managers so they can better do their jobs", while development is defined as "efforts to improve future performance by providing skills to be used in subsequent assignment" (Berman et al., 2013, p. 340). Klinger and Nalbandian (2003) stated that "training provides learning for current responsibilities and skills—and much of this learning focuses on skill building but also can include understanding concepts and theories and increasing self-awareness of one's own personal attributes, perceptions, attitudes, and ways of thinking" (p. 240). In the performance of new jobs, employees expect to have sufficient training for them to perform the duties and responsibilities attached to a certain job. Though some may argue that the acquisition of KSA in a traditional organization is done not mostly or imparted by the existing employees and managers who are familiar with the work, thus they may argue it is more of an informal acquisition (Berman et al., 2013). However, it is important to point out those training remains to be a tool in the transmission of organization-wide policies as well as expectations (Berman et al., 2013). On the other hand, development beef up the potentialities and provide an effective succession planning for the employees. Various organizations are keeping track of the developmental participation of the employees as an expression of their professional commitment (Berman et al., 2013) to the organization.

Table 5.1
The Development of T&D in the Organization

Employee Status	New	Proficient/Old
Purpose	To learn important organization values and norms To establish working relationships and learn how to function within their jobs. To teach the new employee a particular skill or area of knowledge.	Encouraging individuals to accept responsibility for their actions, to address any work-related problems, and to achieve and sustain superior levels of performance. To help employees deal with personnel problems that may interfere with the achievement of these goals, like substance abuse, stress management, etc.
Method	Employee orientation Skills training	Coaching Counseling
Focus	Primarily training	Primarily development

Source: Modified from Werner & DeSimone (2009, p. 10)

A. Training Methods and Strategies

There are various training and development methods that can be adapted in the delivery of learning in the organization. However, we seek to provide an overview of the broad range of learning solutions, many of which can be creatively blended together to provide bespoke solutions to meet individual, team, and organizational needs. In Marchington and Wilkinson (1996), it provides a fram16criteria (cited in Gold, Holden, Stewart, Iles, & Beardwell, 2013):

a. The extent to which methods are individually, or group based;
b. The extent to which they are self-directed and participative (andragogical), or have high levels of control by tutors, trainers and other experts (pedagogical).

185

Figure 5.4
A Framework of Training and Learning Methods

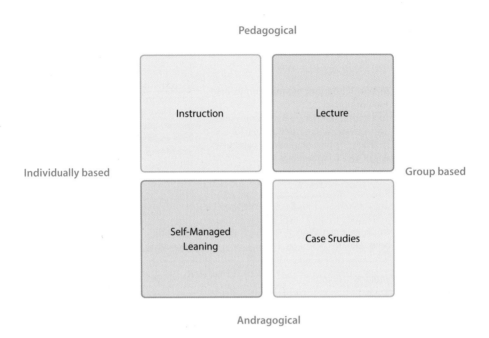

Source: *Marchington and Wilkinson (1996)*

There is no perfect categorization of methods, however. Others may view that training methods are "trainer-or-learner-centered" which may be categorized into (see Hackett, 2003): a. training-centered methods (e.g., lectures), b. learner-centered methods (e.g., self-development questionnaires), and c. coaching. Berman and his colleagues (2013, p. 347) presented six (6) strategic focus of training and development which includes:

1. Helping existing staff to adapt to new tasks as a result of promotion, restructuring, or otaher reassignments (performance);

2. Assisting new employees to get up to date on the unique procedures,

equipment, or standards of the organization (performance and risk management);

3. Confirming that employees are abreast of new laws, procedures, or knowledge pertinent to the organization, the environment, or their jobs (risk management);

4. Ensuring that personnel in jobs critical to the organization's performance—and which have high costs of failure—perform in satisfactory ways (risk management);

5. Using training and development as a tool to ensure that desirable employees and managers stay current and committed to the organization (retention of human capital); and

6. Ensuring that everyone has the KSAs that are consistent with what is needed to help the organization move forward (planning).

B. Training and Development Strategies

There are various training and development methods or strategies that can help develop individuals' knowledge, skills, and abilities (KSAs). Among them include off-the-job training (Off JT), on-the-job training (OJT), and other HRD practices.

On-the-Job Training Methods

On-the-job training (OJT) is the most common training method (Berman et al., 2013), do not cost much and is considered to be less work disruptive. Under this method new or inexperienced employees acquire knowledge, skills, and abilities (KSAs) through observing colleagues and managers or supervisors while performing the job and emulate their job or work behavior. Berman and colleagues (2013) also posited that OJT is not "sink or swim" for new employees, nor is it an employer giving an employee a manual and the name of a supervisor to contact if there is a problem. Bona fide OJT involves a thoughtful and guided approach to learning the job as it is performed. In the conduct of OJT, it is important to consider the physical environment of the training area. Trainee must feel comfortable in order to concentrate on the training process and be able to take all learnings. In the OJT, noise, phone calls, and other interruptions must be avoided enough to bring trainees into a learning mood. Among the popular and widely used OJT training techniques are the following:

- Coaching
- Mentoring
- Job Rotation
- Job Instruction Training
- Apprenticeship

Off-the-Job Training Methods

Off-the-job training (Off-JT) methods are conducted in separate from the job environment, study material is supplied, there is full concentration on learning rather than performing, and there is freedom of expression. Important Off-the-Job Training methods include:

- Lectures and Conferences
- Vestibule Training
- Simulation Exercises
- Sensitivity Training
- Transactional Analysis
- Formal Education

Other Training and Development Methods

- In-House Seminars
- Web-Based Learning
- Formal Education
- Classroom Training
- Self-Paced Training

Career Development (CD)

There are several definitions about Career development (CD). Gilley, Eggland and Gilley (2002) defined it as "a process requiring individuals and organizations to create a partnership that enhances employees' knowledge, skills, competencies, and attitudes required for their current and future job assignments." They emphasized that CD is 'a collaborative effort', because enhanced individual performance contributes to the success of the organization.

Those scholars' (i.e., Gilley, Eggland and Gilley, 2002) perspective can be divided into two distinctive ways; one regards CD as individual progress, thus proceeded in a person's life cycle, while another perspective regards CD as organizational progress that influence a person to perform specific job, or task. In any case, it seems that CD captures the transaction between a person's growth and organization goals. Mcdonald and Hite (2005) noted that, "it involves reciprocal interaction between employee and employer." In this perspective, they stated assumptions of CD. Those assumptions imply that career development pursuit congruence between needs of organization and employees, to ensure achieving strategic goals of organization.

CD involves two distinct processes: career planning and career management. Career planning involves activities performed by an individual, often with the assistance of counselors and others, to assess his or her skills and abilities in order to establish a realistic career plan. Career management involves taking the necessary steps to achieve that plan, and generally focuses more on what an organization can do to foster employee career development.

Mcdonald & Hite (2005) described the emergence and advance of career development. It was suggested by Parsons (1909), Herr (2001), and van Dijk (2004). The primary concern of CD was organization's human resource needs. It focused on matching individual interests and skills with organizational needs. It was changed in mid-90s. As downsizing goes trend in organizations, the perspective of a person's career changed in two ways. First, focus was redirected from monetary condition to personal interest. Second, proficiency and network that ensure job mobility are emphasized rather than loyalty. Mcdonald & Hite (2005) articulated it as "the boundary less career."

But other scholars still advocate the importance of organizational context in career development. Boudreaux (2001), Herr (2001) argued the value of career development to affirm and guide individuals through career transitions, to enhance organizational loyalty for the time employees are with an organization, to encourage motivation and productivity, and to contribute to the larger structure of economic stability remains. Van Dijk, (2004) supports that employees and systems can mutually benefit from the career development process, reinforcing its relevance as a human resource development function.

Figure 5.5
Spectrum of Career Development Activities

Source: Hall (1996)

Those changes are mirrored into career management. Career management is consisted of two ways; career self-management and organizational career management. The major difference of two concepts is that the former is under the control of the individual, while the latter is largely planned and managed by the organization. However, Sturges et al. (2002) argued that two concepts are not mutually exclusive. That is, organizational career management may help to promote career self-management. In their longitudinal study of U.K. graduates, they found limited support of that hypothesis. They also found that career development is associated with organizational commitment.

The psychological process that CD influences employees can be explained by two theories, Hall's 'career success cycle model (Hall, 1977), and Schein's model. (Schein, 1978) Hall (1971) argued that a person set goals and invest efforts. With performance, one feels psychological success and self-esteem. Thus involvement is made, and it cycles by later goal settings. It focuses on career development on individual perspective. This process can be outlined in Figure 5.5 and Figure 5.6 presents the spectrum of career development activities developed by Hall (1996).

On the other hand, Schein and Schein (1978) focused on matching organizational needs and individual needs. Organization needs increasing productivity and profit, and individual needs job security, job satisfaction, and success. He argued career development is systematic approach for satisfying two needs, individual and organizational.

Figure 5.6
Revised Psychological Success Cycle of Goal Setting

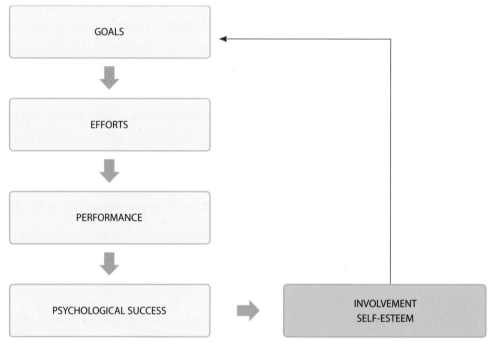

Source: Hall (1977, p. 289)

Organizational Development (OD)

Organizational development (OD) is "a process of enhancing the effectiveness of an organization and the well-being of its members through planned interventions that apply behavioral science concept (Werner & DeSimone, 2009). OD emphasizes both macro and micro organizational changes: macro changes are intended to ultimately improve the effectiveness of the organizational effectiveness by introducing employee involvement programs that require fundamental changes in work expectations, reward systems, and reporting procedures. The role of the HRD professional involved in an OD intervention is generally to function as a change agent. Facilitating change often requires consulting with and advising line managers on strategies that can be used to effect the desired change.

Its essential role is facilitating changes, so it contains many dimensions and strategies. First is human process based interventions. Its focus is improving interpersonal / organizational relationship, and initial development of OD method based on this perspective. It contains feedback and team building. Second is a techno structural intervention. Its purpose is increasing job satisfaction and improving ineffective structure and process. It includes job enlargement, job enrichment, and alternative work schedule. Third is sociotechnical system. It focuses on integrating structural requirement and social requirement in organization. This intervention contains Quality Circle (QC) program, and Total Quality Management (TQM). It is the most widely implemented intervention among organizations. Research suggests that sociotechnical system interventions have greater effect on productivity than either human process-based or techno structural interventions. Last is organizational transformation (OT). It is the change of organization itself, in organizational culture, strategy, knowledge management. It focuses on articulating a new vision for an organization, with the purpose of redefining the desired organizational culture, mission, and strategy. There are four types of OT interventions – cultural change, strategic change, organization learning, and high performance work system. Cultural change involves a complex process of replacing an existing paradigm or way of thinking with another. Strategic change is defined as any fundamental change in an organizational purpose or mission requiring system wide changes. Organization learning emphasizes transferring knowledge by collaborating and sharing expertise and information that is unbounded by status, space, and time. High Performance Work Systems are multifaceted, involving different combinations of the intervention strategies. It includes self-managed teams, quality circles, flatter organizational structures, new flexible technologies, innovative compensation schemes, increased training, and continuous improvement.

There is vast amount of OD literature and relevant theories, because the OD is multidisciplinary area. (T. G. Cummings & Worley, 2001; French & Bell, 1999; Rothwell, Sullivan & McLean, 1995). Egan's (2002) study, for example, collected 27 definitions of OD and made use of a panel of seven experts to highlight the dependent variables in each definition. In addition, there are many approaches and views regarding the nature of OD theory (Cummings & Worley, 2001; French & Bell, 1999; Rothwell et al., 1995; Van Eynde, Hoy, & Van Eynde, 1997). Lynham et al. (2004) worked to synthesize those vast amount theories. They regard performance as "a key outcome emphasis of HRD", and if considering OD as a component of HRD (McLagan, 1989, cited in Lynham et al, 2004). As OD's definitions and Lynham et al.'s (2004) work, primary concern of OD is to helping performance improvement, directly or indirectly.

There are various theories that explains OD intervention that may influence employee's performance in the organization, we'll investigate three theories that influence individual performance because this research pursuit individual interaction.

- *Bridges' Transition Theory:* Bridges (1980) defined three zones of personal transition— an ending, a neutral, and a new beginning — as necessary for successful individual performance through change. According to Bridges, each phase must be completed before an individual can successfully begin the next. Bridges' theory informs HRD professionals about how individuals cope with change. Understanding how individuals cope with change may explain why, after change interventions, individual performance often decreases before it improves (T. G. Cummings & Worley, 2001).

- *Expectancy Theory:* Vroom (1964) and Atkinson and Birch (1970) separately adapted Bernoulli's expectancy theory, originally applied to economics, to explain individual motivation in the context of the system within which they operate. The theory informs HRD professionals of the importance of the value that individuals assign to organizational decisions based on potential individual outcomes and helps to articulate the impact that perceived equity can have on individual and ultimately organizational effectiveness.

- *Locke's Theory of Task Motivation and Incentives:* Locke's (1968) theory of task motivation and incentives asserts that conscious goals and incentives have a direct impact on performance improvement (Knight et al., 2001). The theory therefore highlights goal setting as an integral part of individual performance improvement. Highly confirmed by research, this theory informs the OD professional about how goal setting, task motivation, and the impact of associated incentives can be used for more effective intervention outcomes, particularly those aimed at increased individual effectiveness.

The abovementioned theories may explain the relationship between OD and individual performance drawing on the employees' motivation. An employee has psychological, economical expectation on an organization. An organization provides its resources to fulfill a person's needs, in exchange of service and commitment. This is supported by Workman's (2003) alignment theory. Alignment theory assumes that people working in their perceived best interests strive toward goals that harmonize with those of the organization. The alignment of individual and organizational goals reduces friction between individuals and the organization, thereby increasing job satisfaction (Semler, 1997), and employees who have high levels of job satisfaction are more likely to express sympathy and positive affect toward customers, leading to greater levels of customer satisfaction (Silvestro, 2002; Wallace, Eagleson, & Waldersee, 2000 cited in Workman, 2003).

HRD Needs Assessment, Design, Implementation, and Evaluation

Typically, training and HRD process commence in four phases from the *needs assessment, design, implementation,* and *evaluation.* Figure 5.7 outlines the training and HRD Process Model (DeSimone & Werner, 2012). These are the typical issues confronting HRD specialists in the determination of training and development activities. For example, they may ask questions like, what is the appropriate training method? When

195

is it appropriate to do it? How to design and evaluate it? As a practitioner, scholar, or student of HRD, learning the framework for the HRD process—focusing on each stages—can provide the basic foundation that can capture the overall principles underlying the HRD. As a template for successful identification of HRD interventions, one must precisely understand the nitty-gritty this four-phase approach.

Figure 5.7
Framework for the HRD Process

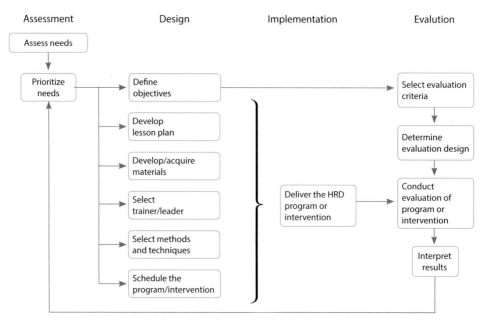

Source: *Werner & DeSimone, 2009*

Needs Assessment Phase

Before designing or implementing a series training program, the need assessment is a necessity. In the HRD parlance, needs assessment is also called as the need analysis. It is the starting point of the HRD process by which an organization's HRD needs is identified and articulated (DeSimone & Werner, 2012). The HRD specialists of officer should be able to identify what problem does exist and whether or not a training solution is appropriate. The needs analysis is crucial because it can provide a microscopic perspective about the organizational and individual needs in order to attain organizational goals and objectives. HRD needs assessment identifies: (a) organizations goals and its effectiveness in reaching these goals; (b) gaps between current skills and the skills needed to perform the job successfully; (c) gaps between employees' skills and the skills required for effective current job performance; and (d) the conditions under which the HRD activity will occur (DeSimone & Werner, 2012).

In practice, there are various issues confronting an HRD specialists or officer with regards the needs assessment. Some have thought that a needs assessment is difficult and can be time consuming because all necessary information for the identification of HRD interventions are already present. Public managers may also view the process of research as immaterial and not necessary, thus they demand immediate action and solution to performance problems. Nonetheless, there is lack of support for the needs assessment. Importantly, an HRD specialist must be able to argue and articulate that needs assessment is needed, and that that through the *needs assessment* the organization can identify specific accomplishment type of learning, expected changes in the behavior and performance, probability of achieving the results, cost benefit analysis of HRD solutions, and also the root causes of performance gaps and determine what type of need (i.e., diagnostic needs, analytic needs, and compliance needs) that is to be addressed.

Training need assessment—an analysis on deficiency between what is expected and what is actually happening—for example, may be explored in order to address issues of performance. In most cases, many organizations employ training to address issues of performance. However they tend to disregard performance problems if they appear to be trivial or if there is no ready solution to it (Klinger and Nalbandian, 2003). Training needs assessment may either be a *general treatment need* or *observable per-formance discrepancies* (Klinger and Nalbandian, 2003). The former contemplates that all employees, without regard of any information as to their work or job performance, must undergo training (e.g., communication training for all employees in constant interaction with the public; supervisory and delegation training for all supervisors). The latter, on the other hand, are determined through performance issues—such as job performance contract or standards not met, low performance evaluation, deadline not met, and among others. Thus, the management or the HRD specialists must observe and determine the fundamental issues surrounding the performance through various means like interview; questionnaires, appraisals, etc. (see also Kaufman, 1997 for some of the potential traps that must be avoided in the training needs assessment). Table 5.2 shows the factors that may bring performance issues, the most probable organizational response as well as personnel activity.

Table 5.2
Organizational Responses to Performance Problems

Situation	Organizational Response	Personnel Activity
1. Problem is insignificant	Ignore it	None
2. Selection criteria are inadequate	Increase attention to selection criteria	Job analysis
3. Employee unaware of performance standards	Set goals and standards and provide feedback	Orientation, performance evaluation
4. Employees have inadequate skills	Provide training	Training
5. Food performance is not rewarded; poor performance is not punished	Provide rewards or punishments and connect them to performance	Performance evaluation, disciplinary action

Source: Klinger Donald, E., & Nalbandian, J. (2003).

Levels of Needs Assessment
Strategic/Organizational Analysis, Task Analysis, and Person Analysis

Organizational Analysis

In the need assessment, organization analysis is a requisite field that must look into consideration. Where is training needed and under what conditions? Thus, it looks at the effectiveness of the organization and determines where training is needed and under what conditions it will be conducted. Why there is a need for the organizational analysis?

- Ties HRD programs to corporate or organizational goals
- Strengthens the link between profit and HRD actions
- Strengthens corporate support for HRD
- Makes HRD more of a revenue generator
- Not a profit waster

In the organizational analysis, the following are the vital sources: a. mission statement; b. HRM inventory; c. skills inventory; d. quality of working life indicators; e. efficiency indexes; f. system changes; and g. exit interviews.

Task Analysis

This is also called as *operation analysis* which refers on the systematic gathering of evidence and data about a specific job or group of jobs. In the need assessment, it basically addresses the issue on *what* must be done to perform the job effectively? This pertains to *task analysis* which provides data about a job or a group of jobs and the knowledge, skills, attitudes and abilities needed to achieve optimum performance. Information can be collected through KSA analysis, performance standards, observe the job/sample the work, perform the job, job inventory questionnaire, review literature about the job, ask questions about the job, and analysis of operating problems. The steps on task analysis appear in Figure 5.8.

Figure 5.8

Steps on Task Analysis

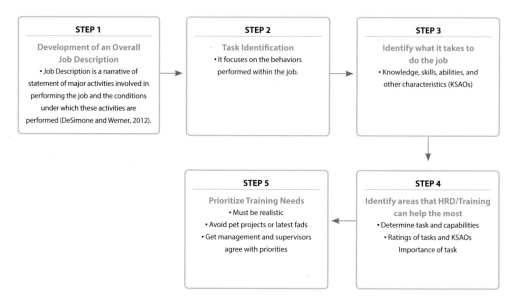

Person Analysis

Lastly, the need assessment must look into the issue of who should be trained and how. It analyzes how well the individual employee is doing the job and determines who are the employees that needs training and of what kind. Basically, the person analysis involves the determination of the overall success of the individual employee performance and also tries to uncover the factors that impacts employee's performance. Information can be gathered from many data sources, determine overall success of the individual, diagnostic analysis, and discover reasons for performance. Specifically, the following are vital sources: performance evaluation, performance problems, observation, work samples, interviews, questionnaires, attitude surveys, and checklists or training progress charts.

Design Phase

After the need assessment stage, the HRD manager or specialists must set for the design phase. However, before jumping into the next phase, the HRD manager or specialists must be able to trash out whether the uncovered issues can and/or should be addressed through an HRD activity. Second, they (HRD manager or specialist) should be able to determine how to effectively translate the results of the needs assessment into a specific training or HRD intervention. Lastly, if the conclusion is to initiate training or HRD activities, the issue that must be addressed is that on how to handle it—should it be designed internally or contract it with an outside vendor, or a combination of the two?

Typically, the design phase includes the following major activities:

1. Define Objectives
2. Develop Lesson Plan
3. Develop and/or Acquire Materials
4. Select Trainer/Leader
5. Select Methods and Techniques
6. Schedule the Program/Intervention

Implementation Phase

When thinking about effective delivery of HRD programs or interventions, it requires a careful and tedious preparation, as well as call for creativity and flexibility. It is important to note that prior to implementing a training or HRD activity, the needs assessment and design phases are substantially or have been completely addressed. There is an assumption that, if HRD activities commences, an important need for training has been identified, and that the program objectives has been spelled out. It is important to consider the current level of expertise that trainees possess in the selection of training methods (see discussions on Training and Development Strategies on this chapter). Basically, novice learners requires learnings that are, basic skills or knowledge that common employee needs to get started. Novice learner may easily get confused or anxious, therefore it is most appropriate to have a more guided, instruction guided, or instruction-centered training centered training methods. On the other hand, as trainees existing level of expertise increases, they become more creative and confident. Thus, the desired or ideal training methods are also likely to shift more toward exploratory or experiential methods

How to get started? In a trainer's perspective, it is important to understand and determine the capacity as well as the motivation of the trainee to learn. The training method may require the development or preparation of a training syllabus or materials; establishment of training norms; and employment varying presentation and teaching methods.

Evaluation Phase

HRD evaluation denotes on "the systematic collection of descriptive and judgmental information necessary to make effective HRD decisions related to the selection, adoption, value, and modification of various instructional activities" DeSimone & Werner, 2012, p. 168). Meanwhile, the effectiveness of HRD was in question constantly. An issue of this argument was about the validity of training evaluation. Training evaluation is "a system for measuring changes whether trainees have achieved learning outcomes, due to training interventions"(Goldstein & Ford, 2002; Kraiger et al., 1993; Sackett & Mullen, 1993, cited in Tan et al, 2003). Many scholars argued about these issues, whether measurement really captures the effectiveness of training. The most widely used criteria are the Kirkpatrick's (1964) model in evaluation of training effectiveness. It outlined four steps or levels of measures of the effectiveness of training outcomes; reaction, learning, behavior, and results. The details of each step are described in Figure 5.7. Though many scholars (i.e., Holton, 1996), criticize Kirkpatrick's model, it is widely used to measure the effectiveness of T&D.

- Determine whether the program is meeting the intended objectives
- Identify strengths and weaknesses
- Determine cost-benefit ratio
- Identify who benefited most or least
- Determine future participants
- Provide information for improving HRD programs
- Reinforce major points to be made
- Gather marketing information
- Determine if training program is appropriate
- Establish management database

Evaluating the effectiveness of training, it must be taken as it addresses the issues of the organizational problems. That is, it must be able to bridge the skills gap in the organization. To prove that such training or HRD intervention is really effective, it must demonstrate a significant impact on the performance of the employees (Klinger & Nalbandian, 2003).

Figure 5.9
Kirkpatrick's 4-Level Evaluation Model

Level 1 (Reaction)
Measuring trainees' feelings for and liking of a training program. Reaction measures may indicate the trainee's motivation to learn; although positive reactions may not ensure learning, negative reactions probably reduce the possibility that learning occurs.

▼

Level 2 (Learning)
Learning was defined as the "principles, facts, and techniques understood and absorbed by the [trainees]" (Alliger & Janak, 1989, p. 331). No change in behavior can be expected unless one or more of these learning objectives have been accomplished (Kirkpatrick, 1994). Learning is most often assessed by giving the trainees tests that tap declarative knowledge (Kraiger et al., 1993).

▼

Level 3 (Behavior)
Behavior defined as transferring knowledge, skills, and attitudes learned during the training to the job (Kirkpatrick, 1994). It is typically measured on the job after a particular amount of time has passed. This is most often assessed through performance appraisal.

▼

Level 4 (Results)
Results were defined as the final results that occurred because the participants attended the program (Kirkpatrick, 1994). These could include increased production, improved quality, decreased costs, reduced frequency and severity of accidents, increased sales, reduced turnover, and higher profits and return on investments.

Source: Tan et al. (2003)

Case Brief

Public Sector HRD: The Case of Korea and Philippines

A competency is a measurable human capability that is required for effective performance. A competency may be comprised of knowledge, a single skill or ability, a personal characteristic, or a cluster of two or more of these attributes. Competencies are the building blocks of work performance (Marrelli, Tondora, & Hoge, 2005). However, Korea's concept of competency is a behavioral characteristics and attitudes of the high performer related with goal achievement of an organization by the national government. The government of Korea further defined *competency model* as the systematic presentation of competencies which public employees in each group classified by grade and job classification should have (MOPAS, 2008; Kim & Jung, 2010). The continuous development of Korean civil service system from the incumbency of President Kim shows a clear line of the development of competency model.

The creation of Open Competition Position System (OPS) and the formulation of its competency model paved the way the constant adoption of competency-based HRM. Following the OPS creation, the Korean government released in 2001 the **Government Standard Competency Dictionary** that served as a guide for developing different competencies of general civil servants as well as the senior officials. The dictionary gave a detailed definition of competencies that are essential to achieve government's strategic goals and to create a common, objective language for talking about competencies (Kim & Jung, 2010). Furthermore, the competency dictionary served as the main reference for the development of competencies that are applicable to different Korean government agencies and groups of employees and/or officials. It can be observed that there is an available different competency models for different ranks or grades at the central government. At present, education and training program for competency development is focused on managerial post – Senior Civil Servants, division managers, and junior managers. The table below shows the competency model for Senior Civil Service and for Junior Managers.

The Education and Training Program for Competency Development through COTI: Korean Model

The new vision that COTI has newly adopted in line with the Lee Myung-bak administration's new operating paradigm is to be a "Leadership Center for a Greater Republic of Korea" that inspires public officials to "Think Big, Think Fast, and Think Fair". It is founded on the president Yoon's firm belief that improved public service training can change the destiny of a nation. As such, civil servants must be fast learners in order to keep up with new trends and cope with emerging challenges and the rapidly changing work climate. Think Big means think the nation beyond your organization, the world beyond your region, the future beyond the present. Think Fast means fast learning, fast communication, fast administrative service. Think Fair means be more ethical, more public-oriented, more caring.

In this light, the institution reportedly has identified new training needs and has revised, to a great extent, the training system, contents, and operation of our programs. However it is afraid that their website does not provide sufficient descriptions of those changes and innovation regarding training programs.

COTI's Training Programs

COTI provide a total of 101 programs for about 10,900 participants. The 101 programs are categorized into six developmental areas and some brief overview of each category can be checked on their website with the number and names of courses. It is not clear though with lack of a specified competency map whether the grade-based development programs are designed systematically competency-based through the process of defining what competences to develop and what approaches to take for public leadership development, not to mention such large numbers of other courses.

Their six training areas are as follows:

1. *Grade-based development programs (13)* for about 3,167 participants; Designed to foster civil service ethics and enhance officials' essential knowledge and competency relevant to grade and responsibilities.

2. *Specific competency development programs (21)* for nearly 1,800 participants; Designed to provide specific competency development programs appropriate to the challenges of the ever-changing environment.t

3. *Global competency training programs (5)* for about 230 participants; Designed to help Korean officials gain global competency with a focus on substantial and practical training content.

4. *International programs (15)* for some 300 foreign government officials; Focus on establishing co-development strategies and cooperative ties between Korea and the countries concerned through a study of and exposure to Korea's national development experiences. Consisted of three different international programs: customized programs for individual countries, official development assistance (ODA) programs, and programs conducted in association with international organizations.

5. *Informatization and E-Learning programs (46)* for some 4,200 officials; Informatization programs - Focus on information skills, policy, and systems to carry out their duties; E-Learning programs – To strengthen individual

competencies and administrative abilities through self-directed learning.

6. *National strategy seminars and customer satisfaction workshops* for 1,200 government officials and field service officials, respectively; National strategy seminars – provide a venue for the president and high ranking officials to share thoughts on important state policy issues; Customer satisfaction workshops – provide field workers opportunity to establish their identity, to take pride in their work, and to communicate with each other The grade-based development structure is presented Figure 5.8:

To briefly introduce an example of innovative training change by reference to his interview with the News and Magazine Power Korea, the New Leader Development Program (G5), the course for new civil servants who passed the civil servant examination, is the case. Every year, many pass the civil servant examination and get training at the institute for six months to a year after which they are dispatched to different ministries based on their grades. As the trainees are people to lead the country for about 30 years, Yoon thought the first training is very important and decided to provide intensive training commensurate to that of military academies. The program was upgraded by having them get special training at the Special Warfare Command, work in 116 small and midsized enterprises (SMEs) and work as global volunteers as teams in order to raise the quality of training and move the trainees' hearts. More than that, Yoon invites the best lecturers to raise the quality of lectures according to his creed "the quality of training is determined by the quality of the lecturers".

Figure 5.10
Grade-Based Development Structure

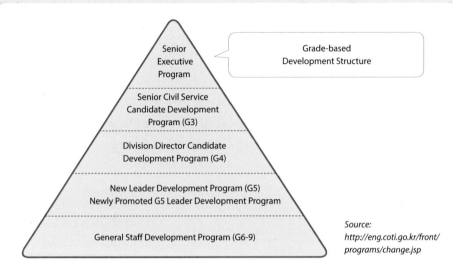

Source:
http://eng.coti.go.kr/front/
programs/change.jsp

HRD System

The COTI has also run an HRD system encompassing general functions such as from assessing self-, 360-degree competency, delivering individual assessment report, planning individual development plan (IDP), and applying for classes to overall learning management modules (LMS). According to their internal document of some user manual, it was mentioned they developed a competency assessment tool with an effort to secure its reliability and validity. The assessment consisted of 9 competencies on the basis of behavior indicators of the high performers at the G2 or the equivalent position level working in public offices for the central government. It is referred as a core leadership competency for the senior civil servants to be equipped with. The 9 competencies are as follows: Communication, Customer oriented, providing vision, Conciliation and integration, Result oriented, Professionalism, leading innovation, Problem awareness and understanding, Strategic thinking. Unfortunately, there is no more explanation of definitions, sub-factors and specific KSA consist each competence.

The user manual conveys a simple guide about how to take self-, and 360-degree competency assessment for the Senior Civil Service Candidate Development Program (G3). It states the assessment items are description of behaviors measured by selection form of five-point scale. In case of the 360-degree assessment, items exclusively describing personal strength and weakness are included.

COTI Training and Development Program: An Assessment

Judging from the glance of menu composition in the assessment user guide and overall information provided on their website, COTI is assumed to have an HRD framework which can be functioned as a precondition for systematic implementation of HRD. It also seems to partly pursue competency-based HRD. However I doubt their seriousness and efforts to search the best approach suitable for development purpose of each training program. Leadership acquisition and development requires a thoughtful strategy, careful candidate selection, appropriate reward, attentive mentoring, and an ongoing and sustained commitment from potential leaders and their respective organizations. Since COTI do not provide even a rough course profile, I can rarely find a clue on how to develop top talented civil servants leading the Republic of Korea and how to realize their ambitious new vision to be a "Leadership Center for a Greater Republic of Korea" that inspires public officials to "Think Big, Think Fast, and Think Fair".

Quoting from the article of models and assumptions for leadership development by Ingraham and Getha-Taylor from review of public personnel administration

2004, they suggest nine assumptions for leadership development after analyzing 10 federal leadership development programs selected as good representing major agencies. Those are as follows: 1) Personal initiative and top-level support are necessary. 2) Ongoing monitoring and continued mentoring are important. 3) There should be a mix of developmental activities. 4) Teaching leadership skills includes teaching life skills. 5) Leadership development includes individual long-term career planning and organizational succession planning. 6) Growing leaders is the rule, buying is the exception. 7) Leadership development = attention to core competencies. 8) Leadership development is needed at all levels. 9) It depends on the organization.

PHILIPPINE GOVERNMENT EMPLOYEES' COMPETENCY BUILDING STRATEGY: AN OVERVIEW

The administration of the public personnel system in the Philippine civil service is delegated upon the Civil Service Commission or the CSC. It is the body tasked by the Philippine Constitution to serve as the central personnel agency of the government. Consequently, it assumes a wide breadth of functions and responsibilities relating to public personnel administration. It is responsible for adopting measures designed to promote morale, efficiency, integrity, responsiveness, progressiveness and courtesy in the Philippine civil service (De Leon, 2001). The CSC's fiat may actually be summed up into four major functions: merit protection and promotion; capability-building or human resource development; quasi-judicial; and organizational development.

The Philippine civil service embraces all branches, subdivisions, instrumentalities, and agencies of the Government. It can likewise be summed-up into three major sectors or subdivisions which are the national government agencies (NGAs), government-owned or controlled corporations (GOCCs) and the local government units (LGUs). Appointments in the Philippine civil service are made in accordance with the principle of merit and fitness. Opportunities for government employment are open to all provided they meet the qualification requirements. A major requirement is an eligibility which is obtained through an examination. For every position in government, minimum standards are set pertaining to education, training, experience and eligibility requirements. However, Fernandez (2003) stated that standards have been upgraded, e.g., a higher minimum passing mark in the eligibility examination from 70 to 80 and a masteral degree for division chief position. Only those who meet the minimum requirements of the vacant position shall be considered for permanent position (Fernandez, 2003).

The Philippine civil service is structured into two major categories, namely, the career service and the non-career service. The career service is the part of the civil service founded on merit and fitness. Its features are competitive examination, opportunity for advancement, and security of tenure. In terms of positions covered, the career service encompasses, among others, those positions, where appointments require prior qualification in an appropriate examination; closed career positions which are scientific, or highly-technical in nature; and positions in the so-called Career Executive Service; career officers appointed by the President of the Republic.

The non-career service, in contra-distinction to the career service, pertains to the part of the civil service characterized by entrance not based on the usual tests of merit and fitness, and tenure is otherwise limited. It covers elective officials; officials holding their positions at the pleasure of the President; chairmen and members of commissions and boards with fixed term of office and their personal and confidential staff; contractual personnel; and emergency and seasonal personnel.

As part of the mandate given to the Philippine Civil Service Commission (PCSC) to develop and retain highly competent workforce, the commission made a policy that every government employees are to be provided with at least two (2) human resource development interventions every year for their personal growth and career advancement. Apart from the major HRD policies of PCSC, different scholarship program (local and foreign) was established to provide educational and other learning opportunities for various levels of personnel for continuing education. The Local Scholarship Program of the commission assists employees pursues graduate studies to enhance the capability of the government employees. Scholarship programs being administered by the CSC have budget allocation from the general appropriation every year. Other government agencies have also established their own educational support programs to assist employees seeking to complete their bachelor's degree and those pursuing their masteral or doctoral studies (Conferido, 1998).

Table 5.3
The Positions in the Philippine Career Service

1st Level	Clerical, trades, crafts and custodial service positions, which involve non-professional or sub-professional work in a non-supervisory or supervisory capacity requiring less than four years of collegiate studies.
2nd Level	Professional, technical and scientific positions involving professional, technical or scientific work in a non-supervisory or supervisory capacity requiring at least four years of college work up to Division Chief level.
3rd Level	Positions in the Career Executive Service

Source: Reforms in the Civil Service: The Philippine Experience, Ms. Corazon De Leon, Former Chairman PCSC (1995-2001)

Up until now, Philippine Civil Service Commission is geared towards building the capabilities of government middle-level managers. Anchored on the assumption that front-line managers are instrumental in igniting and releasing the productive and creative spirit within the organization, it was found appropriate that their managerial skills should be kept abreast with requirements of the changing times (De Leon, 2003). Thus, the Supervisory Development Course and the Advance Management Development Program were instituted in order to enhance the leadership capability of first-line supervisors in the Philippine bureaucracy (De Leon, 2003).

For career executive service (Level 3), there is a separate board that focuses on their capability building programs. They have a series of trainings and other career development interventions intended to provide a range of perspective, experience, attitude, knowledge and skills necessary for their effective performance on the job.

In addition, a Distance Learning Program was conceived as an alternative strategy without prejudice to continuing manpower development. As in correspondence schooling, it consisted of modules on a wide range of topics and courses (De Leon, 2003). Apart from CSC-led HRD interventions for competency development, the concept of decentralized HRD functions to head of national agencies is in place. The agency is responsible for some HRD decision points like training, scholarship, and career development for its own employees. Each agency is responsible for providing training opportunities to employees. Either the agency undertakes an in-house training or sends its employees to external training providers. Funding for such training is sourced from an appropriation from HRD (usually 5% of agency annual budget) and savings and trust funds of a certain government agency.

Comparison

Generally, unlike South Korea having a separate training institute like Central Officials Training Institute (COTI), before 2011, training and capacity development programs for government officials in the Philippines are commonly initiated by renowned universities, other government agencies, CSC and CSC-accredited training institutions. To further boost the capability of government employees, the Philippine Civil Service Commission (PCSC) launched on 26 July 2011 the Civil Service Institute (CSI) that will serve as the premiere training institution for all workers in the country. Training programs under the CSI are specifically designed to enrich the knowledge, skills and attitudes of state workers in line with the CSC's mandate of transforming every civil servant into a *lingkod-bayani* or servant hero.

Training programs offered in Civil Service Institute (CSI) includes courses on values and governance like Values Orientation Workshop (VOW), Public Service Ethics and Accountability, Basic Customer Service Skills, Gender Sensitivity Training, Service Excellence Delivery Program, and Administrative Justice. Courses such as Creating Learning Mindset, High Performance for Public Supervisors, Financial Planning Workshop for First Level employees, Project Management, Powerful Media Relations, Ethical Decision Making for Public Managers, and Future Leadership Program are also integrated in the training program. It appears that CSI's training programs are designed to enhance skills and knowledge of employees to make them more effective in their jobs. These are centered on orientation and reorientation; values development; updating of skills for supervisors, middle managers, clerical force, and technical or professional employees; and personnel development. These imply that the kind of training that government employees will receive would make them more effective civil servants.

However, since it's a newly established institute, and no evaluation of the training program have been initiated yet, there are lots of things to expect as to the aspect of what was earned, changes in behavior, and agency performance – impacts on costs, outputs, and goal accomplishment (Kirkpatrick, 1976).

1. In your opinion, what are the strength of the Korea's training and development program? What do you think are the implications of adopting a centralized training and development system in a developing country, like Philippines?

2. To what extent does your country or agency have come to initiate training and development strategy?

3. What do you think is the advantage of having an identified competencies required in a certain government position?

4 In the design process, what do you think are the advantages and disadvantages of skipping with the agency level (i.e., trainee's immediate agency) training needs assessment? Is it acceptable to have a one-fit-all competencies and training approaches to achieve a certain target competency?

Student Activity

Identify major HRD issues/problems/concerns in your country or organization. For example, the major issues discussed in this chapter include: 1) instructional strategies/design, 2) community education, 3) training program development, 4) needs assessment, 5) program planning and development, 6) CD, MD, and OD, 7) workforce/place diversity and work-life balance issues, 8) International HRD, and 9) E-HRD, etc. In the PBL table provided below, give brief and succinct information on each item. Give your own ideas and comments on the HRD issue(s) you have chosen, including your own opinion and your proposed solution to enhance and improve the overall HRD systems/cultures/structures/processes. Also, discuss your own suggestion(s) for resolving/reforming civil service systems of the country. Lastly, argue on the relevance and importance of the HRD issue(s) you identified and the contribution of your analysis to the current personnel administration and management systems in your country or your organization. Using the Case Analysis Table, please determine the important issues of training and development in your agency or your country.

HRM in the Public Organizations: An Essential Guide

Case Analysis

	Step	Contents		
1	Environments/ Conditions/ Backgrounds	Please explain the situation briefly. (1-2 pages)		
2	Problem Definitions	In your own perspective, please be as specific as possible when pointing out the problem. (2-3 pages)		
3	Actual Case Studies	Please explain by providing specific examples. (Newspaper articles, news clips, or interviews) (2-3 pages)		
4	Alternatives	Possible Alternative(s)	Pros in your Country Context	Cons in a your Country Context
		①		
		②		
		③		
		Please propose more than three policy alternatives. (2-3 pages)		
5	The Best Solutions	Why did you choose this alternative as the best solution? What are the expected effects and potential contribution? (2 pages)		

Reviews

1. Neglecting or undervaluing needs assessment; why and how to cope with it? Can we really forego with the needs assessment process?

2. In the public sector, how does effectiveness of training and development being evaluated? How about the impact of its training measures and programs? What adjustments are needed, if any?

Ending Credits

Research Digest

Performance Management Theory: A Look from the Performer's Perspective with Implications for HRD

The concept of performance management has gained strong attention to improve results in the midst of challenging economic conditions. Many organizations instead of waiting for external improvements such as market growth and technological advances, they looked into their internal capabilities for performance and productivity gains.

Performance management has been defined as management's systematic application of processes aimed at optimizing performance in an organization (Warren, 1982). There is an emphasis on process that somewhat carries a negative connotation in the performer's perspective – something done to people. While a more progressive definition was given by Weiss and Hartle (1997): 'A process for establishing a shared understanding about what is to be achieved, and how it is to be achieved, and an approach to managing people that increases the probability of achieving success' (p. 3), this definition continues to represent a top-down orientation. Performers and their immediate supervisors tend to think performance management is in compliance of something that is required or forced. Likewise, employees do not look at it as helpful or valued element of their job (Coens and Jenkins, 2000).

Traditionally, performance management is viewed to be the responsibility of immediate supervisor (e.g., Barnes-Farrell, 2001; Cardy & Dobbins, 1994; Latham & Wexley, 1994). However, with the presence of different organizational challenges such decentralized workforces, enlarged spans of control, lack of direct experience, evolving performer expectations, etc., caused supervisors not to be effective managers of others' performance. In addition, the tendency of managers never having held one or more of the positions that report to them. Without the expertise, knowledge, and understanding that come with having performed the work, the credibility of feedback is suspect (Coens & Jenkins, 2000). Finally, many of the modern employees now expect to be more involved in determining the performance management that affects them (Mohrman et al., 1989).

Moreover, with the sizeable investment of many organizations for performance management it does not appear that there is a clear evidence of theoretical research supporting organizations manages performance. Despite the availability of relevant and advance models especially work motivation; performance management is described in process terms (e.g. Grote, 1996; Swan, 1991) wherein it starts from objective setting, through formal appraisal, to the start of the next cycle. There may well be theories applied to this but clear connections are weak and average managers would have hard time to grasp such a theoretical support.

There is a vast array of relevant motivational theories that can be utilized in the improvement of performance management. However, managers are apt to the more traditional and sometimes to those theories that have patently weak connections to the distinctiveness of an organization, like the Maslow's hierarchy of needs. Among the modern motivation theories worthy of consideration are: Expectancy Theory (Guest, 1997), Justice Theory (Latham et.al, 2005), Self-Determination Theory (Ryan and

Deci, 2000). Donovan (2001) identified Equity Theory, Expectancy Theory, Cognitive Evaluation Theory, Goal Setting Theory, Control Theory, and Social Cognitive Theory as those that have received the most attention recently.

For the purpose of this study, the writer selected three among the theories and explores its application to performance management: Goal-Setting Theory, Control Theory and Social Cognitive Theory (See Table 5.4).

The descriptions of the above-mentioned theories are enough to show how much motivation theories offer insight and explanation of how performance management works. Goal-setting theory is relevant to the questions raised in Human Performance System such as, "do performance standard exist?" In the same way, control theory provides a solid foundation for critically assessing the feedback elements of performance management approaches. And lastly, social cognitive theory provides explanations in support of performance management. The interaction of the three factors provides a strong systems view of performance. Self-efficacy places emphasis on what performer's think of them, as they set or react to goals, monitor and judge their performance, and correct behaviors using self-regulation mechanisms (Bandura, 1986). Lastly, the same theories mentioned above were considered to look into the performer's perspective. Table 5.5 shows the relation of the three motivational theories to performance management.

Table 5.4

Three Motivation Theories and Performance Management

Goal-Setting Theory	Control Theory	Social Cognitive Theory
Found to be exceptionally reliable, valid, and useful across diverse work situations (Locke et al., 1981). Difficult and specific goals led to higher performance when compared to vague do-your-best goals (Locke and Latham, 2002).	Also referred to as feedback control or cybernetics. It is described in self-regulation terms as an ongoing comparative process aimed at reducing the discrepancy standards for behavior and the observed effects of actual behavior (Carver and Scheier, 1981, 1998).	Motivation is influenced by interaction of three elements: work environment itself, what the performer thinks, and what the performer does (Bandura, 1986). Strong performance requires positive self-beliefs of efficacy in addition to appropriate skills and abilities.

Table 5.5

Performer's Perspective to Performance Management

Goal-Setting Theory	Control Theory	Social Cognitive Theory
It makes a solid case for the use of difficult and specific goals to create the strong situations necessary for substantial achievement (Locke and Latham, 2002). They pointed out that performer's participation heightens the importance of the goal, thereby strengthening goal commitment.	Most performance management does not emphasize feedback (Coen and Jenkins, 2000). Performers taking charge of their own feedback loops helps them obtain the timely feedback they need to make the negative discrepancy adjustments indicated by this theory.	People who see themselves as highly capable of performers tend to embrace difficult goals with above average (Bandura, 1994). Specifically, strong self-efficacy translates to higher level of goal challenge, effort expended in pursuit of established goals, perseverance and resilience.

Performance management is the means by which an organization ensures that their employees understand how they can contribute to the organizational strategic goals. It focuses on the effective management of people in line with the organizational goals and objectives to enhance performance. And, guarantees the creation of a working environment that will allow and enable people to perform their duties and responsibilities to the best of their abilities.

Issue(s)

This article is a conceptual paper that looks into the construct of performance management and challenged and discussed it along two lines: to what degree does theoretical support for performance management exist as it is applied in organizations; and from the performer's standpoint, how performance management might be improved.

Findings

However, findings of this article are quite surprising because despite the positive contributions of performance management in the organization, it seems that it is not effectively implemented. In addition, the availability of relevant theories that have substantial scholarly history and much accumulated evidence of their value are not fully integrated in the performance management process. Many organizations cling to the most common theories instead of applying concepts that is more fitted to the circumstances of their organization. This is a clear loss to organizations; an unacceptable loss that is just because of missing the opportunity in maximizing available and applicable theories to support performance management system.

Along with the less integration of pertinent and significant theoretical works to support construct of performance management, this article have seen the possibility of having alternate forms of performance management. This came out because of the observation that there is no tight feedback system and the role of self-efficacy in support of higher goal achievement was noted. Simply put, the performer's perspective to performance management warrants a serious attention in the organization – the possibility of self-directed performance management.

This article left HRD managers challenging and important things to consider in appreciating what performance management wants to achieve. Besides the above-mentioned gap between the theory in-use and practice and the introduction of self-directed performance management, the following are equally important implications to look into:

a. *A careful study and understanding of organizational performance management system*. This will be vital in the identification of appropriate theoretical base that will support the construct of performance management. Likewise, it will give a clear picture whether or not there is a strong theoretical support for the system;

b. *Performance management system must be working in consonance with the organizational culture.* Such culture will be the basis of relevant theories to be applied;

c. *Motivation is an indispensable aspect of performance management and is contributory to the creation of a high performing organization. Various available motivational theories such as, Goal-Setting, Control, Social Cognition, Self-determination, Feedback Intervention, and Self-Management Theories deserve HRD's serious attention.* These are all theoretical works closely related to performance management that can give a strong theoretical support to it.

d. *The idea of self-directed performance management opened the door to a more cost-saving and motivated employees.* HRD managers have to crucially consider this by taking into account the circumstances of its organization. The organization and the employees may accept or decline this idea. Hence, HRD manager was left with the challenge of helping both the organizations and employees better understand their performance management systems and the performer's perspective.

The article has given vast array of information that described different flaws in the performance management and gave a clearer picture of the importance of relevant theoretical support in the system. It further emphasize that performance management is all about increasing performance - employees and organizational performance. However, despite of organizational continuous development of performance management, there are still more to be done.

With the teachings from this article, successful use of performance management system should include the following:

1. The conduct of a cautious study regarding the existing performance management system and the identification of a relevant and strong theoretical support.

The organization, HRD manager and/or the person in-charge in the monitoring of the performance of the employees must be able to   describe and define the existing performance management system. Meaning, they must understand the system and knows how it actually work in the organization. In particular, it can be done through a performance management system review. This review must be attended by the Head of the organization, HRD manager, Manager(s) in-charge of the employee's performance, and a representative from the employees. They should discuss in here the status of organizational and employees performance, assessment of the existing performance system and the possible actions to be taken in order to improve it.

A committee-type of reviewing or assessing of a current state of performance management system is an effective way to encourage the development a collective approach of solving problems. It is in a way removing the organizational thinking of top-down approach of management that tends to be more imposing rather than encouraging.

After the careful assessment of the performance management, the logical thing to do must be the identification of a strong and appropriate theoretical support. It must be clear that what we want to integrate are motivational theories that will encourage employees reach a high performance. Such a theoretical base must be in congruent with the circumstances of the organization, or to simply put, the culture of the organization. The article has enumerated various motivational theories that are substantial scholarly works and are closely related to the performance management such as, Goal-Setting Theory (Lock & Latham, 1990), Control Theory (Carver and Scheier, 1998), Social Cognition Theory (Donovan, 2001), Self-determination Theory (Deci & Ryan, 1985), Feedback Intervention Theory (Kluger & DeNisi, 1996), and Self-Management Theory (Manz & Sims, 1980; Manz, 1986). The integration of a well-founded and valid theory in the performance management system will result surely to the attainment of a highly performing organization.

2. The organization must ensure the creation of an open and active 'communicating organization.'

Communication is very important in whatever aspect of life. Like in an organization, communication is considered to be a key element to manage performance of employees. It is important for the employees to have regular and frequent communication to deal with different problems of the organization. We must put to note that, the absence of communication is tantamount to detaching employee from the organization, or the organization to the employee.

But, how can we have an open and active communicating organization? This will let us go back to the basics of performance management. *Firstly*, communicate goals and job expectations. Traditionally, goal-setting is a management function but the finding of this article looks at it to be a two-way communication of goals between the organization and individual. Simply put, the participation of the employee in goal-setting must be encouraged rather than to follow the top-down approach. It is important that the organizational vision and goals are crafted with the employees for them to clearly understand how their works fits into the organization, and how they could contribute to the achievement of such organizational goal. Likewise, it will strengthen the commitment in the achievement of goal is higher. The article have made mention about Peter Drucker's concept of "manager's letter" that encourages performers to write to their boss to facilitate communication. This concept is worth exploring to stimulate goal-sharing and communication. Lastly, the supervisor and employees understanding of the job duties will eliminate ambiguities regarding functions in the organizations.

Secondly, communicate feedback. It must be a regular and frequent performance feedback process that will facilitate dialogue between the manager, supervisor and the employee. Consequently, it will foster better communication in the organization. An effective performance management system promotes regular checking of the strengths and weaknesses and allows the performer to participate in the exchange of views. By doing so, it will build performer's confidence and help them improve performance further. Lastly, communicating feedback must not be done once or twice a year. It must be a continuous process of performance review unlike the prevailing organizational norm of doing at the beginning and end of the rating cycle. It must be frequent and regular, which much be determined at the dispense of the manager and/or supervisor. Finally, the organization must foster a performance management system that must include manager, supervisor(s), and employees in the work planning, setting expectations, monitoring performance, developing the capacity to perform, rating and good performance must rewarded.

Source: Performance Management Theory: A Look from the Performer's Perspective with Implications for HRD" by Thomas W. Buchner, University of Minnesota (Published in Human Resource Development International, Vol. 10, No. 1, 59-73, March 2007)

Further Readings

- Berman, E. M., Bowman, J. S., West, J. P., & Van Wart, M. R. (Ed.) (2012). *Human Resource Management in Public Service: Paradoxes, Processes, and Problems.* Fourth Edition. Sage Publications.
- Nigro, L., Nigro, F., & Kellough, J. (2013). The new public personnel administration. *Cengage Learning.*
- Pynes, J. E. (2008). Human resources management for public and nonprofit organizations: A strategic approach (Vol. 30). *John Wiley & Sons.*
- Buchner, T. W. (2007). Performance management theory: A look from the performer's perspective with implications for HRD. Human Resource Development International, 10(1), 59-73.
- Werner, Jon M., & DeSimone, Randy L. (2009). Human Resource Development, Fifth Edition. Cincinnati: South-Western/Cengage Learning.

References

Alliger, G. M., & Janak, E. A. (1989). Kirkpatrick's levels of training criteria: Thirty years later. Personnel psychology, 42(2), 331-342.

Berman, E. M., Bowman, J. S., West, J. P., & Van Wart, M. R. (2012). *Human resource management in public service: Paradoxes, processes, and problems*. Sage.

Bucknall, H., & Ohtaki, R. (2006). Mastering business in Asia: Human resource management. John Wiley & Sons.

Boudreaux, M. A. (2001). Career development: What is its role in human resource development. *In Proceedings of the Academy of Human Resource Development* (pp. 224-231).

Brockbank, W. (1999). If HR were really strategically proactive: Present and future directions in HR's contribution to competitive advantage. *Human Resource Management*, 38, 337-352.

Civil Service Commission - www.csc.gov.ph

Czarnowsky, M. (2008). Executive Development. T+ D, 62(9), 44-45.

Cummings, T. G., & Worley, C. G. (2001). Essentials of organization development and change. South-Western College Publ..

DeSimone R, L and Werner, J, M (2012), Human Resource Development, (6th edition) South-Western Cengage Learning, Canada

Department, C. S. (n.d.). Retrieved December 14, 2012, from Civil Service Management Department: http://www.csmd.gov.af/index.php/about-csmd

Egan, T. M., Yang, B., & Bartlett, K. R. (2004). The effects of organizational learning culture and job satisfaction on motivation to transfer learning and turnover intention. *Human resource development quarterly*, 15(3), 279-301.

Egan, T. M. (2002). Grounded theory research and theory building. Advances in developing human resources, 4(3), 277-295.

Fernandez, Mary Ann. (2003). A Comparative Perspective, 2004. International Public Management Association for Human Resources (IPMA-HR)

French, P. E., & Goodman, D. (2011). Review of Public Personnel.

French, W. and Bell, C. (1999) Organization Development: Behavioural Science Interventions for Organization Improvement. Prentice Hall, New Jersey.

Garavan, T.N., O'Donnell, D., McGuire, D. and Watson, S. (2007), "Exploring perspectives on human resource development: an introduction", *Advances in Developing Human Resources*, Vol. 9 No. 1, pp. 3-10.

Garavan, T. (1991), "Strategic human resource development", *Journal of European Industrial Training*, Vol. 15, pp. 17-30.

Gardiner, P., Leat, M., & Sadler-Smith, E. (2001). Learning in organizations: HR implications and considerations. Human Resource Development International, 4(3), 391-405.

Dirkx, J. M., Gilley, J. W., & Gilley, A. M. (2004). Change theory in CPE and HRD: Toward a holistic view of learning and change in work. *Advances in developing human resources*, 6(1), 35-51.

Gold, J., Holden, R., Iles, P., Stewart, J., & Beardwell, J. (Eds.). (2013). Human resource development: Theory and practice. Palgrave Macmillan.

Hackett, P. (2003). Training practice. CIPD Publishing.

Hall, D. T. (1996). The Career Is Dead--Long Live the Career. A Relational Approach to Careers. The Jossey-Bass Business & Management Series. Jossey-Bass Inc., Publishers, 350 Sansome Street, San Francisco, CA 94104..

Hall, D. T. (1971). A theoretical model of career subidentity development in organizational settings. *Organizational Behavior and Human Performance*, 6(1), 50-76.

Hamlin, B. and Stewart, J. (2010), "What is HRD? A definitional review and synthesis of the HRD domain", *Journal of European Industrial Training*, Vol. 35, pp. 199-220.

Harter, J. K., Schmidt, F. L., & Hayes, T. L. (2002). Business-unit-level relationship between employee satisfaction, employee engagement, and business outcomes: a meta-analysis. *Journal of applied psychology*, 87(2), 268.

Herzberg, F. (1968). One more time: How do you motivate employees (pp. 46-57). Boston: *Harvard Business Review.*

Herr, E. L. (2001). Career development and its practice: A historical perspective. *The Career Development Quarterly*, 49(3), 196-211.

Holton, E. F. (1996). The flawed four-level evaluation model. Human resource development quarterly, 7(1), 5-21.

Im, T., & Shin, H. Y. Evaluating Training and Development for Korean Civil Servants: Challenges and responses.

Kahn, W. A. (1990). Psychological conditions of personal engagement and disengagement at work. *Academy of management journal*, 33(4), 692-724.

Kim, S. & Jung, H. W. (2010). The Competency Management in the Korea National Government. K. U.Leuven, Public Management Institute, 2010

Kirkpatrick, D.L. (1994). Evaluating training programs: The four levels. San Francisco: Berret-Koehler.

Klinger Donald, E., & Nalbandian, J. (2003). Public Personnel Management: Contexts and Strategies. New Jersey.

Knight, D., Durham, C. C., & Locke, E. A. (2001). The relationship of team goals, incentives, and efficacy to strategic risk, tactical implementation, and performance. Academy of Management Journal, 44(2), 326-338.

Kraiger, K., Ford, J. K., & Salas, E. (1993). Application of cognitive, skill-based, and affective theories of learning outcomes to new methods of training evaluation. Journal of applied psychology, 78(2), 311.

Lewis, G. B., & Cho, Y. J. (2011). The aging of the state government workforce: Trends and implications. *American Review of Public Administration*, 41(1), 48–60.

Lynham, S. A., Chermack, T. J., & Noggle, M. A. (2004). Selecting organization development theory from an HRD perspective. Human Resource Development Review, 3(2), 151-172.

Marchington, M., & Wilkinson, A. J. (1996). Core personnel and development. *Institute of Personnel and Development.*

McDonald, K. S., & Hite, L. M. (2005). Reviving the relevance of career development in human resource development. Human Resource Development Review, 4(4), 418-439.

McLagan, P. and Suhadolnik, D. (1989), Models for HRD Practice: The Research Report, American Society for Training and Development, Alexandria, VA.

McLean, G.N. and McLean, L. (2001), "If we can't define HRD in one country, how can we define it in an international context?", *Human Resource Development International,* Vol. 4 No. 3, pp. 313-26.

National Academy of Public Administration (NAPA), (1996). A Guide for Effective Strategic *Management of Human Resources*, Washington, DC. 27

Parsons, F. (1909). Choosing a vocation. Houghton Mifflin.

Rothwell, W. J., & Sullivan, R. L. (Eds.). (2005). Practicing organization development: A guide for consultants (Vol. 27). John Wiley & Sons.

Sackett, P. R., & Mullen, E. J. (1993). Beyond formal experimental design: Towards an expanded view of the training evaluation process. Personnel Psychology, 46(3), 613-627.

Saks, A. M. (2006). Antecedents and consequences of employee engagement. *Journal of managerial psychology*, 21(7), 600-619.

Schein, E. H., & Schein, E. (1978). Career dynamics: Matching individual and organizational needs (Vol. 24). Reading, MA: Addison-Wesley.

Semler, S. W. (1997). Systematic agreement: A theory of organizational alignment. *Human Resource Development Quarterly*, 8, 23-40.

Silvestro, R. (2002). Dispelling the modern myth: Employee satisfaction and loyalty drive service profitability. International Journal of Operations & Production Management, 22(1), 30-49.

Sturman, M. C., Trevor, C. O., Boudreau, J. W., & Gerhart, B. (2003). Is it worth it to win the talent war? Evaluating the utility of performance-based pay. Personnel Psychology, 56(4), 997-1035.

Soni, V. (2000). A twenty-first-century reception for diversity in the public sector: A case study. *Public Administration Review*, 60, 395–408.

Shafritz J. M et al. (2001). Personnel management in Government: Politics and ProcessNew York: Marcel Dekker

Sturges, J., Guest, D., Conway, N., & Davey, K. M. (2002). A longitudinal study of the relationship between career management and organizational commitment among graduates in the first ten years at work. *Journal of Organizational Behavior*, 23(6), 731-748.

Swanson, R. A. & Holton, E. F. (2009). Foundations of Human Resource Development, 2nd Edition. San Francisco: Berrett-Koehler

Swanson, R. A. (2001). Human resource development and its underlying theory. *Human Resource Development International*, 4(3), 299-312.

Tan, J. A., Hall, R. J., & Boyce, C. (2003). The role of employee reactions in predicting training effectiveness. Human Resource Development Quarterly, 14(4), 397-411.

van Dijk, M. S. (2004). Career Development within HRD: Foundation or Fad?. Online Submission.

Van Eynde, D. F., Hoy, J. C., & Van Eynde, D. C. (1997). Organization development classics: the practice and theory of change--the best of the OD practitioner. Jossey-Bass.

Wallace, C. M., Eagleson, G., & Waldersee, R. (2000). The sacrificial HR strategy in call centers. International Journal of Service Industry Management, 11(2), 174-184.

Watkins, K. (1989). Business and industry. Handbook of adult and continuing education, 427.

Werner, J.M. and DeSimone, R.L. (2006), Human Resource Development, 4th ed., Thomson South-Western, Mason, OH.

231

Werner, J. M., & DeSimone, R. L.(2009). Human Resource Development, 5th Ed, US: South-Western Cengage Learning.

Workman, M. (2003). Results from organizational development interventions in a technology call center. Human Resource Development Quarterly, 14(2), 215-230.

Yorks, L. (2005). Nothing so practical as a good theory. *Human Resource Development Review*, 4(2), 111-113.

Chapter 6

Succession Planning: SHRM

Framework

Human Resource Management for Public Organizations: An Essential Guide

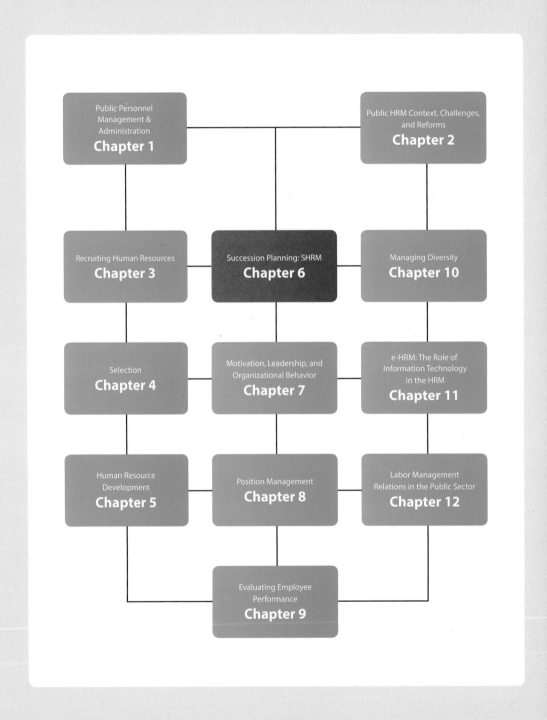

Learning Outcomes

After going through this chapter, you should be able to:

- Define and discuss the strategic human resource management (SHRM)
- Determine the relationship of strategic planning and human resource management
- Identify the issues and problems in the strategic human capital (workforce force) planning
- Discuss the Five-Step Workforce Planning Model
- Determine the critical issues in SHRM
- Discuss and determine the problems and implications of SHRM in the public sector
- Relate the role of succession planning in the SHRM.

Preview

In the management literature, various innovations and trends on organizational transformations have been identified, for example the Strategic Human Resource Management (SHRM) which denotes on the "ideas intended to increase the responsiveness of the human resource function to organizational goals" (Mesch, Perry, & Wise 1995; Schuler 1992; cited in Choi & Rainey, 2002). During the past two decades, Strategic Human Resource Management (SHRM) has been continuously recognized as one of the most influential and powerful ideas that ever emerged in the field of business and management (Salaman, Storey, & Billsberry, 2005). In the public sector organizations, the principles drawn from the SHRM had opened the discussion on the promotion of 'high performance workplaces'—is both a descriptor of the outcomes achieved by innovative work organization, and shorthand for particular sets of human resource practices (Hunter & Hitt, 2000)—and 'human capital management'—an approach to employee staffing that perceives people as assets (human capital) whose current value can be measured and whose future value can be enhanced through investment. In the context of continuously changing circumstances, public managers views that there is a need for proper administration and management of people in the organization in order to stay and remain in the competitive environment. The development of this new trend of strategic human resource management, as an alternative to the traditional bureaucratic control model has attracted managers in a wide variety of organizations. Along this fashion, the public sector organizations has emphasized the important role of human resources in the public sector and focused on strategic management of the workforce to improve efficiency and effectiveness of performance of the public sector. For example, in the U.S. federal government's efforts to improve performance of the public sector by strategically managing the workforce, the Presidential Management Agenda in 2001 has designated strategic human resource management (HRM) as the first goal that federal agencies should achieve (Choi & Rainey, 2002).

Undeniably, human resource represents the most crucial asset in the organization that is capable of providing a vast source of competitive advantage because it's often difficult to duplicate by competitors and hard to substitute even within the same organization. It was argued that SHRM can be used by various organizations—public, private, or non-profit—to acquire and develop valuable human capital. A number of studies have actually demonstrated that SHRM practices, either individually or as a system, are associated with higher levels of performance (see, for example, Huselid, 1995; Huang, 1998). Thus, not least, SHRM has been widely considered as a significant and important framework in the field of management.

Taken together, there occurred a wholesale shift in thinking and in practice relating to people-management over a period of some twenty-plus years. Perhaps not surprisingly, while some observers expected rapid transformation, others were skeptical and academics frequently detected as much 'continuity' as change. Many expected HRM and SHRM to be transient.

Depending how one interprets the contours public personnel management, it is still possible to construct images of rather different landscapes. One stance would be to note that the past two to three decades have been as marked by subcontracting and the loosening of employment contracts as they have moved towards human asset management. In recent months, the 'gang masters' who buy, sell and deploy labour, much of it comprised of workers not legally-entitled to work, and under conditions reminiscent of the nineteenth century let alone the twentieth, have captured the headlines more than HR Directors. Short-term contracts, temporary work, call-center employment, off-shoring and the like have all challenged the simple idea of an unproblematic transition and progression to a more sophisticated, high-value-added, high-performance workforce, high-commitment management, employment nirvana.

Yet on the other hand, it can also be argued that while the contingent workforce has grown, this evidences the 'hard' version of SHRM (the willingness to treat human resources as other resources and not to be fettered by long-standing practices). Alongside this, employment management in the core (and it has also been noted that short-term contract labour has remained at around 7 per cent of the workforce) is now routinely conceptualized in terms of SHRM assumptions, frameworks and logics rather more so than in terms of the erstwhile industrial relations paradigm of the 1960s–1980s. The intervening period has seen a whole series of movements (in theory and practices) which are easily interpreted as expressive of or even re-workings of, the SHRM framework. Key examples include: the learning organization, the resource-based view of the firm, the celebration of the importance of 'knowledge workers', investment in people, high performance work systems and so on. Perhaps most important of all, whether fully realized in practice or not, the idea that it is sensible for an organization in the public or private sector to view its people management in a strategic way is nowadays conventional wisdom

Making Sense of the RealWorld

Development in SHRM thinking has a profound impact on our understanding of its contribution to organizational performance, through increased competitive advantage and added value. Indeed, it becomes clear that whether the focus of SHRM practices is on alignment with the external context or on the internal context of the organization, the meaning of SHRM can only really be understood in the context of something else, namely organizational performance, whether that be in terms of economic value added and increased shareholder value, customer value added and increased market share, or people added value through increased employee commitment and reservoirs of employee skills and knowledge.

As supplementary materials, the following video clips may provide useful information on Strategic Human Resource Management as well as the succession planning.

Title	Gist	Source
How can Strategic Human Resource Management (SHRM) help in modern organizational growth?	The video clip provides information on the role of Strategic Human Resource Management in the organizational performance.	https://www.youtube.com/ watch?v=jWdovBCWTF0
Why Succession Planning is essential: The Case of the Runaway Talent	It provides a basic discussion on the importance of succession planning in the organization—in times wherein employees leave the organization unplanned.	https://www.youtube.com/ watch?v=GZ8C3ie0drw

1. What kinds of SHRM initiatives or strategies are engaged in your department or organization?

2. Among the following tips for successful strategic HR planning, what would you prefer if you were in charge of adopting SHRM initiatives in your organization?

   - Assign a "process champion" to lead each strategic initiative
   - Keep the process simple by focusing on only a few critical issues at a time
   - Involve employees and other key stakeholders, including elected officials

3. What could pubic employers do to better anticipate and plan for labor market conditions? What kinds of SHRM initiatives or strategies are engaged in your department or organization?

4. In what way does an understanding of strategic management contribute to your understanding of strategic human resource management? How would you differentiate human resource management from strategic human resource management?

5. What do you think is the relationship between strategic human resource management and organizational performance?

"I'd like to give you a raise and promotion, but that wouldn't be fair to others who don't stay late or work as hard as you do."

Theory Synopsis

Strategic Human Resource Management (SHRM)

What is SHRM? Various definitions and conceptions have been attached with SHRM based on different context and circumstances. Schuler and Walker (1990) defined SHRM as a "set of processes and activities jointly shared by human resources and line managers to solve people-related business issues" (p. 7). It can be gleaned that SHRM shares some commonalities with the traditional HRM; however, it gives emphasis on the future direction and challenges of the organization. SHRM, as argued by Snell and colleagues (1996), is an organizational system that endeavors to attain a sustainable and competitive advantage through people. Practically, the human resource as one of the most important asset of the organization is to be seriously integrated in the whole organizational plan and proper investment must be afforded for them to enhance their knowledge, skills, ability. No other factors are to be considered on the top list on enhancing the human resource capacity except for the public managers to address the old-fashioned and obsolete knowledge, skills, ability of the employees.

As widely argued, SHRM is not a public management concept or a framework in transient because it is an overarching approach to people management within the organization in a broad, strategic sense. Also, it is concerned with longer-term people issues and macro-concerns about structure, quality, culture, values, commitment and matching resources to future need (CIPD, 2009, p. 1). Boxall and Purcell (2008) denotes SHRM as a "set of activities aimed at building individual and organizational performance (p. 5); while Pynes (2009) refers SHRM as "the identification and implementation of HR activities, policies, and practices to make the necessary ongoing changes to support or improve the agency's operational and strategic objectives" (Pynes, 2009, p. 95). The idea that people, or the human capital of an organization, can play a strategic role in the organization's success is the foundation of the field of SHRM.

One of the issues that have featured prominently in the discussion on the interactions of SHRM and organizational performance is the question of whether the relationship between SHRM practices and indicators of organizational performance is universal or contingent. The universalistic approach suggests that certain types of HRM practices are more effective than others (Pfeffer, 1994; Huselid, 1995). For example, organizations that use innovative recruitment and selection systems should typically have more effective, efficient and motivated workforce than organizations that do not. The contingency approach, on the other hand, suggests that the effectiveness of HRM practices is contingent upon other factors such as organizational climate, culture, competitive strategies, etc. According to this argument, HRM practices that enhance the knowledge, skills, ability and motivation of employees would have a greater impact on performance if the organization is using a strategy that requires highly skilled and motivated employees (Neal, West and Paterson, 2005).

Strategic Planning and HRM

What comes to your mind when we talk about 'strategy'? How would you describe 'strategy'? Think of various words that can be closely associated with the word strategy. Then try to relate the term 'strategy' in a public sector organization based on your own perspective. Again, consider a public organization strategic plan; can you determine the vision statement, mission, objectives and values on it? What do you know about the 'strategic and operational planning process' in an organization (i.e., public, non-profit, or private)?

Historically, the term 'strategy' comes from the Greek word 'strategus' which means commander in chief and was later on adapted and used in English in the year 1656. A Wikipedia entry describes strategy as:

> "A high level plan to achieve one or more goals under conditions of uncertainty. In the sense of the "art of the general", which included several subsets of skills

including "tactics", siegecraft, logistics etc., the term came into use in the 6th century C.E. in East Roman terminology, and was translated into Western vernacular languages only in the 18th century. From then until the 20th century, the word "strategy" came to denote "a comprehensive way to try to pursue political ends, including the threat or actual use of force, in a dialectic of wills" in a military conflict, in which both adversaries interact"

Adapted from: Wikipedia (en.wikipedia.org). Freedman, Lawrence (2013).
Strategy. Oxford University Press. ISBN 978-0-19-932515-3.

Figure 6.1
The Three Traditional Poles of a Strategic Plan

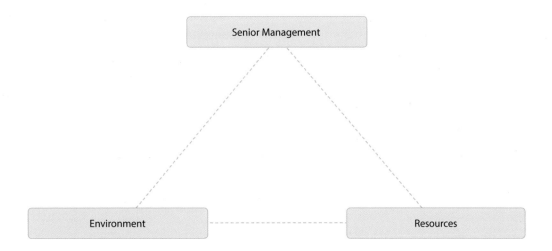

Source: Adapted from Aktouf, 1996

Table 6.1
Reforming the People Side of Government

ISSUE PRIORITIES AND RECOMMENDATONS FROM THE
NATIONAL ACADEMY OF PUBLIC ADMINISTRATION

In order to improve fundamentally the human resources future for the federal government, Presidential leadership in cooperation with key stakeholders such as federal employee unions, managers, executives, senior political appointees, is essential. The four key recommendations for reforming the people side of government follow:

1. Human capital needs to be top priority (not just an HR issue, but an executive priority—White House and every agency)
   a. Assign lead responsibility to senior WH aide and COO in every agency
   b. OMB, OPM, and executive branch agencies should work closely with Capitol Hill on human capital issues
   c. OMB should be more involved in human capital planning/process, linked to budget process and the GPRA (strategic planning and results-oriented management) process, with the support of OPM
   d. OPM should focus more on tools not rules (e.g., workforce planning, helping agencies, technical assistance, best practices, streamline regulations)

2. Recruit, retain, and develop a skilled and diverse workforce, including redefining public service careers and promoting public service
   a. President and key government leaders must speak out about the importance and value of public service on a continuing basis
   b. Require agencies to develop and implement workforce analysis and plans (e.g., what competencies exist now, what are needed in the future to achieve agency missions, what are the gaps?)
   c. Develop policies and encourage inter-intra-governmental and private sector

mobility.

d. Improve and promote quality of work place (i.e., rewarding initiative, motivating workers, encourage risk-taking, stimulate intellectual growth)

e. Improve and promote quality of work life balance through family-friendly policies (e.g., flextime, flexiplace, virtual office)

f. Increase educational outreach efforts

g. Streamline the hiring process to respond to changing market competition

3. Modernize the performance management and training/development systems

a. Link performance management systems to the strategic plan and make it results-oriented

b. Adopt a balanced scorecard approach (e.g., results, client feedback, employee feedback)

c. Adopt a more performance-based incentive and reward system for individuals, teams, and agencies

d. Enhance information systems to support improved performance management systems

e. Invest in human capital development necessary to achieve organizational goals, drawing examples of levels of investment from private sector best practices

4. Decide how much standardization is necessary in the human capital system

a. White House should lead an expedited assessment of the effects of the implementation of individual agency personnel systems and their results (e.g., achievement of agency mission)

b. Simultaneously review the existing regulations associated with Title V to simplify/streamline/improve the human capital system

c. Determine the opportunities for more comprehensive improvements necessary to achieve organizational goals

Source: Klinger and Nalbandian, 2003

Strategy and strategic planning deal with a process of looking at the organization and environment—both today and in the expected future—and determining what an organization want to do to meet the requirements of that expected future. Grant (2002) pointed the important elements in the successful strategic management (see Figure 6.2) where clear goals, understanding the competitive environment, resource appraisal and effective implementation form the basis of the general analysis.

Figure 6.2
Elements of Successful Strategies

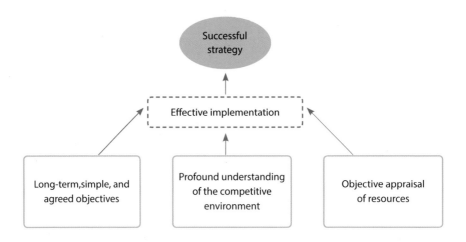

Source: Adapted from Grant, 2002

Strategic and Operational Planning Process

As an innovative approach, SHRM requires that agencies engage in strategic human capital planning and support an agency's strategic plan. Such process may include the following:

- A rational process that enables public organizations to guide their future activities and the use of their available resources

- Establish goals and objectives for the future
- Identify the means and resources to be used in achieving them
- Set the criteria that will be used to evaluate outcomes or results

However, in the public sector organizations there is a need to engage in a more detailed and objective strategic management in the conduct of the affairs of the organization. Strategic management is considered a continuous activity, undertaken by the upper echelon of the organization that requires constant adjustment of three major interdependent poles: the values of senior management, the environment, and the resources available (see Figure 6.1). Strategic management emphasizes the necessity to monitor and evaluate environmental opportunities and threats in the light of an organization's strengths and weaknesses. Hence, any changes in the environment and the internal and external resources must be monitored closely so that the goals pursued can, if necessary, be adjusted. The goals should be flexible and open to amendment, subject to the demands and constraints of the environment and what takes place in the status of the resources.

Figure 6.3
Strategic Management Model

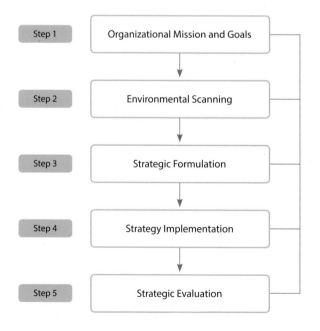

Step 1	Organizational Mission and Goals
Step 2	Environmental Scanning
Step 3	Strategic Formulation
Step 4	Strategy Implementation
Step 5	Strategic Evaluation

Source: Adapted from Bratton, 2005

Strategic Human Capital (Work Force) **Planning**

The strategic Human Capital (Work Force) Planning is one of the most critical components of HRM. It's the process whereby it provides a venue in analyzing and identifying the need for and availability of HR to meet the organization's objectives, planning and job design, hiring (recruitment and selection) and retention, training and development, performance evaluation; recognition and reward; compensations, communication, succession management (forecasting) and planning—assess past trends, evaluate the present situation, and project future events, retirement; employee allocation— internal and external supply of qualified candidates.

The Five-Step Workforce Planning Model

- Step 1: Include HR in strategic plans
- Step 2: Define HR requirements
- Step 3: Developing action plan for implementing HR strategies
- Step 4: Evaluate progress
- Step 5: Manage the change process

Figure 6.4 shows the U.S. Federal Workforce Planning Model starting from (a) setting strategic direction, (b) checking on the supply, demand, and discrepancies in terms of organizational workforce conditions, (c) developing action plan, (d) implementing the action plan, and (e) monitoring, evaluating, and revising whatever aspects that needs to be improved.

Figure 6.4
Federal Workforce Planning Model

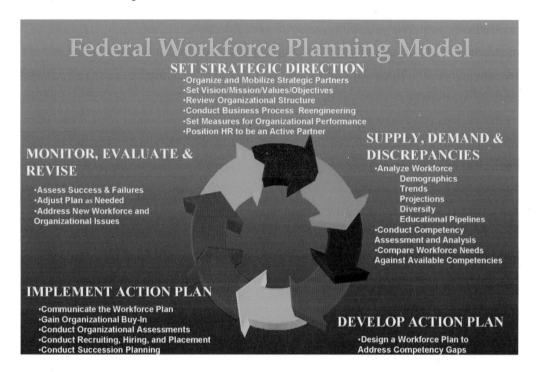

Various studies have argued that human resource is the most important organizational resource; while its effective management is the most critical organizational managerial focus in order to improve performance and productivity. In the United States, for example, the federal government urged all its agencies to encourage capable applicants, retain highly productive employees, and continuously foster employee engagement, and implement sustainable training and development in order to enhance employee capacity and competency. As pronounced by the U.S. General Accounting Office (1999), "Leading performance-based organizations understand that effectively managing the organization's employees – or human capital – is essential to achieve results" (Brewer & Selden 2000).

Issues in SHRM

- Can identify goals and missions in your organizations?
- Can develop both (1) an agency strategic plan and (2)a strategic human capital plan?
- Top-down or Bottom up?
- What barriers might there be to successful implementation of SHRM?
- Who will be responsible for the implementation? Who will evaluate and adjust the planning process?

Problems and Implications of SHRM

- Lack of flexibilities, capabilities, and skills necessary to move HRM to a more proactive role
- Privatization or outsourcing?
- The Problems of coordination and communication; reluctance to change
- Leadership and organizational culture
- Financial cost and political realities
- Maintain the partnership with managers and employees
- Establish a HR planning task force team
- Identify and analyze workforce competencies (strengths and weaknesses)

Succession Planning

Succession planning is the process of planning for the development and placement of people in senior executive positions. It deals with the art and science of planning for the replacement of top executives when they depart – the culmination of a process to identify leadership talent early and cultivate it through training, action learning, mentoring, job rotation, and high potential development programs. It is a process sustained by performance evaluation systems that track and evaluate senior leaders to prepare agencies to fill vacancies when they occur. As Figure 6.5 makes clear, the goal of succession planning is to establish, maintain and nurture the entire pipeline of leadership talent.

Figure 6.5
Goal of Succession Planning

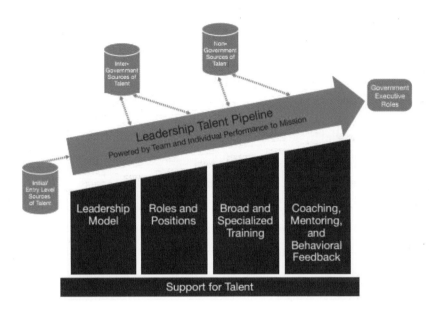

Source: Adapted from Bratton, 2005

The concept of succession planning has long been a subject of study in the private sector, but not in the public sector. Of some 130 studies of succession planning conducted between 1980 and 1993, only five involved the public sector. Nonetheless, succession planning is increasingly discussed in the public sector, and the dangers of not having adequate succession plans and mechanisms in place are becoming more obvious. Succession planning is the means by which an organization prepares for and replaces managers, executives and other key employees who leave their positions, and is critically important to the organization's continued and future success. It includes processes such as how the organization identifies and recruits successors, how it manages transitions from one executive to another and how it develops successors. Succession planning can also involve identifying "high potential" employees and including them in special training and development for future management roles. The practice of succession planning is key to sustaining an organization's initiatives and performance and to ensuring it meets its mission even in the face of turnover. Succession planning in the private sector has been more formalized than in the public sector, which has begun to look at it systematically only recently. Similarly, there has been a lack of focus on succession planning in nonprofits, although the need there is just as pressing. One study examined the effects of turnover in the federal government's Senior Executive Service (SES) and noted: "The loss of experienced executives without adequate replacements can have a substantial, immediate negative effect on an organization."

In addition, labor market conditions over the last several years have combined with demographic and social trends to increase the competition for talent between the public and private sectors. This has led many public agencies to reexamine their approach to managing talent and to consider adopting strategies similar to those of the private sector for attracting and retaining it. While some of these efforts have succeeded, challenges specific to the public sector have made implementing these programs difficult.

A recent literature search shows that while articles on succession in the private sector continue to proliferate, there continues to be a lack of strong public and nonprofit sector models. While there was a sharp increase in the literature beginning in 1980, a lack of successful, proven strategies remained. Ambiguity about the results of many successions and succession planning methods still existed. Further exploration was necessary to determine the factors and strategies in successful transitions. Most of the studies had focused on the origin of the successor (internal or external) and the consequences of the succession (market response, fiscal performance and so on). They concluded that this period was only the beginning of a comprehensive study of succession planning. Schall (1997) echoed their lament about the lack of literature, particularly in the public sector. She noted that serious study of succession planning in the public sector began in 1992 with a National Academy of Public Administration study in response to an anticipated turnover crisis in the SES. Since then, she said, most literature had focused on the transition of the chief executive officer. Finally, she noted an overall lack of focus on successful transition at the agency level, and suggested this was an area for future research.

Case Brief

Smoky Bear is an Underfill

An "underfill" occurs when an employee who is classified at a lower grade is moved up to fill a position at a higher level. One can understand this action if it happens occasionally under management's prerogative of
"other duties as assigned," but there's something awry when an employee is permanently placed in a higher position with accompanying duties and responsibilities without the pay that goes along with that position.
That's just bad planning and wrong thinking by management.

Background

Dough Randall began work with the U.S. Forest Service (USFS) right out of high school as a firefighter in Shasta-Trinity National Forest in Northern California in 1987. Over the next fifteen years, Dough received outstanding performance evaluations and steadily advanced upward, even though the agency began reduction-in-force in the late 1990's. By 2002, Dough held the position of forestry technician (GS-7) and was transferred to the Park Falls/Medford District of Chequamegon-Nicolet National Forest (CNNF) in Wisconsin.

The major responsibilities of the forestry technician position at a GS-7 level are to:

1. Plan and manage the recreation sites and activities on the north end of the district.
2. Serve as coordinator on all equal access issues on the district, with overall CNNF access responsibilities.
3. Serve as primary supervisor for eight Soil Conservation and Senior Executive Program (SCSEP) employees and one seasonal employee.

4. Provide operational coordination in planning and budget.

5. Provide long-range planning and design or recreational facilities.

6. Complete National Environmental Protection Advocates (NEPA) work related recreational improvements.

7. Oversee successful operation and maintenance of recreation facilities on Park Falls area.

8. Supervise Human Resource programs as they relate to recreational facilities.

Dough's performance throughout 2002-04 was consistently rated by his supervisors as outstanding. One tongue-in-cheek narrative of his toilet design literally "gushed over":

Many examples of significant achievements" Restoration of campgrounds, trail clearing and step construction, vegetative mgmt., bathroom construction, concrete work...all very well done, and certainly a success story. On another note, Dough showed me his latest toilet designs...I was flushed with enthusiasm after being in one. His newest has LEXAN clear roof... it's like being in a *House and Gardens* atrium...light, spacious, friendly, spiritually renewing. Dough is clearly a riser in this subject and is pumped with enthusiasm. Don't raise a big stink about the costs of toilets...Dough's much cheaper designs are definitely worth considering. The combination of using WCC senior citizen volunteers, community service crews, home grown timbers sawn from hazard trees, Lexan clear roofs to view the sky, birds and the tress along with a very attractive and functional modern designs are all contributing to this outstanding step forward in the contemporary toilet movement.

Reorganizing the National Forest

Sometimes the "human side" of human resource planning is lost in the rhetoric of downsizing, reorganizing, and reinvention. "Doing more with less" is conveyed as an abstract principle that sometimes is seemingly unconnected to work performed by real people in the field. In June 2001, a part of the Forest Service initiative to reinvent and redefine its mission, the Chequamegon-Nicolet National Forest (CNNF) carried out a series of reorganization moves. The CNNF plan called for the Medford and park Falls ranger districts to be merged into a single district and the workforce downsized by more than 30% in three years. This was accomplished and meanwhile, the recreation program grew significantly, with visitor-use rates increasing by more than 50% in many areas. In staffing terms, this translated into a majority of recreation work previously accomplished by a forester (GS-9), an outdoor recreation planner ((GS-11), and a forest landscape architect (GS-11) that would henceforth be reassigned to Dough Randall, a GS-7 forest technician.

Dough's position description was updated to reflect his reassigned duties. The subsequent job evaluation rated the position at the GS-9 grade. However, this rating did not coincide with the forest's reorganization plans, which reflected national priorities to "do more with less." The forest had only allocated funds for a forest technician at the GS-8 level. Accordingly, Dough agreed to a management compromise—his duties would be reduced to reflect those of a GS-8 rather than higher duties of a GS-9. Accordingly, Dough was reclassified to a GS-8 grade on August 20, 2002.

Dough notified his supervisor Donna Mackey on August 28 that the following duties should be reduced in their level of expected responsibilities:

1. Long-range planning and design of recreational facilities
2. Setting of budgetary priorities
3. NEPA participation
4. Interpretive services

Not only did responsibilities need downsizing, so did performance elements by which Dough's performance would ultimately be evaluated. After all, Dough reasoned, how could management evaluate him against responsibilities that were inaccurately stated? Dough grew increasingly frustrated as management dragged its feet; no changes were made to his performance elements, nor were any of his position responsibilities ever reduced to the GS-8 level. During the same period, Dough's level of work activity actually increased:

> *I have developed community service crews for accomplishment of range goals, been involved in the interpretive plan for the Round Lake Dam, contributed professional input on Forest projects such as Lost Lake Campground, created new designs of toilets, modified and updated the Forest transition plan, assisted others in fishing pier design, created new cooperative agreements and assumed budget responsibility for community service crews, developed rehabilitation plans for Sailor Lake, and been active in the District budgeting process.*

> *None of this should be constructed to mean that I'm unhappy with my work situation, my learning opportunities from management, etc. I'm just requesting that my position description be reexamined, and my grade be established at the proper level.*

Finally, HR specialists in the Milwaukee office agreed to conduct another job evaluation of Dog's position in March 2004. The result was that the forest technician position filled by incumbent Randal recommended to be classified as a GS-9.

Interestingly, the job evaluation report stressed that the primary difference between the work currently performed by Doug Randal and the official GS-8 position description was in Factor 1, "Knowledge Required by the Position." In essence, a GS-9 standard requires incumbent to exercise "broad recreational responsibilities" with knowledge used to "design, coordinate, and execute complete conventional projects" that are "well-precedented in scientific literature and exercise of judgment based on critical analysis and evaluation of project objectives." By comparison, a GS-8 standard does not require that "critical analysis and evaluation" be solely performed by the incumbent. Rather, this knowledge resides in the incumbent's supervisor, who is graded at a higher level. However, the job evaluation confirmed that Doug Randall had regularly used broad discretion in performing the duties of a forest technician during 2001-04.

Clearly, management had two options: (1) remove the work from the position performed by Dough or (2) it could noncompetitively promote Dough to a GS-9 level and presumably pay him for at the GS-9 level for the last three years. With the former option, one can reasonably question whether it would be fair or appropriate to remove work, considering that those duties have been performed for several years.

Finally, on April 29, 2004, Robert Heinny, district ranger, informed Dough by memo that management had made a decision regarding his requested upgrade: Dough would be retained in his current GS-8 forestry technician position, and Doug's supervisor must perform the GS-9 work identified in the desk audit. "This place us in line with the long-term organization plan," Heinny reasoned, and noted, "We plan to recognize you for your extra efforts this past year." Off the record, Heinny let it be known that promoting Dough could "cause resentment from other employees." Doug was dumb-founded, "How does one take back knowledge that I already have?" It seemed illogical to ask to Dough's already overworked supervisor to perform additional duties that Doug had quite capably performed for three years. Dough knew management would not recognize his work as a GS-9 because it was not in the reorganization plan.

1. How can human resources planning prevent long-term underfills?

2. Is it really possible to do more with less in reorganizing?

3. How would you recommend that Doug and the district ranger resolve their dispute regarding Doug's job duties?

This case was adopted from: Reeves, T. Z. (2006).Cases in public human resource management. Thomson Wadsworth.

Student Activity:

Following the steps in the case analysis table, identify the critical factors that may affect the adoption or implementation of a succession planning. You may start on looking at the possible issues such as the availability organizational mechanisms that may foster successful succession planning (e.g., HRD strategies), individual characteristics such as the willingness of the employees to learn and the transfer of skills, and among others. Analyze and identify best practices on succession planning that may be adopted for the public sector organizations.

Case Analysis

	Step	Contents		
1	Environments/ Conditions/ Backgrounds	Please explain the situation briefly. (1-2 pages)		
2	Problem Definitions	In your own perspective, please be as specific as possible when pointing out the problem. (2-3 pages)		
3	Actual Case Studies	Please explain by providing specific examples. (Newspaper articles, news clips, or interviews) (2-3 pages)		
4	Alternatives	Possible Alternative(s)	Pros in your Country Context	Cons in a your Country Context
		①		
		②		
		③		
		Please propose more than three policy alternatives. (2-3 pages)		
5	The Best Solutions	Why did you choose this alternative as the best solution? What are the expected effects and potential contribution? (2 pages)		

1. What do you think is the emerging recruitment and selection "best strategies and practices" emerging across the world? What can be the primary challenges for HR managers for adopting these new strategies and techniques?

2. Do you agree with his argument that we need to change pay and staffing systems as two keystones of success in improving public-sector performance?

Research Digest

Human Resource Practices in State Government: Findings from a National Survey

Facts

This article tries to identify emerging trends and innovations in state personnel systems. Specially, it provides a national comparison in the areas of personnel authority, workforce planning, selection, classification, and performance management. Many state civil service systems have been attacked as rigid, regressive, rule bound, and cumbersome like federal government. In response to these criticisms, in the name of performance and efficiency, various personnel reforms have prevailed through state governments. Most proposals for reforming state civil service systems fit into three broad categories:

1. Reducing the size and scope of the civil service by making it easier to dismiss employees
2. Creating flexibilities within existing civil service system to improve a manger's discretion
3. Abolishing civil service entirely

This survey research addresses the trends and innovations in public personnel systems; the analysis is based on the Government Performance Project (GPP) done by Syracuse University in 1998 and observes what 49 states are currently doing in 5 areas using quantitative and qualitative data.

Findings
1. Personnel authority: asked states to describe the extent to which classification, recruiting, testing, hiring, and performance appraisal procedures were centralized or decentralized.
   - Responses vary from completely centralized to completely decentralized across the key personnel functions; indicating that southern states are significantly more likely to decentralize classification, recruiting, testing than other states. Ex) Nevada v. South Carolina

2. Workforce Planning: a strategy and set of procedures by which the state's future personnel needs are assessed and preparation for HR objectives; without this knowledge, agencies will not maintain a highly productive workforce.
   - The majority of states do little to no formal workforce planning and only five states have implemented a comprehensive plan; WP is lagging behind SP Ex) Illinois and New Jersey

3. Selection Process: most states recognize that their selection systems have to change to meet the demands of the changing labor market; many states have responded by decentralizing the hiring process ex) certified list, using bands of qualified applicants, minimum qualifications rather than ranking scores
   - Kansas' skill-matching programs; Missouri's automated application system; Utah's HR enterprise system-matching applicants' skills with position qualifications

automatically
- Pass/fail examinations in Connecticut, walk in testing in Ohio and Wisconsin, applying online in CA, FL , and signing bonuses in Colorado
- Many states perceive to improve the selection process by granting managers more latitude and adopting technologies and practices that expedite the hiring process.

4. Classification Systems: In an effort to create simplified and more flexible systems, many states have decentralized job classification, adopted broad banding system and reduced the number of job classifications.
- The data indicate that 16 states have delegated some responsibility for classification actions, with 8 of those states delegating all authority to agencies. In Virginia, for example, most classification actions are decentralized to the agencies but the central office still plays a role.
- In total, more than 19 states are considering broad banding and more states are considering broad banding than have actually adopted it. Of the states using broad banding, most started by experimenting in a few agencies before statewide implementation. Minnesota, North Carolina, and Wyoming, for example, concluded that broad banding which give more flexibility to mangers was the answer to streamlining the extensive number of classifications that were malfunctioning.
- Between 1991 and 1998, 30 states reduced the number of job classifications. NY: 7300 to 5075; SC: 2318 to 500; WV: 2000 to 750. cf) GA gain program; with the exception of Georgia, most states are attempting to reduce the number of job classifications by combining, eliminating, or banding classes.

5. Performance Evaluation and Reward Systems
- Critics: these systems have been criticized as being meaningless because of lack of objective appraisal systems, biased ratings; focusing on receiving pay increase rather than improving performance
- Recent innovations include developing performance management system (PMS) that support a performance-driven culture. This approach assumes that by aligning individual and team objectives with agency goals, employees at all levels will have greater ownership of the agency's goals; i.e.) agency and employees' benefits
- Use of performance tools by sates: monetary and non-monetary

Conclusion

- Major findings from this research indicate that various changes are occurring in state civil service systems, i.e., toward a more flexible and varied structure. A number of states are trying to revamp their classifications system by streamlining the process, reducing the number of titles, or adopting broad banding systems. Similarly, several states are adopting performance management systems that link agency and individual goals and subsequently reward high performance. Currently, there is relatively little effort being put into workforce planning, although it does appear to be an agenda item for some states.

- The state personnel system of the future will need to consider vertical and horizontal fit.

    - Vertical fit: alignment of state HRM with strategic planning and management of state government; and

    - Horizontal fit: focus on the extent to which the human resource practices fit together

- In the future, central offices are likely to focus less on micro issues of human resource and more on macro issues, such as change management, employee development and training, managerial consultation, and leadership development.

Further Readings

- Berman, E. M., Bowman, J. S., West, J. P., & Van Wart, M. R. (Ed.) (2012). *Human Resource Management in Public Service: Paradoxes, Processes, and Problems.* Fourth Edition. Sage Publications.
- Lynn, D. B. (2001). Succession Management Strategies in Public Sector Organizations Building Leadership Capital. *Review of Public Personnel Administration*, 21(2), 114-132.
- Pynes, J. E. (2004). The implementation of workforce and succession planning in the public sector. *Public Personnel Management*, 33(4), 389-404.
- Wise, L. R. (2002). Public management reform: Competing drivers of change. *Public Administration Review*, 62(5), 556-567.
- Mesch, D. J., Perry, J. L., & Wise, L. R. (1995). Bureaucratic and strategic human resource management: An empirical comparison in the federal government. Journal of Public Administration Research and Theory, 5(4), 385-402.

References

Applebaum, E., & Batt, R. (1994). The new American workplace. Ithaca, NY: ILR.

Boxall, P. and Purcell, J. (2008), Strategy and Human Resource Management, 2nd ed., *Palgrave* MacMillan, New York, NY.

Bratton, K. A. (2005). Critical mass theory revisited: The behavior and success of token women in state legislatures. Politics & Gender, 1(01), 97-125.

Brewer, G. A., & Selden, S. C. (2000). Why elephants gallop: Assessing and predicting organizational performance in federal agencies. Journal of public administration research and theory, 10(4), 685-712.

Delaney, J. T., & Huselid, M. A. (1996). The impact of human resource management practices on perceptions of organizational performance. Academy of Management journal, 39(4), 949-969.

Freedman, Lawrence (2013). Strategy. *Oxford University Press*. ISBN 978-0-19-932515-3

Grant, R.M. (2002(. Contemporary Strategic Analysis, 4th Edition, Blackwell, Oxford.

Huang, T.C. (1998). The strategic level of human resource management and organizational performance: an empirical investigation", *Asia Pacific Journal of Human Resources*, Vol. 36 No. 2, pp. 59-72.

Hunter, L. W., & Hitt, L. M. (2000). What makes a high-performance workplace. Evidence from retail bank branches (Working paper), Financial Institutions Center, Wharton School, University of Pennsylvania.

Huselid, M. A. (1995). The impact of human resource management practices on turnover, productivity, and corporate financial performance. Academy of management journal, 38(3), 635-672.

Kalleberg, A. L., & Moody, J. W. (1994). Human resource management and organizational performance. American Behavioral Scientist, 37(7), 948-962.

Kochan, T. A., & Useem, M. (1992). Transforming organizations. New York: Oxford University Press.

Klinger Donald, E., & Nalbandian, J. (2003). Public Personnel Management: Contexts and Strategies. New Jersey.

Neal, A., West, M. A., & Patterson, M. G. (2005). Do organizational climate and competitive strategy moderate the relationship between human resource management and productivity?. Journal of Management, 31(4), 492-512.

Mesch, D. J., Perry, J. L., & Wise, L. R. (1995). Bureaucratic and strategic human resource management: An empirical comparison in the federal government. Journal of Public Administration Research and Theory, 5(4), 385-402.

Pynes, J. E. (2009). Human resources management for public and nonprofit organizations:

A strategic approach. (3rd ed.). San Francisco: Jossey-Bass, Inc.

Reeves, T. Z. (2006).Cases in public human resource management. Thomson Wadsworth.

Schall, E. (1997). Public-sector succession: A strategic approach to sustaining innovation. Public

Administration Review, 4-10.

Salaman, G., Storey, J., & Billsberry, J. (Eds.). (2005). Strategic human resource management: theory and practice. Sage.

Chapter 7

Motivation, Leadership, and Organizational Behavior

Framework

Human Resource Management for Public Organizations: An Essential Guide

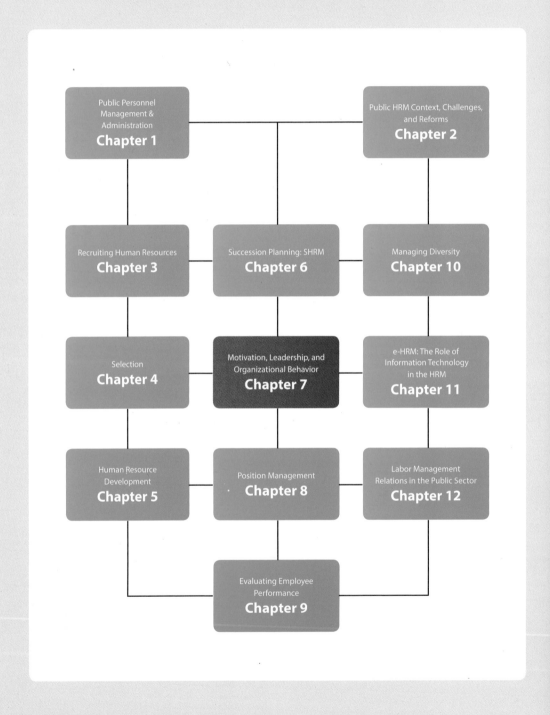

Learning Outcomes

After going through this chapter, you should be able to:

- Define motivation and describe the main approaches to understanding motivation at work
- Understand what is the importance of employee motivation
- Understand how motivation varies given individual characteristics and circumstances
- Discuss determine what are the possible personnel strategies for increasing motivation,
- Identify that influence employee behavior
- Describe outcomes resulting from behavior and tell how they influence future behavior
- State how a supervisor's leadership and expectations for employees can affect their behavior
- Recognize the impact that coworkers and the organization itself have on employee behavior
- Discuss how knowledge, skill, ability, and attitudes influence employee behavior

Preview

Employee motivation has long been a central research topic for scholars and practitioners because of its in enhancing employee job performance. As a result, an abundance of theories and approaches were developed in order to explain the nature of employee motivation either in the public or private sector organization. However, having an effective employee motivation approach has long been one of management's most difficult, important and sensitive challenges for managers (Rainey, 2009). Rainey (2009) concluded that with the abundant topics in management and organizational behavior (OB), there is no conclusive science of motivation that can be derived from theories and research. Public managers have to rely on ideas and available techniques together with the experience, judgment and insights provided by literatures (Rainey, 2009). This is surprising because public management reforms in different countries emphasized the importance of motivating employees to perform at a high level. Thus, implies a degree of managerial competencies on motivating employees. The New Public Management (NPM) paradigm emphasized the importance of performance improvements, initiative, and service orientation characteristics (Pollitt & Bouckaert, 2000; Vigoda-Gadot et al., 2012) to maintain and uplift efficiency and effectiveness of government service. Among other things, the strategic direction of enhancing performance level and advancing a sustainable delivery of valuable public services, management and motivation of employees towards *human capital* must go its way in the public sector organizations. This reiterates that organization's most important resource or asset is the people with their knowledge, skills, and abilities that can drive the organization towards its direction (Rainey, 2009). However, one must also take note that the effects of motivation do not end with performance. Basically, motivated employees commits less work accidents, fewer rates of ethical problems, less employee turnover and lower rates of absenteeism (Jurkiewicz, Massey, & Brown, 1998). Also, motivated employees feel less stress, enjoy their work, and as a result have better physical and mental health (Robison, 2010). Furthermore, motivated employees are more committed to their organizations and show less insubordination and grievance (Jurkiewicz et al., 1998). They are also more creative, innovative, and responsive to customers, thus indirectly contributing to the long-term success of the organization (MANforum, 2009). In short, motivated employees are the greatest asset of any organization.

Along the trend towards *human capital,* public sector agencies recognized the significance of having motivated, engaged, and skilled employees especially in the light of severe cuts to public spending, looming retirement, and public debates over the value of federal employees and their work (MSPB, 2010). Furthermore, understanding the level of employee motivation seemingly was perceived as a sustainable approach for shaping the future of an organization. Given the irrefutable contribution of motivating employees in developing positive work and organizational attitudes among employees, and its capacity on offering public sector organizations a competitive advantage; and better understanding of employee functioning in the public service, there is a need to improve it now more than ever and explore its dimensionalities.

In the public sector organization, managers do face unique challenges in motivating employees (Rainey, 2009). Though public managers may draw lessons and action from existing motivation literatures, the characteristics and context of public sector may render it difficult to maximize motivation initiatives for the employees. Perry and Porter (1982) summarized and suggested a unique context for motivation in public organizations:

- The absence of economic markets for the outputs of public organizations and the consequent diffuseness of incentives and performance indicators in the public sector.
- The multiple, conflicting, and often abstract values that public organizations must pursue.
- The complex, dynamic political and public policy processes by which public organizations operate, which involve many actors, interests, and shifting agendas.
- The external oversight bodies and processes that impose structures, rules, ad procedures on public organizations, including civil service rules governing pay, promotion, and discipline, and rules that affect training and personnel development.
- The external political climate, including public attitudes toward taxes, government, and government employees, which turned sharply negative during the 1970s and 1980s.

Source: Adapted from Rainey, 2009, p. 246

Making Sense of the RealWorld

Public manager's effort to motivate employees may come in different forms. They employ strategies in the nature of intrinsic or extrinsic incentive systems but among them is the use of monetary incentives. However, does money can really give an impact to employees' motivation? Is money the only motivator? To what extent can it influence individual work performance? Though in different context, the use of money as a motivator can be give a relative impact, still its contribution in motivating employees' needs to be established. But how about providing people the sense of autonomy in work? Will it provide a better performance results?

Title	Gist	Source
Dan Pink: The Puzzle of Motivation	Dan Pink presented a strong case against the use of money as a motivator of complex problem solving. He argued on the use of providing autonomy to drive employees to master the skill and good performance in the organizational.	https://www.youtube.com/watch?v=rrkrvAUbU9Y
Dan Pink: Drive—Our Motivations are Unbelievably Interesting	Based on Dan Pink assertions. It illustrates the hidden truths behind what really motivates us at home and in the workplace.	https://www.youtube.com/watch?v=avnHUxSVfVM
Ten Leadership Theories in Five Minutes	There's nothing as practical as a good theory. This is for those who want to learn more	https://www.youtube.com/watch?v=XKUPDUDOBVo

1. Are there stereotypes about motivation of public employees? What are they? Do you think they are true? How have people tried to measure motivation? What difficulties are encountered in measuring?

2. Is motivation the only determinant of an individual's performance? What other factors are important?

3. What is public service motivation? How does Perry define and measure it? Do you consider this an adequate definition and measure?

4. How might civil service reform trends (e.g., at-will employee systems, merit pay systems, and privatization) affect intrinsic motivations such as PSM?

5. In terms of recruitment, selection, and retention, should hiring departments seek out employees with a public service motive, and can it be screened for?

"Winners never quit and quitters never win.
But if you're not a winner, by all means
please quit as quickly as possible!"

The Concept of Motivation

What does motivation mean? Is it an attitude or a behavior, or both (Rainey, 2009)? We are all familiar with the concept; however when asked to give an explicit definition, we start to mumble and have the tendency of providing indeterminate response. In fact, various scholars provide differing definitions of motivation (Kleinginna & Kleinginna, 1981). Also, there are already substantial body of research and theories that explicates the concept of motivation in which scrutinizing will show the complex nature of motivation. For practioners, scholars, and students of public management, motivating employees requires a vivid understanding of the concept before taking any move of motivating employees. Thus, the succeeding discussions will illuminate various features of motivation and the distinct notions on motivating public employees.

Everyone has sense of what does motivation mean. The term is coined from the Latin word for move—*motus* a verb form for *movere*—which basically means to move, stimulate, influence, direct, or excite somebody. Many argue that motivation represents the reasons why people act the way they do, their desires, as well as their needs. Motivation can also be defined as one's direction to behavior or what causes a person to want to repeat a behavior and vice versa (Elliot & Covington, 2001). One of the influential definitions available in the literature is that of Rainey (2009). He defined "work motivation refers to a person's desire to work hard and work well—to the arousal, direction, and persistence of effort in work settings" (Rainey, 2009, p. 248); while various scholars provides an expanded definition into a "set of psychological processes that cause the arousal, direction, and persistence of individual's behavior toward attaining a goal" (Greenberg & Baron, 2008, p. 190; Robbins & Judge, 2008, p. 209). The latter definition highlighted three important elements of motivation: (1) *arousal*—the drive to do something; (2) *direction*—the behavior that is in line with the organizational demand; and (3) *persistence*—the sustainability of the behavior.

There are also other factors that can be gleaned from the definition. It asserts that motivation is an *individual* phenomenon. Meaning, that every individual has unique characteristics—different needs; expectations, values, history, attitudes and goals. Hence, a manager cannot assume that what motivates him will also motivate the employee. And what motivates one employee may not necessarily motivate another.

Denhardt and colleagues (2013, p. 165)) also summarized what motivation *is not.* They stated that *MOTIVATION IS NOT*...

- DIRECTLY OBSERVABLE—It is an internal state or invisible. The behavior or outward expressions of motivation can be observed, however the motivation per se is not.

- THE SAME AS SATISFACTION—As Lawler (1990) posited. "Motivation is influenced by forward-looking perceptions concerning the relationship between performance and rewards, while satisfaction refers to people's feelings about the reward they received" (p. 32). Satisfaction is past oriented while motivation is future oriented (Denhardt et al, 2013).

- ALWAYS CONSCIOUS—Individual do not always know what motivates them in different circumstances. For example, they might act on something out of habit or driven by subconscious needs.

- DIRECTLY CONTROLLABLE—Denhardt et al (2013) pointed out that "Motivation is not something that people do to others; rather it occurs within people's minds and hearts" (p. 165). For example, managers may directly influence the motivation process, but cannot control it (Denhardt et al., 2013).

Measuring Motivation

Various measurement and assessment of motivation has been introduced. They all have tried to measure motivation in different ways that imply varying answers. Rainey (2009) summarized some of the questionnaire items used to measure work motivation.

Table 7.1
Questionnaire Items Used to Measure Work Motivation

1. Job Motivation Scale (Patchen, Pelz, and Allen, 1965)

This questionnaire, one of the few direct measures of job motivation, poses the following questions:

- On most days on your job, how often does time seem to drag for you?
- Some people are completely involved in their job—they are absorbed in it night and day. For other people, their job is simply one of several interests. How involved do you feel in your job?
- How often do you do some extra for your job that isn't really required of you?
- Would you say that you work harder, less hard, or about the same as other people doing your type of work at [name of organization]?

2. Work Motivation Scale (Wright, 2004)

- I put forth my best effort to get the job done regardless of the difficulties
- I am willing to start work early or stay late to finish a job.
- It has been hard for me to get very involved in my current job (reversed)
- I do extra work for my job that isn't really expected of me.
- Time seems to drag while I am on the job (reversed).

3. Intrinsic Motivation (Lawler and Hall, 1970)

Intrinsic motivation refers to the motivating effects of the work itself. Researchers have measured it with items such as these:

- When I do my work well, it gives me a feeling of accomplishment.
- When I perform my job well, it contributes to my personal growth and development.
- I feel a great of sense of personal satisfaction when I do my job well.
- Doing my job well increases my self-esteem.

4. Reward Expectancies (Rainey, 1983)

Some surveys, such as the Federal Employee Attitude Survey, use questions about reward expectations, such as those that follow, to assess reward systems but also as indicators of motivation:
- Producing a high quality of work increases my chances for higher pay.
- Producing a high quality of work increases my chances for a promotion.

5. Peer Evaluation of an Individual's Work Motivation (Guion and Landy, 1972; Landy and Guion, 1970)

For this method of measuring motivation, fellow employees evaluate an individual's work motivation on the following dimensions:
- Team attitude
- Task concentration
- Independence/self-starter
- Organizational identification
- Job curiosity
- Persistence
- Professional identification

Source: Rainey, 2009, p. 249

Intrinsic and Extrinsic Motivation

Motivation, then, is fundamentally an inside job (Bruce & Pepitone, 1998, p.2). It originates from within the individual and causes him/her to be internally stimulated. This type of motivation is called *intrinsic motivation*. Ryan and Deci (2000) consider intrinsic motivation to be the most important and pervasive motivation. Because it is through this kind of natural motivational tendency that humans develop cognitive, social, and physical abilities (p.56). Employing the thesis of self-determination theory (SDT), Ryan and Deci (1985) distinguishes two different types of motivation extrinsic and intrinsic motivation. They characterized intrinsic motivation as doing something that is "inherently interesting or enjoyable" while extrinsic motivation as doing something because there is a condition doing it. Ryan and Deci (2000) defined intrinsic motivation as "the doing of an activity for its inherent satisfactions rather than for some separable consequence." Some author look at intrinsic motivation as the degree in which an individual is "inner-directed, is interested or fascinated with a task, and engages in it for the sake of the task itself" (Utman, 1997). It is also understood as a motivation that comes from within an individual and is often referred to the concepts of spiritual recognition, selflessness or altruism, public service motivation, and prosocial behavior (Park and Word, 2012). Considering the very nature of whistle-blowing as a prosocial behavior, it makes it closer to the intrinsic motivation, which is composed of a sense of altruism and self-interest that reinforces each other to jump into something that promotes ethics or the public's interest (see Mansbridge, 1990).

On the otherhand, extrinsic motivation denotes the performance of a task due to some consideration like pay, reward, recognition, or other tangible benefits (Park and Word, 2012). Following the tenor of SDT, it argued that extrinsic motivation can be classified into controlled and autonomous motivation that is reflected in a continuum. Through an internalization process, a controlled motivation may be developed into an autonomous motivation or a more sense of positive perception, or personal commitment. Thus, this research argues that, the role of extrinsic motivation, may it be in a controlled or autonomous stage may encourage a culture of whistle-blowing, or it may be the other way around.

Frey and Osterloh (2002) distinguish between three forms of intrinsic motivation. In the first, people engage in an activity for its own sake, since they find the activity itself as a source of joy and satisfaction. Examples can be hobbies that one chooses to pursue, or in the work context fulfilling an interesting task. The second form is activities which are tedious and unexciting, but their accomplishment is a source of pleasure. For instance, meeting a deadline at work brings a sense of achievement, albeit the process is sometimes arduous. In the third form of intrinsic motivation it is a matter of compliance with standards for their own sake that propels people to act. These may be ethical standards one feels a need to respect, commitment to group members, or the desire to act according to values of material or procedural fairness. Despite its significance, many a time people act not because they are intrinsically motivated, but rather because external factors prompt them to take action (Ryan & Deci, 2000, p.60). This type of motivation is called extrinsic motivation and it concerns whenever an activity is done in order to attain an outcome that is separable from the activity itself. In a career context, extrinsic motivation means the desire to satisfy needs or goals that are not related to the work itself. For example, work as a mere tool for earning money.

Public Service Motivation (PSM)

Public service motivation (PSM) is a well-established concept that was developed in the U.S. and make known in the organizational behavior and psychological literatures. The idea of PSM revived the essence of public service ethic and public duty (Perry and Wise, 1990); thus is somewhat reflective of an intrinsic work motivation in the public sector (Perry & Hondeghem, 2008; Park & Word, 2012). As Perry and Wise (1990) put it, "public service motivation may be understood as an individual's predisposition to respond to motives grounded primarily or uniquely in public institutions and organizations" (p.368). Public service motivation (PSM) is an important public administration concept (Mann, 2006; Perry & Wise, 1990; Pattakos, 2004) because it gives an explanation of an individual's act for the society (Brewer and Selden 1998, Baarspul & Wilderom, 2011). Public service motivation (PSM) is defined as "an individual's predisposition to respond to motives grounded primarily or uniquely in public institutions and organizations"

(Perry & Wise, 1990, p. 368; Perry, 1996, p. 6). That is, motives—rational, norm-based, effective—are psychological deficiencies that an individual feels the drive to dispose of (Perry, 1996). Hence, PSM is characterized by beliefs, values, and attitudes that manifests greater concern on the interest of the organization and the general public (Perry & Wise, 1990; Perry, 1996; Vandenabeele, 2009). PSM has become an important research area in public management, nationally and internationally (Perry & Hondeghem, 2008). Various studies held that PSM infuence positively various organizational factors such assatisfaction (Bright, 2008), and commitment of public employees (Park & Word, 2012), job performance (Alonso & Lewis, 2001), and among others.

As a well established construct, PSM is composed of four (4) dimensions as developed by Perry (1996) based on an exploratory result, a 24-item scale: 1) attraction to policy-making, 2) commitment to public interest, 3) compassion, and 4) self-sacrifice (Perry, 1997; Coursey, Perry, Jeffrey & Littlepage, 2008). The attraction to policy-making focuses on the commitment to political dynamics in order to bring changes and improve delivery services. Commitment to public interest is the inclination of an individual to serve the general public. Compassion is an emotion-based motivation that drives an individual to do good things for others. Lastly, self-sacrifice is the willingness of an individual to disregard personal or self needs to help others and/or the society.

Table 7.2
Public Service Motivation Items by Subscale

Attraction to Policy Making (5 items)
- Politics is a dirty word. (Reversed)
- I respect public officials who can turn a good idea into law.
- Ethical behavior of public officials is as important as competence.
- The give and take of public policy making doesn't appeal to me. (Reversed)
- I don't care much for politicians. (Reversed)

Commitment to the Public Interest (7 items)
- People may talk about the public interest, but they are really concerned only

about their self-interest.(Reversed)

- It is hard for me to get intensely interested in what is going on in my community. (Reversed)
- I unselfishly contribute to my community.
- Meaningful public service is very important to me.
- I would prefer seeing public officials do what is best for the whole community even if it harmed my interests.
- An official's obligation to the public should always come before loyalty to superiors.
- I consider public service my civic duty.

Social Justice (5 items)

- I believe that there are many public causes worth championing.
- I do not believe that government can do much to make society fairer. (Reversed)
- If any group does not share in the prosperity of our society, then we are all worse off.
- I am willing to use every ounce of my energy to make the world a more just place.
- I am not afraid to go to bat for the rights of others even if it means I will be ridiculed.

Civic Duty (7 items)

- When public officials take an oath of office, I believe they accept obligations not expected of other citizens.
- I am willing to go great lengths to fulfill my obligations to my country.
- Public service is one of the highest forms of citizenship.
- I believe everyone has a moral commitment to civic affairs no matter how busy they are.
- I have an obligation to look after those less well off.
- To me, the phrase "duty, honor, and country" stirs deeply felt emotions.

- It is my responsibility to help solve problems arising from interdependencies among people.

Compassion (8 items)
- I am rarely moved by the plight of the underprivileged. (Reversed)
- Most social programs are too vital to do without.
- It is difficult for me to contain my feelings when I see people in distress.
- To me, patriotism includes seeing to the welfare of others.
- I seldom think about the welfare of people whom I don't know personally. (Reversed)
- I am often reminded by daily events about how dependent we are on one another.
- I have little compassion for people in need who are unwilling to take the first step to help themselves. (Reversed)
- There are few public programs that I wholeheartedly support. (Reversed)

Self-Sacrifice (8 items)
- Making a difference in society means more to me than personal achievements.
- I believe in putting duty before self.
- Doing well financially is definitely more important to me than doing good deeds. (Reversed)
- Much of what I do is for a cause bigger than myself.
- Serving citizens would give me a good feeling even if no one paid me for it.
- I feel people should give back to society more than they get from it.
- I am one of those rare people who would risk personal loss to help someone else.
- I am prepared to make enormous sacrifices for the good of society.

Source: Perry, 1996, p. 9-10

Models of Motivation

In an organization, the relationship that is indispensible is that of an employee-employer relationship. Most of the time, such relationship is perceived to exist in an exchange relationship—both parties are expecting a degree of benefit from each other. This relationship can be explained through a psychological relationship. The psychological contract has been used to analyze the changing employment relationship and has been defined as *"an individual's belief regarding the terms and conditions of the reciprocal exchange agreement between the focal person and another party...key issues here include the belief that a promise* is being made and a consideration offered in exchange for it" (Rousseau, 1989). It can be described as the set of expectations held the individual employee which specifies what the individual and the organization expect to give and receive from each other in the course of their working relationship (Sims, 1994). Schein (1980) and Levinson et al (1962) further agreed that psychological contract is a mutual expectations and the exchange relationship between the two parties – employer and employee – were described as the core of the contract.

However, the unilateral or individual level conception of Rousseau will be adopted. Other author's bilateral conception of psychological contract appears to be acceptable. They argued that psychological contract is the perception of both parties to the employment relationship; organization and individual, of the reciprocal promises and obligations implied in that relationship (Guest and Conway, 2002). This definition however, and others focusing on the bilateral relationship, is in its turn problematic because it compares the expectations at different levels (organizational and individual) (Anderson & Schalk, 1998). Hence, this study will dwell on exploring the violation or fulfillment of the contract can occur when an employee perceives a discrepancy or satisfaction between the promises made by the organization – about its obligations – and the actual fulfillment of these promises (Anderson & Schalk, 1998).

As a well-established model, psychological contract is not an isolated, or a detached concept. Previous studies showed that psychological contract is influenced by a whole range of factors, both individual and organizational. The psychological contract itself also has its effect on a range of attitudes and behaviors. Guest and Conway's model of the causes and consequences of the psychological contracts is one of the more inclusive ones. It encompasses both individual and organizational background factors and policy influences as causes for the state of the psychological contracts and also includes attitudinal as well as behavioral consequences.

Various factors may influence the degree to which the organization or the employee that the psychological contract is unbiased. In the context of human resource management, the extent to which the organization-employee relationship can be determined through some HRM interventions such as in the recruitment and selection process (i.e., selection and placement process). A good fit between the organization and employee or value congruence will be expected to carry out increases the odds that satisfying the employees' needs.

Self-determination Theory (SDT)

Self-determination Theory (SDT) is an encompassing theory of motivation that allows the investigation of social and contextual conditions that hastens or obstructs self-motivation and psychological development in the organization (Deci & Ryan, 1985; Ryan & Deci, 2000b). The essential attribute of SDT is the study on intrinsic motivation (Deci, 1972) and the difference between autonomous motivation and controlled motivation (see Figure 1) (Gagne and Deci, 2005). Deci and Gangne argued that autonomous— though autonomy postulates an act drawn from one's own volition, it doesn't mean being independent with others (Deci & Vansteenkiste, 2004)— motivation refers to the intrinsic motivation wherein the actors act on their own volition; being such act is deemed interesting and satisfying (2005). On the other hand, controlled motivation involves 'acting with a sense of pressure, a sense of having to engage in actions' (Gagne and Deci, 2005). Extrinsic motivation has depicted this kind of motivation since doing an act is influenced by an external goal (see Deci, 1972). Ryan and Deci (2004) identified four types of extrinsic motivation which are represented on a continuum: (1) external regulation, at the one end and over (2) introjected regulation and (3) identified regulation to (4) integrated regulation at the other end (see Figure 1). Base on this conceptualization of extrinsic motivation, Ryan and Deci elaborates that external regulation describes a motivation whenever an individual engage in a certain activity if there is reward expected out of it or an act of evasion of a perceived sanction or punishment. Meaning, the removal of a conditional element of reward or evasion of perceived negative sanction, will eventually lead to the disappearance of the motivation, thus no internalization of motivation. In introjected regulation, they described it as taking on regulations on behavior to behavior but not fully accepting such regulations as part of the self. In this instance, there is the internalization of motivation. For identified regulation, individual willfully identify himself with the value of a goal or a regulation, thus motivation is deemed internalized. Lastly, integrated regulation is an extrinsic motivation which is the closest to intrinsic motivation. In here, the individual is not identified with the regulation but are fully assimilated with it.

SDT gives distinction on how it approaches motivation. The rationale behind this is that, the work motivation, e.g., intrinsic and extrinsic motivations affects 'different processes and contrasting organizational results' (Park and Rainey, 2012). In the cognitive evaluation theory (CET), a sub theory of SDT postulates that external factors like tangible rewards or organizational factors such as regulations, autonomy, events, or communication (see Park and Rainey, 2012) tends to undermine intrinsic motivation (Gagne and Deci, 2005). In the same manner, providing choice about aspects of tasks tend to increase autonomy, thus a shift in the perceived locus of causality from external to internal, and subsequently enhance intrinsic motivation (Zuckerman et al., 1978; as cited in Gangne and Deci, 2005).

Figure 7.1
Continuum of Internalization

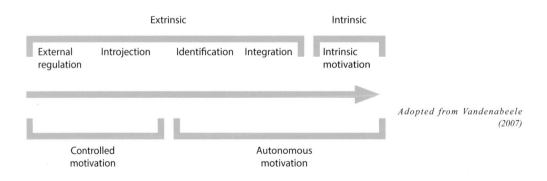

Adopted from Vandenabeele (2007)

Content and Process Theory

One of the most common ways of classifying motivation theories is according to content theories—it answers the question "what motivates the individual?" or dwells on analyzing particular needs, motives, and rewards that may influence motivation (Rainey, 2009; Condrey, 2005, 475); and process theories—it answers question "How one gets motivated?" or focuses more on the psychological processes behind motivation (Rainey, 2009; Condrey, 2005, p. 475).

A. **Content Theories**

Maslow's Hierarchy of Needs—Abraham Maslow (1954) provided the most influential theory that influences most ideas in social science (Rainey, 2009). Maslow depicted the pile of human needs and priorities that start from the bottom (the most basic) up. Maslow suggested that the needs that motivate human behavior can be categorized as follows, moving from bottom to the top of the pyramid.

Figure 7.2
Maslow's Hierarchy of Needs

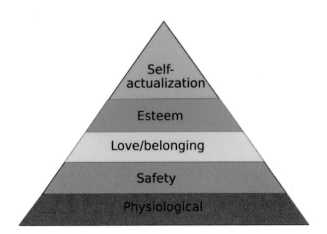

- Physiological Needs – Needs for relief from hunger, thirst, and fatigue and for defense from elements such as food, air, water, and shelter.
- Safety Needs – Needs to be free of the threat of bodily harm such as safety, security, and freedom from danger.
- Love Needs – Need for love, affection, and belonging to social units and groups.
- Esteem Needs – Needs for sense of achievement, confidence, recognition, and prestige.
- Self-Actualization Needs – The need to become everything one is capable of becoming, to achieve self-fulfillment, especially in some are of endeavor or purpose (such as motherhood, artistic creativity, or a profession).

Source: Rainey, 2009, p. 275

Herzberg's Two-Factor Theory—Frederick Herzberg's two-factor theory (1968) suggests that there are two factors that affect individual motivation or the or motivation-hygiene factors (see Figure 7.3). He also suggests that the factors that affect "job satisfaction or motivation are different from the factors that lead to dissatisfaction" (Dendhart et al., 2013, p. 168). He argues that satisfaction of lower-level needs, which he called hygiene or extrinsic factors, does not lead to motivation; it only leads to the absence of dissatisfaction. Only when work the higher order-needs such as interest and enjoyment of the work itself and a sense of growth, achievement, and fulfillment (Rainey, 2009, p. 277).

Figure 7.3
Herzberg's Two-Factor Theory

Hygiene Factors	Motivation Factors
Company policy and administration	Achievement
Supervision	Recognition
Relations with supervisor	The work itself
Working conditions	Responsibility
Salary	Growth
Relations with peers	Advancement
Personal life	
Relations with subordinates	
Status	
Security	

Other Content Theories

- Hackman & Oldham' Job Characteristics Theory
- McClelland's Needs Theory
- McGregor's Theory X and Theory Y

B. Process Theories

Adam's Equity Theory—Equity Theory (Adams, 1963) has been considered as one of the justice theories that explain the relational satisfaction in terms of perceptions of fair/unfair distributions of resources within interpersonal relationships. Adams (1965) gave emphasis on inequity which he defined as, "Inequity exist for person whenever he perceives that the ratio of his outcomes to inputs and the ratio of other's outcomes to other's inputs are unequal. This may happen either (a) when he and other are in a direct relationship or (b) when both are in an exchange relationship with a third party and person compares himself to other" (p. 280). This assertion explicate that employees seeks to sustain an equitable delivery of inputs and outcomes in the job situation.

Inputs in the job refer to the effort or how hard the person works in a particular job, educational level, and qualifications on the job or the inputs are the contributions made by the employee for the organization. Whereas outcome includes pay, fringe benefits, status, and intrinsic interest in the job (Lawler, 1968).

Other Process Theories

- Vroom's Expectancy Theory
- Locke and Latham's Goal-Setting Theory
- Wood and Bandura's Social Learning Theory

Leadership

Leadership is a permanently entrenched part of the socially constructed reality (Meindl et al., 1985; Kuhnert, 2001) and its role in whatever organizational setting is beyond question. Leadership does influence individual behavior and their totality within the organization, and may hinder or influence them to spill the beans of wrongdoings. The shift from the postmodernist paradigm of public organizations follows a changing trend in the leadership theories and approaches like the movement from transformational and servant leadership to group leadership and leadership of organizational culture (Clegg, 1990; Kuhnert, 2001; Holzer and Illiash, 2009). Kuhnert observed that this emerging 'organizational forms need new leadership and leaders who pursue an agenda more consistent with the postmodern principles of non-rationality, de-differentiation, and synthesis' (Kuhnert, 2001). However, coincident with the continuous contextualization of leadership styles, the nature of leadership that is prominent and manifest in the public sector has been an important issue that demands serious attention. The indispensable relationship between politics and administration in the public sector has a unique leadership type that challenges authority and/or dominance in the organization between political leaders and administrative or bureaucratic leaders (Wille, 2009, p. 127). Wille (2009) further characterized political leadership "functions as a sovereign representative of political values and interest, whereas, bureaucrat or administrative leadership represents a subordinate expert adviser and policy executor, concerned about efficiency and not acting from biased, personal or partisan orientations" (p. 127). In the seminal work of Wilson (1999), he described career executives (can be denoted as administrative/ or bureaucratic leaders) as professional line managers and that programs and activities of the federal government depend on their technical and administrative expertise. On the other hand, political executives (can be denoted as political leaders) represent the president, thus they are expected to be committed to the president's agenda and values and/or viewpoints with a limited length of service, and "create an in-and-out system that provides government with new ideas and perspectives" (Wilson, 1999).

Transformational Leadership

Among the leadership development in the modern society is the formulation of tranformational leadership concept (Denhardt, Denhardt, & Aristigueta, 2013). Transformational leadership is a "leadership approach that involves motivating followers to do more than expected, to continuously develop and grow, to increase self-confidence, and to place the interests of the unit or organization before their own; it also invloves charisma, intellectual stimulation, and individual consideration" (Hitt, Miller, Colella, 2011, p. 305). Hitt and colleagues (2011) also provides that transformational leaders do the following things (p. 306):

1. They increase followers' awareness of the importance of pursuing a vision of mission and the strategy required;
2. They encourage followers to place interests of the unit, organization, or larger collective before their own personal interests; and
3. They raise followers' aspirations so that they continuously try to develop and improve themselves while striving for higher levels of accomplishment.

Bass and Avolio (1994) proposed four distinct components of transformational leadership: idealized influence—charismatic role modeling; inspirational motivation—

articulating an evocative vision; intellectual stimulation—leader's ability to increase organization's members focus on problems and to develop creativity or innovative behavior; and individualized consideration—focus on individual strengths through coaching and mentoring. Various scholars argue that these dimensions are interrelated and are important factors that may unfluence norms, values, or changes towards a productive and effective organization (Howell & Avolio, 1993; Jung & Sosik, 2002; Avolio & Bass, 1988). For example, Bass (1985) posited that tranformational leaders often encourages members of the organization to actively work together as team—collective tasks peformance—to foster creativity and innovation in the organization. Transformational leaders articlute clear and appealing organizational vision which is not only beneficial for the organization but also for the employees (Hitt et. Al., 2011). They are more eager to foster and encourage positive organizational outcomes (Avolio & Bass, 1988) such as job performance—cooperative/helping, creative, voice behavior, and effective task performance. Lastly, transformational leadership has long been related with employee behaviors, including task performance and various measures of organizational citizenship behaviors (Podsakoff, MacKenzie, Paine, & Bachrach, 2000). There is increasing evidence that a variety of the relationship between transformational leadership and employee performance (Purvanova, Bono, & Dzieweczynski, 2006).

Transactional Leadership

Transactional Leadership, also known as managerial leadership, focuses on the role of supervision, organization, and group performance; transactional leadership is a style of leadership in which the leader promotes compliance of his/her followers through both rewards and punishments. Unlike transformational leadership, leaders using the transactional approach are not looking to change the future; they are looking to merely keep things the same. Leaders using transactional leadership as a model pay attention to followers' work in order to find faults and deviations. This type of leadership is effective in crisis and emergency situations, as well as for projects that need to be carried out in a specific way.

Directive Leadership

Letting subordinates know what they are expected to do; giving specific guidance; asking subordinates to follow rules and procedures; scheduling and coordinating— tasks: *monitor, plan operations, clarify roles, inform,* delegate; organizational: general management functions (Van Wart, 2005, p. 300)

Engaging Leadership

Engaging leadership is a style of leadership that shows itself in respect for others and concern for their development and well-being; in the ability to unite different groups of stakeholders in developing a joint vision; in supporting a developmental culture; and in delegation of a kind that empowers and develops individuals' potential, coupled with the encouragement of questioning and of thinking which is constructively critical as well as strategic (Alimo-Metcalfe and Alban-Metcalfe, 2008).

Various leadership scholars contends that, leadership development have gone through five stages (see Alban-Metcalfe and Alimo-Metcalfe, 2009). They traced that the traditional conception of leadership started from (1) "trait" theories of the 1930-1950s, (2) behavioral theories of the 1950-1960s, (3) situational and contingency theories of the 1960-1970s, (4) model of distant "heroic leadership" - based on charismatic and transformational leadership (Bass, 1985; House, 1977; Sashkin, 1988; cited in Alimo-Metcalfe, Alban-Metcalfe, Bradley, Mariathasan, and Samele, 2008), and (5) nearby leadership behavior, or engaging leadership (Alimo-Metcalfe and Alban-Metcalfe, 2008).

The Chartered Institute for Personnel Development (CIPD) argue that engaging leadership "emphasizes not on heroism, but on serving and enabling others to display leadership themselves. It is not being an extraordinary person, but rather a somewhat ordinary, vulnerable and humble, or at least a very open, accessible and transparent individual." (2008, p. 11). Like other leadership behaviour such as transformational leadership, engaging leadership encourages teamwork, collaboration, and connectedness, innovations, and creativity (CIPD, 2010).

Among the crucial and important factors that may influence the employees to blow the whistle are leadership (Bhal & Dadhich, 2011; Gundlach et al., 2003; Henik, 2008), work motivation (i.e., public service motivation, extrinsic-oriented motivation), issues that is unique on whistle-blowing (i.e., perceived organizational support, job security, complaint success, job security), and organizational equity factors (i.e., procedural equity perception). Public sector leadership is characterized by an indispensable relationship between politics and administration (Wille, 2009, p. 127) and wherein leadership is in dichotomy: political and career/bureaucratic leadership. Thus, first, this study seeks to ascertain the effects they may lodge on the whistle-blowing behavior through a mediator, intrinsic motivation and extrinsic motivation. This is in contrast with the previous researches that moved from the exploration of mainstream leadership styles and its relationship with whistle-blowing, for example ethical leadership (see Bhal and Dadhich, 2011) and transformational leadership (see Caillier, 2013).

Some Leadership Theories

- Traits Theories
- The Ohio State Leadership Studies
- The Blake and Mouton Managerial Grid
- Fiedler's Contingency Theory of Leadership
- The Path Goal Theory of Leadership
- The Vroom-Yetton Normative Model
- Life-Cycle Theory
- Attribution Models
- Leader-Member Exchange Theory
- Cognitive Resource Utilization Theory

Case Brief

Where Do We Begin?

Imagine yourself as the newly appointed supervisor of a unit that interviews applicants and processes the paper works for unemployment applications. You have inherited eight employees whose experience varies from 3 months to more than 40 years, each with his or her own strengths and weaknesses:

- *SUSAN* is extremely careful and rarely makes mistakes. She is courteous and professional but takes about twice as long as the average employee to interview an applicant and process the paperwork.

- *MARILYN* is much faster but is quite brusque with clients, sometimes resulting in complaints.

- *MARK's* work is average; he handles an appropriate number of cases and makes few errors. But he has been having open, hostile, and time-consuming conflicts with his coworkers over seemingly small matters such as their fans blowing the papers o his desk and the odor of their lunch wrappings in the wastebaskets.

- *TOM,* the newest employee, is fresh out of college. He is young, energetic, and eager to please but does not always use good judgment in handling clients. Last week, he allowed someone who complained to move ahead in line, rightfully angering the other people who were waiting. Still, he does excellent work and seems willing and ready to learn from his mistakes.

- *SHERI* is an outstanding employee. She is quick, efficient, and professional, and she has excellent "people skills." She seems to be a natural leader among her coworkers, and they often seek her advice on difficult matters. She has been invaluable to you in providing constructive suggestions on how to make the application process work more effectively.

- *RALPH* is the most senior employee. Although he has an excellent record, he is going through a very difficult divorce and is only 1 year away from retirement. He has become increasingly preoccupied with these matters. As result, his work has suffered substantially in terms of both amount and quality.

- *TONI* is the social organizer and spends much of her day planning potlucks and bowling nights, gossiping with coworkers and clients, bringing in balloons and donuts, and playing practical jokes on everyone. Although a little socializing is good, you think that she crosses the line to the point where she spends more time on those activities than on assignee tasks.

- *HAN* hates his job and you in equal measure. He complains constantly to all who will listen. He pins up slogans in his office such as the one this week that says, "Only insecure supervisors refuse to delegate." This followed a meeting in which he presented you with a proposal that he be allowed to work from home and that the others employees could handle all of the interviews. When you told him that such arrangement was not feasible; he accused you of not trusting him. As he walked out of your office, he turned and asked snidely, "Haven't you ever had any supervisory training."

You have just received word from the central office that the geographic area your office serves has doubled and that your office will need to serve the increased numbers of clients with no increase in staff. In addition, the contra office has put you on notice that the error rate in paperwork processing has increas4ed 20% over the past 6 months and that your new goal is to decrease it by 10% per quarter for the next three quarters.

1. How can you motivate yourself and your employees to do their best in terms of serving the public?

2. How can you influence motivation in a way that is positive and constructive for you, your co-workers and employees, the organization, and those you serve?

This case was adopted from: Denhardt, Denhardt, & Aristigueta, 2013, p. 161-162

Student Activity:

But, what really are the crucial factors that may motivate employees in the public sector? Try to consider the following and select eight (ranking them from 1 to 8) important terms that may motivate you in work place (Herzberg, 1968; cited in Denhardt, Denhardt, & Aristigueta, 2013, p.163):

1. A positive working relationship with my boss
2. Good pay

3. Lots of freedom on the job

4. Praise for a job well done

5. Interesting and challenging work

6. People with whom I enjoy working

7. Knowing that there will be consequences for poor performance

8. A clearly written job description

9. Chance for promotion

10. A nice office

11. Personal respect

12. A generous retirement program

13. Performance evaluation

14. Doing important work

15. Time off from work

16. Serving the public and making the community a better place to live

17. Regular hours

18. Knowing "inside" information about what is going on at work

19. Opportunity for leering and growth

Share the results of your ranking in the class. What was on your top list? Can you explain it why? What would be motivating you in your job in the future? Would there be any difference with what motivates you in your current job? Why?

In the case analysis table below, please try to identify a case or an issue that think is the most prevalent in motivating employees in the public sector. Define the problem, what are the environmental conditions surrounding it, the alternative courses of action that can be adapted and best solutions for it. You may discuss the results of your analysis in the class.

HRM in the Public Organizations: An Essential Guide

Case Analysis

	Step	Contents		
1	Environments/ Conditions/ Backgrounds	Please explain the situation briefly. (1-2 pages)		
2	Problem Definitions	In your own perspective, please be as specific as possible when pointing out the problem. (2-3 pages)		
3	Actual Case Studies	Please explain by providing specific examples. (Newspaper articles, news clips, or interviews) (2-3 pages)		
4	Alternatives	Possible Alternative(s)	Pros in your Country Context	Cons in a your Country Context
		①		
		②		
		③		
		Please propose more than three policy alternatives. (2-3 pages)		
5	The Best Solutions	Why did you choose this alternative as the best solution? What are the expected effects and potential contribution? (2 pages)		

1. What are the main research objects, hypotheses, arguments, and findings of the assigned articles? What contribution, if any has the research made to the HRM, OB, and PSM fields? How can the research be improved?

2. What are your PSM? Does it affect your job performance? Do you think there is a relationship between PSM and P-O fit? What do your organizations do to motivate employees? What do you wish your organization would do to become more inclusive?

Ending Credits

Research Digest

Leadership and Public Service Motivation in U.S. Federal Agencies

Facts

One of the important research issues and practical challenges in human resource management and organizational behavior in government is to increase employees' motivation, commitment, and job satisfaction, as well as to decrease turnover intentions, thereby increasing government agencies' performance. Although several researchers (e.g., see Alonso and Lewis 2001; Houston 2000; Naff and Crum 1999; Perry 1996; Perry and Wise 1990) have found significant relationships among variables such as Public Service Motivation (PSM), leadership, organizational commitment, job satisfaction, and performance, there remains a need for more research to assess the linkage between antecedents, mediators, and consequences in public organizations. For example, while many organizational experts (e.g., Tett and Meyer 1993) have argued that job satisfaction is an important antecedent of turnover intentions, researchers have reported little evidence about this relationship in the public sector. This study analyzes organizational leadership and work motivation in federal agencies, and tests the hypotheses that these main predictors and other contingent factors relate to job satisfaction, performance, quality of work, and turnover intentions. First, this article reviews the theory of transformational and transactional leadership, and the theory of public service motivation (PSM). Second, this study probes the dimensions and latent constructs of the two leadership styles—transformation-oriented leadership (TOL) and transaction-oriented leadership (TSOL)—as well as both public service-oriented motivation (PSOM) and extrinsically oriented motivation (EOM) using confirmatory factor analysis (CFA). Third, using multivariate regression and a structural equation model (SEM), we empirically test and measure 1) how and to what extent the specific leadership styles (i.e., TOL and TSOL) and motivation styles (i.e., PSOM and EOM) affect outcome variables directly and indirectly (Hypotheses 1a, 1b, 2a, and 2b); 2) how interaction effects between leadership and motivation influence organizational consequences (Hypotheses 1c, 2c, 2d, and 2e); and 3) how different types of endogenous organizational outcomes are associated with one another in the SEM (Hypothesis 3). Finally, this study suggests research and practical implications for future leadership and motivation research in the public sector. Among this very large sample of federal employees, those who perceived their leader as displaying transformation-oriented leadership (TOL, i.e., leadership that is encouraging, supportive, informative, and that emphasizes high standards) also expressed higher levels of public service-oriented motivation (PSOM) and higher levels of job satisfaction, perceived performance and work quality, and lower turnover intentions. The SEM analysis further indicates that TOL has these effects by way of empowerment and PSOM, and that TSOL (transaction-oriented) leadership shows no such relationships.

Transformational Leadership

Bass and Avolio (1994; 1997) characterized transformational leadership as composed of four unique but interrelated behavioral sub-dimensions: inspirational motivation (communicating an appealing vision, using symbols to focus subordinate effort, and modeling appropriate behaviors), intellectual stimulation (increasing follower awareness of problems and influencing followers to view problems from a new perspective; promoting creativity and innovation), idealized influence (arousing strong follower emotions and identification with the leader), and individualized consideration (providing support, encouragement, and coaching and mentoring to followers). Research has found that leaders who show these four behaviors are able to 'realign their followers' values and norms, promote both personal and organizational changes, and help followers to perform beyond their initial performance expectations specified in the implicit or explicit exchange agreement (e.g., Jung and Avolio 2000, 951; Jung et al. 2003).

Transformational leaders also empower followers and make them less dependent on the leader by delegating significant authority to individuals, developing follower skills and self-confidence, creating self-managed teams, providing direct access to sensitive information, eliminating unnecessary control, and building a strong team and employee empowerment culture (Barling et al. 1996; Bass 1985a). Such leaders provide ideological and cognitive frameworks that connect followers' identities to the collective identity of their organization, thereby increasing followers' intrinsic motivation (rather than just providing extrinsic motivation) to perform their job (Bass 1985b). By providing intellectual stimulation (Bass and Avolio 1997), transformational leadership provides and enhances exploratory thinking and creativity by encouraging critical thinking, rationality, and rethinking of ideas by group members (Sosik, Avolio, and Kahai 1998, 112–113). It stimulates their followers to think about old problems in new ways and encourages them to challenge their own values, traditions, and beliefs (Hater and Bass 1988). It helps to develop follower's commitment to long-term goals, missions, and vision and to shift their focus from short-term objectives to long-term and fundamental solutions and objectives.

Hence, transformational leadership can have a direct relationship with organizational performance, as well as affecting individual and work-group performance through its effects on subordinates' satisfaction with their leader, sense of empowerment, and related responses (Howell and Avolio 1993; Hater and Bass 1988; Podsakoff 1996). It has consistently been linked to a number of positive outcomes across samples and cultures (e.g., Bass 1997; Howell and Avolio 1993), leading some scholars to view transformational leadership as an unbounded, parsimonious, and universal theory (Bass 1997; Bass and Avolio 1994). By articulating an important vision and mission for the organization, transformational leaders increase followers' understanding of the importance and values associated with desired outcomes, get them to perform above and beyond expectations, and provide them with higher levels of intrinsic and altruistic motivation (e.g., public service motivation) to work for collective and community goals rather than to pursue self-interest or extrinsic rewards (Conger and Kanungo 1998; Whittington et al. 2004). However, until now, few studies in government agencies have examined the influence processes that account for the positive relationship between the transformational leader's behavior and public employees' job behaviors.

Transactional Leadership

Transactional leadership behaviors include 1) contingent reward leadership, 2) passive management by exception, and 3) active management by exception (see Bass 1998; Bass and Avolio 1994; 1997). Contingent reward behavior refers to "clarification of the work which is required to obtain rewards and the use of incentives and contingent rewards to influence motivation" (Antonakis and House 2002, 9–11; Yukl 2002). Contingent reward leadership can motivate subordinates, but with less positive impact on motivation than that of transformational leadership (Antonakis and House 2002; Bass and Avolio 1997). Passive management by exception includes use of contingent punishments and other corrective action in response to deviations from performance standards. Active management by exception involves correcting mistakes and enforcing rules and regulations; the leader watches subordinates' misbehaviors and actively provides corrective action to avoid routine mistakes (Bass and Avolio 1990; Yukl 2002). The active and passive management-by-exception styles are similar, but differ in that passive management leaders wait until employees' attitudinal or behavioral deviations happen before intervening. The transactional leadership style appeals to subordinates' self-interest and uses extrinsic reward systems; an exchange relationship between leaders and subordinates provides followers with rewards such as wages and promotions for complying with a leader's wishes and orders. Contingent reward involves rewarding followers for attaining specified performance levels.

In transactional contingent reinforcement (reward or punishment), the individual receives a reward from the leader for successful enactment of the role as agreed upon with the leader. For punishment, the leader corrects, threatens, or disciplines the subordinate for failing to achieve a specific standard of performance. Transactional leadership, in sum, concentrates on task accomplishment, rather than on developing followers. The primary influence process involves "instrumental compliance and contingent sanctioning behavior" (Bass and Avolio 1990; Kohn 1993; Podsakoff, Todor, and Skov 1982, 811–812). Antonakis and House (2002) suggest that leaders should show transformational behaviors most often, then contingent reward leadership, then active management by exception, and then passive management by exception. They argue that this hierarchical leadership framework can be traced from a meta-analysis by Lowe et al. (1996), which confirmed that transformational leadership more strongly affects outcome variables than does transactional leadership.

THEORY OF WORK MOTIVATION IN PUBLIC ORGANIZATIONS

Motivating employees remains a crucial challenge for public managers (Mann 2006, 35). Work motivation can be categorized into two distinct types based on different reward systems within applied organizational settings: intrinsic and extrinsic motivation. Intrinsic motivation refers to "behaviors for which there is no apparent reward except the activity itself " whereas extrinsic motivation refers to "behaviors in which an external controlling variable (such as explicit reward, incentive, or threat) can be readily identified" (Cameron and Pierce 2002, 12).4 Intrinsic and extrinsic motivation can have different relationships with behavioral and attitudinal outcomes. The positive effects of intrinsic motivations have long been recognized; that is, intrinsic motivation can enhance job performance and satisfaction (Herzberg 1968; McGregor 1960). Cognitive evaluation theorists further argue that, in general, extrinsic sources of motivation (e.g., extrinsic reward systems or feedback) can be detrimental to employees' intrinsic and internal motivation, especially when those extrinsic sources are perceived as controlling rather than as informative. (For further discussion of the different cognitive evaluation theory perspectives on motivation, see Cameron, Banko, and Pierce 2001; Eisenberger and Cameron 1996; Deci, Koestner, and Ryan 1999; Deci and Ryan 1985; Ryan and Deci 1996). On the other hand, from a social learning theory perspective, extrinsic incentives such as monetary rewards are supposed to increase the level of self-efficacy and self-motivation (e.g., see Bandura 1986).

Recently, self-determination theory (SDT) has analyzed social-contextual conditions that facilitate or hinder self-motivation within organizations (Ryan and Deci 2000). Deci and Ryan (1985) introduced the self-determination continuum that categorizes motivational states as moving from amotivation, to extrinsic motivation, to self-determined or autonomous motivation. These states relate to the different forms of extrinsic motivation—i.e., external regulation, introjected regulation, identified regulation, and integrated regulation. As an individual moves towards internalizing the external regulations and incentives and integrating them with his or her own values, the person moves toward more autonomous and intrinsic motivation (Ryan and Deci 2000). More autonomy in work provides better conditions for intrinsic motivation. SDT thus proposes that organizational factors such as autonomy in work climates and managerial systems enhance intrinsic motivation, resulting in more positive outcomes (Ryan and Connell 1989). Where individuals have more autonomy as opposed to external regulation, they have more opportunities to derive personal fulfillment and satisfaction from the work itself. Ryan and Deci (2002, 12) add, however, that external influence in the form of positive performance feedback can enhance intrinsic motivation. The results we report below provide an example of such dynamics, since they indicate that transformational leadership (TOL) enhances employee empowerment, and that TOL and empowerment both enhance public service oriented motivation (PSOM), which can be conceived as an intrinsic motivation. In turn, PSOM relates positively to job satisfaction, perceived organizational performance and to a lower level of intent to turnover.

Issues

In federal agencies, are the latent constructs of TOL and TSOL conceptually distinct? In a measurement model, do these two latent variables (i.e., endogenous variables) have a positive causal effect on the relevant observable variables (i.e., exogenous variables)?

In federal agencies, are the latent constructs of PSOM and EOM conceptually separate and distinct? In a measurement model, do these two latent variables (i.e., endogenous variables) have a positive effect on the exogenous variables?

Findings

This analysis of a large survey of federal employees finds beneficial effects when the respondents perceive their leaders as transformation-oriented (TOL)—where the leader informs the respondent, supports her or his development and personal welfare, emphasizes high standards, and helps poor performers improve. The analysis also finds beneficial effects of public service-oriented motivation (PSOM). Both TOL and PSOM show strong positive relations to job satisfaction, and perceived performance and work quality, and negative relations to intent to turnover. Transaction-oriented leadership (TSOL) shows similar beneficial relations with the dependent variables, but weaker ones. Analysis of interactions among the variables indicates support for Bass's (1985) contention that transformational leaders also display transactional leadership behaviors; the interaction of TOL and TSOL enhances positive effects on the dependent variables (with the exception of turnover intent). The interaction of TOL and PSOM also enhances positive results on the dependent variables.

The OLS regression analysis and the structural equation model provide further evidence about relations among the variables and about the roles of empowerment, goal clarity, perceived procedural equity (fairness) and objective (i.e., merit-based and communication enhancing) performance appraisal systems. The SEM, in particular, suggests that TOL relates positively to PSOM and to empowerment (with an additional indirect effect on empowerment through goal clarity). That is, TOL fosters PSOM via empowerment in federal agencies. Our finding about the TOL-empowerment-PSOM relationship is also consistent with the findings of an inverse relationship between red tape and PSM (see Moynihan and Pandey 2007) in that red tape would severely attenuate or eliminate the culture of TOL and empowerment in the public sector. Empowerment relates positively to PSOM, and PSOM relates positively to job satisfaction and to lower turnover intentions; job satisfaction then relates positively to perceived performance and quality of work, and relates to lower turnover intentions. We conceive PSOM as an intrinsic motivation and interpret these results as consistent with the perspective of self-determination theory (SDT), that contends that external regulation can reduce intrinsic satisfaction, and greater autonomy (in the present study, due to TOL, empowerment, procedural fairness, and merit-based, communicative performance appraisals) can increase it. They are also consistent with the conclusion in SDT that external influence in the form of supportive and positive feedback can enhance intrinsic motivation. Moreover, they are consistent with Herzberg's emphasis on autonomy as conducive to "motivators" that are predominantly intrinsic. These observations raise the ongoing theoretical challenge of further developing theory about public service motivation as an intrinsic incentive, and how it relates to leadership behaviors, autonomy, and empowerment. Reliance on an employee attitude survey raises concerns about mono-method bias, positive response bias, and subjective measures of the variables, especially the dependent variables. Countering these concerns is the very large, anonymous nature of the survey, which reduce the likelihood, remote in any case, that federal employees can be cowed or duped into providing invalid positive responses. In this and other surveys, federal employees have responded negatively or critically about important matters. Countering concerns about subjective measures are reports of appreciable correlations between subjective and objective performance measures (e.g., see Brewer 2006, 36–37; Walker and Boyne 2006; Wall et al. 2004). Moreover, the pattern of positive responses about TOL and PSOM were by no means preordained. We need to take seriously the evidence provided here, that many federal employees in the stereotypically constraining federal "bureaucracy" perceive their leaders as transformation-oriented, as conceived here. In response to such leadership, they feel empowered and express public service oriented motivation and these responses relate strongly to positive responses on job satisfaction, perceived performance, and turnover intentions. Federal employees frequently express concerns about their pay and promotion systems (as emphasized in EOM), and they could have more heavily emphasized those concerns as influences on their job satisfaction, on perceived performance and on work quality. More research with different methods and more objective outcome measures will clearly be valuable, but the results reported here provide important evidence to confirm, extend, or refute in further studies.

Practical and policy implications include the value of encouraging and training leaders in the behaviors indicated in the TOL measure used here, and in empowering. The results underscore the value of fair, communicative personnel practices that can enhance and reward PSOM. For decades, reform efforts have emphasized pay for performance, and more recently pay-banding, in spite of mixed or disappointing results of such reforms (Alonso and Lewis 2001; Kellough and Lu 1993; Lewis 1991). As analysts have pointed out (e.g., Lyons, Duxbury, and Higgins 2006, 605; Barzelay 2001) reforms in the New Public Management movement in many nations have often emphasized organizational efficiency and effectiveness based on economic rationales that depict managers and employees as heavily dependent on their narrow material self-interests and seeking "to maximize their personal utility." The pursuit of efficiency and effectiveness should and will continue, as should the pursuit of effective pay and incentive systems. The evidence reported here, however, emphasizes the importance of continuing to develop ways to avoid letting such emphases crowd out concerns with encouraging, recognizing, and rewarding distinctive motives and incentives in the public service— public service motivation (Bright 2005, 151; Houston 2005, 81). The evidence further suggests means to do so, through such approaches as transformational leadership behaviors, communication-enhancing performance appraisal systems, clear goals and missions, and empowerment.

Source: Park, S. M., & Rainey, H. G. (2008). Leadership and public service motivation in US federal agencies. International public management journal, 11(1), 109-142.

Further Readings

- Berman, E. M., Bowman, J. S., West, J. P., & Van Wart, M. R. (Ed.) (2012). *Human Resource Management in Public Service: Paradoxes, Processes, and Problems.* Fourth Edition. Sage Publications.
- Park, S. M., & Rainey, H. G. (2008). Leadership and public service motivation in US federal agencies. International public management journal, 11(1), 109-142.
- Denhardt, R. B., Denhardt, J. V., & Aristigueta, M. P. (2013). Managing human behavior in public and nonprofit organizations. Sage Publications.
- Bright, L. (2007). Does person-organization fit mediate the relationship between public service motivation and the job performance of public employees?. Review of public personnel administration, 27(4), 361-379.
- Locke, E. A., & Latham, G. P. (2002). Building a practically useful theory of goal setting and task motivation: A 35-year odyssey. American psychologist, 57(9), 705.
- Moynihan, D. P., & Pandey, S. K. (2007). The role of organizations in fostering public service motivation. Public administration review, 67(1), 40-53.
- Park, S. M., & Rainey, H. G. (2007). Antecedents, mediators, and consequences of affective, normative, and continuance commitment empirical tests of commitment effects in federal agencies. Review of Public Personnel Administration, 27(3), 197-226.

References

Alban-Metcalfe, J., & Alimo-Metcalfe, B. (2009). Engaging leadership part one: competencies are like Brighton Pier. International Journal of Leadership in Public Services, 5(1), 10-18.

Alimo-Metcalfe, B., Alban-Metcalfe, J., Bradley, M., Mariathasan, J., & Samele, C. (2008). The impact of engaging leadership on performance, attitudes to work and wellbeing at work: A longitudinal study. Journal of health organization and management, 22(6), 586-598.

Alonso, P., & Lewis, G. B. (2001). Public Service Motivation and Job Performance Evidence from the Federal Sector. The American Review of Public Administration, 31(4), 363-380.

Anderson, N., & Schalk, R. (1998). Editorial: The psychological contract in retrospect and prospect. Journal of organizational behavior, 19(637-647).

Baarspul, H. C., & Wilderom, C. P. (2011). Do employees behave differently in public-vs private-sector organizations? A state-of-the-art review. Public management review, 13(7), 967-1002.

Bhal, K. T., & Dadhich, A. (2011). Impact of ethical leadership and leader–member exchange on whistle blowing: The moderating impact of the moral intensity of the issue. Journal of Business Ethics, 103(3), 485-496.

Bass, B. M., & Avolio, B. J. (1994). Transformational leadership and organizational culture. The International Journal of Public Administration, 17(3-4), 541-554.

Brewer, G. A., & Selden, S. C. (1998). Whistle blowers in the federal civil service: New evidence of the public service ethic. Journal of public administration research and theory, 8(3), 413-440.

Caillier, J. G. (2013). Transformational leadership and whistle-blowing attitudes: Is this relationship mediated by organizational commitment and public service motivation. The American Review of Public Administration, 0275074013515299.

Condrey, S. E. (Ed.). (2005). Handbook of Human Resources Management in Government. John Wiley & Sons.

Coursey, D., Brudney, J. L., Littlepage, L., & Perry, J. L. (2011). Does public service motivation matter in volunteering domain choices? A test of functional theory. Review of Public Personnel Administration, 31(1), 48-66.

Deci, E. L. (1972). Intrinsic motivation, extrinsic reinforcement, and inequity. Journal of personality and social psychology, 22(1), 113.

Deci, E. L., & Ryan, R. M. (1985). Intrinsic motivation and self-determination in human behavior. Springer Science & Business Media.

Denhardt, R. B., Denhardt, J. V., & Aristigueta, M. P. (2013). Managing human behavior in public and nonprofit organizations. Sage Publications.

Elliot, A. J., & Covington, M. V. (2001). Approach and avoidance motivation. Educational Psychology Review, 13(2), 73-92.

Frey, B. S., & Osterloh, M. (Eds.). (2002). Successful management by motivation: Balancing intrinsic and extrinsic incentives. Springer Science & Business Media.

Gagné, M., & Deci, E. L. (2005). Self-determination theory and work motivation. Journal of Organizational behavior, 26(4), 331-362.

Guest, D. E., & Conway, N. (2002). Communicating the psychological contract: an employer perspective. Human Resource Management Journal, 12(2), 22-38.

Gundlach, M. J., Douglas, S. C., & Martinko, M. J. (2003). The decision to blow the whistle: A social information processing framework. Academy of Management Review, 28(1), 107-123.

Greenberg, J., & Baron, R. A. (2008). Behavior in organizations.

Herzberg, F. (1968). One more time: How do you motivate employees (pp. 46-57). Boston: Harvard Business Review.

Hitt, M. A., Miller, C. C., & Colella, A. (2009). Organizational behavior--A strategic approach

(2nd ed.). Pennsylvania State University: John Wiley Sons, Inc.

Holzer, M., & Illiash, I. (2009). 8. Russian bureaucracy as an alternative model of leadership. Public Sector Leadership: International Challenges and Perspectives, 145.

Howell, J. M., & Avolio, B. J. (1993). Transformational leadership, transactional leadership, locus of control, and support for innovation: Key predictors of consolidated-business-unit performance. Journal of applied psychology, 78(6), 891.

Jung, D. I., & Sosik, J. J. (2002). Transformational leadership in work groups the role of empowerment, cohesiveness, and collective-efficacy on perceived group performance. Small group research, 33(3), 313-336.

Jurkiewicz, C. L., Massey Jr, T. K., & Brown, R. G. (1998). Motivation in public and private organizations: A comparative study. Public productivity & Management review, 230-250.

Kleinginna Jr, P. R., & Kleinginna, A. M. (1981). A categorized list of emotion definitions, with suggestions for a consensual definition. Motivation and emotion, 5(4), 345-379.

Mansbridge, J. J. (Ed.). (1990). Beyond self-interest. University of Chicago Press.

Mann, G. A. (2006). A motive to serve: Public service motivation in human resource management and the role of PSM in the nonprofit sector. Public Personnel Management, 35(1), 33-48.

Meindl, J. R. (1995). The romance of leadership as a follower-centric theory: A social constructionist approach. The Leadership Quarterly, 6(3), 329-341.

Park, S. M., & Word, J. (2012). Driven to service: Intrinsic and extrinsic motivation for public and nonprofit managers. Public Personnel Management, 41(4), 681-710.

Park, S. M., & Rainey, H. G. (2012). Work motivation and social communication among public managers.

The International Journal of Human Resource Management, 23(13), 2630-2660.

Pattakos, A. N. (2004). The search for meaning in government service. Public Administration Review, 64(1), 106-112.

Perry, J. L., & Porter, L. W. (1982). Factors affecting the context for motivation in public organizations1. Academy of management review, 7(1), 89-98.

Perry, J. L., & Wise, L. R. (1990). The motivational bases of public service. Public administration review, 367-373.

Perry, J. L. (1996). Measuring public service motivation: An assessment of construct reliability and validity. Journal of public administration research and theory, 6(1), 5-22.

Perry, J. L., & Hondeghem, A. (Eds.). (2008). Motivation in public management: The call of public service: The call of public service. Oxford University Press.

Pollitt, C., & Bouckaert, G. (1999). Public Management Reform: A Comparative Analysis: A Comparative Analysis. Oxford university press.

Podsakoff, P. M., MacKenzie, S. B., Paine, J. B., & Bachrach, D. G. (2000). Organizational citizenship behaviors: A critical review of the theoretical and empirical literature and suggestions for future research. Journal of management, 26(3), 513-563.

Purvanova, R. K., Bono, J. E., & Dzieweczynski, J. (2006). Transformational leadership, job characteristics, and organizational citizenship performance. Human performance, 19(1), 1-22.

Rainey, H. G. (2009). Understanding and managing public organizations. John Wiley & Sons.

Ryan, R. M., & Deci, E. L. (2004). Avoiding death or engaging life as accounts of meaning and culture: comment on Pyszczynski et al.(2004).

Ryan, R. M., & Deci, E. L. (2000). Self-determination theory and the facilitation of intrinsic motivation, social development, and well-being. American psychologist, 55(1), 68.

Utman, C. H. (1997). Performance effects of motivational state: A meta-analysis. Personality and Social Psychology Review, 1(2), 170-182.

Van Wart, M. (2005). Dynamics of leadership in public service: Theory and practice. ME Sharpe.

Vandenabeele, W. (2009). The mediating effect of job satisfaction and organizational commitment on self-reported performance: more robust evidence of the PSM—performance relationship. International review of administrative sciences, 75(1), 11-34.

Vigoda-Gadot, E., & Beeri, I. (2012). Change-oriented organizational citizenship behavior in public administration: The power of leadership and the cost of organizational politics. Journal of Public Administration Research and Theory, 22(3), 573-596.

Wille, A. (2009). Political and administrative leadership in a reinvented European Commission. Public Sector Leadership: International Challenges and Perspectives, 125-144.

Position
Management

Framework

Human Resource Management for Public Organizations: An Essential Guide

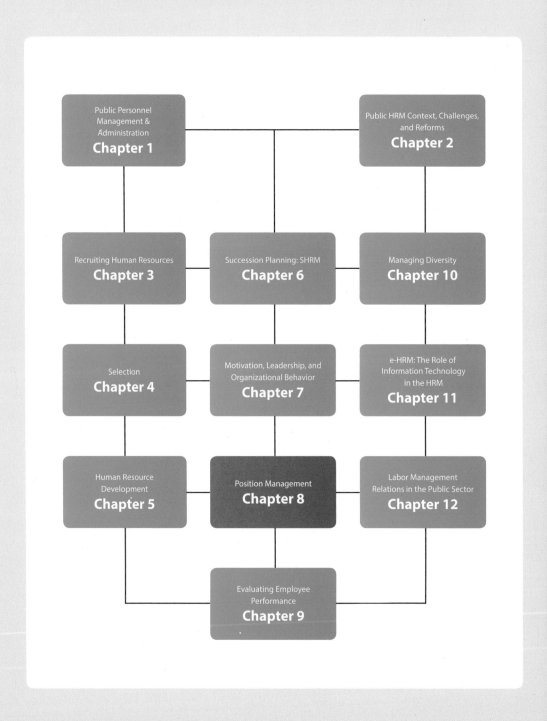

Public Personnel Management & Administration
Chapter 1

Public HRM Context, Challenges, and Reforms
Chapter 2

Recruiting Human Resources
Chapter 3

Succession Planning: SHRM
Chapter 6

Managing Diversity
Chapter 10

Selection
Chapter 4

Motivation, Leadership, and Organizational Behavior
Chapter 7

e-HRM: The Role of Information Technology in the HRM
Chapter 11

Human Resource Development
Chapter 5

Position Management
Chapter 8

Labor Management Relations in the Public Sector
Chapter 12

Evaluating Employee Performance
Chapter 9

Learning Outcomes

After going through this chapter, you should be able to:

- Identify the major concepts that are attached with position management and classification.
- Be able to identify the importance of position management as a human resource management function.
- Determine the prevailing personnel strategies, their differences and degree of importance in the civil service.
- Understand the developmental evolution of position management or classification and how it took its course in the public sector arena.
- Develop background knowledge of position management as it pertains to Human Resources
- Understand broadbanding and its application in the public sector organizations.
- Identify organizational components related to position management
- Summarize organizational gaps and strategic processes to mitigate them
- Learn new trends in the job analysis process.

Preview

Position Management allows a manager (or their designee) to request that an open or budgeted position be routed for review and approval; request a new position or change a position. Position Management activities should happen *prior to* an employee being placed into a position. This ensures that the employee is appropriately compensated, receives the correct benefits, and that the correct department is charged for the position. In most cases, position management activities happen before the recruitment for the position begins, job postings, interviewing, hiring, changes in title or job happens, salary adjustments, promotions, and transfers.

Position Management Coordinates Three (3) Components:

A. *Position*—a Job independent of an Employee, e.g., Administrative Assistant

B. *Person*—an Employee, e.g., Reynald Ugaddan

C. *Job*—the union of Position and Person, e.g., Reynald Ugaddan in the Administrative Assistant position

Position Management is part of important functions of HRM. This is put in place to track positions, do trend analyses and provide information about the work force. It is generally thought to be a dry science of little interest to anyone but a few specialists in human resource departments. Such a notion is full of irony and paradoxes, if not outright misconceptions. In the US Federal Agencies, it was already recognized that the public sector manager must incessantly evaluate organization's ability commitments, to fulfill goals and objectives that constitute the federal agency's mission and purpose. They also declared that "comprehensive evaluation of available resources and capabilities are essential in identifying the organizational changes needed to support strategic business goals" (OPM, 2015). At OPM, they have organizational design and position classification professionals that can assist in reviewing existing resources and processes and creating a foundation for organizational change (OPM, 2015). They also assistance in assessing current management of an organization's positions, and can develop a framework for an effective position management program.

Making Sense of the RealWorld

In a position management analysis, it is important to consider and "review the types, grades, and numbers of positions in comparison with functions and workload; review position descriptions for accuracy and clarity; compute supervisory ratios; and assess career paths, career ladders, and the balance between support positions and those assigned to perform the mission-oriented functions of the organization" (OPM, 2015). We will deliver to you a written analysis of our findings along with recommendations for. With this, it can be able to deliver valuable recommendations for achieving greater efficiency and cost-effectiveness.

Title	Gist	Source
Human Resources, Job Design and Work Measurement	The video clip provides information on the role of Strategic Human Resource Management in the organizational performance.	https://www.youtube.com/watch?v=5uiRSnSJOcE
What is Job Characteristics Theory?	A very thorough and succinct summary of the Hackman & Oldham model.	https://www.youtube.com/watch?v=oxxQuCTVgqY

1. Do you think delegations of authority in the pay and classification areas lead to favoritism and systematic violations of the merit principle by managers?

2. Should public employers be required to negotiate pay rates with employee unions?

3. Would a rank-in-person system work well where you are employed?

"It may be a difficult position to fill. We need to hire a brilliant person who isn't smart enough to know we're underpaying him."

Position Management

Why should a public HR manager be concerned about position management? Position management is the skillful use of people to accomplish the organization's mission while conserving average grade levels and controlling personnel costs. It uses a systematic approach to determine the number of positions needed, the skills and knowledge required, and the grouping and assignment of duties and responsibilities to achieve the maximum efficiency and economy in the work force. It is a significant aspect of each supervisor and manager's personnel management responsibility. Simply put, position management used to describe activities that revolve around establishing, modifying and inactivating positions. In essence, position management can be defined as an approach that ensures careful design of position structures which blends the skills and assignments of employees with the goal of successfully carrying out the programs, goals and mission of an organization (NASA, n.d.).

Sound position management reflects a logical balance between employees needed to carry out the major functions of the organization and those needed to provide adequate support; between professional employees and technicians; between fully trained employees and trainees; and between supervisors and subordinates. But who conducts position management? Each supervisor "conducts" position management every time he or she changes or establishes a position to perform some of the organization's workload. Effective position management results from a conscious effort to organize and assign the work in the most efficient and economical manner. Although position management is a continual process, each department should be audited periodically with an emphasis on overall position management improvement. These audits may be conducted in conjunction with the periodic classification surveys, but can be initiated by management at any time as deemed appropriate.

By using position management wisely, managers can have the privilege of adjusting their own positions and organization structures to meet local conditions. In addition, each supervisor can gain some direct advantages from practicing sound position management. Position management can be improved by applying some established guidelines, using common "symptoms" to locate and diagnose problems, and following tested methods to correct the problems found.

Types of Personnel Strategies

Berman and his colleagues (2013) posited three important types of personnel strategy (see Figure 8.1). The first type pf personnel strategy is election wherein selection is done through democratic process. The public chooses through popular voting those who will make and execute the laws and, and in some instances those who may interpret them as well. Berman et al (2013) postulated that, "the electoral systems emphasize values, debate, political responsiveness, and generalized (rather than expert) knowledge of government" (p. 178). In different contexts, elected officials serve in a given term of office, for example, in the case of the Philippine local government system, an elected official is eligible only for 3 terms with 3 years in each terms in his/her held position—however, after completion of the full 3-year terms and if he/she wishes to have another political start he/she must wait for the next election to start anew. This strategy gives birth to the so-called "political career" in the Philippine political framework.

The second personnel strategy is by appointment made by elected officials. Practically, they serve on the discretion of the appointing authority and at most times, they are temporary in nature and the length of service is co-terminus with the appointing authority's term of office. Such position includes cabinet secretaries that are appointed by the President, assistant secretaries, executive assistants, confidential employees, and policy related advisers and consultants. This is a common practice that displays the spoils system in the government service. Appointment is done as a fulfillment of political promises for the supporters and political accommodation of immediate or distant family members in the civil service. However, this has been criticized and court battles have been lodged against erring political officials in the indiscriminate politicking in the appointment process. This is perceived to be a mockery in the civil service system if such appointment is devoid of merits and qualifications.

The third personnel strategy is rule-based selection. It emphasizes on merit and based on the qualifications and competitive selection of applicants (Berman et al., 2013).

Figure 8.1
Types of Personnel Strategies

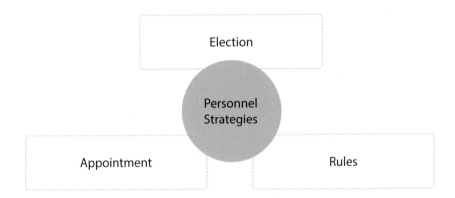

Source: Berman et al., 2013

Position Classification System

Position classification is a means for organizing work into groups and levels (pay grades) on the basis of duties and responsibilities. It is a process for reviewing job duties, classifying positions on the positions to salary grades that reflect their relative worth and market value. Specifically, it is position management process of formally specifying the duties, responsibilities, grade, and level of compensation assigned to a certain position. Historically, the country of origin of position management is the United States. It took its roots in the 17th century wherein the patronage system, social class, and regional representativeness are the predominant system—it is basically elitist and staid and the merit principles were mere coincidental (Berman et al., 2013, p. 181). Legislations that entail the promulgation of position classification was enacted in 1853 and later repealed in 1923. However, the classification was solely based on the salary structure and not on the duties and job responsibilities. In the early 1900s, the scientific management of Frederick Taylor has opened the development of position classification processes which advanced the essentiality of work analysis. In a bid towards merit systems in the federal civil service, the United States federal government enacted Classification Act of 1923 and then was repealed by Classification Act of 1949—which created classes and series of positions. The textbook law mandates that in order for the merit system to be effective, duties and specific qualifications are to be identified in the various groups of positions (Stahl, 1971). Then, in the 1990s, the civil service reform agenda brought influence to the age of new human resource approaches. From this period and until now, innovations on organizational processes, flexibilities, and reforms on personnel policies are the key concepts. Figure 8.2 provide a schematic flow of the evolution of position management.

There are various reasons why managers hate position classification. Naff (2003) pointed some of them such as the following:

- Creates rigid, narrow boundaries between jobs
- Increase structural hierarchy
- Demands centralization and uniformity
- Limits competitive salaries
- Fails to keep up with changing technology
- Impedes employee development
- Creates conflict between mangers and the classifiers

Figure 8.2
Position Management Journey

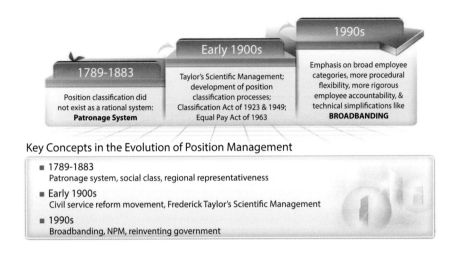

Source: Based from Berman et al., 2013.

There are two fundamental merit strategies that exist (see also Table 8.1 for their differences): rank-in-job approach and rank-in-person approach.

Rank-in-job Approach

This is a traditional position classification system that the criteria for filling a given position, as well as the level of compensation assigned to it are based on the job itself, and not on the person who might fill it (Huddleston, 1987). The position held by the job holder is the basis of rank and salary. It is based on General Schedule (**GS**) system. In case of the United States, the U.S. Office of Personnel Management (OPM) defined GS as, "the broadest subdivision of the classification system covered by title 5. It includes a range of levels of difficulty and responsibility for covered positions from grades GS−1 to GS−15. It is designated by "GS" for supervisory and nonsupervisory positions at all of these grade levels. (Most positions above grade GS−15 are included in the Senior Executive Service (SES) which is outside the General Schedule)" (OPM, 2009, p. 3). The merit selection relies on various grades or levels (Berman et al., 2013). Grade, on the other hand, is "the numerical designation, GS–1 through GS–15, which identifies the range of difficulty and responsibility, and level of qualification requirements of positions included in the General Schedule" (OPM, 2009, p. 4). Figure 8.3 shows an example of a GS—2015 General Schedule of US Federal Employees.

Figure 8.3

2015 General Schedule of US Federal Employees

SALARY TABLE 2015-GS
INCORPORATING THE 1% GENERAL SCHEDULE INCREASE
EFFECTIVE JANUARY 2015

Annual Rates by Grade and Step

Grade	Step 1	Step 2	Step 3	Step 4	Step 5	Step 6	Step 7	Step 8	Step 9	Step 10	WITHIN GRADE AMOUNTS
1	$ 18,161	$ 18,768	$ 19,372	$ 19,973	$ 20,577	$ 20,931	$ 21,528	$ 22,130	$ 22,153	$ 22,712	VARIES
2	20,419	20,905	21,581	22,153	22,403	23,062	23,721	24,380	25,039	25,698	VARIES
3	22,279	23,022	23,765	24,508	25,251	25,994	26,737	27,480	28,223	28,966	743
4	25,011	25,845	26,679	27,513	28,347	29,181	30,015	30,849	31,683	32,517	834
5	27,982	28,915	29,848	30,781	31,714	32,647	33,580	34,513	35,446	36,379	933
6	31,192	32,232	33,272	34,312	35,352	36,392	37,432	38,472	39,512	40,552	1,040
7	34,662	35,817	36,972	38,127	39,282	40,437	41,592	42,747	43,902	45,057	1,155
8	38,387	39,667	40,947	42,227	43,507	44,787	46,067	47,347	48,627	49,907	1,280
9	42,399	43,812	45,225	46,638	48,051	49,464	50,877	52,290	53,703	55,116	1,413
10	46,691	48,247	49,803	51,359	52,915	54,471	56,027	57,583	59,139	60,695	1,556
11	51,298	53,008	54,718	56,428	58,138	59,848	61,558	63,268	64,978	66,688	1,710
12	61,486	63,536	65,586	67,636	69,686	71,736	73,786	75,836	77,886	79,936	2,050
13	73,115	75,552	77,989	80,426	82,863	85,300	87,737	90,174	92,611	95,048	2,437
14	86,399	89,279	92,159	95,039	97,919	100,799	103,679	106,559	109,439	112,319	2,880
15	101,630	105,018	108,406	111,794	115,182	118,570	121,958	125,346	128,734	132,122	3,388

Source: the U.S. Office of Personnel Management (OPM)

Rank-in-person Approach

Pay and organizational status determined by educational backgrounds, administrative qualifications, special abilities, and relevant experiences. This is a system in which the candidate carries with him or her rank, or set of qualification independent of the particular position being performed at a given moment. To illustrate the "rank-in-person" concept, a military officer carries the same rank and level of pay regardless of his or her current position.

Table 8.1
Job vs. Rank Classification

Job (Open) Merit Strategy	Rank (Closed)Merit Strategy
Focus on work: "Job makes the person"	Focus on individual: "Person makes the job"
Entry based on technical qualifications	Entry based on general qualifications and lone term potential
Lateral entry allowed	Lateral entry discouraged or prohibited
Promotions based on open competition in most cases	Promotion based on evaluation by superiors
Grade level maintained as long as performance is satisfactory	Expectation that rank will increase over time; an "up-or-out" philosophy will screen out incumbents
Career development is largely the responsibility of the incumbent	Career development is largely planned by the organization through specified career paths.
Tends to focus on/produce specialists	Tends to focus on/produce generalists

Source: Berman et al., 2013, p. 180

Broadbanding System

Broadband is a pay and classification approach that combines two or more grades into broad pay bands—broader job titles and broader pay ranges. Can move in a more flexible way (horizontally and vertically). Broadbanding involves the combining of multiple salary grades into a few and smaller job and pay "bands" with significantly larger ranges (Milkovich & Newman, 2002). Broadbanding allows the organization to have greater leeway of assigning job (NAPA, 1991). Each band may have a minimum and maximum pay rate but usually does not have a traditional midpoint. It may not be feasible to use a traditional pay range midpoint for control and analysis because the pay range is so broad and encompasses such a wide level of skills. Table 8.2 shows the difference of broadbanding and traditional classification and Figure 8.4 displays the broadbanding framework.

What is the importance of broadbanding? Here are some of the major reasons why various organizations implements broadbanding (NAPA, 2003, p. 5):

- Recruit and retain a quality workforce.
- Create a performance-focused organization where pay is based on performance, not longevity or entitlement.
- Give managers greater authority to manage their workforces (e.g. assigning, paying, assessing performance).
- Simplify an overly complex human resource system.
- Operate in a more business-like manner.
- Emulate the success of other broadband systems.
- Improve organizational effectiveness.
- Provide pay increases to deserving employees.
- Increase the value of management responsibilities.
- Design an HRM system for a new agency created by consolidating six organizations.

Table 8.2
Broadbanding vs. Traditional Classification and Grade Level Example

Classification	Grade	Banding Title	Band Level
Department Director	18	Senior Executive	9
Deputy Director	17	Executive	8
Assistant Director	16	Executive	8
Division Administrator	15	Senior Administrator	7
Lawyer2	14	Senior Advisor	7
Division Administrator 1	14	Senior Administrator	7
Bureau Chief 2	13	Administrator	6
Lawyer 1	12	Advisor	6
Bureau Chief 1	12	Administrator	6

Supervisor 2	11	Supervisor	5
Supervisor 1	10	Supervisor	5
Lead Worker	9	Senior Professional	4
Professional 3	9	Senior Professional	4
Professional 2	8	Professional	3
Specialist 3	8	Senior Specialist	3
Professional 1	7	Professional	3
Technician 4	7	Senior Technician	3
Specialist 2	6	Senior Specialist	3
Technician 3	6	Senior Technician	3
Specialist 1	5	Specialist	2
Administrative Assistant 4	5	Senior Administrative Support	2
Technician 2	5	Technician	2
Administrative Assistant 3	4	Senior Administrative Support	2
Technician 1	4	Technician	2
Clerical Worker 4	4	Senior Administrative Support	2
Administrative Assistant 2	3	Administrative Support	1
Clerical Worker 3	3	Administrative Support	1
Administrative Assistant 1	2	Administrative Support	1
Clerical Worker 2	2	Administrative Support	1
Clerical Worker 1	1	Administrative Support	1

Note: Banding reduces both the number of grade (pay) levels and the number of job titles. Pay ranges for banding are wider than grade levels to accommodate the multiple grade levels that have been incorporated by the band. Banding also accommodates high-level individual contributor positions, such as lawyers, at band levels equivalent to positions that have supervisory responsibilities.

Source: National Academy of Public Administration, Modernizing Federal Classification: An Opportunity for Excellence, Washington D.C.: NAPA, 1991

Figure 8.4
Framework for Broadbanding

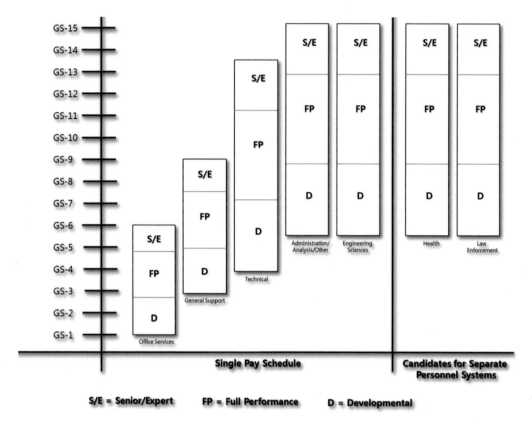

Source: National Academy of Public Administration, Modernizing Federal Classification:
An Opportunity for Excellence, Washington D.C.: NAPA, 1991, p. 45

Exhibit 8.1
Position Rating Summary Sheet and Sample Grade Determination Chart

Position Classification Title:
Assistant Librarian

Factors	Final Rating	Final Points
Physical Environment	1	5
Knowledge, training, and education	5	75

Intellectual skills and effort	5	34
Physical skills and effort	2	20
Experience	4	40
Interactions with others	4	20
Confidentiality	2	10
Occupational risks	1	5
Complexity	3	15
Supervision received	4	30
Supervision given	2	10
Supervision scope	3	20
Judgment and initiative	4	60
Accountability	4	30
Total Points		374

Score Range	Grade
200-224	1
225-249	2
250-274	3
275-299	4
300-324	5
325-349	6
350-374	7
375-399	8
400-424	9
425-449	10

Job Design, Job Analysis, and Position Descriptions

Job design and job analysis are two crucial factors on creating a balanced jobs within the context of ever changing work environment and external challenges in the public sector organizations (Berman et al., 2005). In all organizations—public or private sector organizations—hiring is of primordial importance to the overall organizational productivity. Public sector managers put all efforts on identifying job descriptions in support to HRM functions (i.e., recruitment, selection, orientation, training, work plans, compensation, performance reviews). Job descriptions explain the key responsibilities of the actual position, reporting relationships and work environment.

In developing job description, the first step in writing or rewriting job descriptions—documents the major duties, responsibilities, and organizational relationships of a job—is job analysis. The UIS OPM defines job analysis as "a systematic examination of the tasks performed in a job and the competencies required performing them; a study of what workers do on the job, what competencies are necessary to do it, what resources are used in doing it, and the conditions under which it is done." A job analysis is NOT an evaluation of the person currently performing the job. Job analysis is "a wide variety of systematic procedures for examining, documenting, and drawing inferences about work activities, worker attributes, and work context." (Sackett & Laczo, 2003, p. 21).Job analysis is an in-depth study of a job and it provides all information necessary for a certain job. In the State of Colorado, job analysis is understood to be "a process used to identify the important tasks of a job and the essential competencies an individual should possess to satisfactorily perform the job" (State of Colorado, 2002). It is crucial because it serves as the official record of the classification of the job and is used to make many other personnel decisions. Job analysis involves methods for learning about the tasks involved in doing a job and/or the knowledge, skills, abilities and other characteristics (KSAOs) that a worker needs to have to do the job (or, to do it well), and the context in which a job is performed. From these definitions, you should see that there are two types of job analysis: job-oriented (aka task-oriented or work-oriented) and person-oriented (worker-oriented).

Figure 8.5
Purposes of Job Analysis

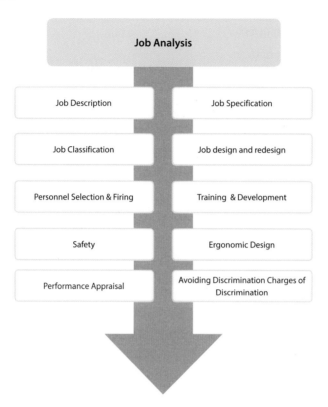

There are two basic formats of job analysis: Narrative or Factor Evaluation System (FES). The former, the narrative format, typically provides statement of major duties and responsibilities, descriptions of the control over the position, and statement of special qualification requirement. On the other hand, FES is a method most used to assign grades to non-supervisory positions in GS occupations. FES is a distinctive way in which descriptions for positions covered by FES standards are written. This format consists of a brief listing of the major duties in terms of the non FES evaluation factors. It matches exactly the way FES classification standards are written. In the U.S. Federal agencies, commonly there are nine FES factors which include:

- Factor 1: Knowledge required by the position
- Factor 2: Supervisory control
- Factor 3: Guidelines (the degree of freedom that is allowed in a position to act and

make decisions of importance)
- Factor 4: Complexity
- Factor 5: Scope and effect
- Factor 6: Personal contacts
- Factor 7: Purpose of contacts
- Factor 8: Physical demands
- Factor 9: Work environment

Exhibit 8.2
Example of a Factor Evaluation System Sheet

Factor Evaluation System
Position Evaluation Statement

Title, Series, and Grade
Organization
Position #
Job Code #

Evaluation Factor	Factor Level	Points Assigned	Comments
Knowledge Required			
Supervisory Controls			
Guidelines			
Complexity			
Scope and Effect			
Personal Contacts			
Purpose of Contacts			
Physical Demands			
Work Environment			

Total Points =

Grade Conversion = GS –

Classification Standards Used:

Source: NIH/OHR/SPB, Reviewed February 2006

The Position Analysis Questionnaire

Position Analysis Questionnaire (PAQ) is "a generic, worker-oriented, structured job analysis questionnaire that could be used in the analysis of most jobs in the labor force" (McCormick & Jeanneret, 1988). This approach focuses on "generalized worker behaviors describing how a job is done."

Table 8.3
Structure of the Position Analysis Questionnaire (PAQ)

Division	Definition	Subdivisions	Example Job Elements
Information Input	Where and How Does the Worker Get the Information Used in the Job?	Sources of job information; Discrimination and perceptual activities	Use of written materials Estimating the speed of moving things
Mediation (mental) processes	What reasoning, decision-making, planning, & information processing activities are used in performing the job?	Decision making and reasoning Information processing Use of stored information	Reasoning in problem solving Encoding/Decoding Using Mathematics
Work Output	What physical activities does the worker perform, and what tools or devices are used?	Use of physical devices Integrative manual activities General body activities. Manipulation/ coordination activities	Use of keyboard devices Handling objects/ materials Climbing Hand-arm manipulation
Interpersonal Activities	What is the nature of contact and with whom?	Communications Interpersonal relationships Personal contact Supervision and coordination	Instruction Serving/catering Personal contact with public customers Level of supervision received

Work situations and job context	In what physical and social contexts is the work performed?	Physical working conditions Psychological and sociological aspects	Low temperature Civic obligations
Miscellaneous		Work schedule, method of pay, and apparel Job demands Responsibility	Irregular hours Specified (controlled) work pace Responsibility for the safety of others

New Trends in Job Analysis

Competency Modeling

A technique popularized in business, designed to identify the "core competencies" that are necessary for a person to be a successful part of an organizations goals. This is similar to job analysis, but it is usually .ore focused on a close connection between the individual competency requirements and the broader goals of the organization. More focused on the things that jobs or occupations within an organization have in common, as opposed to identifying the differences between jobs. More likely to identify broad level descriptors. On the down-side, the broadness of the descriptors sometimes means that competency models for any job sound alike. Especially because there is no clear-cut definition of what is meant by the term "core competency."

Cognitive Task Analysis

An emphasis on finding the actual mental processes or activities used by experts to complete the job. For example, in a task-based analysis of the job pilot, we might have the task "Determine current location." A worker-based analysis might include related skills or abilities: "Knowldege of maps & compasses", "visual acuity", "visualization ability". A Cognitive task analysis would attempt to determine which of many ways to work out current location is being used by expert pilots, and how that would differ from non-experts. Uses techniques and concepts from cognitive psychology. Can be time consuming and expensive.

Job Characteristics Model

Hackman & Oldham' Job Characteristics Theory—Hackman and Oldham (1980) developed a job characteristic model that identifies how jobs can be enriched to help people feel more motivated. The model, as seen in Figure 8.6, suggests that five core job characteristics foster three critical psychological states that, in turn, lead to high internal work motivation.

Figure 8.6
Hackman and Oldham's Job Characteristics Theory

Job Charateristics Model

Core job Charateristics	Critical Psychological States	Outcomes
Skill variety Task identity Task signficance	Meaningfulness	Work motivation
Autonomy	Reponsibility	Growth satisfaction / General satisfaction
Feedback from job	Knowlege of results	Work effectiveness

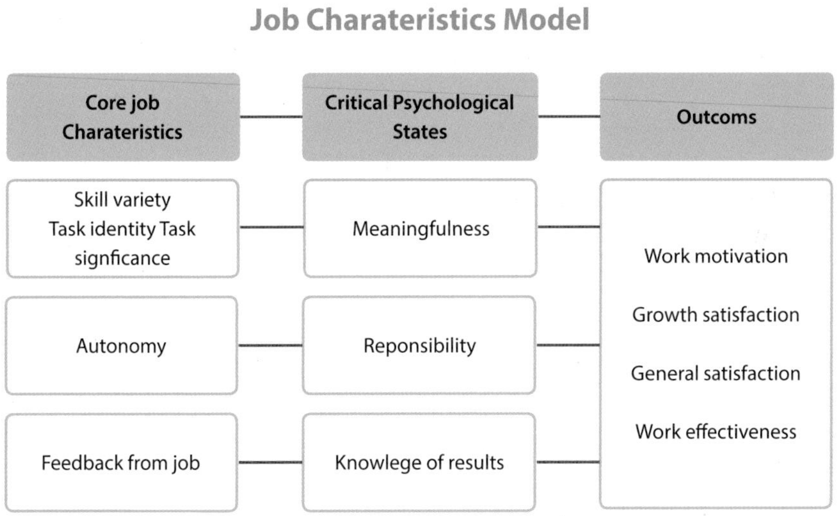

The first three job characteristics are skill variety - the degree to which a job requires the use of a multitude of skills; task identity - the extent to which a task requires that one individual will perform it from beginning to end; and task significance - the level of impact a job has over the lives of people inside and outside the organization. Tasks that fulfill these three criteria contribute substantially to employees' perception of their work as meaningful, important, and valuable.

The fourth job characteristic, *autonomy*, refers to the degree to which employees have freedom, independence, and discretion to plan, schedule, and do their work. According to Hackman and Oldham (ibid. p.79), high level of autonomy nurtures a self-responsibility, since employees then view their work outcomes as directly linked to their own efforts. The last job characteristic is *feedback*, which helps employees understand the results of their work. Therefore, high degree of direct and clear feedback about the effectiveness of ones work can help direct efforts in the right way.

In the past, research has been quite skeptic whether the job characteristic model applies in the public sector (Wright, 2001). Yet, more recent works strongly advocate its practicability as a mean to reduce turnover and absenteeism as well as a way to increase job satisfaction, organizational relatedness, and productivity (Durant et al., 2006). Job design is, therefore, a very lucrative theory for the public manager. But, it has its own limitations – it can only motivate employees who have high growth needs, i.e. they want to be given more tasks and responsibility, and at the same time they have the knowledge and skills to tackle new assignments (Hackman and Oldham, 1980). Though, the lack of competencies can be overcome by proper education and training (Hackman, 1987).

Case Brief

Case #1: Reinventing Civil Service in Georgia

On July 1, 1996, the state of Georgia radically changed its personnel system by ceasing to grant civil service protection to incoming employees. After that date, incoming employees are considered "unclassified," which removes them from the jurisdiction of the State Personnel Board and essentially makes them at-will employees. Eventually, no state employees will be covered by the traditional civil service protections afforded under the State Personnel Board. At least four factors seem to have contributed to the ability of Georgia to pass and uphold such radical legislation:

- Georgia being a right-to-work state
- Gubernatorial success in passing a legislative agenda
- Editorial support from the largest newspapers in the state
- Support from bureaucratic leaders in government

Under the new provisions, employees do not have property interest or tenure rights over their jobs, which mean that supervisors will have more discretion in termination proceedings. In addition, recruiting and selection will be done on an agency-by-agency basis. Even before 1996, some agencies had removed themselves from the civil service system so that 18% of state employees were unclassified. By 1998, the proportion had increased significantly to 33%, and the projections are that by 2006, nearly 90% of the state's employees will be unclassified.

To date, the changes have resulted in no prominent abuses such as political intervention, bureaucratic nepotism, or managerial bullying; nor have they resulted in widespread organizational changes. Observers will watch this case carefully because of the ramifications. Of particular interest will be whether examples of spoils appointments become evident and evidence of how a widespread reduction in force (RIF) will affect a system without bumping rights.

Case #2: Job Design

A moderate-sized division realizes that a series of functions are being performed at too high a level. The assistant director of the division has come to act as the Web master, information technology (IT) troubleshooter, and public relations officer for the division. These additional roles prevent him from focusing on operations, which is his role according to his job description. Rather than creating a second assistant director to handle the regular operational workload, the division wanted to create specialized functions. The division now interacts with the public a great deal though its web page, which needs daily maintenance and updates; this role is not yet considered a full-time job. The division also needs a local IT troubleshooter to fix easy systems problems and to manage software purchases; complex problems can be referred to the organization's IT department. Furthermore, because of the Web presence, the division wants to be more proactive in providing good public relations stories as well as educational messages to the public. At first, the hope was that all these functions could be performed by the same person who would provide excellent job enlargement. However, after with the people in these positions in other organizations, the job analysts found that the array of skills seemed too different, and was concerned that combining them into one job would diminish job specialization too greatly. The division ultimately decided to hire an IT troubleshooter and web master as well as separate public information officer who would take over a number of community outreach responsibilities. The IT-Web master would report to the public information officer, wo would in turn report to the assistant director.

Case #3: Job Analysis

A fire department has requested that the human resource division review two series—the firefighter series and the emergency management technician (EMT) series. When the fire department expanded into firs-responder services in the 1980s, firefighters did not do medical services generally. Personnel were even segregated by vehicles—fire trucks and ambulances. Over time, however, the expectation of new firefighters recruits to be able to perform basic first-responder responsibilities had become routine, and the city could not afford to maintain a large presence exclusively for firefighting when less than 10% of the calls were fire service—most were EMTs, and sizeable portion was for various types of rescue services and hazards materials cleanup. After reviewing existing positions, sending questions to all those affected, conducting focus group interviews, and even performing a number of ride-alongs, the human resource department proposed a new joint firefighter-EMT series. The new series would pay better, but increase the training and job requirements substantially. Hiring would cease in the old series until those classifications had no incumbents, at which time they could be eliminated.

1. If you are the HR manager, how would you approach this problem?

2. What do you think are the most important components of job design?

This case was adopted from: Berman et al., 2005

Student Activity:

Evaluate a position using FES

1. Determine the grade level by assigning a factor level and the corresponding number of point to each of the nine factors in the position description.

2. Convert the total point value of all the factors to a grade using the established FES point conversion chart.

3. Record the results of the evaluation.

Case Analysis

	Step	Contents		
1	Environments/ Conditions/ Backgrounds	Please explain the situation briefly. (1-2 pages)		
2	Problem Definitions	In your own perspective, please be as specific as possible when pointing out the problem. (2-3 pages)		
3	Actual Case Studies	Please explain by providing specific examples. (Newspaper articles, news clips, or interviews) (2-3 pages)		
4	Alternatives	Possible Alternative(s)	Pros in your Country Context	Cons in a your Country Context
		①		
		②		
		③		
		Please propose more than three policy alternatives. (2-3 pages)		
5	The Best Solutions	Why did you choose this alternative as the best solution? What are the expected effects and potential contribution? (2 pages)		

Reviews

1. Would a rank-in-person system work well where you are employed?

2. If you are an employee or a government official, what do you think are the most prevalent issues or challenges in the public sector position management?

3. Ponder on this: You are a manager whose best worker has "topped out"; that is, the employee is at the top step of her pay grade. Furthermore, her job is properly classified. Unfortunately, the government jurisdiction for whom you both work is 20% to 30% below the market in most positions. You know that the person will leave soon if the situation is not altered. You could assign a few people to her to justify a reclassification and pay increase, although it would not make much sense.

4. What do you think is best approach, "generalist" or "specialist"? Like rank-in-person as generalist approach, rank-in-job and broadbanding as specialist?

5. How do you define broadbanding (i.e., broadbanded pay grade structures)? What is the most important/critical lesson for a successful implementation of broadbanding? If you were a HR manager, are you willing to initiate a Broadbanding system in your agency? Why or why not? Can you illustrate specific cases which support your arguments? If necessary, what other reform initiatives should be accompanied by broadbanding?

Ending Credits

Research Digest

Broadbanding Trends in the States

Facts

Recent decades have witnessed dissatisfaction with traditional public human resource practices. Narrow job classifications connected to discrete pay ranges were heralded as innovative when implemented more than a century ago. The system promised transparency in pay scales, equity across workers, equitable pay for comparable work, and an efficient link from job skills to job description to compensation. Solutions create their own problems, however, and critics now claim that this once-innovative system creates too many barriers. For example, because workers are slotted into discrete job descriptions, managers have no flexibility to develop workers beyond the narrow confines of the specific job tasks for which they are hired; constraints on pay grades restrict managers from rewarding top performers or from hiring experienced newcomers at more than the entry level; and the tight link between job and pay provides no means for inserting performance into the equation. For an elaboration of civil service reforms that attempt to overcome these weaknesses, see Hays and Sowa (2006), Battaglio and Condrey (2006), Hays and Kearney (2001), Selden, Ingraham, and Jacobson (2001), and Thompson and LeHew (2000). This article examines one of the more popular strategies that attempt to overcome the shortcomings of traditional classification and compensation schemes.

Broadbanding is a reform that replaces narrow job classifications with large bands. Also known as *paybanding*, it collapses salary grades into wider pay bands, allowing more discretion for managers and simplifying the hiring and promotion process (Hays, 2004; Pynes, 1997). The concept has multiple benefits for both management and worker (see Human Resources Management Panel, 2003a, 2003b, 2003c). Because it simplifies complex, outdated job classifications, it allows managers to promote workers from one job to another without having to go through the formal job reclassification process. It promotes increased job flexibility by putting less emphasis on titles and position hierarchy; facilitates reorganization and job mobility; eliminates status distinctions among team members who are in different pay grades; and creates a performance-focused organization where pay is based on performance, rather than on longevity or rank.

As with so many reforms, however, the difference between theory and practice can be wide. Skeptics cite a laundry list of problems when broadbanding is actually implemented: Work may be shifted from higher- to lower-level positions; it allows management too much discretion and leads to favoritism and pay inequity; it increases the range of tasks that employees may be asked to perform, which can lead to job dissatisfaction, poor performance, and increased stress; and it can be used as an excuse to reduce the number of workers (American Federation of State, County and Municipal Employees, 1997). To reconcile the arguments for and against implementation, we investigated the degree to which broadbanding has been adopted in the states and then queried three states' experiences.

Issue(s)

Determine the extent of broadbanding in state civil service systems and the factors that affect its adoption.

Findings

The purpose of this study was to investigate whether broadbanding works as well in practice as it does in theory. To do this, we surveyed the 50 states and recorded whether they have, or have not, implemented a broadband system. We then selected three states that have implemented it and report the reasons for, and results of, that implementation. It would be an exaggeration to say that the results are mixed. In fact, they are abysmal. Broadbanding has not achieved greater flexibility for managers or more maneuverability for workers. It has not enabled pay for performance.

It has not made the work of the manager easier, other than reducing some of the paperwork that used to be required when a worker was being reclassified. The majority of states seeks a more streamlined HR system and has investigated broadbanding. After investigating it, and learning from those who have implemented it, most turn away and continue a search for a system more likely to work. Among the states that implemented broadbanding, they did so with multiple goals. It was only one initiative among a package of intended changes. The other changes include simplification of outmoded job classifications, reduction of unused job titles, and creation of a more meaningful employee reward system.

Usually, the states that considered broadbanding but did not implement it stated that not enough compelling research existed. Among those that did implement, some used pilot programs as a trial run. Pilot programs suggest that there is hesitation for a complete overhaul. In the case of Delaware, "We didn't see where it would provide enough benefits to make it worthwhile to overhaul our entire system. We decided instead to review the strengths and weaknesses of our current classification system and make appropriate changes there" (D. Jefferson, personal communication, May 28, 2007). The most significant lesson learned by states that have implemented broadbanding is that success is highly dependent on changes to all consequential components. Broadband reforms must include more than simply a change in job class structure. We conclude that the neglect for secondary although significant elements is a recipe

Whalen, C., & Guy, M. E. (2008). Broadbanding trends in the states.
Review of Public Personnel Administration.

Further Readings

- Berman, E. M., Bowman, J. S., West, J. P., & Van Wart, M. R. (Ed.) (2012). *Human Resource Management in Public Service: Paradoxes, Processes, and Problems.* Fourth Edition. Sage Publications.
- Whalen, C., & Guy, M. E. (2008). Broadbanding trends in the states. Review of Public Personnel Administration.
- Pynes, J. E. (2008). Human resources management for public and nonprofit organizations: A strategic approach (Vol. 30). *John Wiley & Sons.*

References

Berman, E. M., Bowman, J. S., West, J. P., & Van Wart, M. R. (Ed.) (2012). Human Resource Management in Public Service: Paradoxes, Processes, and Problems. Fourth Edition. Sage Publications.

Hackman, J. R., & Oldham, G. R. (1980). Work redesign (Vol. 72). Reading, MA: Addison-Wesley.

Milkovich, G. T., & Newman, J. M. (2002). Compensation (7th edn). Boston: McGraw-HillIrwin.

Naff, K. (2003). Why managers hate position classification. Public personnel administration: Problems and prospects, 126-43.

National Academy of Public Administration (NAPA), (1996). A Guide for Effective Strategic Management of Human Resources, Washington, DC. 27

National Academy of Public Administration (NAPA) (1991). Modernizing Federal Classification: An Opportunity for Excellence, Washington D.C.

Sackett, P. R., & Laczo, R. M. (2003). Job and work analysis. Handbook of psychology.

Stahl, O Glenn, 1971, Sixth Edition, Public Personnel Administration, Oxford and IBH Publishing Co. New Delhi

Evaluating Employee Performance

Framework

Human Resource Management for Public Organizations: An Essential Guide

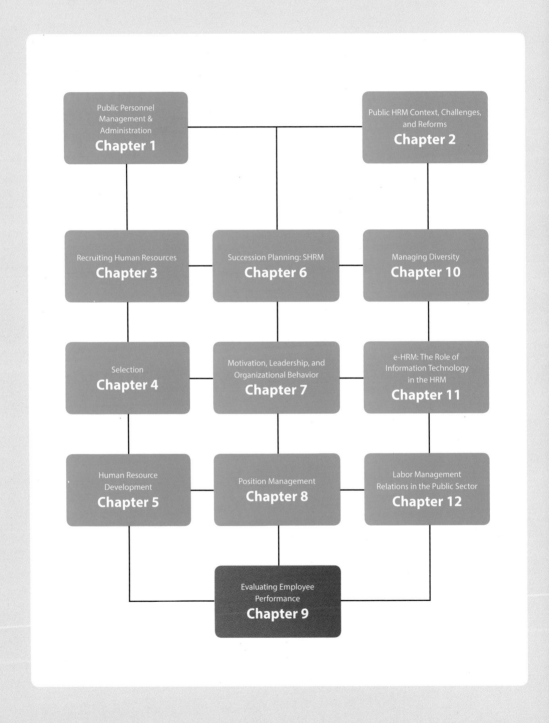

Learning Outcomes

After going through this chapter, you should be able to:

- Clarify the goals of performance evaluation/appraisal
- Describe the role of appraisal in different personnel system
- Identify the contemporary work trends and their challenges to the appraisal function.
- Differentiate between performance-based and person-based performance evaluation criteria
- Distinguish among several examples of performance appraisal methods
- Discuss the characteristics of an effective performance appraisal system
- Describe the relationship of performance appraisal to the sanctions functions and particularly its role in creating a sense of fairness in an organization.
- Determine ways on how to enhance public sector employee performance appraisal system
- Learn how to do an evaluation

Preview

One of the most challenging components of human resource management is the performance management which is the "process of identifying, measuring, managing, and developing the performance of the human resources in an organization" (Sage, 2008). From the recruitment and selection process, HRD, position management, and determination of pay scale, the human resource manager will get into determining the performance orientation of the employees in relation with the organizational performance. The components of performance management provides an effective, efficient, and acceptable mechanisms that ensures the use of information (e.g., performance evaluation) for improving individual productivity and the achievement of organizational goals and objectives. As public sector organizations have come to view human resource not a mere factor of production, but an important capital for the performance of its societal roles, performance management has become one of the important aspects of HRM. As Klinger and Nalbandian (2003) had described on the shift of public organizations towards strategic HRM, "public agencies have come to view human resources management in more of a strategic light—looking for the connections between human resources policies and management and agencies and goals and objectives, performance management has become at least as important as position management" (p. 261). Any "deliberate act that intended to affect employee performance falls under the category of performance management" (Klinger & Nalbandian, 2003, p. 261).

But how does performance being managed in the organization? Among them, which will be the focus of this chapter is performance appraisal or evaluation. In these days, performance appraisal is a crucial aspect of performance management (Klinger & Nalbandian, 2003). In this chapter, the term appraisal and evaluation were used interchangeably. Performance appraisal is one piece of performance management. It is understood to be an ongoing process of evaluating employee performance. Performance appraisals are reviews of employee performance over time.

Figure 9.1

A Generic Performance Management System

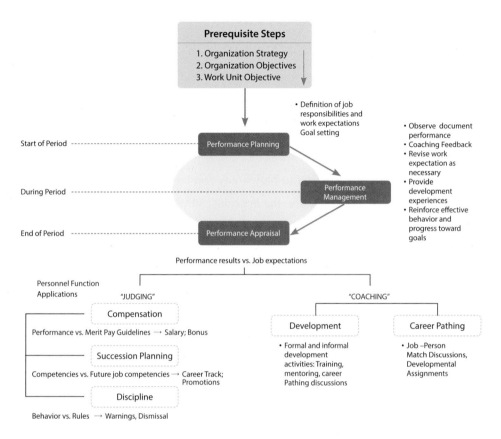

Source: Spencer, L. M., & Spencer, P. S. M. (2008). Competence at Work models for superior performance. John Wiley & Sons. (p. 265)

A typical Performance Management System (PMS) cycle is displayed in Figure 9.1. The starting point of the process—*performance planning*— includes defining job responsibilities and work expectations for a given performance period. During the period, the *performance management* comes to play through coaching feedback, reinforce effective behavior and progress towards achieving the goals. And the end of the period is the performance appraisal that formally launches the evaluation of process. As shown in the process, the results of performance appraisal can provide useful information for "judging" and "coaching". In the *judging* side (judgmental), PA results can be used to determine fix or performance-based-pay, a basis for succession planning, and for disciplining employees. While in the *coaching* side (developmental), it involves development efforts such as training, mentoring, and other interventions that can possibly enhance employee competencies; and career pathing—planning for future job assignments that are designed to introduce specific experiences and/ or competencies. Performance appraisal leads to organizational decisions regarding promotion and pay-allocational decisions, the process becomes more complicated; it is accompanied by heightened legal scrutiny for civil rights violations and employee demands for reasons behind decisions. Where the results of an unsatisfactory appraisal lead to disciplinary action or denial of an organizational reward, due process;

Performance appraisal is supposed to play a key role in the development of employees and their productivity. Theoretically, the appraisal of performance provides employees with feedback on their work, leading to greater clarity regarding organizational expectations and to a more effective channeling of employee ability and effort.

Guiding Principles for Evaluating Employee Performance

Clearly, the importance of performance appraisal systems (PAS) has gained recognition in the public sector organizations. Within an organizational performance management process, employee appraisal systems are emphasized as crucial personnel management or policy tools that relate the performance goals and achievements of employees to those of the organization and its programs (Nigro, Nigro, & Kellough, 2007). There is this major assumption that, the greater performance by individual employees will lead to improved organizational performance. Nonetheless, for us to ensure that such performance can be linked to organizational performance, an effective and reliable performance appraisal system should be in place. The basic principles in evaluating employee performance must include the following:

- The organization's mission should determine important performance goals
- Evaluation techniques must fit performance goals
- Performance evaluation techniques must be valid and reliable
- Cooperation between management and rank-and-file employees is as important as the technique selected

- Performance evaluations should report both strengths and weaknesses
- Managers should determine whether to develop in-house expertise or to contract out for the service

Even though the performance appraisal is a linked with employee and organizational productivity, the process remains to be unsatisfactory for both the employees and supervisors (Klinger & Nalbandian, 2003). In some organizations, performance appraisal is not taken seriously because they thought it to be a waste of time and effort. It also became a source of conflict between the management and the workforce, such as in federal government of US in 1994 with regards the pay-for-performance for the civil servants (Klinger & Nalbandian, 2003). Employee performance appraisal is perceived to be one of the most difficult and vague aspects of HRM because "the more appraisal systems are made objective, the more it's evident there is no way to avoid subjectivity" and "although communication of negative information is difficult, not communicating it can be worse" (Berman et al., 2012, p. 374-375).

Making Sense of the RealWorld

Traditionally, performance evaluation has been regarded as a necessary and basic personnel function.

Different countries might have some sort of performance appraisal (or performance evaluation) system in the form of performance agreement, typical trait-rating methods, and/or 360-degree feedback as a supplementary evaluation. Employee performance evaluation could be executed by the personnel authority of each agency and performance of government employees could be evaluated regularly. Based on the result of performance appraisal, incentives and/or discipline could be provided to government employees. The following video clips provide some useful and additional information in the conduct performance appraisal.

Title	Gist	Source
Performance Management – 6 Simple Steps	Learn the basic but important skills on evaluating employees.	https://www.youtube.com/watch?v=IHpAacOQTk0
Performance Reviews: Performance Evaluations & Appraisal	Learn about Different Types of Employee Performance Evaluations. How to Conduct an Employee Performance Review or Appraisal	https://www.youtube.com/watch?v=KcGhX7Htk9U
Awkward Performance Review	Anticipate some of the awkward instances that may compromise an objective performance evaluation process.	https://www.youtube.com/watch?v=gdp4sPviV74

1. What do you think is the rationale behind employee performance appraisal?

2. Is there one best way to measure performance, or are different methods needed for different employees groups? Who should evaluate employee's performance (such as supervisor, peers, or subordinates)?

3. What factors will affect performance appraisal in the 20th century? Or in the future?

4. Will behavioral science research better explain the mysterious decision-making processes involved in performance appraisal?

5. How will performance appraisal programs be changed as a result of changing work force, governmental regulation, or the complexity of management jobs?

**"Before we begin your performance review,
I took the liberty of ordering you some comfort food."**

Performance Appraisal

Performance appraisal (PA) is defined in different ways: (1) the experts perspectives—which describe what should be happening in the guise of performance appraisal; (2) cognitive and interpersonal processes underlying performance appraisal; (3) organizational perspective—based on how organizations currently do performance appraisal (Devries, Morrison, Shullman, & Gerlach, 1986). Devries et al (1986) defined PA base on organizational perspective, and they put it as, "the process by which an organization measures and evaluates an individual employee's behavior and accomplishments for a finite time period" (p. 2). Typically, evaluations are done annually and are initiated by the immediate supervisor or manager and results are used as a basis for administrative decisions (e.g., promotion) that affects the employee (Devries et al., 1986).

There are various issues that impede or foster the process of performance appraisal. Designing an appraisal system requires a commitment and clear understanding from all elements of the organization such as the leadership, employees, and the union (Berman et al., 2012). For practitioners, there has been a habit of asking basic and troublesome questions about performance appraisal. These questions fall into the five categories listed next. These issues, as a whole, constitute the major policy and operational decisions that are made whenever PA systems are developed, changed, or even dropped. For example, the issue on what really is the reason for doing performance appraisal—why there is a need for such? This question will give an elaborate explanation on the purpose of performance appraisal (e.g., increasing employee's productivity, improving manager-employee relationships, or simply supporting other human resource programs like salary administration) and whether or not it's influence to organizational performance worth considering for an investment. The components or characteristics of an effective performance appraisal remain an issue. Still, questions have been raised on how to define "effective performance appraisal" emphasizing on the identification of core measurement variables. There are various methods used in the performance appraisal, however, it remains to be bleak what is the most effective approach, for example can we consider the Management by Objectives (MBO) as the most appropriate and reliable appraisal method? Is there one best way to measure performance, or are different methods needed for different employees groups? Who should evaluate employee's performance? What is the role of PA in the larger personnel and management picture? How should PA systems be designed and implemented in an organization? How can an existing PA system be changed to better serve the current needs of an organization? Is there a way to introduce a PA program that will get a more enthusiastic response from employees? What factors will affect PA in the 20th century? Or in the future? Will behavioral science research better explain the mysterious decision-making processes involved in PA? How will PA programs be changed as a result of changing work force, governmental regulation, or the complexity of management jobs?

The above-mentioned issues will be the focus of this chapter. We will try to provide answers to those questions and give light on some blurry aspects of employee performance appraisal in the public sector.

Rationale for Performance Evaluation

What value really can an organization and the individual get from performance appraisal? Why do we appraise or evaluate performance? If performance evaluation is done in an objective and careful manner, it can give colossal value for both the organization and the individual. On the other hand, if it is handled haphazardly, it can lead to some negative organizational outcome such as less productivity and individual outcome such as lesser job satisfaction.

For Klinger and Nalbandian (2003), they summarized some of the reasons for the management in conducting performance appraisal:

1. Communicate management goals and objectives to employees. It is clear that performance appraisal reinforces managerial expectations. After instructing what to do, it is management's responsibility to follow through by providing feedback on how performance matches the stated criteria.

2. Motivate employees to improve their performance. The purpose of providing feedback, or constructive criticism, is to improve performance. Appraisal, then, should encourage employees to maintain or improve job performance.

3. Distribute organizational rewards such as salary increases and promotions equitably. One of the primary criteria of organizational justice and quality of employee work life is whether rewards are distributed fairly.

4. Conduct personnel management research. Logic suggests that if jobs have been analyzed accurately, and if people have been selected for those jobs based on job-related skills, knowledge, and abilities, their subsequent on-the-job performance should be satisfactory or better. If not, one might suspect defects in the job analysis, selection, or promotion criteria—or in the performance appraisal system itself.

Klinger and Nalbandian (2003, p. 262)

For Condrey (2005), he posited that performance appraisal is a decision-making tool that can provide managers appropriate and rational decisions that are directed towards effective organizational and individual effectiveness and well-being. He further conveyed that the purpose of performance appraisal is numerous and that it can be grouped into two broad categories—judgmental and developmental.

Judgmental purposes adheres with the management system, or command-and-control, model of authority and are explicitly linked to extrinsic rewards and punishments (Condrey, 2005, p. 500). On the other hand, *developmental* emphasizes on determining the potentials of an individual—enhancement of competencies, knowledge, skills, and abilities. See Figure 9.1 for a more elaborate understanding on the difference and directions of judgmental and developmental purposes of performance appraisal.

> **Point to ponder**: Can judgmental and developmental purposes simultaneously mixed in the same appraisal process?

Performance Factors to Evaluate

Now that we basically understand why there is a need for performance appraisal, the next thing to do is to determine what performance factors are to be considered in the appraisal. The most widely used evaluation factors are those that are judgmental approaches which can be categorized as trait-based appraisal, behavior-based appraisal, and results-based appraisal. The knowledge, skills, and abilities (KSAs), personal traits or characteristics, activities or work behaviors, and results can all serve as criteria for assessing performance (Milkovich & Boundreau, 1991; cited in Condrey, 2005, p. 502). Thus, we may focus and take these three as the main performance factors.

Trait Evaluation

This approach focuses on identifying the "physical or psychological characteristics of a person" (Sage, 2008). It requires the evaluation of an individual's personal characteristics that are deemed necessary and important for the job (Berman et al., 2012). For example, inquisitiveness, conscientiousness, and general cognitive ability have been shown to have a reasonable link to job performance (Sage, 2008, p. 292). However, measuring performance based on traits requires the accurate use of job descriptions and the utilization of trained evaluators in order to make the ratings more credible (Berman et al., 2012). Due to the presence of many evaluation items, the critical issue is that, whether or not the manager and the individual agreed that the performance factor is valid and the measured rating is accurate. The basic requisite, however, and the bottom-line should be on the satisfaction of whether or not there is a clear and unambiguous link between the trait and the successful performance of the job in the organization. See Exhibit 9.1 for an example of a Trait-based Appraisal (included also are factors for Behaviorally Anchored Rating Scale (BARS) and Management by Objectives (MBO).

Exhibit 9.1
Example of Trait Appraisal, Behaviorally Anchored Rating Scale (BARS), and Management by Objectives (MBO)

Employee Name: _____	Agency: _____		Review Period: _____		
	Outstanding	Good	Satisfactory	Fair	Unsatisfactory
Job knowledge					
Interpersonal relationship					
Quantity of work					
Quality of work					
Dependability					
Initiative					
Supervisory skills					
Supervisor: _____		Date: _____			
Comments:					

Source: Berman et al., 2013, p. 379

Behavioral Evaluation

In this approach, the focus is on the behaviors of the employees—or simply what someone has actually done and says. Behaviors are the activities and tasks individuals engage in the performance of their jobs; results are the activity outcomes (Daley, 1992; Landy & Farr, 1983; Murphy & Cleveland, 1995). Generally, behaviors are much better option than the appraisals on traits. Behaviors are observable unlike traits that are hard to discern, thus can more valid basis in measuring individual performance. The objectivity of judging or evaluating individual based on observable behaviors are more reliable due to the fact that evaluation are based on observed and not mere assumptions or perceptions. It is easy for the evaluator to determine the direct linkage of the behavior and the performance—whether such behavior has something to do with the job. In addition, if evaluation of behaviors is to be applied in all jobs of the same type, it would lead to a uniform evaluation and could possibly provide a comparison of results among the employees. Still, though behavioral appraisal can be more acceptable than trait appraisal, the basic requisite should be satisfied—that is, the behavior has a direct link with the work or job performance. A typical example of this approach is the Behaviorally Anchored Rating Scales (BARS). Exhibit 9.2 is an example of behavior appraisal instrument (see also Exhibit 9.1).

Exhibit 9.2
Employee Performance Evaluation Form

Left anchors	Rating	Right anchors
	5	Could be expected to meet deadlines No matter how unusual the circumstances, By increasing efforts until the work is done.
Could be expected to meet deadlines comfortably by delegating the less important duties to others		
	4	Could be expected always to meet deadlines on time by delegating most of the work to others
Could be expected to meet deadlines within a reasonable length of time		
	3	Could be expected to offer work at home after failing to get work out on the deadline day once in a while
Could be expected to fail to meet deadlines on a regular basis, but be ready to devote personal time to catching up		
	2	Could be expected to be behind schedule All the time, but appear to work hard to catch up
Could be expected to be behind schedule and display little effort to catch up		
	1	Could be expected to ignore deadlines and get work in on time only infrequently

Rating Instructions: Select the statement that best reflects the work behavior of the employee.
Note: This is an example of one of the possible items that could be used on a BARS rating instrument. In addition to selecting the statement that best identifies the employee's typical behavior, the rater could also be asked to write examples of the employee's work to support the selection made.

Results Evaluation

Results evaluation is simply an outcome-based approach that seeks to measure one's contribution to the success of the organization (Berman et al., 2012). Normally, an organization really wants to measure the results because this is the main interest and an effective measurement of its success. However, in terms of measuring the individual contribution to such organizational results would be hard to determine. There are various factors that may be considered in deriving at the actual organizational performance results which might render it hard to calculate individual input. The adaption of this approach to be reliable and valid, all factors that are outside the control of the individual in the performance of their jobs must be taken into account. Thus, it should be assessed in the context wherein the organization and individual have agreed on performance measurements, considering all other factors beyond the individual

Exhibit 9.3
Example of MBO Goal-Setting Approach (a Participatory Technique)

Employee Name: _____   Rating Period: _____

In the coming six months, the following objectives will be pursued and success will be determined by these associated results.

Objectives	Results Sought
1. Train field workers well	Preparation of five staff members to assume supervisory duties at field offices in rural areas.
2. Improve quality of services to walk-in clients	Conduct search for and locate the most willing/able employee to take on receptionist duties as required.
3. Achieve better cost control over long-distance telephone use	Hold staff meeting to discuss the problem of telephone charges and appoint a committee to formulate a plan to achieve a 15 percent reduction charges.

Agree to on: _____
                         (Date)

Agreed to by: _____
                           (Evaluatee)

_____
(Evaluator)

control, and agreed on the level of performance to be achieved. The most common example on this approach is the use of Management by Objectives (MBO) which was introduced in 1950 (Berman et al., 2012).

Performance-based and Person-based Evaluation

Considering the three factors—trait, behavior, and results, there are two basic criteria that can be viewed in the same respect: performance-based and person-based.

Person-based Rating System	Performance-based Rating System
The rater compares employees against other employees or against some absolute standard.	Measures each employees' behaviors against previously established behaviors and standards.

Point to ponder: What are the limitations that you can identify in the adaption of either of the three evaluation factors? Can you think of any remedy to mitigate such limitation(s)? What is the best option to take among these three factors? Why?

Actors in the Evaluation

Conventionally, the main actors in the evaluation are the employee and the immediate supervisor who is tasked or responsible on evaluating the performance (Mohrman, Resnick-West, and Lawler, 1989). Of course, due to various performance appraisal methods that are available for the public sector to adapt, actors may as well change—especially on the side of evaluators (e.g., clients or the public, co-workers, subordinates, etc.). Table 9.1 summarized the common performance evaluators and a brief description on each of them.

Table 9.1
Who Does Evaluation?

Evaluator	Description	Issue(s)
Supervisor	The supervisor is deemed to be the most knowledgeable individual that knows about the person to be evaluated as well as the job.	■ The threat of subjectivity due to some causes such as personality conflict. ■ In the advent of ICT, work environment may have changed and that supervisors may not know well about the job.
Self	The employee evaluates his own work performance. This is anchored on the belief that the individual knew his own strengths and weaknesses.	■ This is more effective in developmental appraisal but could be an issue in judgmental evaluation. People hardly accept some weaknesses.
Peer	The peers (i.e., coworkers) evaluates employee's performance that knew the job well and also interacts with the employee, thus can be able to observe behaviors directly.	■ It can be less objective due to personality conflicts and personal biases.
Subordinate	Subordinate evaluation are usually adapted to measure or assess managerial job performance	■ Subordinate's evaluation must be confidential. Subordinates may not engage into this type of evaluation because of fear of retribution.
External or Outsider	This denotes to clients or customers evaluations. Public customers are tax payer thus deserve to take evaluations of employees in the public sector organizations.	■ It employs simple scales that are most of time subjective. ■ Clients or customers are not trained to be evaluators, thus bias may arise.

Team Management	Seeks to address both developmental (done by the supervisor) and judgmental (done by the other team managers) purposes.	▪ The evaluation may not provide a well-coined developmental and judgmental purpose because it is done by two different evaluators.
Experts/ Consultants	Performance evaluation done by an external group or individual (e.g., central personnel office, or private consultants).	▪ Instead of evaluating the activities, behaviors, tasks, and responsibilities, the analysis evaluates the employee's performance level on those same items.
360o Degree Evaluation or Multiple raters (see Figure 9.3)	The combination of supervisor, subordinate, peer, self, customer (if applicable) is the basis of 360-degree feedback. It can obtain feedback from a variety of sources in addition to the supervisor, including subordinates, peers, and customers or clients	▪ This requires time and money, thus costly.

Figure 9.2
The Multi-source Assessment Model

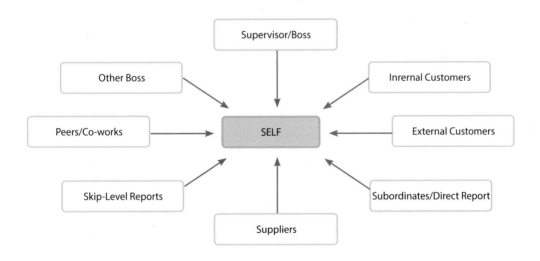

Timing for Evaluation

Questions are being asked on when is the perfect, if not the most appropriate timing for evaluation. When should it commence? And when should it end? There are two popular approaches when it comes to timing: (1) *anniversary date approach* and (2) *focal point approach*. The anniversary date approach posits that, the evaluation is in accord with the anniversary of employment of an employee. While in the focal point approach, the evaluation is done the same time. The issue is easy to identify. For the anniversary date approach, though it gives the supervisor the opportunity to focus on individual performance, it can't provide a mechanism of comparison—which is absent because the evaluation is done alone on the individual. On the otherhand, the focal point approach, however, it gives an opportunity to compare performance of various employees; the supervisor is being stretched and may miss the focus on individual performances.

> **Point to ponder**: What do you think is the most appropriate techniques to be employed in the public sector? Explain your answer.

Evaluation Methods

Before going through with the various methods of performance evaluation, take a look into the typical performance evaluation process (see Figure 9.3).

Figure 9.3
The Performance Evaluation Process

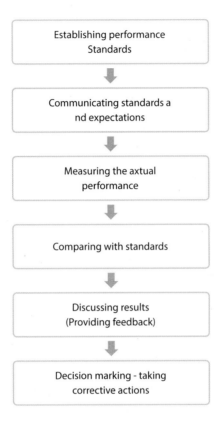

Recently, many public organizations have developed, implemented and adapted various performance evaluation methods such as Management by Objectives (MBO), BARS techniques, narrative methods, and among others which encourages the an objective design of evaluation process. In participatory reviews, the employee is included in the process of setting performance objectives. While having some disadvantages in public organizations (e.g., MBO processes are more time-consuming than other appraisal methods in terms of setting goals, reviewing employee progress, and completing appraisals), the MBO process is understood to improve organizational communication, clarify expectations for rewards, and increase the commitment of employees to goal attainment (Freyss, 2004). Employees are also evaluated on job-related behaviors associated with specific positions. Such evaluation techniques are relatively common ways of measuring job-related employee performance in the public sector. For example, behavioral observation scales (BOS) ask raters to report the frequency of specific job-related behaviors achieved by employees. In addition, behavioral anchored rating scales (BARS) rely on actual descriptions of important job behaviors that are developed and "anchored" alongside a performance scale for evaluators to select the description of behavior that best matches actual employee behavior for the rating period (Rarick & Baxter, 1986).

One of the challenging aspects of human resource management is the successful implementation of performance appraisal system (Gabris & Ihrke, 2000, p. 41). Typical barriers to effective performance appraisal include "1) absence of trust in the organization, 2) supervisory training and top management support, 3) rater accountability, 4) overall evaluation of the system itself" and "these can be overcome by nonthreatening feedback, not using numerical rating standards, and ensuring multiple sources of data" (Berman et al., 2012, pp. 401-402). While these performance appraisal techniques are mainly used to provide extrinsic rewards to public employees, it is critical to examine how these techniques and systems are emotionally perceived and affectively accepted by public workers, and further, to investigate which organizational factors might impact the acceptability of PAS in public agencies.

Figure 9.4
The Performance Appraisal Measurement Methods

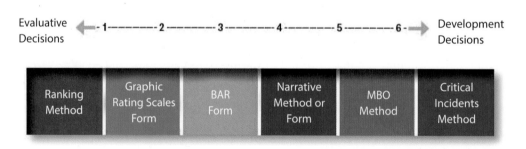

Source: Sage, 2008

- The *critical incidents method* is a performance appraisal method in which a manager keeps a written record of positive and negative performance of employees throughout the performance period.

- The *Management by Objectives (MBO)* method is a process in which managers and employees jointly set objectives for the employees, periodically evaluate performance, and reward according to the results. MBO is also referred to as work planning and review, goals management, goals and controls, and management by results.

- The *narrative method* or form requires a manager to write a statement about the employee's performance.

- The *graphic rating scale* form is a performance appraisal checklist on which a manager simply rates performance on a continuum such as excellent, good, average, fair, and poor. The continuum often includes a numerical scale, for example from 1 (lowest performance level) to 5 (highest performance level).

- The *Behaviorally Anchored Rating Scale* (BARS) form is a performance appraisal that provides a description of each assessment along a continuum. Like with rating scales, the continuum often includes a numerical scale from low to high.

- The *ranking method* is a performance appraisal method that is used to evaluate employee performance from best to worst. There often is no actual standard form used, and we don't always have to rank all employees.

New Approaches

First, is the management approach which is less with questions of measurement issues (e.g., validity and reliability). Its central objectives: employee acceptance and organizational utility. A typical example of this is the MBO Approach which is more concerned with the workability of the performance appraisal system within the organization. Also, it stresses the importance of the organizational setting (social, psychological, and technical). Second, is the TQM approach which is different approach from traditional systems that focus on the individual employee (i.e., accurately measuring and controlling the performance of each worker). It relies on group appraisals and rewards (e.g., team evaluations). Also, increasing employee participation and setting the entire process in a "developmental" frame of reference

Overall, however, public employers have not moved away from individual performance appraisals to any significant extent because

Lastly, the Technology: Electronic Performance Monitoring. It is the process of observing ongoing employee actions using computers or other nonhuman methods. The number of employees monitored through EPM has increased drastically in the past 20 years. In the early 1990s, about one third of employees were being monitored electronically. By 2001, approximately 78% were monitored electronically, and in 2010 that number more than likely increased even more. The reason for this steep increase is that EPM apparently is an effective means of increasing productivity. EPM allows management to know if employees are actually working or doing personal things during work hours. The biggest upside to EPM seems to be that it provides information for concrete results-based performance evaluations. Certainly, this is a valuable, outcome. However, some researchers and practitioners argue against EPM because of a number of factors including ethical questions concerning such monitoring, legal concerns over employee privacy, and apparent increases in stress due to constant monitoring of performance. So, the question is whether or not organizations should use EPM systems.

Rater Error

During the performance appraisal process, there are common problems that we face. However, knowing these common problems, we can take measures to avoid them. So in this section we discuss the problems first with simple ways to avoid each of them as an individual. Then we discuss what the organization can do to overcome these problems on an organization-wide basis. We can actually overcome multiple problems with the same method.

Figure 9.5
The Performance Appraisal Problems

Common Problems	Avoiding Problems
Bias	Develop Accurate Performance Measures
Stereotyping	Use Multiple Criteria
Halo Error	Minimize the Use of Trait-Based Evaluations
Distributional Errors	Use the OUCH and Blanchard Tests
Similarity Error	Train Your Evaluators
Proximity Error	Use Multiple Raters
Recency Error	
Contrast Error	
Attribution Error	

Source: Sage, 2008

Contemporary Challenges to Performance Appraisal

Figure 9.6
Top Ten Problems in Managerial Appraisal

Top ten reasons for ineffective managerial appraisals

Reason for Ineffective managerial appraisals	Percentage
1. Unclear performance criteria / ineffective rating instruments	83.0
2. Poor working relationship with the boss	79.0
3. Superior lacks information on actual performance	75.0
4. Lack of ongoing performance feedback	67.0
5. Overly negative / second guessing review	63.0
6. Perceived political reviews	54.0
7. Lack of focus in management development / improvement	42.0
8. An ineffective link to reward systems	50.0
9. Superior lacks rating skills / motivation	33.0
10. Review process lacks structure / consistency	29.0

source: Longenecker(1997)

- Technical Problems
  - The identification of specific work outcome is quite difficult
  - What standards of performance can reasonably be expected regarding those outcomes?
  - Rating errors and bias
  - Behavior-based systems or trait-based systems vs. actual work outcomes

- Managerial problems
  - Did existing performance appraisal systems help managers manage?
  - Poor informal and formal feedback

- Organizational problems
  - Performance appraisals were not administratively relevant to organizational functions such as planning and budgeting.

Tips for Developing Valid and Reliable Performance Appraisal Instruments

Use a job analysis to develop the appraisal instrument. You may also develop a behavior-oriented or results-based instrument rather than a personal trait-oriented instrument. Give evaluators specific written instructions on how to use the performance appraisal instrument.

Case Brief

To Protect and to Serve

The motto of the Los Angeles Police Department is "to protect and to serve." How are Angelenos being "served" by the chief of police forcing his police officers to write a set number of traffic tickets each month? All that's going to do is make the public even madder at the department and that's not a smart thing to do in the aftermath of the Rodney King incident. The race riots in South Central Los Angeles and the racist revelations of Mrk Furhmann during the O.J. Simpson trial.

Tension between whites and blacks regarding police performance is nothing new in the City of Los Angeles; the city has a long history of racial tension going all the way back to the 1960s with the bitter infighting between Mayor Sam Yorty and Councilman Tom Bradley. It was later continued between Chief Daryl Gates and Mayor Bradley. In 1998, it later spilled over in conflict between the Chief and the Union, the Los Angeles Police Protective League (LAPPL), who became embroiled in a seemingly neutral issue regarding the measurement of police officer productivity.

Police Chief Bernard C. Parks, who was the department's first black chief and a positive contrast to his predecessor, Daryl Gates, was known as a nonsense administrator. Chief Parks did little to endear himself to the troops in 1997 when he unilaterally eliminated the three-day work week that was widely supported, but which Parks argued had the effect of reducing services to the community.

Further deterioration occurred when Chief Parks restructured the grievance process and proposed changes in the city charter that would have strengthened his own decision-making authority. The most recent flash point happened when Chief parks announced a renewed departmental focus on individual officer accountability as the key component of his community-policing program.

Performance evaluation criteria would be developed in each of LAPD's divisions, by which officer performance could be quantitatively compared against all other officers in the same division. Predictably, LAPPL President Garth Moran criticized the chief's approach as a numbers game that was not in the best interests of the community.

League President Moran was particularly incensed with a performance productivity plan devised by Captain Booby Hanson, who recently had been put in command of LAPD's Harbor Division. Moran criticized Hanson for allegedly improperly comparing officers along the following eleven categories:

- Issuance of traffic and parking citations
- Conducting field interviews
- Quality of incident reports
- Correctly responding to radio communication
- Following arrest procedures
- Safety skills
- Maintenance of equipment
- Reliability
- Judgment of equipment
- Attendance
- Performance-improvement log entries

Moran attacked the chief's performance evaluation program as "smoke and mirrors" to hide the fact that quotas were being mandated from the top. Key LAPD officials vehemently denied that the performance evaluation criteria caused the creation quotas. They maintained that the criteria simply helped supervisors determine whether officers are doing their jobs or being productive.

In an effort to promote more light than heat on the subject, Chief Park's asked his Chief of Staff, Commander Don Kalishman, to meet with League President

Moran, and see if greater understanding could be attained regarding the chief's new productivity focus. Garth Moran (GM) agreed to meet with Don Kalishman (DK). The following excerpts are taken from their conversation at the San Fernando Valley Division Headquarters:

GM:	Don, the captains in LAPD are scared because the chief's breathing down their necks about this new productive thing. They're afraid of being criticized, so they all want their numbers to be up. You know, give us more citations and arrests. These are "quotas" and this isn't in anyone's bet interest.
DK:	Look Garth, I don't believe in quotas, it's merely a way of measuring officer performance. It's done all the time in corporate America.
GM:	Are you kidding me? Measuring individual performance is not where it's anymore; employee performance evaluations have gone the way of the dinosaur. The new cutting-edge techniques, such as Total Quality Management (TQM), put evaluation emphasis on teams and group incentives. Your system encourages officers to compete against one another rather than working as a team.
DK:	Productivity statistics were not intended to be the sole measurement of an officer's job productivity, but they certainly are a key indicator of what officers are doing out in the field. It's not the numbers that matter; the chief wants us to focus on the end result. Are we "mission-driven" and results-oriented?" There was one officer who came up with some good suggestions for building a better working relationship between the North Hollywood Hispanic community and the department. That's the kind of result that the chief wants to encourage.
GM:	There you go again with that bullshit jargon that doesn't mean anything to the rank-and-file officers. We're supposed to be doing "community policing" in LA, but no one knows what the means either. Under community policing, the officer should get to know his community or barrio so the citizens are involved on fighting crime. This requires time for the officers for the officers to stop and talk to neighbors while they're out on patrol. So where does this philosophy fit into the chief's focus on productivity? If you take the time to get to know the community, your numbers will be down. So what in the hell does the chief want—to churn out the arrests and citations or slow down and get to know people in the communities?

DK:	You know, Garth, the only officers who have complained about the chief's productivity emphasis are the ones who are unproductive. I believe in making certain that the officers who work for me really work hard and aren't just killing time in a Starbucks getting to know the neighborhood. We understand that occasionally even the best officer will have an off day but, come on, we've got to have minimum standards and criteria over the a period of time by which to find out who the loafers are in this department.
GM:	I really resent your comments about my fellow officers. There out of there busting their busting their buns on the streets while you and your MBA types in the Parker Center concoct some new performance evaluation scheme that isn't even state-of-the-art. For example, hasn't always been left to officer discretion to decide whether to issue a citation? This new system forces us to inflate those numbers whenever possible. And whatever happened to teamwork? This new system will result in several officers at a crime scene each trying to take credit as the arresting officer. Everyone will want to "hot dog" it to get those numbers way up.
DK:	I'm not trying to put anybody down and, by the way, I've put my time in and out in the field just like everyone else. I started out as a detective in the violent crimes divisions; later on, I become a captain of the patrol division and commanding officer of criminal investigations. I'll have you know that, for what it's worth, I didn't get an MBA; I've got an MPA from Cal State, Dominguez Hills. I'm certainly aware of TQM and the quality movement, but frankly, all that "continuous quality improvement" stuff and "self-directed work teams" business just doesn't cut it in police work, particularly in a city like Los Angeles. Our philosophy is that even though an officer in the field depends on support and backup from fellow officers in case of emergency or during an investigation, police work is still basically handled by an individual officer. It isn't a team that decided to give a citation to a speeding motorist or initiate a chase on foot; it's the beat cop and that's the type of work that can be easily documented for productivity.
GM:	Sorry, I wasn't putting down your degree. In fact, I'm getting a BA in Criminal Justice fro Cal Site, Fullerton. But it seems to most of us in the union that you guys have forgotten your roots and what really works out here in the field. It's just that the chief's quantitative rating system sets an illegal quota that punishes officers who fail to reach arbitrary goals in ticket writing and other police duties. It isn't fair to the officers or the citizens of Los Angeles. Officers should be judged by their overall performance in the field, as witnessed and documented by front-line supervisors.
DK:	Well, frankly we've tried that approach and it doesn't work very well. We let sergeants set individual objectives for each officer and these usually turned out to be unrealistically low because no one wanted to crack the whip. So we went back to a system that relied on hard data and compared officer's pe4formances to one another. Well, I see that it's about time to end things for today. Maybe we can meet again next Monday, if you want.
GM:	That would be fine for me. Oh, by the way, we're getting a little bit pissed off with allowing captains and lieutenants, who aren't even these officers' supervisors, to change evaluation ratings given out by sergeants. These people don't know the officers, but they've got in mind some set percentages of how many officers should fall into certain rating categories. That's unfair to evaluate someone you don't even know. Maybe that's an issue we could discuss in the future.

1. Discuss the advantages and disadvantages of the chief's new performance productivity plan.

2. What are the prospects for TQM and team approaches to performance evaluation in paramilitary agencies?

3. What recommendations would you make for implementing a performance evaluation system at the Los Angeles Police Department?

This case was adopted from: Reeves, T. Z. (2006).*Cases in public human resource management*. Thomson Wadsworth.

Student Activity:

The evaluation concept, which follows, is a typical example of Management by Objectives (MBO) which is applied in evaluating the overall performance of the participants in all aspects of the program. In this section, you are asked to understand the whole process of the MBO and fill-up Table 2 base on the descriptions provided in Table 1.

Management by Objectives (MBO) and Performance Appraisal

As a new approach in evaluating the MPA participants, the MBO approach will be adapted to reflect a proactive program management. As a principle, MBO is a result-oriented approach that encourages an active participation of all stakeholders in the program. Specifically, the performance evaluation strategy will require the participants to identify tangible goals while in the duration of the program. The academic supervisor will ensure that the participant are properly guided in the formulation of goals and objectives, help to achieve desired outcome, and evaluate on how well the participants perform based on the determined objectives. Figure 9.7 shows the MBO Process.

Figure 9.7 The MBO Process

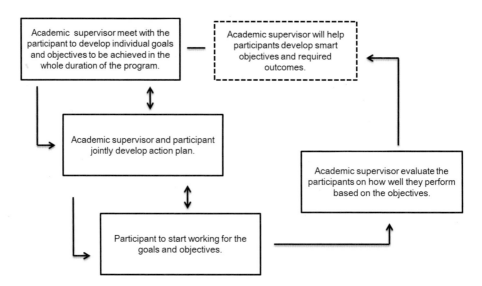

Primary flow

The performance plans requires three major areas (tracks) of responsibility for the participants and define a performance goal for each track: (a) *Research Track— Track 1*, (b) *Academic Track—Track 2*, and (c) *Activity Track—Track 3*. The academic supervisor will evaluate the participant's progress towards his/her goal in four phases. The MPA office, through the MPA Dean and Program Director will help give an evaluation on *Track 3* as they coordinate invitations from KOICA and plan and execute activities for the participants. You will also note, the evaluation will not be in a numeric rating, rather will assign color—green (excellent), yellow (satisfactory), and red (unsatisfactory)—and provide comment on the participants goal achievements in each track (Table 2).

Performance Evaluation Criteria

The participants' success in achieving the performance objectives will be based on the following criteria (see also Table 1):

a. Research Track (Track 1)

- Completion of research plan. As the program is into e-Government and e-Policy, the research agenda must at least center on e-Government research and/or its specific services, strengthening public administration capacity, etc.
- Completion of thesis proposal. This will be the result of the 1-year education and training program participation in GSG-SKKU.
- Participation in domestic or international conferences on public policy, public administration, eGovernment, or other related gatherings.

b. Academic Track (Track 2)

- Projected grade in each enrolled courses are achieved (to have a grade of not less than A).
- Completion of International Summer Semester (ISS). This summer program of SKKU offers various courses taught by known academicians from all over the world.
- Excellent in-campus behavior. The total demeanor of the participants will be evaluated based on their in-campus behavior, deportment, manner, or conduct.

c. Activity Track (Track 3)

- 100% participation on various activities planned and executed by MPA office.
- Exposure to various e-Government systems available in Korea.
- Learning the principles and strategies in the development of Korean e-Government system.
- Excellent off-and-in-campus behavior. Participant's total demeanor during the conduct of activities and/or their whole stay in Korea.

Table 9.2 Four-Phased Evaluation Criteria

Sub-Activity Tracks	Goal-Setting Phase			
	Preparation Stage	Phase 1	Phase 2	Phase 3
Track 1: Research	Identification, presentation, and submission of research agenda.	Submission and presentation of research plan.	Completion of thesis proposal.	Completion and submission of thesis; Participation in domestic or international conferences on public policy, public administration, e-Government, or other related activities.
Track 2: Academic	Participation in the preliminary seminars; identification of possible elective courses.	To get a mark of not less than A in all courses enrolled in the fall semester; excellent in-campus demeanor.	Completion of Internship Program; get a mark of not less than A in all enrolled courses in winter semester; excellent in-campus demeanor.	Completion of International Summer Semester (ISS); get a mark of not less than A in all enrolled courses in winter semester; excellent in-campus demeanor.

Track 3: Activity	Participation in all activities planned and executed by MPA Office; exposure and learning the Korean e-Government system and strategies; excellent off- and-in-campus demeanor.	Participation in all activities planned and executed by MPA Office; exposure and learning the Korean e-Government system and strategies; excellent off- and-in-campus demeanor.	Participation in all activities planned and executed by GMPA Office; exposure and learning the Korean e-Government system and strategies; excellent off- and-in-campus demeanor.	Participation in all activities planned and executed by GMPA Office; exposure and learning the Korean e-Government system and strategies; excellent off- and-in-campus demeanor.

Color-Performance Management Board. Performance will be monitored and measured through a color-coding system. This scheme will provide a regular check-up of individual research, academic, and activities; and will be able to arrest issues that will help the participant(s) to keep in the right track of the program.

Table 9.3 Performance Management Board

Sub-Activity Tracks	Goal-Setting Phase			
	Preparation Stage Aug	Phase 1 Sept - Nov	Phase 2 Dec - Mar	Phase 3 Apr - Jul
Track 1: Research				
Track 2: Academic				
Track 3: Activity				

⬤ Green (Excellent), ⬤ Yellow (Average), ⬤ Red (Unsatisfactory)

Note: Green (70%-100%), Yellow (40%-69%), Red (0%-39%)

Case Analysis

	Step	Contents		
1	Environments/ Conditions/ Backgrounds	Please explain the situation briefly. (1-2 pages)		
2	Problem Definitions	In your own perspective, please be as specific as possible when pointing out the problem. (2-3 pages)		
3	Actual Case Studies	Please explain by providing specific examples. (Newspaper articles, news clips, or interviews) (2-3 pages)		
4	Alternatives	Possible Alternative(s)	Pros in your Country Context	Cons in a your Country Context
		①		
		②		
		③		
		Please propose more than three policy alternatives. (2-3 pages)		
5	The Best Solutions	Why did you choose this alternative as the best solution? What are the expected effects and potential contribution? (2 pages)		

Reviews

1. Can judgmental and developmental purposes simultaneously mixed in the same appraisal process?

2. What are the limitations that you can identify in the adaption of either of the three evaluation factors? Can you think of any remedy to mitigate such limitation(s)?

3. What is the best option to take among these three factors? Why?

4. What do you think is the most appropriate techniques to be employed in the public sector? Explain your answer.

Ending Credits

Research Digest

Does the Form Really Matter? Leadership, Trust, and Acceptance of the Performance Appraisal Process

Facts

Performance appraisal traditionally has two major purposes, broadly conceived as developmental and summative. Developmental approaches focus on enhancing employee performance by identifying opportunities for employee growth and marshalling organizational resources to support that growth. Summative approaches are judgmental in nature and are explicitly linked to extrinsic rewards such as promotions or pay (Daley, 1993; Moussavi & Ashbaugh, 1995). Whatever the purpose, Carson, Cardy, and Dobbins (1991) proposed that performance appraisal makes three critical assumptions: Employees actually differ in their contribution to the organization, the cause of this difference is due (at least in part) to individual performance, and supervisors are actually able and willing to distinguish between performance attributable to individual performance and to other sources. These assumptions have been, and continue to be, challenged in the literature on performance appraisal (Bowman, 1999; Cook, 1995; Martin & Bartol, 1998; Roberts, 1998). Despite the problems with these assumptions and performance appraisal in general, the public sector seems destined to continue the practice (Golembiewski, 1995).

This research seeks to explore an overlooked fourth assumption. Performance appraisal assumes that employees and supervisors accept the process as legitimate. In this study, legitimacy is defined in terms of whether employees believe the process adequately evaluates individual performance and rewards good performance. If they do, the summative and developmental purposes of appraisal will be fulfilled. Employees will respond to information received in the appraisal process and alter their behavior to receive promised rewards (promotion, pay, etc.). Supervisors, on the other hand, will use the processes to identify employee needs for development and fitness for promotion or additional pay. If employees and supervisors do not accept the performance appraisal process as legitimate, then its purposes are thwarted regardless of the quality of the instrument or the processes supporting it (Dipboye & Pontbriand, 1981; Hedge & Teachout, 2000; Landy, Barnes, & Murphy, 1978; Lawler, 1967).

Issue(s)

This study seeks to measure employee and supervisor acceptance of the appraisal process and explore variables that may shape this acceptance. In line with recent research conducted by Hedge and Teachout (2000) and Gabris and Ihrke (2000), this study examines the role of leadership and trust in influencing acceptance of the appraisal process. Unlike these other studies, this research examined the role of a particular leadership approach, servant leadership, and proposes that trust serves as a moderating variable between leadership and employee attitudes toward the appraisal process.

Findings

A number of findings emerged from this study. First, in line with previous studies (Hedge & Teachout, 2000; Reinke & Baldwin, 2001), trust emerged as the most important predictor of an attitude toward a performance appraisal process, in this instance, acceptance of the process. This supports the literature suggesting that no analysis of performance appraisal is complete that does not acknowledge its essentially interpersonal nature (Bowman, 1999) and its place as part of the ongoing relationship between the supervisor and employee. This does not mean that other factors are not important. The ANOVA conducted in this study supports the concept that a broad understanding of the system is essential to acceptance of the process. Therefore, whether done within the context of a formal training session or not, HR managers must ensure that employees and supervisors understand the performance appraisal system.

Furthermore, the negative effects of perceptions concerning socializing with the boss were also demonstrated. Clearly, perceptions that favoritism exists undermine employee and supervisor perceptions of the fairness of an appraisal process and therefore reduces acceptance. This finding lends support to provisions in organizational codes of ethics or in HR policies concerning the importance of appropriate professional relationships. At its best, the variables proposed in this study explained 30% of the variance in levels of acceptance, leaving a large amount of variance unexplained.

Future research should incorporate more variables, such as the last rating received, to help further our understanding of what affects acceptance of a performance appraisal process. Perhaps the most startling finding of this study was the difference between supervisors and employees. Although there was no statistically significant difference in their levels of acceptance of the existing appraisal process, there were striking differences in the predictors of acceptance. Although this may not conclusively prove the adage "where you stand depends on where you sit," it certainly provides support. For supervisors, the only salient variable was the perceived utility of the form. This result is consistent with Murphy and Cleveland's (1991) stress on the importance of practicality criteria and the results of other empirical research into the importance of the length and complexity of the form (Longenecker & Fink, 1999; Roberts, 1992). Supervisors, in other words, are more interested in the practical utility of the form than in the interpersonal issues surrounding appraisal. This may be a form of avoidance, but it points to a problem in the appraisal process. If interpersonal issues such as trust are as important as this and similar studies suggest, a supervisor's unwillingness or inability to acknowledge the importance of interpersonal issues can lead to misunderstandings and conflict in the appraisal process.

In short, as part of the training program on the appraisal process, HR managers need to place increased focus on the interpersonal issues surrounding appraisal and less focus on such technical topics as "filling out the form." The true magnitude of the problem is illustrated in the regression analysis involving employees. For employees, the only important predictor of their level of acceptance of the appraisal process was their perceptions of their supervisor's leadership. Specifically, employees who perceived their supervisors as more like servant-leaders were more likely to accept the appraisal process. This suggests that Gabris and Ihrke (2000) are correct that leadership behaviors play an important role in shaping employee attitudes toward the appraisal process.

How does leadership make a difference? The intriguing differences in the regression analyses in this study suggest a solution. When both employees and supervisors are included in the analysis, trust emerges as the most potent predictor of acceptance. When employees and supervisors are separated, trust disappears as a predictor but leadership emerges as the only significant predictor for employees. The high correlation between trust and servant leadership suggests the answer: From an employee's standpoint, trust and leadership may not be distinctly different. Rather, trust and leadership are deeply intertwined. Such an interpretation is consistent with Kramer's (1999) conclusion that trust is a history-dependent process and Lewicki and Bunker's (1996) construct of successively deeper levels of trust. Leadership and trust coexist in a self-feeding cycle that moves either toward ever-deeper levels of trust or the complete breakdown of trust. The cycle is fueled by the participant's perceptions of the behavior of others in the relationship. The findings in the regression involving only employees suggest that leadership sets the stage for trust to emerge. Finally, it is important to remember that the construct of servant leadership is a values-based approach to leadership. The emphasis this construct places on stewardship and ethics once again points to the importance of ethical behavior in an organization, particularly for supervisors. In short, ethics cannot be an afterthought in an organization. Instead, a concern with ethics, and particularly the fostering of stewardship, should form the cornerstone of a public organization's culture.

Reinke, S. J. (2003). Does the form really matter? Leadership, trust, and acceptance of the performance appraisal process. Review of Public Personnel Administration, 23(1), 23-37.

Further Readings

- Berman, E. M., Bowman, J. S., West, J. P., & Van Wart, M. R. (Ed.) (2012). *Human Resource Management in Public Service: Paradoxes, Processes, and Problems.* Fourth Edition. Sage Publications.
- Condrey, S. E. (Ed.). (2005). Handbook of Human Resources Management in Government. John Wiley & Sons.
- Pynes, J. E. (2008). Human resources management for public and nonprofit organizations: A strategic approach (Vol. 30). *John Wiley & Sons.*
- Reinke, S. J. (2003). Does the form really matter? Leadership, trust, and acceptance of the performance appraisal process. *Review of Public Personnel Administration*, 23(1), 23-37.
- DeVries, D. L., Morrison, A. M., Shullman, S. L., & Gerlach, M. (1986). Performance appraisal on the line. *Center for Creative Leadership.*
- Durant, R. F., Kramer, R., Perry, J. L., Mesch, D., & Paarlberg, L. (2006). Motivating employees in a new governance era: The performance paradigm revisited. Public Administration Review, 66(4), 505-514.

References

Berman, E. M., Bowman, J. S., West, J. P., & Van Wart, M. R. (2012). Human resource management in public service: Paradoxes, processes, and problems. Sage.

Condrey, S. E. (Ed.). (2005). Handbook of Human Resources Management in Government. John Wiley & Sons.

Daley, D. M. (1992). Performance appraisal in the public sector: Techniques and applications. Abc-clio.

DeVries, D. L., Morrison, A. M., Shullman, S. L., & Gerlach, M. (1986). Performance appraisal on the line. Center for Creative Leadership.

Freyss, S. F. (Ed.). (2004). Human resource management in local government: An essential guide. International City/County Management Association.

Gabris, G. T., & Ihrke, D. M. (2000). Improving Employee Acceptance Toward Performance Appraisal and Merit Pay Systems The Role of Leadership Credibility. Review of Public Personnel Administration,

20(1), 41-53.

Kevin R. Murphy, & Jeanette Cleveland. (1995). Understanding performance appraisal: Social, organizational, and goal-based perspectives. Sage.

Klinger Donald, E., & Nalbandian, J. (2003). Public Personnel Management: Contexts and Strategies. New Jersey.

Landy, F. J., & Farr, J. L. (1983). The measurement of work performance: Methods, theory, and applications. Academic Pr.

Mohrman Jr, A. M., Resnick-West, S. M., Lawler III, E. E., Driver, M. J., Von Glinow, M. A., & Prince, J. B. (1989). Designing performance appraisal systems: Aligning appraisals and organizational realities. Jossey-Bass.

Nigro, Lloyd G., Felix A. Nigro, and J. Edward Kellough. 2007. Th e New Public Personnel Administration. 6th ed. Belmont, CA: Th omson/Wadsworth.

Rarick, C. A., & Baxter, G. (1986). Behaviorally anchored rating scales (BARS): An effective performance appraisal approach. SAM Advanced Management Journal, 51(1), 36-39.

Reeves, T. Z. (2006).Cases in public human resource management. Thomson Wadsworth.

Spencer, L. M., & Spencer, P. S. M. (2008). Competence at Work models for superior performance. John Wiley & Sons. (p. 265)

PART 3

THE CORE ISSUES AND SPECIAL TOPICS IN HUMAN RESOURCE MANAGEMENT

Managing Diversity

Framework

Human Resource Management for Public Organizations: An Essential Guide

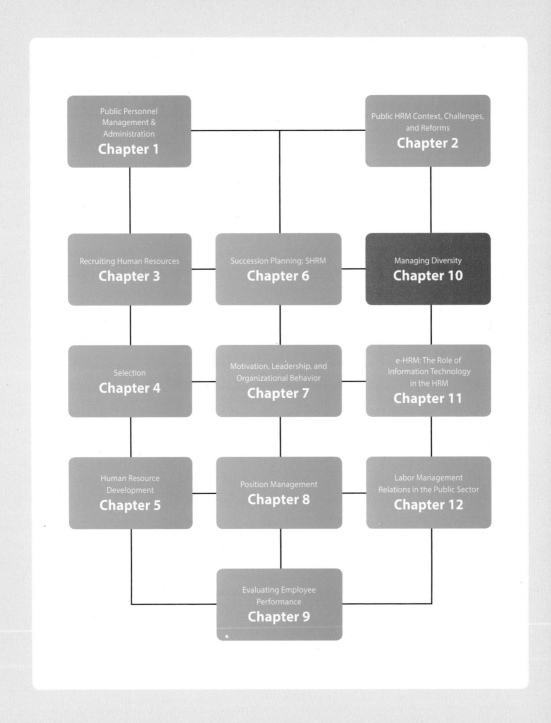

Public Personnel Management & Administration
Chapter 1

Public HRM Context, Challenges, and Reforms
Chapter 2

Recruiting Human Resources
Chapter 3

Succession Planning: SHRM
Chapter 6

Managing Diversity
Chapter 10

Selection
Chapter 4

Motivation, Leadership, and Organizational Behavior
Chapter 7

e-HRM: The Role of Information Technology in the HRM
Chapter 11

Human Resource Development
Chapter 5

Position Management
Chapter 8

Labor Management Relations in the Public Sector
Chapter 12

Evaluating Employee Performance
Chapter 9

Learning Outcomes

After going through this chapter, you should be able to:

- Discuss how workforce diversity differs from both EEO and AA, and describe how workforce diversification leads organizations to actively manage diversity by making changes in the organization's structure and processes.
- Identify how workforce diversity will affect specific human resource management policy and practice: recruitment and retention, job design, education and training, benefits and rewards, and performance measurement and improvement.
- Determine the characteristics of an effective management of diversity.
- Discuss why managing diversity is important to strategic human resources management

Preview

Various organizations—public and private organizations have become more diverse as to age, gender, race, ethnicity, and nationality (Slocum & Hellriegel, 2011). Diversity can be described "not only as the mixture of backgrounds and competences but also as valuing and using people's competences, experience, and perspectives to improve government efficiency and effectiveness, and to meet public servant's professional expectations" (OECD, 2009, p. 5). In OECD countries, the emphasis on a diverse workforce was inspired to increase social mobility, equity, and quality in service delivery (OECD, 2009). It encourages the participation of all segments of the society in governance, that is moving from the sexist and work dynasty—singly-dominated and controlled workplace—white Americans, or a men's club bureau depicting the rigid and rheostat government. Since the 1960s, the demand for equal work opportunity—the equal employment opportunity (EEO), regardless of gender, biographical and educational information, physical condition and other uniquely and evident personal attributes, dominantly raised an issue and a serious societal phenomenon. Civil rights movement advanced for the legislation of equal employment opportunity (EEO), affirmative actions (AA), anti-harassment policy initiatives—national and organizational policy, and also equal treatment policy agenda (i.e., pay, benefits, rewards, and other organizational outcomes). The demand for workforce diversity radiates and was accepted as a political and social policy in different contexts. In 2005, there was an increased number of women in the senior managerial leadership, for example in Korea and Japan with 42% and 20%, respectively; LGBTs, persons with disabilities, and racially diverse workplace. However, the satisfaction of workforce diversity brings many benefits as well as problems. Undoubtedly, diversity helped achieve major policy outcomes, for example addressing the challenges of an ageing society; and strengthening people's trust in public governance. For Kandola and Fullerton (1998), there are three advantages of a diversified workforce: "(1) proven benefits: "recruitment of scarce labor and skills, reduction in employee turnover, reduction in absenteeism, enhanced organizational flexibility; (2) debatable benefits: enhanced team creativity and problem solving, improved decision making, improved customer service and responsiveness, improved quality; and, (3) indirect benefits: improved morale, increased job satisfaction, better public image, increased competitive edge" (cited in Gold et al., 2013, p. 348).

There are instances wherein, due to an embedded culture of 'workforce dynasty', or solely controlled and dominated by a particular ethnicity and/or gender—masculinity or good 'ol boy's mindset, there are instances of harassments—verbal harassment, physical harassment, visual harassment, and sexual harassment (Slocum & Hellriegel, 2011). It does create an atmosphere of diverse and unique workforce diversity; however, it gives rise to issues of bullying which engenders the fair treatment in the organization; decline on job satisfaction as well as the motivation to work. The process of inviting workforce diversity in the organization requires subsequent effective measures on workforce inclusion. Inclusion was defined as a proactive behavior that makes each person in the organization welcome and feels valued in the organization ('What is the Difference', 2011). It is different to that of diverse organization because it describes solely the workforce characteristics of the organization—presence of diversified race, gender, or those with other sexual orientation. Figure 10.1 shows the women's percentage in top management positions in the OECD member countries.

Figure 10.1
Women in top management positions compared to their share in central government (2010)

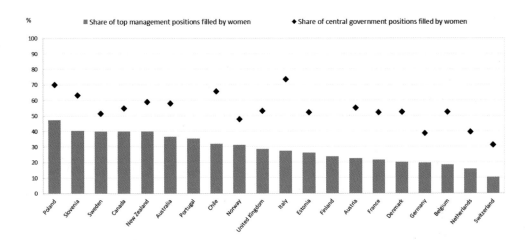

Source: OECD 2011 Survey on Gender in Public Employment.

The inclusive organizational environment provides a platform that accepts differences and united work to develop an organizational culture with unique talents ('What is the Difference', 2011). In building an inclusive organization, the role of top management leadership is crucial. Like developing an organizational environment conducive for positive individual and organizational behavior, leaders should take the lead on undertaking the effort towards inclusive, though diversified organization. Subsequent to inclusion efforts, the development of a sustainable diversity and its effective management matters. Continuous training and development, requires leaders to sustain and continue with the process of inviting and integrating diverse workforce from different segments of the society.

Making Sense of the RealWorld

As a phenomenon, workplace diversity creates diverse issues that warrant a profound understanding. Its complexities, for example, require the leaders to fathom what the controversies are in order to effectively identify plan of actions; and in general to effectively lead the organization. For the members of the organization, it is necessary to understand the workplace diversity issues and know how it affects the employee-to-employee relationship, the whole performance of the organization, as well as issues specific to the organization.

Workforce diversity was viewed in two different perspectives: (1) *the melting pot* and (2) *garden salad (or salad bowl)*. The "melting pot" metaphor is described as the mixing and amalgamation of different cultural characteristics into one strong culture. It is also compared with the melting of various metals over a sweltering hot fire while in a melting pot to produce a new metal—stronger and unique. The concept of "the melting pot" was popularly used also with the growing multicultural nations like U.S., Korea, as well as European countries. People of different race, ethnicity, national origin, language, religion, and other unique individual characteristic have come to the U.S. or Europe to live in and establish a society that embraces and merges various cultural origins into a one and strong and healthy culture. While the idea that "the melting pot" is offering may be theoretically acceptable, it remains to be a myth because practically people remain separate and still connected and immersed is with their own cultural identities.

The "garden salad or the salad bowl" on the other hand, asserts that there is unity in diversity. From the phrase itself, the "garden salad" is composed of several vegetables of different types, tastes, and quality. The metaphor describes the presence of different cultural orientations are held together—while maintaining its unique characteristics to create a dynamic society.

Title	Gist	Source
Diversity management: making the difference	This video shows the benefits of diversity and encourages you to make the difference in your organization.	https://www.youtube.com/watch?v=PKiTEog37NY

1. How does workforce diversification differ from EEO or AA? Isn't this just an "old wine in new bottles?"

2. How do you see diversity in your workplace? Has anyone experienced reverse discrimination in the workplace? Should AA be changed or abolished? Is AA value symbolic or substantive?

3. Do you participate in diversity training exercises at work? What do you think about those exercises? Have they changed the way you think? Do you feel it is an important aspect to be taught?

4. What role do you feel diversity plays in our lives? How can you apply it to your everyday lives? How do you think it will play out in the future? (Workplace, children, future leaders, etc.)

"We need to focus on diversity. I want
you to hire more people who look
different, but think just like me."

Workforce Diversity

As the society is developing, the workforce is becoming socially more diverse—includes differences in employees and applicants characteristics in terms of race, gender, ethnicity, national origin, language, religion, age, eductaion, intelligence, and disabilities. This is simply what we call, workforce diversity that creates "the range of variations among human beings in the workforce" (Klinger & Nalbandian, 2003, p. 168). Various scholars defined diversity in different ways. For example, Loden (1996) refers diversity as a critical individual characteristics that influences one's principles, prospects, as well as on how an individual perceive own self in relation with others in the organization. According to Loden (1996), the core dimension of diversity includes human characteristics such as age, ethnicity, gender, mental and physical abilities, race, and sexual orientation; while communication style, eductaion, family status, military experience, organizational role and level, religion, first language, geographical location, income, work experience, and work style constitute the secondary dimension (Pynes, 2008, p. 87). Diversity emphasizes more on power differences rather than individual differences, thus advocates intergroup interaction (Konrad, Prasad, & Pringle, 2006).

Pitts (2006), acknowledges three distinct areas of research commonly found in the diversity literature — "integration and inclusion, management programs, and diversity efforts — notes a void in the research as to whether diversity efforts lead to improved organization outcomes" (as cited in Pynes, 2008, p. 87).

Why human resource diversity is necessary? What it can bring to the organization? Aside from the constitutional, legal, and/or moral compliance of equal employment opportunity (EEO) and affirmative action (AA), "evidence is growing that managing diversity leads to greater service effectiveness, efficiency, and productivity" (Pynes, 2008, p. 92). For the U.S. Federal government, a diverse federal workforce is capable to advance and achieve an agency's mission (Federal Employees Viewpoint Survey [FEVS], 2014). Diversity can bring potential benefits and may enhance creativity and innovation to the organization believing that individuals who possess diverse or different characteristics and perspectives are good for the organization (Page, 2007). Many argued that there are lots of advantages an organization can get from adapting diversity. It can possibly lead to a vibrant organization that can provide quality and diverse ideas— which may be an opposing or concurring ideas and viewpoints—that are provided by diverse human resource. Nonetheless, organizations must recognize and respect such diverse and distinctive characteristics of the employees and provide them the autonomy to use their knowledge, skills, and abilities; diversity helps to increase an understanding of the community and the marketplace and also increase the quality of team problem solving (Cox, 2001; Naff & Kellough, 2002).

Data from the OECD (2014) illustrates the increasing trend of women representation in the public sector. Yet women in few countries have more than 40% representation in top echelons of the civil service, and mainly occupying 'female-dominated'—relatively lower-paid occupations (OECD, 2014). This phenomenon of women employment status is caused by glass ceiling, which "refers to the artificial barriers that block the advancement of women and minorities to upper - level managerial and executive positions within organizations" (Pynes, 2008, p. 91).

In the recent U.S. Federal Employees Viewpoint Survey (FEVS), federal agencies show that 55% of the respondents described that the management supports diversity in all ways (FEVS, 2014). From 2012, the FEVS identified three diversity categories such as veteran status; lesbian, gay, bisexual, transgender (LGBT); and people with disabilities. While it brings a positive note for diversity, the work satisfaction of those who belong to the above-mentioned categories remains to be low compared to their counterparts. The differences in the level of satisfaction allows public managers to determine mechanisms that could help all employees feel valued, supported, and treated fairly (FEVS, 2014, p. 35).

Generally, diversity highlights the development and implementation of organizational initiatives that (1) increase the numerical representation of historically excluded groups; (2) empower a diverse workforce once it is in place to participate fully in organizational decision making; and (3) ensure the inclusion of a diverse workforce in every aspect of organizational life (Kossek & Lobel, 1996).

Equal Employment Opportunity

The equal employment opportunity (EEO) is designed to protect the employees from undue discrimination in the employment and processes and decisions (Klinger & Nalbandian, 2003). In the U.S., Title VII of the Civil Rights Act of 1964 emphasized the importance of social equity in the employment process that prohibit discrimination against employees on the basis of race, sex, creed, religion, color, or national origin. The primordial objective of EEO is the achievement of a more equitable distribution of job opportunities. In the context of U.S. Federal government, the enforcement of EEO is done by the Equal Employment Opportunity Commission (EEOC) pursuant to Title VII of the Civil Rights Act of 1964.

Affirmative Action

Affirmative action (AA) or positive discrimination is "designed to deal with the failure of passive non-discrimination to eliminate discrimination by enforcing diversity—a demographically representative workforce—through more results-oriented and operational intrusions into recruitment, selection, and other personnel functions" (Miller, Fayneese, Reyes, & Shaffer, 1997; cited in Klinger & Nalbandian, 2003, p. 161). For example, a representative bureaucracy—government bureaucracy more representative of the people—will be more responsive to the people's needs. The main assumption however is that, the values influencing a bureaucrat's policy preferences derive at least in part from racial or ethnic background and gender; policy of favoring members of a disadvantaged group who suffer from discrimination within a culture. AA is defined as systematic effort to increase the employment representation of groups who have historically been denied opportunities for employment or advancement. The nature of positive discrimination policies varies from country to country. Some countries, such as in the Philippines, specific quota is not employed, instead members of minorities are given preference in selection processes. India, use a quota system, whereby a certain percentage of jobs or school vacancies must be set aside for members of a certain group.

Passive representation focuses on the demographic composition of the bureaucracy. While active representation focuses on the effect of minority (gender) representation on policy outputs and outcomes. Contrasting AA with EEO, AA does not only prohibit the discrimination but also oblige the "employers, unions, and employment agencies to take positive steps to reduce underrepresentation through the preparation and implementation of affirmative action plans (AAPs)" (Klinger & Nalbandian, 2003, p. 163).

AA has important symbolic value: a commitment to AA in government sends the message to other segments of society that discrimination against minorities and women is no longer tolerable. AA is the symbol of the nation's commitment to end discrimination against minorities and women to make government more responsive to their interests. Affirmative action (AA) emerged from a concern for EEO wherein the early approaches (the late 1940s) dwells on unlawful to withhold federal employment on the basis of race or ethnicity; active recruitment of minorities and women. Generally, AA is designed to facilitate managerial planning to address the under-representation of women and minorities in certain job categories. Since 1970s, goals and time tables (referred to as quotas) have become the most commonly thought of approach to AA.

EEO, AA, and Managing Diversity

The three concepts should not be confused with each other. They may be viewed as interrelated and interconnected. Equal employment opportunity (EEO) and affirmative action (AA) is legal requirements designed to bring women and minorities into the workforce. Managing diversity requires more than just compliance with laws. The management of diversity consists of " management processes to create a supportive work environment for employees already on board, and to develop and fully include all of them in order to make the organization more productive " (U.S. Merit Systems Protections Board, 1993, p. xiii).

Three distinct phases of diversity management

1. *EEO/AA*: Focused on passive representation (quotas)
2. *Valuing diversity* (symbolic approach): Celebrations of diverse characteristics
3. *Managing diversity* (managerial approach): Work diversity and organizational goals

Table 10.1 displays the detailed differences of EEO, AA, valuing differences, and managing diversity.

Table 10.1
Difference of EEO, AA, Valuing Differences, and Managing Difference

	Diversity under duress	Equal Opportunity	Augmented Affirmative Action	Valuing Differences	Managing Diversity
How driven?	**Situationally,** by a pressing problem	**Legally,** resting on widely shared sense of discrimination too long ignored r tolerated	**Legally and politically,** reinforced by special extensions beyond equal opportunity— in legislation, the courts, and political mandates in contention	**Interpersonally,** by emphasizing greater inclusion for all and hence, higher comfort levels	**Strategically,** by tying progress on diversity to organization goals, cultures, structures, policies, and reward systems
Posture re differences?	Minimal tolerance and time-bounded only	Focuses on basic equality in one particular and hence does not emphasize range of personal differences	Focuses on preferential treatment for specific interests or protected groups	Acknowledges differences, and seeks to reduce potential for conflict between them	Builds cultures, norms, structures, and skills so that all employees can fully develop their differences, personal as well as social-cultural

Dominant metaphor	Diversity as temporary deviation	"Open doors to all"	Encouraging, or forcing, preferential allocations by schedules, timetables or quotas	Raising consciousness about differences and their significance	Reinventing or reengineering work to accommodate diversities
Basic orientation?	Ad hoc, with minimal or no intent to maintain	Remedy past wrongs by broad proclamation applicable to all new job entrants	Remedy past wrongs with great urgency and targeting	Enhance appreciation of differences and, ideally, acceptance of them	Build infrastructure, culture, and skills that maximize learning for individuals and organizations.
Underlying model of integration (or lack thereof)	Rigidity enforced parallelism or separatism of new entrants	Assimilation over time to existing norms and practices by new entrants—an organizational "melting pot", or successful; adaptation by individuals to existing structure, policies, and culture	A congeries of protected interests as contesting with, if not dominating over, the traditional concept of a loyal and efficient work force	Diverse entrants retain own features, at least for an extended period, but with lessened abrasion for all and with the possibility of some emergent common ground	Organization policies structures, and cultures will induce systems appropriate for specific collections of employees different work histories, and developmental stages
Basic limitations	Intended to return to status quo ante, with a probable backlash	Assumes that "equal opportunity" over time will result in equitable allocations to all ranks	Violates sense of equity of meritocrats; may risk lower competence and performance; and raises probability of a backlash	Generally, may reduce creative tension, lower frequency of useful confrontations, and diminish sense of urgency about moving toward common goals. Specifically, focuses on personal rather than organizational performance	Requires long-term, intensive effort; traditional prescriptions for management infrastructure are not helpful models

Source: Golembiewski, R. T. (1995). Managing diversity in organizations (Vol. 45879). University of Alabama Press. (p. 48-49)

405

Also, to provide a further explanation on the specific differences between EEO/AA and managing diversity Figure 10.2 summarized this information.

Figure 10.2
Specific Difference between EEO/AA and Managing Diversity

EEO/AA	Managing Diversity
Mandatory	Voluntary
Legal, social, moral justification	Productivity, efficiency, and Quality
Focuses on race, gender, ethnicity	Focuses on all elements of diversity
Changes the mix of people	Changes the systems/operations
Perception of preference	Perception of equality
Short term and limited	Long term and ongoing
Grounded in assimilation	Grounded in individuality

Managing Diversity

To manage diversity, employers must first understand and then manage their organizational cultures. The organizational culture is defined as the values, beliefs, assumptions, expectations, attitudes, and norms shared by a majority of the organization's members. Wilson (1989) believes that "every organization has a culture that is a persistent, patterned way of thinking about the central tasks of and human relationships within an organization. Culture is to an organization what personality is to an individual. Like human culture generally, it is passed from one generation to the next. It changes slowly, if at all" (p. 91). Not only do organizations possess a dominant culture, but subcultures can emerge as well. Subcultures often develop to reflect common problems, situations, or experiences that employees face.

Organizational culture is perceived to be valuable when it helps to orient new employees to expected job - related behaviors and performance levels. A strong culture can minimize the need for formal rules and regulations because values, traditions, rituals, heroes and heroines, and the informal communication network that provides information and interprets messages sent through the organization serve to reduce ambiguity (Deal & Kennedy, 1982). Employers must be aware that an entrenched organizational culture can be a liability when the shared culture will not react to change or change to strengthen the organization's effectiveness.

Figure 10.3
General Framework for Managing Diversity

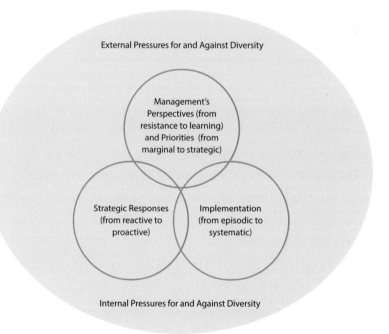

Source: Harvey, C. P., Allard, M. J., & Allard, M. J. (2002).
Understanding and managing diversity: readings, cases, and exercises. Prentice Hall.

Figure 10.3 presents an outline of the general framework, which shows that different steps in the process of managing diversity are related and can occur simultaneously. In practice, most U.S. organizations have assembled a more diverse workforce in response to external and/or internal pressures. For example, customers, suppliers, civil liberties groups, or others representing social, legal, economic, and other imperatives might exert extremal pressures to hire more people of color. At the same time, diversity champions, employee groups, or change managers might apply internal pressures for diversity in organizational hiring. The unique set of pressures brought to bear on a single organization combine to influence managers' perspectives, priorities, and strategic responses. Other managers may assemble more diverse workforces even when there are few pressures to do so. Their choices affect strategic responses and implementation, which, in turn, alter pressures for diversity.

Exhibit 10.1
Major Sources of Advantage/Disadvantage in Managing Diversity in the Public Sector

1. **LEGAL**: Failure to manage diversity will result in high costs of litigation as well as of adverse judgments by the courts.
2. **COSTS**: The costs of doing business will be higher with failure to manage diversity—communication will be more difficult, employee involvement will be reduced, relationships will be strained if not adversarial, and so on, as organizations become more diverse.
3. **INTERGROUP CONFLICT**: A special case costs, with broad implications for the quality of working life, labor-management relationships, the quality of unionization—conflict, will be greater where managing diversity is less successful.
4. **ATTRACTIVENESS TO POTENTIAL AND ACTUAL EMPLOYEES**: Failure in managing diversity will be a major disincentive for existing as well as potential employees, which is of special significance in the public in the public sector which has well-known disadvantages in recruitment and retention. This attractiveness holds not only for minorities, who will form larger portions of the pool of employees, but also for others interested in a public work force that "looks like America" (e.g., Schmidt, 1988).
5. **ATTRACTIVENESS TO BUDGETING AUTHORITIES**: Government agencies derive their life's blood from complex executive-legislative views of requests for appropriations, and poor performance in managing diversity may

well become a growing factor in adverse reviews.

6. **ATTRACTIVENESS TO CLIENTELE OR CUSTOMER**: Unsuccessful diversity efforts may well have direct implications for how an agency serves its clients or customers. The latter will become increasingly diverse over time, their needs presumably will be more accessible to diverse work forces and managements, and the comfort level for both service provider and client/ customer should increase (esp. Thomas, 1990, 1991).

7. **ATTRACTIVENESS TO MANAGERS AND EXECUTIVES**: More management is not only tasking subordinates with diversity goals, but performance on those goals is taken into increasing account re promotions and salary judgments (e.g., Brown and Harris, 1993).

8. **CREATIVITY AND PROBLEM SOLVING**: Many observers argue that organizations successful in managing diversity will bring broader perspectives, different experiences, and lessened attachment to past norms and practices, all of which can be expected to have a positive effect on creativity and problem-solving.

9. **SYSTEM FLEXIBILITY**: Agencies with successful diversity efforts will be more accustomed to dealing comprehensively with a changing environment, and hence more fluid and perhaps less standardized, as well as arguably more efficient and effective in responding to environmental turbulence.

10. **SYSTEM LEGITIMACY**: Success in managing diversity is associated with core values in our political and social philosophy, and hence that success also should have regime-enhancing tendencies.

11. **SYSTEM IMAGE**: Successfully managing diversity provides another opportunity for government to exercise leadership as model employer.

Source: Golembiewski, R. T. (1995). Managing diversity in organizations (Vol. 45879). University of Alabama Press.

Paradigms of Diversity within Public Organizations

There are four diversity paradigms that are within the public organization (Thomas & Ely, 1996): (1) discrimination-and-fairness perspective (DFP); (2) Access-and-legitimacy perspective (ALP); (3) Learning-and-effectiveness perspective (LEP); and (4) Valuing-and-integrating paradigm. The discrimination-and-fairness perspective (DFP) complies with the conditions provided in EEO and AA. Its primary goals are to provide access and equal opportunity in the recruiting and hiring processes. It focuses on descriptive representation; not likely to explore how employees' differences can improve organizational processes and outcomes. The access-and-legitimacy perspective (ALP) professes passive and active representation relationship; produce policy outputs that meet the needs of all citizens. The learning-and-effectiveness perspective (LEP) is the model is founded on understanding and valuing the notion that cultural differences exist. It also seeks to integrate, as opposed to assimilate or differentiate, diverse individuals within the agency; work group diversity promotes creativity and innovativeness. The valuing-and-integrating paradigm (creating a multicultural organization) seeks to build directly on the learning-and-effectiveness paradigm and incorporate aspects of the other two paradigms. Also, it encompasses the goals of three perspectives such as access, democratization, effectiveness, and service to stakeholders; seeks to create a multicultural climate; support and emphasize the individual perspective and culture.

Managing multiculturalism is a process, not a program that encourages agencies to examine themselves critically and move forward as they learn. By creating an organizational culture we can enhance the agency's overall mission, cost efficiency, and effectiveness. The intrinsic benefit to diversity is the resulting natural inclusion and acceptance of worth of individuals. Workforce diversification or multicultural organization is about changing work processes to reflect the diversity and creativity of unique perspectives that exist within an organization and creating a culture that encourage diverse workers to stay and contribute over time

Diversity Friendly Polices

Modern-day employers usually provide programmed assistance to employees in resolving work/family conflicts in order to best to optimize employee productivity. The employers' goal is to mitigate or minimize employee tardiness, absenteeism and other workplace disruptions. Five solutions employers utilize to assist employees address work/family conflicts.

- Child Care programs
- Elder Care programs
- Parental and Military leave
- Adoption assistance
- Domestic partners coverage

Work/life balance is a top career priority Employees are working longer hours than they have in the past Changes in the world of workers' attitudes have made studying the relationship between work and family important Generation New Millennial introduced employee-friendly policy.

Two primary factors to consider when seeking implementation of employee-friendly policies: (1) employer attitudes and (2) the power of peers. First, for "work comes first" supervisors, the administration of employee friendly programs can be difficult. Second, employee-friendly programs are more easily implemented for similar work groups, and are a major component of employee job satisfaction. Other factors to be considered are the cost—tangible vs. intangible costs for program implementation. Inability of public sector organizations to pass on any program costs to the marketplace and the authorization/negotiation of what comprises the benefit program or package.

Flextime

A workplace initiative that provides the employee tremendous latitude in determining what hours they will be at work.

Wellness Programs

A workplace initiative that offered by some employers as a combination of educational, organizational, and environmental activities designed to support behavior conducive to the health of employees in a business and their families. Wellness programs generally consist of health education, screening, and interventions designed to change employees' behavior in order to achieve better health and reduce the associated health risks. Wellness program is characterized by:

- These programs are designed to alter unhealthy personal habits and lifestyles and promote behaviors conducive to health and well-being.
- Studies have indicated improved morale, organizational commitment, employee retention and increased productivity as the hallmarks of successful wellness programs.
- These programs are available in 92% of state governments, 65% of local governments, and 46% of private sector employers.

As society has become more health-conscious, employers have developed an interest in developing programs for their employees. Challenges to program provision include:

- Accessibility to desired programs
- Range of activities offered.
- Convenience and privacy
- Measurable employer return on investment for program provision

Four relevant initiatives that typify a balanced program:

- Stress reduction
- Wellness programs
- Safety initiatives
- Employee assistance programs

Stress reduction programs may also include:

- Estimate more than 10M people in the nation's workforce suffer from stress-related problems.
- The prevention, detection, and management of negative stress are beneficial to both employer and employee.
- 64% of local governments and 52% of private sector employers have engaged stress-reducing programs

Organizational benefit...

- What can managers do to ease stress?
- Follow a consistent management style.
- Ensure tasks are well-defined and responsibilities are clear.
- Promote career development and career security.

What can employees do at work to ease stress?

- Identify sources of stress.
- Avoid unrealistic expectations of yourself.
- Review your priorities and lifestyle.

What can employees do at home to ease stress?

- Exercise regularly.
- Begin to rid your life of clutter.
- Spend time each day in a relaxing activity.

Safety Initiative Programs

These programs are designed to protect employees from an unsafe workplace environment. Federal and state law mandate guidelines to ensure employee workplace safety.

Employee Assistance Programs (EAP)

These programs are designed to improve employee health and assist the employee with coping with personal problems. Who owns the personal information shared in EAP sessions?

Components of an employers' comprehensive EAP program:

- Counseling and referral for employees and their families.
- Staff with a solid clinical background and knowledge of providers for referral.
- Broad health coverage (including mental health) in the benefit package.
- Staff familiarity with the health package to ensure that provider services are covered.
- Confidential services.
- A training component for employees, supervisors, and managers.

Family and Medical Leave Act (FMLA)

Provides eligible workers with up to 12 weeks, during any 12-month period, of unpaid leave for personal illness, childbirth or adoption, caregiving to a child, caregiving to an elder parent, or spouse with a serious health concern.

Other Employee-Friendly Policies – Flexible Work Arrangements

Employers and employees must weigh convenience and productivity when identifying options that may work for the organization. Options include:

- Flex option
- Telecommuting
- Part-time work
- Voluntary reduced work time
- Temporary work
- Leave sharing and pooling
- Job sharing

Flex Option. This type of program allows for a differential in starting/quitting times, but mandates a required number of hours to be completed in a work cycle.

Compressed work week. Number of hours worked per week is condensed into fewer days. Number of public sector employees utilizing this work option increased from 1992 (29%) to 2002 (43%). 8 in 10 federal employees work flexible schedules (U.S. Dept. of Labor)

- Used by 79% of federal-level employers
- Used by 14% of state-level employers
- Used by 60% of private sector firms

Telecommuting. Employees working in non-traditional work locales (i.e. home, satellite locations, on the road). In U.S. 26M employees in telecommute.

Part-time work. Employees regularly working fewer than 35 hours per week. Overall part-time employment rate for U.S. – 13% while in Japan is equivalent to– 25% of workforce and in Florida – 20% of state government workforce. One of the advantages of part-time is that, attractive option for new parents while it is somewhat disadvantageous because no employer no employer benefits offered.

Voluntary Reduced Work Time. Employees' voluntary reduction of work hours and compensation. This approach is beneficial because employers may reduce labor costs. Employees may better be able to address caregiving responsibilities, alternative program to employee layoffs, can function as a transition phase into retirement.

Leave Sharing and Pooling. An employee-to-employee job benefit whereby healthy workers donate sick time or other benefits to coworkers in crisis. This is more prevalent in federal and state government than for private sector firms. It allows an organization to send a message of concern for employees in distress. Also, it allows an organization to fill in gaps not clearly or completely covered by insurance, cope with medical emergencies, or assist with financial hardship.

Job-sharing. Enables to employees to split the responsibilities, hours, salary, and (often) the benefits of a full-time position. This approach provides a solution to severe financial restraints, reduction of absenteeism, or a tool to heighten productivity. However, issues on how benefits are arranged, promotion opportunities, and the determination of who has seniority may impede its effective implementation.

Case Brief

An African American Woman Among the Good Ol' Boys in Indiana

Whenever I hear terms as college mascots, such as "Aggies," "Hokies,"
and "Hoosiers," I envision "good ol' boys" of the white, redneck variety.
I certainly can't imagine African American ever referring to themselves
by such names.

President William Clinton
The White House
1600 Pennsylvania Ave. NW.
Washington, DC 20500

Dear Mr. President:

I applaud you for taking the initiative in attempting to improve race relations in this country; believe me, it is sorely needed. Having just gone through horrendous experiences with the U.S. Forest Service, I am of the opinion that the first place that needs investigation are the federal agencies – specifically, the U.S. Forest Service. I believe this agency is the bastion of institutional racism. Are you aware, Mr. President, that there were thousands of complaints filed against this agency for harassment and racial discrimination within the last few years? Doesn't that tell you something is wrong?

As a fifty-two-year-old African American employee of USFS, I was systematically forced to resign. I had to make a choice if I wanted to retain a modicum of my health and my sanity. I had to give up the benefits of eight years that I had accumulated through very hard work. Now, I must try to start all over because of harassment and discrimination by a male supervisor who did not live the color of my skin and who resented my abilities.

Before becoming employed by the federal government, I worked in private industry. I was a graduate assistant in a Department of Public Administration during my college years. I have never received a poor evaluation nor was I ever dismissed from any position.

Through the years, I had heard from federal employees about the "good ol' boy network" and how people's lives were ruined by it. Therefore, in 1986, when I was approached about becoming a federal employee, I gave the invitation a good deal of thought before giving my answer. I was also told there was a desperate need for accountants. Emphasis was made on the fact that not only was my employment credentials impeccable, but the USFS would benefit in their diversity program because I am a black female with a permanent handicap. After two years, I finally decided to apply for a position and received a direct hire from the Office of Personnel Management (OPM).

At the time I was hired, I was the only black in my section and one of only three in the entire building. Shortly after entering the USFS, I received a GS-9 rating and performed well, despite suffering brain aneurysm, which caused me to be unable to work for almost a year. Upon my return, I was presented with an opportunity to upgrade to a GS-11 status by transferring to the Hoosier National Forest in Bedford, Indiana, for a position as a budget and accounting officer.

My only preconceptions of Indiana were from the movies; I'd been inspired by the film *Hoosiers* and touched by *Breaking Away*. At the time I was unaware of the fact that Indiana held the record for the state with the most number of Ku Klux Klan lynchings of blacks. I soon discovered that Bedford was a blue-collar community that made no effort to conceal the fact that African Americans were not welcome in their town. However, the time on the job was quite enjoyable. When I mad the transfer, I found the forest supervisor, a white male, easy to work with and very supportive of diversity. Within a few months, I was appointed Diversity Program manager as part of my collaborative duties.

The supervisor respected me and accepted my recommendations. At the end of the first year in the position, I received an outstanding performance rating and a quality step increase award. According to the regional African American diversity coordinator, I was the first African American woman in the region to receive such an award.

However, in less than two years, this supervisor retired. Then came the acting supervisor who wanted a "white only" shop. He had no respect for women in general and African American women in particular. To date, there is no African American employed by the Hoosier National Forest. One African American male is housed in the building, but he is employed by the Washington office. Through my years in that office working for this supervisor, I applied numerous times for a transfer, but to no avail. I soon became aware that I was being blackballed, even though this fact was continuously denied.

As you expect, through the years, snide and unpleasant remarks had been directed to me in meetings or whenever the opportunity permitted. My supervisor resented the fact that I have a relative that is an undersecretary in the government and used this on numerous occasions to make unfair or cutting remarks; others did the same. With a supportive supervisor, those remarks would have been discredited. However, when the supervisor becomes the leader of disparaging remarks, there is very little that can be done to dissuade others. I was consistently and continuously the object of such behavior. When I spoke up and expressed my displeasure with this type of treatment, it made bad matters worse.

Working with this supervisor soon became so stressful that my health began to deteriorate. I went to work daily feeling as though I was walking to my death, constantly faced with defending myself in situations where I had little, and in some instances, no input. That was no life for anyone to have to endure. Finally, I followed department guidelines and filed a complaint with EEO. However, that action only exacerbated an already unbearable situation.

The lies and assumptions were too much to handle. Neither my supervisor nor any member of the Hoosier Strategy Team took responsibility for his or her actions; they attempted to lay all blame at my feet. I was the only African American in leadership and I had no real voice. Consequently, after months of pain and agony, and having been diagnosed to be suffering with a spastic colon from stress, I decided the best thing for my peace of mind and to improve my health was to resign. Currently, Hoosier Forest is all white; the supervisor got what he wanted.

In May 1996, I resigned and returned to my home in New Mexico at my expense. I not only lost all my job benefits from the past eight years, I had lost my good reputation as an outstanding employee.

In June 1997, I was more or less forced to accept what the Forest Service offered. As you probably know, one is sworn to secrecy regarding settlements. I can understand why that action is necessary – if I were the person responsible for destroying another person's life and reputation through falsehoods and institutional racism, I too would be ashamed to be associated with this action! Not one person on the Hoosier National Forest who was involved in helping to destroy my life and reputation has been held accountable. Nor has anyone been transferred because of their actions. It's business as usual. They go along happily in their day-to-day activities while I have been slandered.

I know that the Department of Agriculture secretary sent out numerous memos instructing the regional supervisors to find a speedy resolution to the numerous complaints. However, lower-level management continues to force and intimidate ex-employees to "get it over with" and to accept mediocre settlements. Now at age fifty-two, I am again attending the university in an attempt to prepare myself to compete in this youth-oriented job market. I know I could have refused the settlement offer; however, I was so sick of the lies that were associated with my name, I had to get out from under it as quickly as possible.

Mr. President, I sincerely hope this letter gives you a little insight into what it is like to be an African American female in the Forest Service. Just check the statistics in that agency – the record speaks for itself. As your former Secretary of Agriculture stated, "it's time to close down the plantation which is known as the Forest Service." Please contact me if you would like additional information.

The best of luck to you in all your endeavors.

Respectfully,

Cheryl Boulden

cc: National Task Force on Race Relations
    Rep. Albert R. Wynn
    Rep. Elijah E. Cummings

1. If you were appointed human resources representative for Hoosier National Forest, how would you go about investigating the allegations made by former employee Cheryl Boulden?

2. What approach would you take to make the Hoosier National Forest's Affirmative Action Plan more effective?

3. What type of Employee Development and Training Plan would you draw up for the managers, supervisors, and employees of Hoosier National Forest?

This case was adopted from: Reeves, T. Z. (2006).*Cases in public human resource management*. Thomson Wadsworth.

Student Activity:

Diversity Self-Awareness Questionnaire

The questionnaire below can help you work on your self-awareness by examining your communication skills in relation to diversity. You will better understand what areas you need to work on in order to become a better communicator and a more effective leader in your diverse organization.

Instructions: Next to each question place the number that best describes your own actions and beliefs.

1 = almost always 2 = frequently 3 = sometimes 4 = seldom 5 = almost never

1. _____ Do you recognize and challenge the perceptions, assumptions, and biases that affect your thinking?

2. _____ Do you think about the impact of what you say or how you act before you speak or act?

3. _____ Do you do everything you can to prevent the reinforcement of prejudices, including avoiding using negative stereotypes when you speak?

4. _____ Do you demonstrate your respect for people who are not from the dominant culture by doing things that show you feel they are as competent and skilled as others, including handling them responsibility as often as you do others?

5. _____ Do you encourage people who are not from the dominant culture to speak out on their concerns and respect those issues?

6. _____ Do you speak up when someone is making racial, sexual, or other derogatory remarks, or is humiliating another person?

7. _____ Do you apologize when you realize you might have offended someone due to inappropriate behavior or comments?

8. _____ Do you try to know people as individuals, not as representatives of specific groups, and include different types of people in your peer group?

9. _____ Do you accept the notion that people from all backgrounds have a need to socialize with and reinforce one another?

10. _____ Do you do everything that you can to understand your own background, and try to educate yourself about other backgrounds, including different communication styles?

Source: Adapted from Sonnenschein, W. (1999). The diversity toolkit: How you can build and benefit from a diverse workforce. Contemporary Books. (p. 47)

HRM in the Public Organizations: An Essential Guide

Case Analysis

	Step	Contents		
1	Environments/ Conditions/ Backgrounds	Please explain the situation briefly. (1-2 pages)		
2	Problem Definitions	In your own perspective, please be as specific as possible when pointing out the problem. (2-3 pages)		
3	Actual Case Studies	Please explain by providing specific examples. (Newspaper articles, news clips, or interviews) (2-3 pages)		
4	Alternatives	Possible Alternative(s)	Pros in your Country Context	Cons in a your Country Context
		①		
		②		
		③		
		Please propose more than three policy alternatives. (2-3 pages)		
5	The Best Solutions	Why did you choose this alternative as the best solution? What are the expected effects and potential contribution? (2 pages)		

Reviews

1. Why should organizations respond to the growing clamor for diversity in the workplace?

2. What do you think is the appropriate framework in managing diversity? The melting pot or the salad bowl approach? What do you think are the effective means to achieve this?

3. How does an organization design a program that satisfies and supports the needs and goals of both employer and employee?

Ending Credits

Research Digest

Diversity, Representation, and Performance: Evidence about Race and Ethnicity in Public Organizations

Facts

In the past twenty years, the growing percentages of racial minorities in the United States have brought diversity to the attention of public management and policy scholarship. Public administration research has recently considered an abundance of diversity-related issues, including racial integration of federal agencies (Cornwell and Kellough 1994; Kellough 1990; Kellough and Elliott 1992), private versus public sector diversity management initiatives (Dobbs 1996), and problems with diversity program implementation (Riccucci 1997; Von Bergen, Soper, and Foster 2002). Universities have created courses in diversity management, which have led to a number of new textbooks in the past ten years (Chemers, Oskamp, and Costanzo 1995; Henderson 1994; Riccucci 2002).

However, much of the work on diversity stems from a normative view that any diversity leads to positive consequences (Wise and Tschirhart 2002). With few exceptions (Wise and Tschirhart 2000), the research has not attempted to assess the real value of diversity. Many, if not most, articles on diversity that appear in the core public management journals are case studies of diversity programs, statistical analyses of workforce trends, or "best practices" studies. Although case studies can be valuable tools through which to build theory, they should be supplemented by quantitative research. Work in social psychology and business administration has been using quantitative methods to test hypotheses connecting diversity and performance (Wise and Tschirhart 2000).

Demographic changes warrant the attention of further research. In 1980 whites made up 80 percent of the total U.S. population.[1] By 2000, that figure had decreased to only 69 percent, while all other racial and ethnic groups in the United States had increased. This represents a substantial population shift in a relatively short period of time, and evidence suggests that diversity will continue to increase into the twenty-first century (Johnston and Packer 2000). Globalization and related economic changes in the United States have combined to create unforeseen levels of racial and ethnic heterogeneity. Along these same lines, more people are speaking languages other than English at home, people with disabilities are becoming more functional with better technology and changing social attitudes, and the baby boom population has increased the number of retired, older citizens.

The United States is becoming increasingly diverse on a number of dimensions. The labor force is experiencing similar trends, and estimates project that white men will account for only 37 percent of the U.S. workforce by 2008.[2] Studies have shown that U.S. workers are becoming older and more balanced with respect to gender and race, particularly in the public sector (Bond, Galinsky, and Swanberg 1998; Johnston and Packer 1990). The typical assumption is that these changes in the workforce and population require greater efforts toward hiring and retaining diverse employees. Some research argues that diversity is necessary in order for organizations to be "competitive" (see particularly Thomas 1991). However, whether diversity among agency employees results in increased organizational performance is an empirical question that is rarely tested in the public administration literature (Wise and Tschirhart 2000).

Issue(s)

This article takes on three interrelated questions as its focus. Does racial diversity increase or decrease organizational performance? Does racial representation—matching agency employees to characteristics of the target population—increase or decrease performance? Are these relationships different for street-level bureaucrat diversity and manager diversity?

Findings

Given these results, what can we say about the impact of diversity on performance? Of the six relationships tested between diversity and performance, three were statistically significant (table 6). Interestingly, all three significant relationships were between teacher diversity and performance. Manager diversity was unrelated to performance in all three cases. This suggests that, for racial diversity, the impact of street-level bureaucrats on performance could be stronger than the impact of management. What muddles these findings, however, is that the impact of these street-level bureaucrats varied according to the performance outcome being measured. For the low-level indicator—dropout rate—we see a negative relationship between teacher diversity and performance. For the mid-level indicator—TAAS pass rate—we see a positive relationship, and for the high-level indicator—percentage of students scoring above 1110 on the SAT—we again see a negative impact. In this context—public education— one must wonder why high levels of teacher diversity are related to students dropping out of school, students not doing well on the SAT, and students passing the TAAS exam, all at the same time. The model contains extensive controls for student and community characteristics that would tend to correlate with lower achievement. Perhaps individual-level indicators play more of a role in dropping out of school and doing well on the SAT than in passing the TAAS exam.[13] For example, the adjusted R^2 for the model with dropout rate as the dependent variable is only 0.329, and for SAT it is only 0.342. The explained variance jumps to almost 60 percent for the TAAS model. Perhaps schools have more control over whether a student passes the TAAS than whether he or she drops out or does well on the SAT. Alternatively, since the TAAS pass rate is unquestionably the most important performance indicator on which school districts are evaluated, it could be that teachers focus much more energy on TAAS preparation than on other factors. The coefficient for teacher diversity in the TAAS model is substantially larger than the coefficients for SAT and dropout rate, indicating that, positive or negative, the impact of teachers is greatest on the TAAS exam.

This raises another issue as to performance: the indicator used to gauge performance can affect conclusions drawn about how managers and employees contribute to outcomes. Using only the TAAS exam as a performance indicator, this evidence would lead one to conclude that racial diversity among street-level bureaucrats contributed positively to organizational performance. However, adding two additional performance indicators permits one to paint a more complete picture, albeit one with more ambiguity. There is no consistent relationship here between racial diversity and performance. The next step in this line of research might be to disaggregate even further the performance outcomes, such that differences between majority and minority student test scores were explored.

These findings are not surprising when taken in the context of other evidence on diversity effects. There is no clear pattern among studies on diversity effects as to strength or direction of impact, and the present study confirms that trend. Manager diversity simply does not matter. Teacher diversity matters, but differently according to performance indicator. Future research should seek to understand more about the relationship between teacher diversity and performance. Qualitative research and well-executed, richly formulated case studies could answer questions about the teacher-student dynamic that cannot be understood through large N, quantitative work. Can a more consistent pattern be shown between representation and performance? Of six relationships tested, four were statistically significant, indicating that racial representation is sometimes relevant and sometimes not. Unlike with the diversity models, we see that managerial representation is significant in all three cases, while teacher representation is significant in only one case. Interestingly, manager representation contributes positively to performance for all three indicators. When managers match the target population by race, or come close to matching it, the organization performs better. In a sense this is not surprising, since managers are in a position to set policies that encourage performance by all students. It is perhaps this capability—policy-setting—that sets managers apart from teachers and leads to more of an impact at that level. For teachers, we again see a negative relationship develop for the percentage of students scoring above 1110 on the SAT exam. For representation, as with diversity, there are no entirely consistent conclusions to draw about the relationship between race and ethnicity and performance. This conclusion—that there are no consistent patterns to draw between representation and performance—leads to a second conclusion, and one that is a primary contribution of this study: diversity and representation affect performance differently. While manager representation was related to the three performance indicators in a positive and statistically significant manner, manager diversity was unrelated to performance. Teacher representation was related to performance in one of three cases, while teacher diversity was related to performance in all three. This speaks to the salience of the target population in drawing conclusions about race, ethnicity, and performance. When talking about the role of management and the impact of diversity, it is important to consider the role of the target population. These results suggest that diversity among the target population produces an imperative for diversity among managers—or, put differently, representation matters. These results indicate that if target population diversity is low, then the need for diversity among managers is low. If target population diversity is higher, then the need for diversity among managers is higher. Matching diversity between the two levels—public managers and target population—produces the most positive and consistent relationship between ethnicity and performance. As mentioned earlier, however, the relative size of the minority group may be a relevant consideration, and these results should be taken cautiously, since the size of the minority population may be an intervening factor.

This study represents one examination of the effects of diversity and representation on performance outcomes in one of many policy settings. Four major conclusions are produced. First, there is no entirely consistent relationship shown between the impacts of diversity and representation on organizational performance. This does not mean that diversity and representation do not matter—they do matter, in significant ways, in seven out of twelve relationships tested. The direction of impact, however, is inconsistent. Second, the impact of diversity and representation varies according to the performance indicator used. This suggests that studies using only one performance outcome might overstate or understate the true impact of race and ethnicity. Third, the impact of diversity and representation varies according to level of analysis. Managers affect performance differently than street-level bureaucrats. Finally, diversity and representation affect performance differently. The overall level of diversity in an organization should not be considered the same as representation within the organization. Results drawn from studies of diversity effects and representative bureaucracy, then, should not attempt to build on research in the other area of study. The field would benefit from continued attention to the impact of diversity on performance; these findings on race and ethnicity in public education do not necessarily inform the effects of other types of diversity on performance in other policy settings. Conducting serious empirical inquiry into the nature of diversity and representation in different settings would provide more answers and assist in building the literature.

Source: Pitts, D. W. (2005). Diversity, representation, and performance: Evidence about race and ethnicity in public organizations. Journal of Public Administration Research and Theory, 15(4), 615-631.

Further Readings

- Berman, E. M., Bowman, J. S., West, J. P., & Van Wart, M. R. (Ed.) (2012). *Human Resource Management in Public Service: Paradoxes, Processes, and Problems.* Fourth Edition. Sage Publications.

- Pynes, J. E. (2008). Human resources management for public and nonprofit organizations: A strategic approach (Vol. 30). *John Wiley & Sons.*

- Klinger Donald, E., & Nalbandian, J. (2003). Public Personnel Management: Contexts and Strategies. New Jersey.

- Pitts, D. W. (2005). Diversity, representation, and performance: Evidence about race and ethnicity in public organizations. Journal of Public Administration Research and Theory, 15(4), 615-631.

- Kellough, J. E., & Naff, K. C. (2004). Responding to a wake-up call An examination of federal agency diversity management programs. Administration & society, 36(1), 62-90.

- Bradbury, M. D., & Kellough, J. E. (2008). Representative bureaucracy: Exploring the potential for active representation in local government. Journal of Public Administration Research and Theory, 18(4), 697-714.

- Golembiewski, R. T. (1995). Managing diversity in organizations (Vol. 45879). University of Alabama Press.

References

Cox, K. B. (2001). The effects of unit morale and interpersonal relations on conflict in the nursing unit. Journal of Advanced Nursing, 35(1), 17-25.

Deal, T. E., & Kennedy, A. A. (1982). Corporate cultures: The rites and rituals of organizational life. Reading/T. Deal, A. Kennedy.–Mass: Addison-Wesley, 98-103.

Golembiewski, R. T. (1995). Managing diversity in organizations (Vol. 45879). University of Alabama Press.

Harvey, C. P., Allard, M. J., & Allard, M. J. (2002). Understanding and managing diversity: readings, cases, and exercises. Prentice Hall.

Hellriegel, D., & Slocum, J. W. (2011). Organizational behavior (13th ed.). Belmont, CA:

Cengage South-Western.

Klinger Donald, E., & Nalbandian, J. (2003). Public Personnel Management: Contexts and Strategies. New Jersey.

Kandola, R., & Fullerton, J. (1998). Diversity in action: Managing the mosaic. CIPD Publishing.

Konrad, A. M., Prasad, P., & Pringle, J. (Eds.). (2005). Handbook of workplace diversity. Sage.

Kossek, E. E., & Lobel, S. A. (Eds.). (1996). Managing diversity: Human resource strategies for transforming the workplace. Cambridge, MA: Blackwell Business.

Loden, M. (1996). Implementing diversity (p. 16). Chicago, IL: Irwin.

Naff, K. C., & Kellough, J. E. (2002). A changing workforce: Understanding diversity programs in the federal government. Human capital, 355-410.

Miller, F., Reyes, X. A., & Shaffer, E. (1997). The Contextualization of Affirmative Action A Historical and Political Analysis. American behavioral scientist, 41(2), 223-231.

OECD. (2014). Government at a Glance 2014. Retrieved from: http://www.oecd.org/gov/43926778.pdf

OECD. (2009). Government at a Glance 2009. Retrieved from: http://www.oecd.org/gov/43926778.pdf)

OECD 2011 Survey on Gender in Public Employment

Pitts, D. W. (2006). Modeling the impact of diversity management. Review of Public Personnel Administration, 26(3), 245-268.

Pynes, J. E. (2008). Human resources management for public and nonprofit organizations: A strategic approach (Vol. 30). John Wiley & Sons.

Reeves, T. Z. (2006).Cases in public human resource management. Thomson Wadsworth.

Sonnenschein, W. (1999). The diversity toolkit: How you can build and benefit from a diverse workforce. Contemporary Books.

e-HRM:
The Role of Information
Technology in the HRM

Framework

Human Resource Management for Public Organizations: An Essential Guide

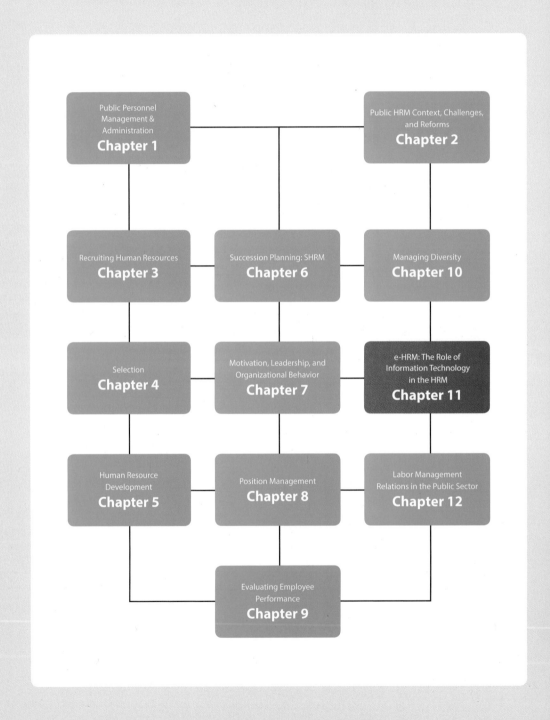

Learning Outcomes

After going through this chapter, you should be able to:

- Define e-HRM
- Determine the goals of e-HRM
- Explain the impact of e-HRM technology in public personnel management
- Discuss the features and characteristics of human resources information system (HRIS)
- Explain how an HRIS is useful when undertaking human resources planning
- Understand how technology is promoting changes in organizational structures and job design
- Understand why information technology resource policies are important

Preview

The changing environmental context—technological change—noted in chapter 2 of this book brought significant changes in the way public organization is administered and managed. The government is now employing the internet in expanding the scale of its services for the people. From the 'brick and wall' service approach, it moved towards a virtual or ubiquitous organization that is capable of delivering services to the citizens, engage the people in the society for active participation in governance, and improve organizational performance anytime and anywhere. A popular buzzword in the NPM era is 'e-Government' which enables the public organizations to level-up their efforts through information technology and internet. In the public organization workplaces, computers and technology now play a major role in redesigning traditional routine jobs and is expected to be a major contributor to productivity in the future. However in order to this, organization needs to hire employees with competencies, knowledge, skills, abilities, and creativity (Cortés & Rafter, 2007; Podolsky, 2003; Stowers & Melitski, 2003) that are capable of soothing with technological developments.

The rapid development of information communication and technology (ICT) and the World Wide Web (or the internet) during the last decade has enhanced the adoption of electronic Human Resource Management (e-HRM). Basically, e-HRM is the adoption of web-based technologies in order to provide an advanced HRM services within an organization. It embraces e-Recruitment and e-Learning the first field of HRM that make extensive use of web-based technology. It is "a network-based structure built on partnerships and typically mediated by information technologies to help the organization acquire, develop, and deploy intellectual capital" (Lepak and Snell, 1998). It is also understood as the process of planning and application of information systems for all actors involved in the HR activities and/or functions (Strohmeier, 2007). Ruël et al. (2004) have defined it differently; he described it as "a way of implementing HR strategies, policies and practices in organizations through a conscious and directed support of and/or with the full use of web-technology-based channels".

The role of e-HRM has been recognized by HR practitioners in that it became a 'common organizational practice' (see Clark, 2006; Strohmeier, 2007). This is all because of the perceived contribution of e-HRM on increasing efficiency; improve service delivery, reduction of cost, and strategic development and transformation of human resource management in the organization (Parry, 2011; Lengnick-Hall & Moritz 2003; Ruël et al., 2006; Martin et al., 2008). Then, if this is the prevailing assumption and practical contribution of e-HRM—increasing the value and competitive advantage of the organization through HR functions—in the organization, there is a need for the extensive understanding and deployment of different infrastructural requirements as well as needed resource (see, for example Dierickx & Cool 1989). These are the driving forces that may boost-start an innovative and advanced organization system. Although challenges are expected along the way such as, acceptability of new system to the organizational culture, leadership commitment to engage in the advancement from typical HR functions to electronically embedded HR systems, and the employee's attitudes and/or behavior towards the new system, HR technologies can be able to sustain growth and organizational performance.

Making Sense of the RealWorld

Among the popular human resource system innovations is the human resource information systems (HRIS). It has been widely adopted in the private sector and gaining popularity in the public sector as well. The system have a provided an effective integration of information communication and technology (ICT) and human resource management functions. The prospect that the ICT has been offering can bring a competitive advantage that can attract, develop, and retain human capitals for the organization. It will take a serious and effective amalgamation of the two dimensional system—technological system and HR system—to bring considerable changes in the organizational human resource processes and practices.

Title	Gist	Source
New Human Resource Information System	The video clip shows an example of HRIS software. The main idea, however, is to understand the necessity of enhancing the HRM in the organization.	https://www.youtube.com/watch?v=PhJQDskcAro&spfreload=1

1. How could the adoption of information technology devolve HR functions to management and employees? Can you think of possible illustrations or examples of this in the organization?

2. How does e-HRM associated with strategic human resource management (SHRM)?

3. What are the main trends in the utilization of IT in HRM around the world? Are your organization's daily HRM operations heavily reliant on computer and IT? What types of IT tools are used to accomplish HR functions?

4. What are the operational, relational, and transformational impacts on HRIS? What are the barriers and success factors that affect HRIS adoption?

Copyright 2002 by Randy Glasbergen.
www.glasbergen.com

"Whenever we upgrade our software, I see an
increase in productivity. Everyone finds something

e-HRM

The contemporary human resource management in the private and public organizations has radically changed due to changes in the environmental context. For example, the HR functions can be delivered by an outsourced organization or specialists, experts, or specialized HR professionals, and most recently through information technology (see Ulrich 1996; Tremblay, Patry & Lanoi, 2008). The latter has brought out the concept of electronic human resource management (e-HRM). e-HRM has been defined in various ways, for example as a mechanism in implementing HR policies and processes, HR transactional activities, and the traditional HR M functions (e.g., recruitment, selection, training and development, performance management, and among others). As a tool in the implementation of HR strategies, e-HRM is defined as 'a way of implementing HR strategies, policies and practices in organisations through a conscious and directed support of and/or with the full use of web-technology-based channels' (Ruel, Bondarouk, & Looise, 2004, p. 281). Recently, however, Bondarouk and Ruel (2009, p. 507) gave a profound definition based on the definitions and conception given by various scholars of e-HRM as:

"An umbrella term covering all possible integration mechanisms and contents between HRM and Information Technologies aiming at creating value within and across organizations for targeted employees and management."

The definition of includes the integration of four factors that are common in the conception of e-HRM: (1) content of e-HRM—any HRM practices that can be supported by information technology; (2) Implementation of e-HRM—adoption and appropriation of e-HRM; (3) Targeted employees and managers—devolution of HRM functions through e-HRM; and, (4) e-HRM consequences—value creation and value capture (see also Lepak, Smith and Taylor 2007). Thite and Kavanagh (2009) also pointed out that e-HRM can be utilized in the organization's transactional activities as well as innovating the traditional HRM functions, for example recruitment and selection (see Breaugh & Starke, 2000), training and development, performance management, and transformational activities of the organization. For recruitment, Breaugh & Starke (2000) identified a number of objectives which includes (a) lessening the cost, (b) speed of filling job vacancies, (c) psychological contract fulfillment, (d) satisfaction and retention rates, (e) quality and quantity of applicants, and (f) diversity of applicants (Kavanagh & Thite, 2009, p. 281). In these objectives, online or e-Recruitment system can provide a significant and positive impact which can foster the attainment of the objectives (Kavanagh & Thite, 2009).

In a wider and different perspective, e-HRM has been used in various functions and it involved a degree of complexity (Martinsons, 1994). e-HRM was able to provide services that are directly linked to the line managers as well as employees, thus do not limit the functions to the top tiers of the organizational leadership. This concept denotes the devolution of HRM functions to the lower tiers of the organization through e-HRM; and the shift from labor intensive to technology intensive organization (see Florkowski & Olivas-Lujan, 2006). In essence, e-HRM provides the opportunity for the devolution of HR functions to management and employees. These become possible through management and employee's access of intranet or other web-technology channels. As a result, it empowers the management and employees to exercise and perform some HR functions at their own pace and freedom. It also gives the opportunity for the HR department to focus on other HR functions necessary for the advancement of organizational goals and objectives. As a whole, e-HRM has been continuously argued to have a great impact on operational, functional, and transformational functions of the organization (see Lepak & Snell, 1998); cost reduction on some HR functions such as recruitment, enhancing human resource services, and widening the organizational orientation (see also Ruel et al., 2004). As it has been observed, there are three types of e-HRM (see Figure 11.1 & 11.2). These are described respectively as *operational e-HRM* (e.g., administrative functions such as payroll system and personnel data management), *relational e-HRM* (e.g., supporting and/or transforming HRM functions such as recruitment—e-Recruitment, selection, performance management, and among others); and, *transformational e-HRM* (e.g., strategic human resource management practices and processes for example, knowledge and management).

Figure 11.1
Three Types of e-HRM

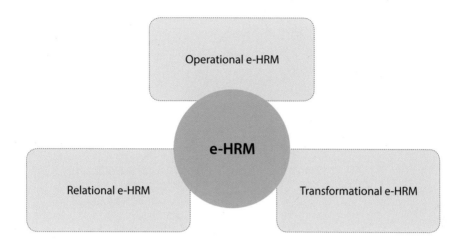

Thus, it encourages organizational efficiency (Buckley, Minette, Joy & Bartel, 2004) and the acceleration towards a human resource management (see Snell, Stueber, & Lepak, 2002) which emboldens its adoption in different organizations (Stroehmeier, 2009).

In the advent of technological development, there are various concepts that came out in relation with the human resource management (HRM). Among them is the concept of human resource information system (HRIS) and virtual HRM. e-HRM is not the same as HRIS (Human resource information system) which refers to ICT systems used within HR departments (Ruel et al., 2004). Nor is it the same as V-HRM or Virtual HRM - which is defined by Lepak and Snell as "...a network-based structure built on partnerships and typically mediated by information technologies to help the organization acquire, develop, and deploy intellectual capital" (Lepak & Snell, 1998).

Figure 11.2
HRM Functions

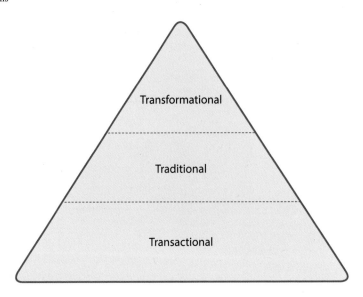

- Transactional (65-75%)
  - Benefits administration, Record keeping, Employee services

- Traditional (15-30%)
  - Recruitment, Selection, Training, Performance management, Compensation, Employee Relations

- Transformational (5-15%)
  - Knowledge management, Strategic redirection and renewal, Cultural change, Management development
  - Added value

Lastly, getting into the understanding of the importance and relevance if e-HRM in the organization—public or private sector organizations, what should be the acceptable approach for transformation of reform? Authors like Werlin (1992) stress the need for a "top down" politically-driven, all-encompassing reform process to address such problems. Thus, Werlin cites the example of countries such as Korea, argues that reforming central bureaucracies is primarily a problem of political will and government capacity to effectively use persuasive and manipulative (rather than coercive and corrupting) forms of power. Esman (1991), on the other hand, advocates a "bottom up" approach. He claims that system-wide reforms disrupt familiar routines and threaten established centers of powers without demonstrating convincingly their effectiveness. He prescribes, instead, incremental, confidence-building measures, such as training, new technologies (e.g., microcomputers), introduced with staff participation and focused at the level of individual programmes or organizations.

Goals of e-HRM

e-HRM is seen as offering the potential to improve services to HR department clients (both employees and management), improve efficiency and cost effectiveness within the HR department, and allow HR to become a strategic partner in achieving organizational goals. Traditionally HR goals have been broken into three categories: maintaining cost effectiveness, the enhancement of service for internal customers, and addressing the tactics of the business. With e-HRM there is a fourth goal added to the three categories and that is the improvement of global orientation of human resource management. HR functions that e-HRM assist with are the transactional and transformational goals. Transactional goals help reduce costs and transformational goals help the allocation of time improvement for HR professionals so that they may address more strategic issues. To add to this operational benefits have become an outcome of the implementation of e-HRM.

The process of payroll is an example of this, with HR being able to have more transactions with fewer problems. e-HRM has increased efficiency and helped businesses reduce their HR staff through reducing costs and increasing the overall speed of different processes. e-HRM also has relational impacts for a business; enabling a company's employees and managers with the ability to access HR information and increase the connectivity of all parts of the company and outside organizations. This connectivity allows for communication on a geographic level to share information and create virtual teams. And finally e-HRM creates standardization, and with standardized procedures this can ensure that an organization remains compliant with HR requirements, thus also ensuring more precise decision-making.

Use of e-HRM Technology

E-Learning is an umbrella term and broadly refers to any learning facilitated using electronic means. E-learning can capitalize on a variety of delivery media depending on the approach taken (see Table 11.1 for the e-Learning Methods):

- Printed media (including textbooks, but also online text and online magazines and journals)
- Audio (e.g. traditional audio tapes, CDs, mp3s, wav, and other electronic file formats)
- Video (e.g. traditional video tape, CD-ROM, interactive video, DVDs, video streaming, satellite or cable transmissions)
- Other combined media including hypermedia, collaborative software or social networking technology (e.g. web sites, discussion forums, e-mail, blogs, wikis, MySpace, YouTube, and Second Life).

Table 11.1
E-Learning Methods

e-Learning Methods	Explanation
Computer-based training (CBT) or technology-based training, computer-managed instruction (CMI), computer-aided (assisted) instruction (CAI), computer-based learning (CBL)	Interactive training experience using a stand-alone computer, when no collaboration and access to external resources is necessary; media used include CD-ROM, DVDs, interactive video
Multimedia-based training (MBT)	Training experience that combines text, colors, graphics, audio, and video to engage the learner; MBT can range from a simple graphical presentation of text to a complex flight simulation
Distance learning (or education)	Learner and tutor are in different locations; the approach uses both synchronous and asynchronous communication; the course provider usually provides online support and supplies students with a course pack, including printed and audio visual materials; courses follow a predetermined curriculum and schedule
Open learning (or education)	Learner has complete control over how, what, when, where, and at what pace learning occurs; any type and combination of media may be used

Open distance learning (ODL)	Umbrella term that covers both open and distance learning
Virtual learning environment (VLE) or virtual classroom	Online environment in which learning takes place
Web-based training (WBT) or online learning (or education), Internet-based training (IBTs)	Any training and learning that takes place online, that is, via the World Wide Web
Mobile learning	Any T&D that involves mobile technologies. Mobile technologies include personal digital assistants (PDA), cell/mobile phones, MP3 players

- Digital collaboration
  - The online collaboration between learners tends to increase learning and learning transfer
  - Groupware (electronic meeting software)
  - Lotus Notes is the most common Groupware
  - Synchronous/Asynchronous communication (e-Learning Communication Typology see Table 11.2).

Table 11.2

E-Learning Communication Typology

Synchronous	Asynchronous
Virtual learning environment (VLEs)	e-mail
Instant messaging services	Discussion forums/weblogs
Audio and video conferencing	Threaded discussions
Digital chat rooms	Self-paced learning
Shared whiteboard applications	
Application sharing	

- Blended learning (hybrid blend of e-Learning and face-to-face)

As one of the most advanced and popular e-HRM, e-Learning have various advantages as well as disadvantages that can be seen on its implementation. Figure 11.3 summarized the advantages and disadvantages of e-Learning.

Figure 11.3
Advantages and Disadvantages of e-Learning

Advantages	Disadvantages
▪ Cost advantages	▪ Basic computer skills necessary
▪ Improves computer skills	▪ Use of computers might cause apprehension
▪ Self paced	▪ Not suitable for certain content
▪ High degree of learner control	▪ Privacy concerns if based online
▪ Choice over learning environment	▪ Requires self-motivation to learn
▪ Interactive	▪ Learners may feel isolated from instructors and peers
▪ Tracking of learner progress and engagement is easy	▪ Lack of human contact in general
▪ Real time feedback	▪ Technical difficulties impede access
▪ Consistent delivery method	
▪ Variety of formats and methods available	
▪ Consistent content	
▪ Unlimited access in terms of time and locale	
▪ Better support / help functions / knowledge base than other methods	
▪ Appeals to several senses simultaneously	
▪ Increased benefits through the combination with traditional training methods	
▪ Can be both synchronous and asynchronous	
▪ Accommodates different learning styles	

Rapid e-Learning Solutions

The key characteristics of e-Learning solutions include:

- It has a short development time;
- Subject Matter Experts (SMEs) act as key source of content development ;
- It can be created using standard presentation software;
- It allows for easy assessment and tracking of training;
- Auxiliary multimedia tools (including flash applications) can be used to enhance training experience;
- Training units can be undertaken in minutes rather than hours; and
- It can be synchronous as well as asynchronous.

HRM and e-HRM

- *e-Job Design and Job Analysis.* Information of listing skills and competency mapping are placed on the net. System matches the listing skills and competency mapping and produces the output by identifying the employee suitable for a particular task.

- *e-Human Resource Planning.* Computer programs are developed and used extensively for the purpose of planning human resource requirements based on the data and the information available. Programs indicate the number of employees required at each level for each category of the job.

- *e-Recruitment.* Organisations advertise job vacancies through the World Wide Web (WWW) or send the info directly to the most competent people through e-mail. Job seekers send their applications through e-mail using internet and place their CV's in the World Wide Web (WWW) thru various jobsites.

- *e-Selection* has become popular with the conduct of various online tests, contacting candidates through e-mail, conducting the preliminary interviews and final interview through audio/video conferencing.

- *e-Performance Management* is a software on employee performance appraisal provides a number of statements and sub statements on each of the performance category. Appraiser selects and clicks the appropriate rating for each statement. System generates a detailed report by the time the appraiser has moved all the performance categories and sub factors. In the report modification, comments can be added or deleted by the appraiser and a final report can be prepared by the manager.

- *e-Training & Development* denotes on online training and online executive development. Employees can learn various skills by staying at the place of their work. Participants can complete course work from wherever they have access to a computer and an internet. e-learning is enabled by the delivery of content via all electronic media, including the internet, intranet, satellite broadcast audio/video tape, interactive TV and CD-ROM.

- *e-Compensation Management.* Almost all the organizations started using computers for salary fixation, salary payment, salary calculations, fixation and calculation of various allowances, employee benefits, welfare measures and fringe benefits

- *e-Grievance Redressal.* Employees send their grievance through e-mail to the superior concerned who in turn solves the problems / redress grievances and communicates the same to the employee. This reduces the time in the process and avoids face to face interaction.

- *e-HR Records.* HR records are created, maintained and updated with the help of computers easily and at a first rate and have good storage in place with real time back up.

- *e-HR Information.* HR information is generated, maintained, processed and transmitted to the appropriate places or clients with the help of software with high speed and accuracy.

- *e-HR Audit.* The standard human resource practices or the desired HR practices are fed into the computer. The data and info regarding the actual practices are also fed into the computer. The software automatically completes the HR audit and produces the audit report. The HR manager can then modify the report by deleting or adding any comments.

Figure 11.4
HRM Practices and the e-HRM Implications

HRM Practices	Implication of e-HRM
Analysis and designs of work	Employees in geographically dispersed locations can work together in virtual teams using video, email and the internet.
Recruiting	Post job openings online, candidates can apply for jobs online.
Selection	Online simulations, including tests, videos and email, can measure candidates' abilities to deal with real-life business challenges.
Training	Online learning can bring training to employees anywhere, anytime.
Compensation and benefits	Employees can review salary and bonus details and seek information about and enrol in benefits plans.

HRIS

The rapid growth in the use of the internet and information technology in human resource management has resulted in the development and implementation of Human Resource Information Systems (HRIS) and electronic Human Resources Management (e-HRM) systems (Kavanagh, Thite, & Johnson, 2012; Marler & Fisher, 2013; Stone & Dulebohn, 2013).

Human Resources Information Systems (HRIS) was defined by Kavanagh et al. (1990) as a "system used to acquire, store, manipulate, analyze, retrieve, and distribute information regarding an organization's human resources. An HRIS is not simply computer hardware and associated HR-related software. Although an HRIS includes hardware and software, it also includes people, forms, policies and procedures, and data." Primarily it emphasizes on the computerization of HR activities including employees and data since a company that does not have a computerized system still has an HRM system on paper. So the stress here is more on the systems and processes that are used by HR professionals (as users of HRIS) than on electronic functions which e-HRM proposes to all employees in the organization (as users of e-HRM). In another words, as Kavanagh et al. (2011) state, e-HRM tends to be more application and HR-function focused (e.g., e-recruitment and e-training), and an HRIS is more focused on the systems and technology underlying the design and acquisition of systems supporting the move to e-HRM.

Figure 11.5
Model of an Organizational System Centered on HRIS

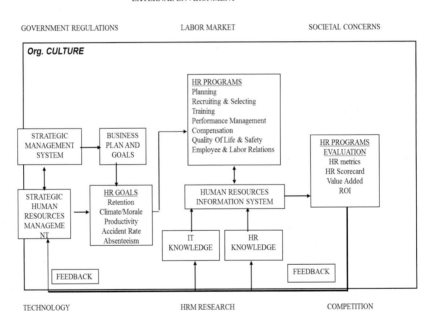

Source: Kavangh & Tithe, 2009

Embracing New Technology

The modern age produced various developments that left all organizations to work hard in order to compete in this challenging environment. Functions and activities have expanded, and impregnated knowledge workers whose responsibilities extend beyond the physical execution of work to include planning, decision making, and problem solving. Also, the spread of E-commerce and the rise of virtual workers brought new challenges for the public organizations to accept and deal with.

Types of HRIS

Electronic Data Processing (EDP): automated processing of routine informatio
- Data & files storage
- Transaction processing
- Summary reports transactions

Management Information System (MIS): emphasis on integration of data
- Information retrieval
- Categorizing data
- Standard report generation

Human Resources Management System (HRMS): information for management use
- Report formation based on managerial needs
- Categorization by management level
- Audit function of HRM

Decision Support System (DSS): focus on managerial decisions
- Interactive for user
- "What if" analyses
- Generation of decision alternatives

- Utility analyses

Biggest Advantages and Limitations of HRIS

First, HRIS can reduce manual handling and paperwork or enables greater impact of paperwork on business operation such as on reports, analysis, negotiations and communications. Limitation includes that; HRIS can't eliminate human judgment calls, can't provide truly exhaustive information, and can't adequately handle new information or social information. Technology is only a tool. People remain the true core of any organisation; and technology influenced by social & managerial issues. The ability to harness HRIS depends on the organization size, management commitment and support, availability of resources, culture, structure, systems, managerial competence & employee motivation. When well used, technology can be a partner in progress and a building block.

Point to Ponder:
WHAT HR FUNCTIONS MIGHT YOU USE AN HRIS TO SUPPORT?

Definitely: Hire/commencement, payroll, leave, allowances, terminations, salary packaging, personal information, i.e., contact details, bank account details, next of kin, basic access and security functions, basic reporting.

Possibly: Performance appraisal, performance data, position data, qualifications, training and development, web-based services, workflow, on-line library/KM, recruitment, Health and Safety, scenario-ing, MIS, DSS, Executive Information System (EIS).

WHAT REPORTS MIGHT YOU SUGGEST FOR AN MANAGEMENT INFORMATION SYSTEM (MIS)

Possibilities include:

- Staff profile reports, i.e., by age, reporting structure, location, service, performance appraisal, performance, salary level, type of employee, names
- Reports on qualifications, training and development
- Reports that track retention and attrition, performance, health and safety incidents and costs

WHAT QUESTIONS MIGHT YOU USE A DECISION SUPPORT SYSTEM (DSS) FOR?

Possibilities include:

- Scenarios – i.e., what is the impact if more recruitment, reduce in some area, hire at different qualification levels
- To fill a vacancy, who is qualified and fits other criteria such as age, service, experience etc.
- What is the profile of the highest performing sales staff
- Based on attrition and age profiles, what is business likely recruitment needs over the next 5 to 10 years.

Case Brief

Meddevco Korea

Meddevco Korea is a large multinational corporation that operates in the medical devices sector. The firm employs around 33,000 people in five divisions and has operations in 120 countries. 66% of the multinational's revenue is generated from products which are less than two years old and 80% of employees are working on products that are less than two years old. These figures illustrate the highly competitive and fast paced nature of the medical devices sector. This sector is also characterized by high levels of regulatory control and a need to comply with industry norms. Meddevco Korea is headquartered in the United States, China, and Korea. The information needs of a firm of this size are substantial and it would be next to impossible to collect, store and analyze HR related information without the use of a fully integrated global HRIS. Moreover, the diversity of the workforce, the multiplicity of skills required in the different divisions and product lines, and the pressure of compliance necessitate a perfectly orchestrated T&D effort.

Needless to say those HRIS T&D applications play a major role in managing the T&D function. Meddevco Korea uses a HRIS by PeopleSoft (now Oracle) to manage the majority of its global HR processes, including e-recruitment and performance appraisals. With regard to data entry into the system, the corporation operates a strict 'no customization unless legally required' policy to ensure data compatibility across the system. In the US, most HR services are centralized in a HR Shared Services Center. The corporation has a dedicated HRIS Center in Asia and negotiations are ongoing to implement an Asian HR Shared Services Model. The company uses a number of different payroll systems in Asia for compliance reasons. All employees in the corporation have access to a company intranet called My Meddevco, which also includes a learning portal that provides access to online training programs, which employees can utilize at work and at home. The intranet also includes a knowledgebase and detailed company information including a full listing of all employees and their job titles and location. Employee transfers and promotions are also listed. A number of years ago, the corporation made the decision not to use the Training Module included in PeopleSoft and opted for a training management system called SABA to coordinate and manage training initiatives, for example, the recent roll-out and training for the use of SAP (an ERP system) for production facilities was managed through SABA.

In addition, Meddevco Korea has recently commenced using the Talent Management Module included in PeopleSoft to identify and track high performing employees for promotion. Every employee is required to complete an online Talent Profile, which is similar to an online CV and which can be updated by the employee. The combination of systems and applications and the careful analysis of HR information contained therein allow the organization to develop and implement a global T&D strategy. However, the firm also faces some challenges arising from the use of these systems. As the organization largely grew through acquisition, a number of legacy systems still co-exist with the global HRIS among some of its subsidiaries. Data compatibility issues also derive from the use of SABA, which is not part of PeopleSoft. In addition, the firm is also using SAP and it is questionable whether Oracle (the owner of PeopleSoft) will support data exchanges with a system supplied by its chief competitor. Furthermore, because Meddevco Korea did not involve the workforce in the implementation process of the Talent Management system, employees are reluctant to complete their Talent Profiles. Moreover, the need to customize the HRIS locally to comply with national legislation in its subsidiaries further complicate the collection and transfer of data within the global HRIS.

The example of Meddevco Korea illustrates how large organizations employ HRIS to manage their workforce and how they leverage human resource development through the use of HRIS T&D applications, learning portals and specialized learning management systems. However, it is also apparent that careful planning is essential to avoid compatibility issues and to ensure a consistent global flow of HR and T&D related information.

1. What should Meddevco have done to avoid some of their problems?

2. How could Meddevco now solve the problems created by not involving employees during the implementation of the HRIS?

3. What else should Meddevco do now to improve the operation of their system?

Student Activity:

e-HRM has been a popular catchphrase that public organizations have yet to explore. There is hesitance, especially on emerging countries due to the long exposure to traditional human resource practices. However, they also have recognized that an improvement must be initiated, if not, a considerable strategic change must be adopted. Following the steps provided in the case analysis table, play the role of a HRM strategists and develop a road map for the integration of e-HRM system in the public sector organization.

HRM in the Public Organizations: An Essential Guide

Case Analysis

	Step	Contents		
1	Environments/ Conditions/ Backgrounds	Please explain the situation briefly. (1-2 pages)		
2	Problem Definitions	In your own perspective, please be as specific as possible when pointing out the problem. (2-3 pages)		
3	Actual Case Studies	Please explain by providing specific examples. (Newspaper articles, news clips, or interviews) (2-3 pages)		
4	Alternatives	Possible Alternative(s)	Pros in your Country Context	Cons in a your Country Context
		①		
		②		
		③		
		Please propose more than three policy alternatives. (2-3 pages)		
5	The Best Solutions	Why did you choose this alternative as the best solution? What are the expected effects and potential contribution? (2 pages)		

Reviews

1. What are the key success enablers in the adoption of e-HRM?

2. To What extent does usage of e-HRM applications, predict HRM value creation? Does a TOL factor, considered to be a contextual factor, have a moderation effect on the relationship between user acceptance factors and e-HRM usage? Refer to the research model developed by Wahyudi and Park (2014) below

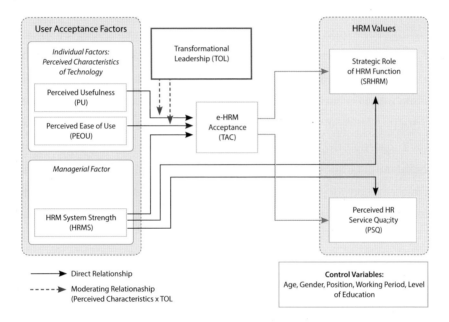

3. How can information systems and IT be used for internal coordination and external coordination? What are intranets, and what is knowledge management? How does IT influence organization design and service quality?

4. Using the organizational model presented in this book, explain why and how national culture and organizational culture influence the nature and importance of the HRIS function.

5. Justify and argue for the need for an HRIS.

6. Explain how an organization that is yet to use technology to automate its HR function can graduate from EDP to MIS and finally to DSS?

Ending Credits

Research Digest

Unveiling the Value Creation Process of Electronic Human Resource Management: An Indonesian Case

Facts

The advancement of information and communication technologies (ICT) is altering the way of life and work, including business and government practices. It is believed that ICT development drives business processes and strategies of change. In human resource management (HRM), for example, organizations have finally realized the growing importance of using ICT in leveraging their HRM functions. Moreover, there is an increasing demand for the HRM function to be more efficient, effective, and capable of supporting the strategic goals of every business function, thereby leading to the organizational adoption of electronic human resource management (e-HRM). e-HRM has been considered as a means for an organization to innovate itself, both in private and public, in response to the demands and changes in the business.

Today, the use of e-HRM is a common practice in many organizations, profit and nonprofit, and is expected to create value for them. Consequently, academic interest in e-HRM has increased in an attempt to investigate the value creation of e-HRM. Lepak and Snell (1998) suggested that e-HRM investment goals include the transformation of the HRM function to a strategic business partner. Strohmeier (2007) found that research on e-HRM has shown to alleviate the administrative burden as well as produce an increased accuracy of results and quality of HR activities. Similarly, Ruel et al. (2007) suggested the following four goals: cost reduction, improving HR services, improving strategic orientation, and global orientation. However, despite the great potential for HR functions to create value beyond administrative outcomes, in practice, many organizations utilize e-HRM more for an "automating" approach that focuses primarily on administrative efficiency rather than supporting strategic "human capital management" processes (Foster, 2010). According to Foster (2010), while process-based administrative tools are used by more than 90% of organizations, strategic HR technology tools have a much lower organizational penetration rate, typically at the 30% to 40% level (Foster, 2010).

It is expected that the adoption of information technology in the HR system will change the relationship between employees and the HR Department. Moreover, the dependency and interaction between employees and computers may increase. Therefore, the e-HRM implementation process must take into account the challenges of both management change and technology acceptance. Incorporation of the Technology Acceptance Model (TAM) into recent e-HRM studies has resulted in the notion, that the use of e-HRM by targeted employees is highly determined by the level of usefulness and the ease of use of the technology (Ruta, 2005).

Issue(s)

Determine what are the key success factors and enablers in the adoption of e-HRM.

To what extent does usage of e-HRM applications predict HRM value creation?

Is TOL considered to be a crucial contextual factor that provides moderation impacts on the relationship between user acceptance factors and e-HRM acceptance?

Findings

The study suggests that e-HRM usage/technology acceptance (TAC) is a strong predictor of PSQ. However, this study reveals that e-HRM usage does not make the HRM function more strategic. According to the findings, the value in the form of service quality is created through the implementation of e-HRM. The success factors are also very clear, as the acceptance of e-HRM is predicted by the perceived of usefulness and HRM strength. What does that mean for HR professionals? As the findings of this study indicate, e-HRM implementation is not perceived as a key trigger for changing the HRM function to be more strategic. In accordance with Steijn and van den Muyzenberg (2012), e-HRM can help an organization to become more strategic but only where the traditional HR functions have already played a strategic role and consciously used e-HRM to achieve such goal. HRM professionals should pay attention to this. That is, the strategic role of HRM cannot be created only by relying on the adoption of technology. e-HRM could lead to strategic HRM only when an organization has a set of internal and external resources as well as traditional HRM systems that could initiate, implement, and actualize certain organizational strategies per se. We also hypothesized that a certain level of TOL within an organization may have a moderating effect on the relationship between PU/PEOU of employees and e-HRM acceptance; however, the result suggests that TOL has no significant moderating effect. This study has some implications for practice, and moreover, it provides an insight for organizations to find the right strategy to obtain the maximum benefit from the adoption and implementation of e-HRM.

Source: Wahyudi, E., & Park, S. M. (2014). Unveiling the Value Creation Process of
Electronic Human Resource Management: An Indonesian Case. Public Personnel Management, 43(1), 83-117.

Further Readings

■ Berman, E. M., Bowman, J. S., West, J. P., & Van Wart, M. R. (Ed.) (2012). *Human Resource Management in Public Service: Paradoxes, Processes, and Problems.* Fourth Edition. Sage Publications.

■ Condrey, S. E. (Ed.). (2005). Handbook of Human Resources Management in Government. John Wiley & Sons.

■ Pynes, J. E. (2008). Human resources management for public and nonprofit organizations: A strategic approach (Vol. 30). *John Wiley & Sons.*

■ Kavanagh, M. J., & Thite, M. (Eds.). (2009). Human resource information systems: Basics, applications, and future directions. Sage.

■ Wahyudi, E., & Park, S. M. (2014). Unveiling the Value Creation Process of Electronic Human Resource Management: An Indonesian Case. Public Personnel Management, 43(1), 83-117.

References

Bondarouk, T. V., & Ruël, H. J. M. (2009). Electronic Human Resource Management: challenges in the digital era. The International Journal of Human Resource Management, 20(3), 505-514.

Breaugh, J. A., & Starke, M. (2000). Research on employee recruitment: So many studies, so many remaining questions. Journal of management, 26(3), 405-434.

Buckley, P., Minnette, K., Joy, D., and Michaelis, J. (2004), 'The Use of an Automated Employment

Recruiting and Screening System for Temporary Professional Employees: A Case Study,' Human Resource Management, 43, 2/3, 233–241.

Cortés, M., & Rafter, K. M. (2007). Nonprofits & technology. Emerging Research for Usable.

Clark, L. (2006), 'Henkel Rolls Out e-Recruitment across Europe,' Computer Weekly, 1, 24, 14.

Dierickx, I., & Cool, K. (1989). Asset stock accumulation and sustainability of competitive advantage. Management science, 35(12), 1504-1511.

Esman, M. J. (1991). Management dimensions of development: perspectives and strategies. Kumarian Press.

Florkowski, G. W., & Olivas-Luján, M. R. (2006). The diffusion of human-resource information-technology innovations in US and non-US firms. Personnel Review, 35(6), 684-710.

Lengnick-Hall, M. L., & Moritz, S. (2003). The impact of e-HR on the human resource management function. Journal of Labor Research, 24(3), 365-379.

Lepak, D. P., & Snell, S. A. (1998). Virtual HR: Strategic human resource management in the 21st century. Human resource management review, 8(3), 215-234.

Lepak, D. P., Smith, K. G., & Taylor, M. S. (2007). Value creation and value capture: a multilevel perspective. Academy of management review, 32(1), 180-194.

Martin, G., Redddington, M., and Alexander, H. (2008), Technology, Outsourcing and Transforming

HR, Oxford: Elsevier.

Martinsons, M. G. (1994). Benchmarking human resource information systems in Canada and Hong Kong. Information & Management, 26(6), 305-316.

Parry, E. (2011). An examination of e-HRM as a means to increase the value of the HR function. The International Journal of Human Resource Management, 22(05), 1146-1162.

Podolsky, J. (2003). Wired for good: Strategic technology planning for nonprofits. John Wiley & Sons.

Ruël, H. J. M., Bondarouk, T., & Looise, J. C. (2004). E-HRM: Innovation or irritation. Utrecht: Lemma Publishers.

Snell, S. A., Stueber, D., & Lepak, D. P. (2002). Virtual HR departments. Human resource management in virtual organizations, 81.

Stowers, G. N., & Melitski, J. (2003). Introduction to symposium. Public Performance & Management

Review, 321-324.

Strohmeier, S. (2007). Research in e-HRM: Review and implications. Human Resource Management Review 17(1): 19-37.

Thite, M., Kavanagh, M. J., & JOHNSON, R. D. (2012). Evolution of human resource management and human resource information systems.

Tremblay, M., Patry, M., and Lanoie, P. (2008), 'Human Resource Outsourcing in Canadian

Organizations: An Empirical Analysis of the Role of Organizational Characteristics, Transaction Costs and Risks,' International Journal of Human Resource Management, 19, 4, 683–715.

Ulrich, D. (1996). Human Resource Champions. Harvard Business School Press: Boston

Werlin, H. (1992). Linking decentralization and centralization: A critique of the new development administration. Public Administration and Development, 12(3), 223-235.

Labor-Management Relations in the Public Sector

Framework

Human Resource Management for Public Organizations: An Essential Guide

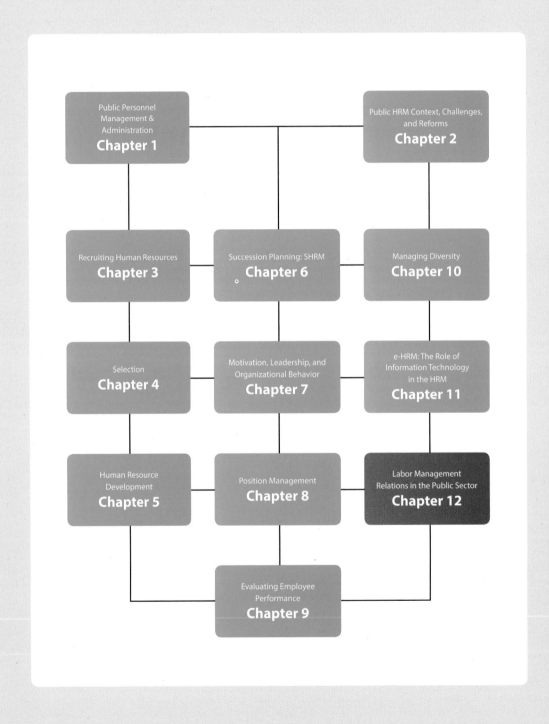

Learning Outcomes

After going through this chapter, you should be able to:

- Discuss the emerging trend of labor-management relations in the public sector.
- Determine the differing opinions between the management and employees regarding unionization.
- Present some of the prevailing differences in labor-management relations between identified nations.
- Identify the impacts of union on personnel processes and policies.
- Determine applicable approaches in dealing with public sector unionism.

Preview

The role of labor unions on various organizational processes is well acknowledged. In a democratic society, the right to organize is in consonance with the internationally recognized right of every individual, provided that such purpose of organization is not contrary to existing laws, moral, or orders. Despite this recognition, however, there are still societies and countries that perceive the presence of labor unions as a barrier to organizational effectiveness and advancement. Labor unions were seen as an anti-organizational movement that perceived to [always] go against the change initiatives in the organization. On the other hand, some gleans labor unions has a unique mechanism that is able to facilitate changes in the organizational working environment because it is capable of initiating and proposing policies not just in the organizational level to nationwide and in the international arena.

Labor unions in the private organizations operate as a labor cartel within the market economy and thus affect the profitability of firms, economic growth, the supply of labor, and consumer prices. Public sector unions function as a monopoly provider of labor within a bureaucratic-political realm. Public sector unionism introduces an unelected body into policy-making, thereby undermining the sovereignty of the state. Public sector employees are able to influence through political lobbying of their — employer-sponsors or politicians, who may seek to enhance union employment as a means of expanding their constituency.

Despite the prevalent challenges in the political power of labor unions in many countries, they remain important actors in modern society (Heins, 2004). Their continuous presence in different organizational set-up (i.e. private, public) is a proof that they exist as a stable democratic entity within a democratic society. Labor unions have been actively lobbying for the interest of union members and employees (i.e. job security, wage hike, good working conditions, health benefits, etc.) and their role was deemed crucial in the call for continuous training and development, work-life balance policy adoption, and goes to the extent of environmental protection, and sustainable consumption and production (Heins, 2004). Thus, labor unions are not just initiators or lobbyists for employees' welfare but also have great potential to impact organization's sustainable consumption and its production in one way or another.

Making Sense of the RealWorld

Title	Gist	Source
Do Labor Unions Still Matters?	In the modern age the existence of labor unions is an issue. Looking back in the historical development of trade unions, the issues aren't the same compared with present. Thus, do they still matter?	https://www.youtube.com/watch?v=amU5RX1uN1M
Andrew Klavan: Behold! Your Public Sector Unions at Work	The video clip presents brief information about the public sector unions. It exposes the 'charming charm' of unionized civil servants and the rationale of their formulation as compared to the private sector.	https://www.youtube.com/watch?v=su4PwZCWUdg

1. Do management and labor have fundamentally conflicting interests?

2. Should all public employees who are not supervisors or managers be allowed to bargain collectively with their employers? Should all but essential public employees be allowed to strike their private sector counterparts? Should employees in a bargaining unit be required to pay a representation fee to the union, even if they are not members?

3. Can collective bargaining and the merit principle really coexist in practice?

4. Does unionization and collective bargaining make it hard for managers to motivate workers and to effectively manage performance? Should supervisors be allowed to bargain collectively with public employers?

5. Is privatization or contracting out more often than not a strategy for "breaking" public employee unions?

"I'll be home late. I've joined a support group for women who need a reason to stay at work until the house is picked up and dinner is on the table."

Employee Unions

In 2009, it is interesting to note that membership in public sector union surpassed membership in private sector unions for the first time in U.S. history. This, however, cannot be generalized but the trend all over the world went on this phase. The growth in public sector unionism is part of 60-year trend fueled by a decline in private sector union membership and the legalization of public sector unionization (Norcross, 2011). As unions have risen in size and influence in the public sector, they have correspondingly fallen in the private sector (Calo, 2006).

Trade unions have traditionally been regarded as important instruments for protecting workers' interests in the workplace. In a unionized context, the union is one mechanism through which an employee can attempt to restore equity to the employment relationship (Brett, 1980). However, the decline in union density worldwide in recent times seems to signify a weakening of their influence (Aminuddin, 2008; Bramble, 2001; Benson & Zhu, 2008; Heery & Salmon, 2002). Membership decline, structural changes in employment, management practices, membership participation and democracy, the legislative framework, and the political influence of unions have been under scrutiny in the developed countries (Waddington& Whitson, 1993). Non-unionism is more prevalent in some sectors of the economy than others. However, unions continue to be a powerful presence in the public sector and parts of the manufacturing sector (for example, the aerospace and automotive industries).

In the United States, the tremendous growth in public employee unionization and collective bargaining is a phenomenon whose beginnings are generally traced back to the issuance of EO 1098 by President John F. Kennedy in 1962 which formally legitimatized bilateral relationships between unions and management in the U.S. federal government. Since then more than one-half of all the state and local government workers joined employee organizations and other states have enacted legislation enabling collective negotiations or meet and confer arrangements for one or more employee groups (Riccucci, 2007, p. 340). Also, the opposing approaches to labor-management relations of President Clinton and Bush are an interesting aspect to look into. They may serve as a principle for HRM practitioners in dealing with the public sector labor unionism – either to isolate or engage labor union in order to implement comprehensive changes necessary to reform government.

The 1993 creation of National Partnership Council (NPC) during Clinton's administration, which promoted the use of labor-management cooperation in order to advise the president on labor matters, was deemed essential in achieving National Performance review for government reform objectives (EO 12871). It also required agencies to establish individual partnership councils and increase union involvement in agency decision-making. In this regard, President Clinton's labor-management relations strategy relied heavily on high performance work system (HPWS) theory to create an organization based on employee involvement, commitment and empowerment, not employee control.

As a result of the adoption of high performance work system model, some opined that Clinton's labor-management partnership have resulted in savings, efficiency, higher productivity and greater focus on customers. In addition, the labor and management partnership allows the management and federal employees to work together to solve problems that hinder effective delivery of federal services. However, there are still questions whether or not the National Partnership Council worked in the minimization of adversarial relations between labor and management representatives in the federal government.

The labor-management relations approach of President Bush is in total conflict with President Clinton's labor-management partnership technique. Upon assumption to office, Bush revoked the executive order issued by Clinton which created the National Partnership Council. He also issued subsequent orders requiring federal contractors to notify employees of their right not to pay portion of their union dues that goes to funding political activities; and, prohibiting agencies from forcing contractors to enter into agreements with unions.

The Bush administration's approach follows the concept laid by "political administration model" of management that encourages the exclusion of unions in the consequential decisions in the workplace as a means of enhancing organizational performance. It appears that employing this model is not just an attempt to expand presidential control over the bureaucracy but rather an effort to totally control the whole bureaucracy. In his management reform program, The President's Management Agenda" (PMA), the role of federal employee unions was not mentioned unlike in Clinton's administration the role of unions are emphasized.

The arguments laid in the adoption of high performance work system model appear to be reasonable and feasible approach that can lead to higher level of performance. In this technique, employee unions are expected to respond in a non-programmed manner to changing circumstances in the organization; and, are characterized by participatory management to the nth degree. Cooke (1994) averred that in a high performance work systems, employee participation programs contributed more to value added per employee in unionized firms, while gain-sharing programs contributed more to performance in non-unionized firms.

The Clinton administration's Office of Personnel Management viewed the partnership strategy as a mechanism by which unions and management handled most significant issues in the government. Janice Lachance, the OPM Director during Clinton's incumbency characterized federal sector labor relations as follows: "Partnership is the high wire act and collective bargaining is the safety net." Subsequently, reports indicates that since the formulation of National Partnership Council, active and successful collaboration of labor and management resulted in savings, efficiency, higher productivity and greater focus to delivering services to the citizens.

Seemingly, Clinton's labor-management relations strategy appears to be strategic in the HRM perspective operating within a strongly democratized government institution. The recognition of the employees' right to collective bargaining and pulling them towards an active collaboration with the management is an acceptable technique in such context. Evidently, this approach is fundamentally different from the traditional hierarchical approach, otherwise known as the control-oriented approach.

Differing Attitudes and Views on Labor Unionism

An attitude is a hypothetical construct that represents an individual's degree of like or dislike for something. Attitudes are judgments that express verbally an individual's degree of preference for an entity, and can be indicative of a behavioral intention or a typical behavioral tendency (Eagly & Chaiken, 1993). Consequently employees who believe in the need for strong trade unions are more likely to join a trade union. Generally the literature on union-joining identifies a number of broad, if sometimes competing, explanations. A worker's decision to become a member of a trade union is best viewed as a function of both the presence of a union in the workplace and individual preferences for membership (Green, 1990; Hartley, 1992). In the latter case membership is perceived to be a function of individual and instrumental characteristics. Alternatively union availability in the workplace is argued to be facilitated or constrained by certain structural factors such as firm size and occupational composition and/or the institutional regime and unique historical experience in a particular country.

A number of individual characteristics have been advanced that influence workers' demand and membership of trade unions. These include age, gender, education, occupational level, and the instrumentality of union membership. Historically the short-term and marginal experience of women in work relative to the male labor force, it has been suggested, has tended to discourage female workers from adopting a collectivist response to the issues of pay and conditions (Lockwood, 1966; Hyman & Price, 1983). Women were also perceived to be more passive and less confrontational than men, resigned to existing job conditions, and so less likely to engage in conflict and strikes (Fiorito, Gallagher, & Greer, 1986; Wheeler & McClendon, 1991; Schur & Kruse, 1992).

Attitudes toward trade unions may be associated with different educational levels. Educational level can plausibly be interpreted as a proxy measure of social class position. It can be expected that those with higher levels of education are less likely to perceive a need for strong trade unions. Similarly, being in a higher level occupation may adversely affect attitudes to trade unions. Usually a concomitant of such occupations are high levels of discretion, job autonomy, and high trust relations (Brown,

2000).

Political orientation can be expected to have a significant impact on union attitudes and membership. Given the relatively strong association between social democratic parties and trade unions in many European countries it is likely that respondents with a left-wing political orientation are likely to be positively disposed toward trade unions (Hague, Harrop, & Breslin, 1998).

The emergence of laws, source of power through the political process is available for public sector unions to influence their employers are some of the reasons that can be considered in their continuous growth. It is also worthy to note that, basic psychology tells us that human behavior is purposeful and goal directed. It is therefore reasonable to assume that, whereas private sector employees are increasingly less inclined to seek representation of their interests through third party intervention, public sector employees are seeking such representation as it is deemed to be in their perceived best interests to do (Calo, 2006).

There are differing views from employees and managers on employee unionism—some are positive and some are negative (Berman et al., 2012). Table 12.1 and 12.2 summarized the differing views of employees and managers regarding unions (adapted from Berman et al., 2012).

Table 12.1
Employees Views of Unions

Positive
▪ Way to solve discontent with job or working conditions
▪ Amplify their voice and help keep management honest
▪ Yield results unattainable through concerted individual efforts
▪ Enjoy feeling of solidarity
Negative
▪ Unresponsive union leaders
▪ Unflattering stereotypes
▪ Questionable benefits
▪ Tendency to support "one size fits all" solutions
▪ Unnecessary to accomplish worker aims

Table 12.2
Managers Views of Unions

Positive
▪ Contribute to work place democracy
▪ Allow one-stop bargaining
▪ Ensure a level playing field
▪ Prefer to work with member-supported union representatives
▪ then disparate groups
Negative
▪ Spiking costs
▪ Push down productivity
▪ Impede organizational change
▪ Concentrate more on advancing employee interests than on citizen interests
▪ Rigid, binding labor contracts
▪ Erosion of managerial rights
▪ Reflexively pro-employee and anti-management

It is also interesting to look at the difference of the private and public sector unionism. The context and/or the environment where they operate provide also a difference on how labor union operates. See Table 12. 3 below.

Table 12.3
Difference between Public and Private Sector Unionism

Difference	Private	Public
Benefits	Scope of negotiations is broad	Many non-bargained benefits are provided and scope of negotiations is narrow
Multilateral Bargaining	Bargaining is a two-party process	Dispersed authority; bargaining involves more players and more complex approval processes
Monopoly vs. Competition	Businesses are subject to market forces; consumers can shop	Government is a monopoly and not subject to market forces; product/service substitution difficult.
Strike	Strikes are legal and a legitimate tool	Strikes occur but they are illegal and they can be punished
Sovereign vs. Free Contract	Doctrine does not apply	Doctrine of sovereignty maintains that government has responsibility to protect all societal interests; inappropriate to share power with interest groups.
Political vs. Economic	Decisions can have political impacts, but they are economic decisions	Decisions have economic impacts but are based on political criteria

Iron Triangle

As popularly known, the term "iron triangle" (see Figure 12.1) describe the dynamics of policy-making between the law-making body (or Congress), interest groups, and governmental bureaucratic agencies. The interrelation of these factors can possibly create a self-sufficient and independent interaction in which the parties can produce the individual purposes. Sometimes, this interrelation is perceived to be impracticable because the interest of the public or citizens is disregarded in the process—due to limited check and balance. Special interests groups are frequently a key element in the iron triangle since they can create a governmental situation in which their lobbyists have an undue influence on government, for example the labor unions. Thus, labor unions may play a critical role on shaking the government and on pushing policies in the policy window.

Figure 12.1
Iron Triangle

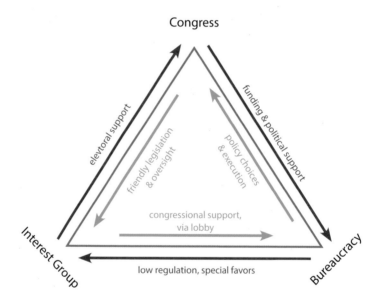

Source: Figure taken from http://study.com/academy/lesson/the-iron-triangle-definition-theory-examples.html

In this regard, the labor union can possibly impact different human resource management processes and policies such as:

- Recruitment, testing, and selection
- Promotions

- Training and development
- Position classification
- Grievances
- Employee discipline
- Dismissals and layoffs
- Reductions in Force (RIF)
- Productivity
- Privatization

Problems for Public Employee Unions

As the issue of public sector unionism is getting into its high attention, the following challenge comes up front. First, fiscal challenges—in times of fiscal retrenchment, devolution of financial and programmatic responsibilities, and contracting out limited union financial resources and the bargaining power. Second, the structural Challenges—technological change: job displacement, the impact of privatization, downsizing, and reinvention, and the inevitable demographic changes or the call for representation of new members of the workforce. Lastly, the strategic (choice) challenges—in which calls on the issues on how unions could effectively address the threats of tax resistance, globalization, and privatization? And, how can unions demonstrate their ability to participate in productivity gains and compete with the private sector?

The challenges are not only left for the unions themselves. The public managers have to face the serious challenges the unions can bring in the whole public organization. The have to address the strike issues, or to be prepared on how to effectively cope with unions' right to strike in nonessential services. Also, they should develop and adapt best mechanisms to motivate employees in a unionized environment as to the fairness of promotions, position reclassification, and job enrichment.

Participative Decision Making (PDM) Approach

In the effort of reinventing public sector labor-management relations, it requires a more collaborative relationship that involves extensive employee participation in organizational decision making at all levels; and recognize all employees as stakeholders in the operations of their organization. The concept of Participative Decision Making (PDM) or the Participative Management (PM) is known for many other characteristics such as shared leadership, employee empowerment, employee involvement, dispersed leadership, open-book management, or industrial democracy" (Steinheider, Bayerl, & Wuestewald, 2006). See Figures 12.2, 12.3, and 12.4 for some of the models that depict the participative management.

Figure 12.2
Partnership-Process Model (Masters & Albright, 2005)

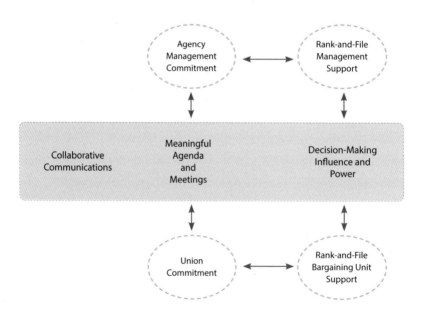

As it has been confirmed, the PDM's impacts on individual worker productivity, job satisfaction, personal growth and development, and willingness to change (see Kearney & Hays, 1994). However, it requires a foundation of trust and mutual respect among managers and workers, a strong level of commitment, win-win expectations, and workable mechanisms.

Figure 12.3
Partnership Internal Stakeholders Model (Masters & Albright, 2005)

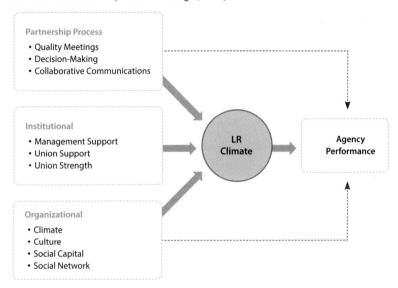

Figure 12.4
Partnership Success Factors (Masters & Albright, 2005)

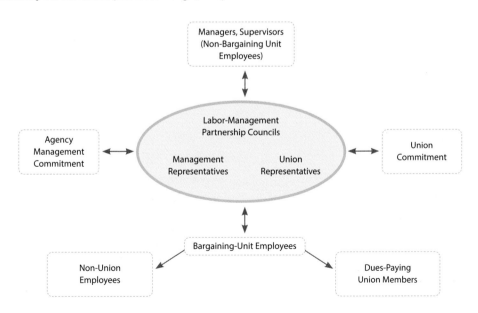

Philippine Public Sector Unionism

Nonetheless, in the case of the Philippines, the growth of the public sector unions was tripled while there is a considerable decline in the number of union membership in the private sector. From 3.57 million in 1995, union membership for both private and public sectors went down to 63% (1.918 million) in 2007 (Aganon, Cerrano, & Serteza, 2009). This became a natural consequence of the continuous effort of the government to integrate employees' unions in the organizational decision-making process and encouraged their formation in all governmental entities. While in the private sector, the decline may be attributed in the economic downturn, inefficient labor relations management, increasing global economic and capital mobility, rapid pace of technological innovations in production, and restructuring of national economies from manufacturing to services (Aganon et. al, 2009). Aganon and colleagues (2009) further argued that the labor unionism decline is caused by the public sector reforms like privatization of some major public services, rise of contingent employment arrangements and mounting resistance of employers to unionization. Moreover, one of the apparent characteristic of Philippines public sector unionism is the negative perception which the agency heads has of employees' unions; government employees need to hide whenever they campaign for union membership. Marasigan De-Lima (2003) observed that majority of the agency heads resists o reluctant to accept public sector unions and has no other goal than their demise.

The union decline in the Philippines has various reasons to attach in its incessant decrease. Some argues that labor unions have contributed to their own decline because they were not able to deal with the changes in the organizational environment. The organizing and mobilizing schemes are tied with the traditional approaches. They focused mainly on the workplace and did not explore the possibility of expansion and are confined to the issues and concerns within their organization. Furthermore, the chronic identification of their efforts that is purely for 'our members' approach limits their efforts to be extensive or for the general working populace.

Labor relations in the Philippines have evolved in dramatic transition of the country from being a foreign controlled to a fully emancipated nation. Filipino people revolted against the Spanish conquerors due to excessive work impositions and hard labor. Though we can't argue that there is a labor relation that can be gleaned from those tumultuous days, at least people have organized themselves in an effort to advance humane working conditions and commensurate wages for their labor. Following through the historical path, the peak of leadership transformation from being a democratic to autocratic governance during the incumbency of President Marcos gave birth to a more aggressive and radical labor unionism in the Philippines. The decisive collective actions and vigor of labor movements during this turbulent period rejuvenated the aspirations of the labor sector to be treated as a human being and not as a mere component of production.

The Philippine Labor Law has an explicit and encompassing definition of labor relations[1]. Book V of the Labor Code characterized labor relations deals with labor organizations, collective bargaining, grievance machinery, voluntary arbitration, conciliation and mediation, unfair labor practices (ULP), strikes, picketing, and lockouts. Separate but related labor standards law is also in place and continuously evolving and undergoes amendments and improvements[2]. Labor Standards laws are provided in Books One to Four of the Philippine Labor Code as well as Book VI thereof which deal with working conditions, wages, hours of work, holiday pay and other benefits, conditions of employment of women, minors, house helpers and homeworkers, medical and dental services, occupational health and safety, termination of employment and retirement.

Government employees like other labor forces in the private sector has the right and granted assurance of protection by the Labor Code of the Philippines. The right to organization is one of the recognized basic rights of each Filipino citizen. The right of government employees to self-organization is not a statutory creation. Instead, it is a natural and constitutional right guaranteed to every working citizen. This constitutional

---

1 Labor Relations refers to the part of the labor law which regulates the relations between employers and workers.

2 Labor Standards refers to that part of labor law which prescribes the minimum terms and conditions of employment which the employer is required to grant to its employees.

guarantee is found in three (3) separate articles of the 1987 Philippine Constitution[3]:

1. Section 8, Article III (on Bill of Rights): "The right of the people, including those employed in the public and private sectors, to form unions, associations or societies for purposes not contrary to law shall not be abridged."

2. Section 2 (5), Article IX-B (on Constitutional Commissions): "The right to self-organization shall not be denied to government employees."

3. Section 3, Article XIII (on Social Justice and Human Rights): "It shall guarantee the rights of all workers to self-organization, collective bargaining and negotiations, and peaceful concerted activities, including the right to strike in accordance with law."

However, though the Philippines Constitution clearly provides for the right to organization or association for the government employees, an enabling act or order is needed to enforce it. Yes, one can claim that no one, even the state has the right to obstruct any individual citizen to organize as provided by the constitution, except when such organization is against public morals, laws, and/or orders; but to exercise fully this constitutional right, an enabling act must be provided. Furthermore, Marasigan De-Lima (2003)[4] states that, one of the features of this government employees right to organization includes the right to leave and cancel his membership with said organization or to abstain from joining one.

In the context of labor relations in the Philippines, public sector unionism is viewed as an organization of government employees established for the promotion and furtherance of their interests. The Civil Service Commission of the Philippines identifies the following as the labor union's reasons of existence:

---

3 The 1987 Philippine Constitution provides the fundamental basis for the respect of the right of each individual to organize. The Right to unionize is in consonance with this provision of the constitution.

4 Director IV, Personnel Relations Office, Civil Service Commission, Philippines

a. As a mechanism to promote harmonious relationship between the rank-and-file employees and management;

b. As a force to compel management to faithfully observe the democratic processes relating to the merit system;

c. As a factor in influencing the enactment of legislations which will further protect and uplift employees' welfare;

d. As a partner of management in policy-making, policy-implementation and policy-monitoring.

e. As a watchdog of the people in preventing graft and corruption;

f. As an agent of change in bringing about a more efficient public service delivery.

g. As a negotiating agent for improved terms and conditions of work, particularly those which are not fixed by law;

h. The coverage of the constitutional guarantee is limited to responsible public sector unions. What is meant by a responsible public sector union5?

Philippine Public Labor Management Relations Reforms

The radical change in the public sector labor management relations reform in the Philippines was inspired by the aspirations of the government to advance good governance. The Civil Service Commission (CSC) actively initiated the revival of the commission's mechanism of solving labor disputes and provides leadership and assistance in the implementation of policies relative to union matters. The CSC restored the defunct labor management relations system which was abolished in 1994 and starts the challenging work of promoting a responsive public sector unionism as a partner for effective governance. Hence, the government has encouraged the formation of labor unions in each agency and engages the unions in organizational affairs and important

5 A responsible government union is one which: a) makes government employees aware not only of their rights but also of their responsibilities; b) knows not only to make impositions or demands but also to listen to reason; looks upon Management not as rival but as partner to social and economic progress; and c) balances its interests with those of the management and the agency as a whole.

policy-making issues.

 The government of the Philippines labor management relations policy reform can be compared to the U.S. approach during the incumbency of President Clinton. The 1993 creation of National Partnership Council (NPC) during Clinton's administration, which promoted the use of labor-management cooperation in order to advise the president on labor matters, was deemed essential in achieving National Performance review for government reform objectives (EO 12871). It also required agencies to establish individual partnership councils and increase union involvement in agency decision-making. In this regard, President Clinton's labor-management relations strategy relied heavily on *high performance work system* (HPWS) theory to create an organization based on employee involvement, commitment and empowerment, not employee control[6]. The U.S. government's labor-management relations strategy relied heavily on high performance work system (HPWS) theory for its theoretical justification. This strategy endorsed worker teams, work redesign, and employee involvement generally as well as quality management and reengineering techniques specifically

As a result of the adoption of *high performance work system* model in the labor management relations, many scholars and administrators observed that this approach resulted in savings, efficiency, higher productivity and greater focus on customers. In addition, the labor and management partnership allows the management and federal employees to work together to solve problems that hinder effective delivery of federal services. However, there are still questions whether or not the National Partnership Council worked in the minimization of adversarial relations between labor and management representatives in the federal government.

The labor management relations reform in the federal agencies of U.S. and the Philippines brought common consequential organizational and individual positive outcomes. Though there is no available empirical research that can prove the claim, the general reports from the Civil Service Commission (CSC) Philippines, reflects

---

6 The main idea of HPWS is to create an organization based on employee involvement, commitment and empowerment, not employee control.

affirmative results from the labor and management partnership. It is a two-way benefit: (1) the presence of highly engaged labor unions and cooperative management in the demands for organizational reforms, employees' welfare and benefits enhanced job satisfaction, reduced turnover intention and increased the organizational effectiveness; and (2) the proactive involvement of the labor unions in the affairs of the organization and in policy-making initiatives resulted to a more comprehensive and well-entrenched organizational policies.

The labor management relation of the Philippines depicts the contentious policy approaches made by Presidents Clinton and Bush in the United States. Getting deeply to the policy approach and strategy of the government, Philippines approach can be compared to the President Clinton's labor-management relations strategy that relied heavily on high performance work system (HPWS) theory for its theoretical justification. This strategy endorsed worker teams, work redesign, and employee involvement generally as well as quality management and reengineering techniques specifically. The approaches may be a perfect reference on how to effectively deal with the evolving role of government employees labor unions in the advancement of organizational goals and mission.

The arguments laid in the adoption of the Philippines labor management relations practice endorses the *high performance work system model.* This approach appears to be reasonable and feasible technique that can lead to higher level of performance. In this technique, employee unions are expected to respond in a non-programmed manner to changing circumstances in the organization; and, are characterized by participative management to the nth degree. Cooke (1994) averred that in a high performance work systems, employee participation programs contributed more to value added per employee in unionized firms, while gain-sharing programs contributed more to performance in non-unionized firms.

The Clinton administration's Office of Personnel Management viewed the partnership strategy as a mechanism by which unions and management handled most significant issues in the government. Janice Lachance, the OPM Director during Clinton's incumbency characterized federal sector labor relations as follows: "Partnership is the high wire act and collective bargaining is the safety net." Subsequently, reports indicates that since the formulation of National Partnership Council, active and successful collaboration of labor and management resulted in savings, efficiency, higher productivity and greater focus to delivering services to the citizens.

Seemingly, the Philippines labor management relations strategy appears to be strategic within a strongly democratized government institution. The recognition of the employees' right to collective bargaining and pulling them towards an active collaboration with the management is an acceptable technique in such context. Evidently, this approach is fundamentally different from the traditional hierarchical approach, otherwise known as the control-oriented approach.

In a highly unionized setting like Philippines, *high performance work system* approach creates an opportunity for the labor union to remove them from the perception of traditional adversarial role in the organization. Their collaborative role in the labor-management partnership will give them the feeling of responsibility, hence, will do more and contribute more for the organization. Some scholars (example Roche and Geary, 2002) argues that union members are interested in having more involvement in the workplace and, increasingly, less interested in adversarial relations, instead favoring more cooperative relationships with management. In the aspect of HRM, unions have the capacity to promote the use of innovative HR practices. One argument, building on the concept of X-inefficiency (Liebenstein, 1966) is that unions may engender "shock" and "voice" effects leading the management to adopt more progressive, efficiency-enhancing HR innovations (Verma, 2005). Thus, the isolation of employee unions in the organization would be a make or break for the organization. The potentials of labor unions' participation may lead to improved management practice or for the management to use more progressive HR policies and practices.

However, taking from the apparent positive gains of the labor-management partnership, the question of 'too much involvement' of employee unions in the decision-making should be taken carefully. They may influence the whole organizational process and gaining control of it, while thinning management command. Also, management should be cautious that in a unionized setting, union leaders will likely influence the extent to which HR innovations are successfully or unsuccessfully implemented. The role of the union leadership may be equally important, hence, worker's attitudinal and behavioral reactions to HRM innovation can be influenced by the guidance they received from their local union leaders.

The adoption of *Political Administration Model* encourages the use of command and control approach to personnel management. The intention of implementing the leader's political and policy agenda by having all the governmental apparatus to be managed from his perspective is wanting and will eventually create an organizational unrest. The clash in the organization will not be solely focused between the political appointees and career federal employees but also between the government and the established employee unions. Isolating the unions will just boost their morale to organize and advance their right to collective bargaining while weakening their motivation to work for the government. As a consequence, the leader's agenda will be subordinated by mere internal organizational priorities.

Case Brief

Holiday Time for Prison Guards

Arbitrators are frequently called in when an impasse is reached between a union and management regarding the meaning of a clause within the Collective Bargaining Agreement (CBA). The Arbitrator is charged with resolving the impasse by applying accepted standards or criteria for interpreting unclear and ambiguous language. One criterion is whether past workplace practices constitute a de facto understanding; another criterion is to determine what the negotiators of the CBA intended when they originally wrote the clause. At times, these two criteria are seemingly contradictory.

Background

Gregory George is a sergeant with the Western New Mexico Correctional Facility

(WNMCF) in Grants, New Mexico. He is a classified employee and a member of a bargaining unit, Local #3422 of the American Federation of State, County, and Municipal Employees (AFSCME). Sgt. George has accrued twenty-four hours (three days) of holiday compensatory time by May 2000 and was informed by his supervisor, Lt. Ethan Carlson that this time would need to be taken before June 18, as the last available date before the end of the fiscal year. Lt. Carlson stated that he was simply complying with a directive from the WNMCF warden and departmental authorities to require all hourly employees to take compensatory time earned by working holidays before the beginning of the next fiscal year. It was also departmental practice to schedule compensatory time, if all possible, rather pay for hours accrued.

Lt. Carlson apprised Sgt. George that he had a choice of several dates to select as holiday compensatory time off, but it would not be permissible to choose days in the next fiscal year. Stg. George declined to select days in May or June and reiterated his desire to use holiday compensatory time in conjunction with the Independence Day in July, which fit into long standing plans to attend a feast day with his family at nearby Zuni Pueblo Reservation. Lt. Carlson refused George's request and scheduled George for June 3, 4, and 5, 2001; these days were in conjunction with George' regular days off and before the end of the fiscal year. Sgt. George was extremely upset and went to see his union steward, who consulted the CBA. According to Article XII.B. of the Collective Bargaining Agreement between New Mexico Department of Corrections and AFSCME Local #3422 (January 29, 2000-January 29, 2001), the following conditions for using compensatory time were in effect:

> Employees required to work on the day a holiday is observed shall be compensated at a rate as authorized by the rules of the State Personnel Board. Such compensation may be in cash or compensatory time. To the extent that such payment is to be made in the form of compensatory time, the following shall prevail.

1. The date to be taken as compensatory time off shall be scheduled by agreement between the supervisor and the employee.
2. If for any reason the scheduled date cannot be honored, the supervisor and the employee shall select another day for the compensatory time off to be taken as soon thereafter as predictable.

The union steward reviewed the CBA clause and exclaimed, "It's just as I thought—this language is clear and unambiguous regarding holiday compensatory time; it must be scheduled on a mutually agreed date by the employee and supervisor. The department cannot allege extenuating circumstances just because of the fiscal year violates Article XII.B."

Following review by the Local's Grievance Review Committee, Sgt. George and the union decided to pursue arbitration and ask the arbitrator to award the following as a remedy: (1) compensation for holiday compensatory time that George was required to take and (2) to compel the department to cease its practice of requiring employees to use accrued holiday compensatory time before the fiscal year's completion.

When presented with Sgt. George's grievance, the department contended that it did not violate its CBA with the union based on the following reasons:

(A) Article III of the CBA, "Management Rights and State Personnel Board Rules," allows the department to schedule days off.

(B) Article XII.B> is not an absolute right and must be understood in harmony with the entire CBA.

(C) The department has a long-standing practice of scheduling holiday compensatory time to meet management's scheduling needs.

(D) Purposes of "sound fiscal management" require that holiday compensatory time not be carried over into another fiscal year.

(E) George's supervisor made a reasonable effort to accommodate him by providing George with a block of time during which he could select days for holiday comp time.

After much discussion and negotiation, the union and management were unable to resolve the issue be agreeing on a common understanding of what the CBA intended as guidelines on this issue. However, both parties stipulated the issue to be arbitrated as follows:

> Did the Department violate Article XII.B. of Collective Bargaining Agreement by requiring the Grievant to request his holiday compensatory time off be scheduled before the end of the fiscal year; and when Grievant failed to refused to make such request, by unilaterally scheduling the grievant off for certain days before the end of the fiscal year on holiday compensatory time?

The two sides were now ready to present their solutions for the impasse to the arbitrator.

Interpreting the CBA on Compensatory Time

The arbitrator heard evidence and testimony from the union and management at the arbitration hearing, most of which focused on two considerations: (1) what the negotiators had meant to articulate when they agreed to the current CBA and (2) past workplace practices when scheduling compensatory time.

What Negotiators Meant to Say

The CBA between the Department of Corrections and AFSCME, Local #3422 went into effect on January 29, 2000, and was due to expire on January 29, 2002. Negotiations between the department and union commenced on or about September 18, 1998, and continued for approximately thirteen months, during which a number of proposals and counterproposals regarding holiday pay were considered by the parties. Previous CBA between the parties had included the following language in Article XII.B. concerning "Holidays":

> Employees required to work on the day a holiday is observed shall be compensated at a rate as authorized by rules of the State Personnel Board. Such compensation may be in cash or compensatory time.

Under this language, supervisors simply scheduled holiday compensatory time, oftentimes without consulting employees. Consequently, during fall 1998, AFSCME negotiators proposed the following language for contract inclusion:

> Employees who are required to work on a day that is observed as a holiday shall be compensated at the arte of two and one-half times the hourly rate of pay or granted compensatory time at the rate of two and on-half times the regular rate of Pay. The choice of compensatory time or wages shall be made by the employee. All such hours worked shall be counted for the purpose of computing overtime. An employee need not have forty (40) hours of work in order to qualify for this holiday pay arte.

Departmental negotiators rejected the concept that an employee could choose either compensatory time or wages for time worked on holidays. Instead, the department team proposed the following article on December 12, 1998, which was incorporated into the CBA.

Holidays

A. Legal public holidays shall be observed as prescribed by statue and regulations of the State Personnel Board.

B. Employees required to work on the day a holiday is observed shall be compensated at a rate as authorized by the rules of the State Personnel Board. Such compensation may be in cash or compensatory time. To the extent that such payment is to be made in form of compensatory time, the following conditions shall prevail:

1. The date to be taken as compensatory time off shall be scheduled by agreement between the supervisor and the employee;

2. If for any reason, the scheduled date cannot be honored, the supervisor and the employee shall select another date for the compensatory time off to be taken as soon thereafter as practicable.

In addition to the CBA, members of the bargaining unit were also governed by rules and regulations passed by the State Personnel Board. State Personnel Board Rule 6.12., adopted January 2, 2000, was adopted before the current CBA and implements the following provisions:

Holiday Pay

A. Employees required to work on the day a holiday is observed shall be compensated at two-and-one-half times the usual hourly rate of pay for all hours actually worked on the holiday.

B. Employees not required to work on the day a holiday is observed shall be compensated at their hour arte of pay for the number of hours they would have worked.

C. Part-time employees whose normal work schedule does not include the day a holiday is observed shall not be compensated for the holiday.

Within a month following ratification of the current CBA, the State Personnel

Board revised Rule 6.12. "Holiday Pay" as follows:

Holiday Pay (revised)

A. When a holiday falls on an employee's regularly scheduled work day and the employee is not required to work, the employee shall be compensated in cash payment at their usual hourly rate of pay for the number of hours they would have normally worked.

B. Employees required to work on the day a holiday is observed shall be compensated at two and one-half times the usual rate of pay for all hours actually worked on the holiday. Such compensation shall be in the form of straight time cash payment for all hours actually worked and additional premium compensation, at the agency's discretion of either compensatory time off or cash payment at one and one-half times the usual hourly rate of pay for all hours actually worked. It is strongly suggested that employee requests for compensatory time off be honored by agencies on a priority basis.

C. Part-time employees whose normal work schedule does not include the day a holiday is observed shall not be compensated for the holiday.

Thus, the CBA and the State Personnel Board Rules included employee preferences as a factor to be considered when scheduling holiday compensatory time.

The Precedence of Departmental Past Practices

Despite giving employees preference a role in deciding when holiday comp time would be scheduled, the department and union agreed in Article III.6 of the CBA that "Management retains the right to determine scheduling and all other actions necessary to carry out Department functions." It was a long-standing past practice of the Department of Corrections to schedule as much holiday compensatory leave as possible before the fiscal year's conclusion, although it was apparently never totally able to reach this goal and would either carry over a small amount of comp time or pay leave to a few employees.

The department's aforementioned policy was determined at the cabinet secretary's level and implemented by the Administrative Service Division as well as the respective wardens. No evidence was produced at the arbitration hearing to indicate that the policy of mandatory scheduling of holiday compensatory time before conclusion of the fiscal year emanated from other state authorities, that is, the Department of Finance and Administration, General Service Department, State Auditor, or by state statute.

The Arbitrator's Award

The following review of the testimony, evidence, and arguments presented during the arbitration hearing, the arbitrator made the following points in his award:

- The language contained in Article XII.B of the controlling Agreement is clear and unambiguous. The dates to be taken as compensatory time off shall be scheduled by agreement between the supervisor and the employee.
- If, for any reason, the scheduled date cannot be honored, the supervisor and the employee shall select another date for the compensatory time off to be taken as soon thereafter as practicable.
- State Personnel Board Rule 6.12 also is clear in its intent: "It is strongly suggested that employees' requests for compensatory time off be honored by agencies on a priority basis. Arbitrators, like the courts, use commonly accepted set of rules to interpret ambiguous or unclear contract language. These standards apply evidence from outside the Agreement and evidence contained within the Agreement itself.

- However, the parol evidence rule holds that external evidence cannot be admitted for the purpose of changing or contradicting clearly written language. In other words, the parties are presumed to have meant what they wrote, and arbitration must enforce the terms as written. If language is unclear (its meaning unpredictable or ambiguous then external criteria, for example, past practice, bargaining history prior settlements, or financial constraints, may be used to interpret language (Along with internal evidence).

- Both parties were represented by experienced negotiating teams who are presumed to literally intend what the controlling language in Article XII. B. Says "The date to be taken as compensatory time shall be scheduled by agreement between the supervisor and the employee." This language supersedes past practices, which included supervisor dictating when leave would be scheduled and requiring leave to be used before the conclusion of the fiscal year.

- Finally, even though clear and unambiguous language was stated in the contract article, parties to an agreement may amend or add to it by subsequent agreement or memorandum of understanding. Although the CBA is the chief instrument that guides the parties in their relationships, there frequently arises an occasion when it is necessary to clarify the Agreement in some manner. This is what a side agreement does. Side agreements are very commonly used because they are found to be useful. But until and unless a MOU is negotiated regarding Article XII.B., clear and unambiguous language is controlling.

The arbitrator ordered that the provisions of Article XII.B. of the CBA be strictly enforced, whereby covered employees must agree to dates selected for holiday compensatory time. The arbitrator did not order the department to reimburse Sgt. George for three days of holiday compensatory time, because a requested remedy by the union was not contained within the original issue statement.

1. To what extent do you agree or disagree with the arbitrator's decision? What modifications, if any, would you have made in the arbitrator's decision?

2. Is the language in the CBA sufficiently clear and unambiguous, or how might it be modified by MOU?

3. Assess from management and labor perspectives how you would attempt to modify the current CBA when planning for negotiations with the next CBA?

This case was adopted from: Reeves, T. Z. (2006). Cases in public human resource management. Thomson Wadsworth.

Student Activity:

The labor union is perceived to be either an employees' association that is management-friendly or the other way around. Position yourself in either on the side of the management or the labor unionist. Towards a PDM approach, identify what are the salient factors that may interfere in the process. Bring out all these issues in the case analysis table.

HRM in the Public Organizations: An Essential Guide

Case Analysis

	Step	Contents		
1	Environments/ Conditions/ Backgrounds	Please explain the situation briefly. (1-2 pages)		
2	Problem Definitions	In your own perspective, please be as specific as possible when pointing out the problem. (2-3 pages)		
3	Actual Case Studies	Please explain by providing specific examples. (Newspaper articles, news clips, or interviews) (2-3 pages)		
4	Alternatives	Possible Alternative(s)	Pros in your Country Context	Cons in a your Country Context
		①		
		②		
		③		
		Please propose more than three policy alternatives. (2-3 pages)		
5	The Best Solutions	Why did you choose this alternative as the best solution? What are the expected effects and potential contribution? (2 pages)		

Reviews

1. What are the main findings and arguments of Thompson' article (2007)? What are the core characteristics of a new personnel system for DHS and DOD?

2. How can you evaluate President Bush's management reform tactic/strategy/policy (e.g., expanding managerial authority in the workplace denying union bargaining rights) on labor-management relations?

Ending Credits

Research Digest

Public Labor Management Relations

This paper is a concise review of the article written by James R. Thompson of the University of Illinois - Chicago entitled, "Federal Labor Management Relations Reforms under Bush: Enlightened Management or Quest for Control?"

This article chronicled development in labor-management relations practices in the US federal sector for the period of 2001-2006 of President Bush administration. It gave a detailed discussion of the reforms made by the Bush administration adopting the political management model of governance and its challenges it brought to the public sector unionism. It also recounted the development of labor relations practices in the US public sector from the incumbency of President Kennedy, Reagan, Nixon, and Clinton.

Chronology of Labor-Management Relations in the US Federal Sector

1912 – Federal employees first gained the right to organize collectively under the Lloyd-Lafollette Act of 1912. However, this act does not give the right for the employees to bargain collectively with the management.

1962 – President Kennedy issued Executive Order (EO) 10988. It allows labor unions to collectively bargain with the management but extremely limited. Issues relating to pay and benefits are excluded from negotiation, instead to be determined by the President and the congress without the labor union participation.

1969 – President Nixon issued Executive Order (EO) 1149 which replaced EO 10988. This EO created an administrative structure for the bargaining process.

1978 – Enactment of the Civil Service Reform Act of 1978 which codified the federal employees' right to collectively bargain. The law, Federal Service Labor-Management Relations Statutes (FSLMRS) incorporated the restrictive provisions of EO 10988 and 11491 by prohibiting negotiations of pay and benefits and prohibiting strikes by the federal employees.

1993 – President Clinton issued Executive Order (EO) 12871 creating a National Partnership Council including union and management officials to advise the President on matters involving labor-management relations in the executive branch. In this period, a separate analysis shows a decline in the four major dispute indicators: (1). Unfair labor practice charges; (2). Bargaining impasses; (3). Appeals to the FLRA; and, (4). Arbitration cases.

Labor-Management Reforms under Bush Administration

President George W. Bush (2001) took an aggressively adversarial stance toward the federal employee unions. He issued Executive Order (EO) 13203 revoking 12871, dissolving the National Partnership Council and rescinding agency directives in support of the order.

Subsequent to the September 11, 2001 Twin Tower attacks, President Bush's restrictive approach to collective bargaining in the federal government gained additional impetus because of a proposal to create a Department of Homeland Security (DHS). This new department has given the power to create its own personnel system in adherence to existing Civil Service Law, merit principles, prohibited personnel practices, and substantially free hand with regard to matters of compensation, performance management, and labor management relations.

In general, the new personnel system at DHS vest line managers with considerably more authority over matters of pay, hiring, and discipline and appears to have a clear infringement of the enabling statute, which expressly requires the new personnel system must ensure collective bargaining.

Likewise, the problematic provision of the Department of Defense (DoD) for their civilian employees is a replication of the DHS personnel system. Hence, its validity was challenged in the US District court. In the instant case, the judge ruled in favor of the unions and enjoined DoD from implementing the labor relations portion of the law because it did not protect collective bargaining rights or ensure the fair treatment of employees facing major disciplinary actions.

The labor-management reforms of the Bush administration can be understood as either an attempt to expand presidential control over the bureaucracy or to make operational movements. It is crystal clear that there is a managerial agenda behind the dilution of collective bargaining rights of the federal employees. There is this perception that managers are greatly limited in how they can use available financial and human resources to manage the programs; red tape; and, excessive control and mechanism that troubles bureaucratic processes. In short, the administration is operating on the premise that enhanced managerial control of workplace is conducive to high performance. It is an idea that gains legitimacy from the new public management movement.

The Clinton and Bush Labor-Management Strategy: A Comparison

President Clinton's labor-management relations strategy relied heavily on high performance work system (HPWS) theory for its theoretical justification. This strategy endorsed worker teams, work redesign, and employee involvement generally as well as quality management and reengineering techniques specifically.

On the other hand, Bush` strategy has not endorsed the application of HPWS principles to the federal workplace. Employee and/or union empowerment ideas show up nowhere in the President's Management Agenda (PMA), instead the strategy for improving the agency performance relies on (a) competitive sourcing, (b) the application of new technologies, and (c) performance incentives to increase the productivity and effectiveness of the federal workforce.

The contention that Bush administration's approach to labor-management relations was shaped primarily by considerations of bureaucratic control is given credence by the apparent influence within the administration of what has been called a "political administration model" of management. According to Neserczuk et al., "the permanent government," (p. 2) a network that includes the career civil service and its allies in the Congress, the leaders of federal unions and the chiefs of managerial and professional associations representing civil servants stands as the primary obstacle to such a program. They argued that in order for Bush to overcome resistance and implement programs he needs to rely on his political appointees. From the positions of leadership held, these appointees can impose president's control on a reluctant civil service. For this reason, President Bush revoked Clinton's order on partnership and demonstrated that his approach to federal reforms will emphasize political responsibility and accountability to the taxpayers.

Outcome of the Bush Labor Relations Strategy

The Bush administration's plan to expand managerial authority in the workplace has also been flawed. Separate federal courts have ruled portions of the new personnel system at DoD and DHS illegal on the grounds that they effectively denied union bargaining rights. Apart from these legal issues, the proposed reforms have a number of potentially adverse implications for the federal workers. From the inception of labor-management relations in the US federal sector, the following are more likely to result:

- Program implementation will be impeded because of the conflict between the career employees and political appointees;
- The labor-management relations environment will be characterized by extreme hostility between parties; and,
- With little union trust in the dispute resolution process, litigiousness will increase with more and more issues referred to the courts for resolution.

The Bush administration took a different management approach. He made used of the Political Administration Model in his dealings with the federal employee unions. Upon assumption to office he has taken series of aggressive, anti-union actions, cancelling an executive order issued by his predecessor that directed federal agencies to cooperate with union representatives in addressing common issues, withdrawing collective bargaining rights from multiple groups of federal employees based on national security considerations, and significantly narrowing the scope of issues over which unions in two of the largest federal departments are permitted to (Riccucci, 2007). President Bush's regulations evidently would want to enhance managerial control of the workplace believing to improve organizational performance. It was part of the administration's grand plan to exclude employee unions from consequential decisions in the workplace as a means of enhancing organizational performance. Conversely, the political administration model seemingly does not fit in the highly bureaucratic and hierarchical nature of the federal government. Such argument can be attributed from, firstly, the political appointees wrongly believed that they could gain control and issue commands to the careerists who are in strong resistance to maintain stability in the workplace. Secondly, the intense isolation for the employee unions resulted to extreme hostility between parties. The unions actively engaged to political activities or parliamentary actions, legal remedies that increased litigation which involved actions against the state, and informal bargaining or quasi-collective bargaining agreements.

Conclusion

From a realpolitik perspective, the Bush administration cannot be faulted for attempting to leverage its political advantage to expand presidential authority within the workplace. However, the short-sighted strategy that was employed may mean that the achievement of policy objectives such as those laid out by Nesterczuk et al. (2001), for example to "eliminate duplication across the bureaucracy and create a leaner workforce to manage the remaining functions" (p. 1), will be delayed or perhaps even denied. And from a policy perspective, regardless of how the lawsuits turn out, workplace conditions in DHS and DoD are likely to deteriorate. The unions are likely to encourage the filing of employee grievances as a means of impeding the success of the pay-for-performance systems that are part of MaxHR and NSPS and that have been upheld in court. The unions will also undoubtedly look for further opportunities to challenge the administration in court on its labor-management policies. As is so often the case in the public sector, the employees, most of whom simply want to get the job done, will suffer the fallout.

Source: Thompson, J. R. (2007). Federal Labor-Management Relations Reforms Under Bush Enlightened Management or Quest for Control? Review of Public Personnel Administration, 27(2), 105-124.

Opinion

The article laid important concepts and techniques that are material for labor-management relations in the public sector. The labor-management strategies of Bush and Clinton may serve as a guiding tool for the promotion of a harmonious organizational atmosphere characterized by a progressive partnership of the labor and management sector.

It is crystal clear that there is a great challenge confronting HR professionals in the public sector relating to the inescapable increase in density of public sector unionism. The trend in labor unionism because of the apparent legalization of public sector unionization revealed that there is a significant increase in their membership while a thinning trend in private sector unions. In some countries, apart from the 'disturbing' collective bargaining activities lodged by the labor sector, the influences of public sector labor unions are manifested not only within the organization but also outside of its supposed limited spheres – the workplace. Unions have a lot say on how the country is run, because they have the ability to influence what laws are passed, have a lot to say about who gets elected to public office, and are sometimes in equal footing with the management, if not powerful over them.

Labor relations are extensively and comprehensively regulated by law in the public sector. Seemingly, the Clinton's labor-management relations strategies are labor-friendly while Bush administration's approach is more of a management-friendly. In this context, the political component of labor-management relation is decisive in shaping the future of public sector employees' labor union. Employee labor unions may actively serve as partners, and on the other hand can be isolated to advance leader's or management's prerogative in running the affairs of the government. However, such management strategy poses serious and inevitable damage like organizational unrest and an implied surrender of management total control.

Lastly, the article did not only present practical experiences of different approaches to labor-management relations, but it also reminds HR practitioners of the importance of labor relations in the public sector. Considering the continuous growth of public sector labor unionization, labor relations remain an important competency in human resource management. The widespread collective bargaining initiatives lodged by teachers and other public employees in different countries calls for the strengthening of labor relations competency of HR practitioners. In a unionized or non-unionized setting, HR managers always have a dual responsibility: protection of organization's interest and to make employer-employee relationship stronger. Their role involves a balancing duty during negotiations; and, they are obligated to represent the management side while engaging bargaining agreements with the labor unions in good faith to reach a satisfactory agreement both for the management and labor. This responsibility can be delivered efficiently through a continuous competency building for the HR managers and practitioners in the public sector. Training and continuing education for them (HR managers/practitioners) should be planned and put into operation as an intelligent response to the challenges the employee labor union may bring.

Further Readings

- Berman, E. M., Bowman, J. S., West, J. P., & Van Wart, M. R. (Ed.) (2012). *Human Resource Management in Public Service: Paradoxes, Processes, and Problems.* Fourth Edition. Sage Publications.
- Riccucci, N. M. (Ed.). (2007). Public personnel administration and labor relations. ME Sharpe.
- Riccucci, N. M. (2007). The changing face of public employee unionism. Review of Public Personnel Administration, 27(1), 71-78.
- Thompson, J. R. (2007). Federal Labor-Management Relations Reforms Under Bush Enlightened Management or Quest for Control?. Review of Public Personnel Administration, 27(2), 105-124.

References

Aganon, M.E., Serrano, M. R., & Certeza, R.A. (2009).Union Revitalization and Social Movement Unionism in the Philippines: A Handbook, Retrieved from http://library.fes.de/pdf-files/bueros/philippinen/07130.pdf

Aminuddin, M. (2008), Human Resource Management: Principles and Practices, Oxford University Press, Kuala Lumpur.

Berman, E. M., Bowman, J. S., West, J. P., & Van Wart, M. R. (Ed.) (2012). Human Resource Management in Public Service: Paradoxes, Processes, and Problems. Fourth Edition. Sage Publications.

Benson, J., & Zhu, Y. (Eds.). (2008). Trade unions in Asia: An economic and sociological analysis. Routledge.

Bramble, T. (2001). Australian union strategies since 1945. Labour & Industry: a journal of the social and economic relations of work, 11(3), 1-25.

Brett, J. M. (1980). Why employees want unions. Organizational Dynamics, 8(4), 47-59.

Brown, S. L. (2000). Union transitions among cohabitors: The significance of relationship assessments and expectations. Journal of Marriage and Family, 62(3), 833-846.

Calo, T. J. (2006). The psychological contract and the union contract: A paradigm shift in public sector employee relations. Public Personnel Management, 35(4), 331-342.

Cooke, W. N. (1994). Employee participation programs, group-based incentives, and company performance: A union-nonunion comparison. Industrial & Labor Relations Review, 47(4), 594-609.

Eagly, A. H., & Chaiken, S. (1993). The psychology of attitudes. Harcourt Brace Jovanovich College Publishers.

Fiorito, J., Gallagher, D. G., & Greer, C. R. (1986). Determinants of unionism: A review of the literature. Research in personnel and human resources management, 4, 269-306.

Green, F. (1990). TRADE UNION AVAILABILITY AND TRADE UNION MEMBERSHIP IN BRITAIN*. The Manchester School, 58(4), 378-394.

Hartley, J. F. (1992). Joining a trade union.

Heery, E., & Salmon, J. (Eds.). (2002). The insecure workforce. Routledge.

Heins, B. (2004). The role of labour unions in the process towards sustainable consumption and production: Final report to the United Nations Environment Programme (UNEP), Division of Technology, Industry and Economics (DTIE), Paris, France. Available at www.ecologic.de/download/projekte/1850-1899/1883/1883_study.pdf

Hyman, R., & Price, R. (Eds.). (1983). The New Working Class? White-collar Workers and Their Organizations: A Reader. Macmillan.

Kearney, R. C., & Hays, S. W. (1994). Labor-management relations and participative decision making: Toward a new paradigm. Public Administration Review, 44-51.

Leibenstein, H. (1966). Allocative efficiency vs." X-efficiency". The American Economic Review, 392-415.

Lockwood, David. (1966). Working-Class Images of Society. Sociological Review 14:249-67.

Masters, M. F., & Albright, R. R. (2005). Dealing with Conflict. Management Skills: A Jossey Bass Reader, 579-605.

De-Lima, M. (2003). Director IV, Personnel Relations Office, Civil Service Commission, Philippines

Norcross, E. (2011). Public sector unionism: A review (No. 11-26, pp. 1211-1249). Mercatus Center Working Paper.

Riccucci, N. M. (Ed.). (2007). Public personnel administration and labor relations. ME Sharpe.

Roche, W. K., & Geary, J. F. (2002). Advocates, critics and union involvement in workplace partnership: Irish airports. British Journal of Industrial Relations, 40(4), 659-688.

Schur, L. A., & Kruse, D. L. (1992). Der Differences in Attitudes toward Unions. Industrial & Labor Relations Review, 46(1), 89-102.

Steinheider, B., Bayerl, P., & Wuestewald, T. (2006). The effects of participative management on employee commitment, productivity, and community satisfaction in a Police Agency. In annual meeting of the International Communication Association, Dresden International Congress Centre, Dresden, Germany.

Retrieved from http://www. allacademic. com/meta/p93097_index. html.

Verma, A. (2005). What do unions do to the workplace? Union effects on management and HRM policies. Journal of Labor Research, 26(3), 415-449.

Waddington, J. & Whitston, C. (1993). Research as Engagement: Trade Unions in the 1990s, in Forrester, K. & Thorne, C. (eds.), Trade Unions and Social Research, Aveburt, England: 24-44.

Wheeler, H. N., & McClendon, J. A. (1991). The individual decision to unionize. The state of the unions, 47-83.

Index

514

About the Authors

Sung Min Park (sm28386@skku.edu) is currently an associate professor in the Department of Public Administration & Graduate School of Governance at Sungkyunkwan University (SKKU). He has also served as assistant professor in the Greenspun School of Environmental and Public Affairs (SEPA) at the University of Nevada in Las Vegas. Park conducts research on management and human resource management in the public sector, focusing on leadership; values and motivations; organizational culture and structure; organizational behavior and performance; human resource development; IT management; and entrepreneurship management in the public, private, and nonprofit sectors. His academic work appears in American Review of Public Administration; Review of Public Personnel Administration; International Public Management Journal; Public Personnel Management; International Review of Administrative Sciences; Public Management Review; International Journal of Human Resource Management; and International Review of Public Administration. In 2005, Sung Min Park received Sage Publications' Best Doctoral Conference Paper Award presented by the Public and Nonprofit Division of the Academy of Management. In 2006, Bill Collins Award for the outstanding doctoral student paper was presented to him at the 2006 Southeastern Conference for Public Administration. In 2008, he received the 2007 Review of Public Personnel Administration (ROPPA) Best Article Award, conferred jointly by the American Society for Public Administration and Sage Publications. In the same year, he also received the 2007 Academy of Management (AOM) PNP Division Best Dissertation Award. In 2013, when he returned to Korea, he received the SKKU-Fellowship (Young Fellow) Award for Excellence in Research and Teaching, conferred by Sungkyunkwan University. Until now, Park has served as a director of the Global MPA Program in the Graduate School of Governance at SKKU and has worked as a managing editor of Korean Social Science Journal. He is also serving as a guest reviewer/referee of a wide range of internationally renowned ISI indexed journals. He received his B.A. degree from Yonsei University in 1997 (from the Department of Political Science and International Studies) and his M.I.A. degree from Columbia University in 2002 (from the School of International and Public Affairs).

Reginald G. Ugaddan (rgu1216@skku.edu) is a Researcher at Sungkyunkwan University's Research Center for Public Human Resource Development. Prior to his graduate career in South Korea, he served as a civil servant at a local government office in the Philippines. That position exposed him to the intricacies of human resource management in the public sector, which later inspired him to pursue a graduate degree in public administration. His research interests are diverse and consist of human resource management in the public sector, public management, public sector leadership, and organizational behavior. His current research endeavors include whistle-blowing, employee engagement, public service motivation, leadership, entrepreneurial orientation, Confucianism, and creativity in public sector organizations. In addition, he serves as a quantitative research methods lecturer for the Global Master's of Public Administration (GMPA) in the Graduate School of Governance at Sungkyunkwan University.

Acknowledgments

We would like to express our gratitude to Nikia Brown, Hyunjung Hu, and Nakyung Lee for their thoughtful comments in the completion of the book. We also want to thank the PSM Research Team who continues to push excellent research works on public HRM and HRD, public management, leadership, motivation, and organizational behavior and who gave inspiration in the writing of this book.

Sung Min Park
Reginald Ugaddan